Oxford & Cherwell Valley Co........e
........ford ....pus

THE USES OF REFORM

*'Godly Discipline' and Popular Behavior
in Scotland and Beyond, 1560–1610*

BY

MICHAEL F. GRAHAM

E.J. BRILL
LEIDEN · NEW YORK · KÖLN
1996

The paper in this book meets the guidelines for permanence and durability of the Committee on Production Guidelines for Book Longevity of the Council on Library Resources.

Library of Congress Cataloging-in-Publication Data

Graham, Michael F.
    The uses of reform : "godly discipline" and popular behavior in
Scotland and Beyond, 1560–1610 / by Michael F. Graham.
        p.   cm. — (Studies in medieval and Reformation thought, ISSN
0585-6914 ; v. 58)
    Includes bibliographical references and index.
    ISBN 9004102612 (alk. paper)
    1. Reformed Church—Scotland—Discipline—History—16th century.
2. Reformed Church—Scotland—Discipline—History—17th century.
3. Church of Scotland—Discipline—History—16th century.   4. Church
of Scotland—Discipline—History—17th century.   5. Reformed Church–
–France—Discipline—History—16th century.   6. Church of Scotland–
–Discipline—History—17th century.   7. Scotland—Church history.
8. France—Church history.   I. Title.   II. Series.
BX9078.G73   1996
262'.052411—dc20
                                                                                96–5481
                                                                                    CIP

Die Deutsche Bibliothek - CIP-Einheitsaufnahme

Graham, Michael F.:
The uses of reform : "godly discipline" and popular behavior in
Scotland and Beyond ; 1560–1610 / by Michael F. Graham. –
Leiden ; New York ; Köln : Brill, 1996
    (Studies in medieval and reformation thought ; Vol. 58)
    ISBN 90–04–10261–2
NE: GT

ISSN   0585-6914
ISBN   90 04 10261 2

For Elizabeth and Davey, who were there from the beginning,
and Kate and Sean, who arrived in the midst

CONTENTS

MAPS

TABLES

ABBREVIATIONS

Aber. Recs.	John Stuart, ed., *Extracts From the Records of the Burgh of Aberdeen, 1398-1625*, 2 Vol., (Aberdeen: Spalding Club, 1844, 1848)
AD Tarn	Archives départementales du Tarn, Albi
APS	*The Acts of the Parliaments of Scotland, 1124-1707*, 12 Vol., (London: HMSO, 1814-75)
ARG	*Archiv für Reformationsgeschichte*
Ars.	Bibliothèque de l'Arsenal, Paris
Aymon	Jean Aymon, ed., *Tous les synodes nationaux des églises reformées de France*, 2 Vol., (The Hague: Charles Delo, 1710)
BKC	Alma B. Calderwood, ed., *The Buik of the Kirk of the Canagait, 1564-1567*, (Edinburgh: Scottish Record Society, 1961)
Bruce	William Cunningham, ed., *Sermons by the Rev. Robert Bruce, Minister of Edinburgh*, (Edinburgh: Wodrow Society, 1843)
BSHPF	*Bulletin de la société de l'histoire du protestantisme français*
BUK	Thomas Thomson, ed., *Acts and Proceedings of the General Assemblies of the Kirk of Scotland*, 3 Vol., (Edinburgh: Bannatyne and Maitland Clubs, 1839-1845)
Calderwood	Thomas Thomson, ed., *The History of the Kirk of Scotland by Mr David Calderwood, some time minister of Crailing*, 8 Vol., (Edinburgh: Wodrow Society, 1842-9)

Canon. Recs.	"Extracts From the Records of the Burgh of the Canongate Near Edinburgh," *Maitland Club Miscellany* 2, (Edinburgh: Maitland Club, 1840), pp. 281-359
Dun KS	Henry Paton, ed., *Dundonald Parish Records. The Session Book of Dundonald, 1602-1731*, (Edinburgh: Bute Society, 1936)
Edin. Recs.	*Extracts From the Records of the Burgh of Edinburgh, 1403-1589*, 4 Vol., (Edinburgh: Burgh Records Society, 1869-82)
ERT	*Commissariat of Edinburgh: Register of Testaments 1514-1700*, 2 Vol., (Edinburgh: Scottish Record Society 1897-8)
Fasti	Hew Scott, ed., *Fasti Ecclesiae Scoticanae*, 9 Vol., (Edinburgh: Oliver and Boyd, 1915-51)
Hist. Ecc.	G. Baum and E. Cunitz, eds., *Histoire ecclesiastique des églises reformées au royaume de France*, (attributed to Theodore Beza), 3 Vol., (Nieuwkoop: B. de Graaf, 1974)
JMD	Robert Pitcairn, ed., *The Autobiography and Diary of Mr James Melvill, minister of Kilrenny*, (Edinburgh: Wodrow Society, 1842)
Knox	David Laing, ed., *The Works of John Knox*, 6 Vol., (Edinburgh: Wodrow Society, 1846-64)
NLS	National Library of Scotland, Edinburgh
NRH	Office of Her Majesty's Registrar General, New Register House, Edinburgh
Pit. Crim.	Robert Pitcairn, ed., *Ancient Criminal Trials in Scotland*, 3 Vol., (Edinburgh: William Tait, 1833)

Quick John Quick, ed., *Synodicon in Gallia Reformata*, 2 Vol., (London: Parkhurst and Robinson, 1692)

RCPG R.M. Kingdon and J.F. Bergier, eds., *Registres de la Compagnie des Pasteurs de Genève au temps de Calvin*, (Genève: Droz, 1964-)

Recueil Gén. Isambert, Decrusy and Taillander, eds., *Recueil général des anciennes lois françaises*, 28 Vol., (Paris: Belin-Leprieur, 1824-33)

Row John Row, *The Historie of the Kirk of Scotland*, 2 Vol., (Edinburgh: Maitland Club, 1842)

RSCHS *Records of the Scottish Church History Society*

Spottiswoode John Spottiswoode, *History of the Church of Scotland*, 3 Vol., (Edinburgh: Bannatyne Club, 1847-51)

SPR James Kirk, ed., *Stirling Presbytery Records, 1581-1587*, (Edinburgh: Scottish History Society, 1981)

SRO Scottish Record Office (main), Register House, Edinburgh

StAP Mark Smith, ed., *The Presbytery of St. Andrews, 1586-1605: A Study and Annotated Edition of the Register of the Minutes of the Presbytery of St. Andrews*, (St. Andrews University Ph.D. Thesis, 1986)

StAKS D. Hay Fleming, ed., *Register of the Minister, Elders and Deacons of the Christian Congregation of St Andrews 1559-1600*, 2 Vol., (Edinburgh: Scottish History Society, 1889-90)

StART *Commissariat of St. Andrews: Register of Testaments 1549-1800*, (Edinburgh: Scottish Record Society, 1902)

StAUM   St. Andrews University Muniments

WRH   Scottish Record Office (modern records and mic-
                            rofilms of manuscripts deposited elsewhere), West
                            Register House, Edinburgh

ACKNOWLEDGEMENTS

While this study bears my name alone, I have been blessed by the help and encouragement of many. The project was born with Carlos Eire's suggestion that Reformed consistory courts might make an interesting topic for a research paper. That they did, but the research paper never seemed to end. Erik Midelfort was quick to see the potential for more in the subject, and I have valued greatly his guidance and criticisms along the way. Raymond Mentzer was very kind and generous with his advice on the French angle, and in helping me see the "pan-Calvinist" elements in the subject. My work in Scotland was aided substantially by Michael Lynch, G.W.S. Barrow and the Scottish History Department at Edinburgh University, where I was made to feel most welcome while far away from home. James Kirk also saved me a great deal of time and helped me focus some of my ideas with good advice one very rainy morning in Glasgow. But most of all, I would like to thank Martin J. Havran, who pored over every page of an earlier version of this work, finding ways to improve most of them. Even when we did not agree, the debates improved the final product.

I have also been helped along the way by the staffs of several libraries and archives. First mention should go to Alderman Library at the University of Virginia, particularly its interlibrary loan department. The staffs of the Scottish Record Office, the Registrar General's Office for Scotland, and the National Library of Scotland, all in Edinburgh, and the Muniments Room at the St. Andrews University Library were also unfailingly kind, courteous and deadly competent. In addition, I am indebted to the librarians and archivists at the British Library in London, the Bibliothèque de l'Arsenal in Paris, and the Archives Départmentales du Tarn in Albi. All quotations from the OPR (old parish registers) series deposited in the New Register House, Edinburgh, are made with the permission of the controller of Her Britannic Majesty's Stationery Office.

On the technical and financial side, I would like to thank Joe Wynne and Rea Klosky for help with the mysteries of data processing. Joe Stoll of the Laboratory for Cartographic and Spatial Analysis at the University of Akron developed the maps for the book, working from sketches supplied by Elizabeth Armstrong. The Corcoran Department of History and the Graduate School of Arts and Sciences at the University of Virginia were generous with financial support, as was the dean's office at Coker College. Funds from the National Endowment for the Humanities allowed me to participate in Hans J. Hillerbrand's seminar on religion and social change in the sixteenth century at Duke University in the summer of 1995, giving me time to hone this manuscript, and fellow scholars with which to discuss it. My colleagues at Coker College and the University of Akron have been very supportive as the book has evolved into its final form, and I thank them for their patience and understanding. Finally, Heiko Oberman of the University of Arizona contributed many useful criticisms, and I am grateful to him for including this book in the *Studies in Medieval and Reformation Thought* series. Needless to say, any errors which remain are mine alone; none of the above should be held guilty by association.

INTRODUCTION

The complaint that society was beset by unprecedented disorder was common in the sixteenth century, as it has been in other times. Jean Calvin, Martin Bucer and other leading figures in the Reformed tradition saw around them a society of men and women at odds with God and with each other, a society in which base instincts ruled, unchecked by civil authorities and the existing ecclesiastical establishments. The old ties of feudal paternalism and the Universal Church were breaking, but nothing had yet emerged to replace them. Society was overflowing with eschatological expectation, but ordinary people seemed woefully unprepared for the day of reckoning. Children no longer respected parents, masters could no longer control their servants, widespread infidelity threatened the institution of marriage (and brought with it the threat of divine vengeance), and the lower orders knew no shame.

The truth of these complaints is hard to gauge from the distance of more than 400 years. What is undeniable is that they are a common refrain in the literature of the period, and that various remedies were suggested. This study is concerned with one of those remedies: the type of church discipline which has been termed "Calvinist," although such labeling obscures the fact that its true origins lie not with Calvin but in the writings of Johannes Oecolampadius and Bucer, and in their attempts to recreate what they considered to have been the institutions of the primitive Christian Church. Thus it would be better to call this "Reformed Church Discipline," due to the fact that its theorists felt that they were re-forming the primitive church, and that the churches which adopted it called themselves "Reformed."

By "Reformed Church Discipline" I mean a system which sought to modify the behavior of individual church members through a network of church courts, usually called consistories, staffed by ministers and lay elders and deacons. These courts (which also had responsibility for poor relief and other aspects of local church administration) were theoretically to be independent of civil authorities, and they had the power to impose sanctions, including the highest sanction of excommunication, without reference to any civil magistrate.

Thus the institution and practice of Reformed Church Discipline was an effort by churches acting on their own to convert reformed doctrine into practice, and to move the religious changes which were taking place from the realm of theology and worship into the realm of everyday life. The church members whose lives were to be reformed might be active members of gathered, voluntary congregations, or they might simply be residents of a region in which a Reformed Church, with Reformed Church Discipline, had been institutionalized. Supporters of this system felt that the state and its officials should act as a "nursing mother" to the church, to assist and support it, but that they should not have any supervisory power over its disciplinary courts. Not surprisingly, this last point was controversial wherever the state was officially reformed, and debate on the matter—between Oecolampadius and Ulrich Zwingli, between Bucer and the Strasbourg city council, between Calvin and the Genevan magistrates, and between Scottish presbyterian ministers and King James VI—continued throughout the sixteenth century.

The combination of extensive lay participation and independence from civil authority made these Reformed consistories (to use the generic term) unique in early modern Europe, and distinguished them from the pre-Reformation church courts as well. From their seats of authority, "pious laymen of good repute" and their ministers watched a seemingly endless procession of adulterers, fornicators, blasphemers, gamblers, murderers, Sabbath-breakers, drunkards, dancers, witches, quarrelers and other sinners march by. Never before had the taverns, living rooms and (where they existed) bedrooms of Europe been subjected to such close surveillance. The disciplinary efforts of the consistories represent an early example of an attempt at social engineering on a societal scale.

The object here is to trace briefly the intellectual and practical origins of this system, and then to examine closely its imposition and practice in one region—lowland Scotland—in the late sixteenth and early seventeenth centuries. A comparative look at the disciplinary system developed in the Huguenot churches of France at the same time will demonstrate how the concept could play a different role in another environment, where the state was more hostile but the congregation perhaps more enthusiastic. This study is both qualitative and quantitative, with a collection of approximately 6000 disciplinary cases, gathered from numerous localities, providing the quantitative basis upon which many conclusions will be reached. But human behavior cannot be described and assessed through statistics alone, and considerable attention will be devoted to the language employed—by offenders, witnesses, ministers and elders—and the nature of the behaviors and attitudes described. No such study has previously been offered for Scotland. Historians of French and continental Protestantism have completed some analogous research, and this study owes a debt to those scholars, as will become apparent. In particular, the comparative aspects of this study would have been impossible without their efforts. Surprisingly, no one has as yet undertaken a major study of comparative Reformed discipline.

In Scotland, these theoretically independent church courts, the kirk sessions and (later) presbyteries, were established in a nation whose legal system was, even by sixteenth century standards, primitive. Thus the consistories grew alongside the secular courts and came to complement them in an era which saw a renewed effort to tame what seemed to contemporaries a particularly violent and disorderly society. In France, on the other hand, the *consistoires* were careful to distinguish themselves and their procedures from the pre-existing legal system. They and the discipline they imposed helped the Reformed community define itself in a hostile world, whereas in Scotland a heavier emphasis was placed on reforming, or at least neutralizing, the enemy within. In both countries, these church courts and their members found themselves at odds with traditional institutions such as the family, the extended kinship network, the crown and aristocracy, and already-established local authorities who viewed the new church courts as unwelcome meddlers. In both countries, they had to find a way to use and cooperate with these authorities and institutions, while still maintaining their own independence. And, in both countries they had to learn to get the maximum effect out of what were largely symbolic punishments. Examination of their successes and failures, and of the ways they adapted themselves to local conditions, can tell us a great deal about the practical implications of ideas in the Reformation period, and of the impact of religious changes on everyday life. Further, the reactions of those subject to discipline reveal something about popular attitudes and culture, and the extent to which the Reformation was a grassroots movement.

CHAPTER ONE

THE FOUNDATIONS OF REFORMED DISCIPLINE

If your brother sins against you, go and tell him his fault, between you and him alone. If he listens to you, you have gained your brother. But if he does not listen, take one or two others along with you, that every word may be confirmed by the evidence of two or three witnesses. If he refuses to listen to them, tell it to the church; and if he refuses to listen even to the church, let him be to you as a Gentile and a tax collector. Truly, I say to you, whatever you bind on earth shall be bound in heaven, and whatever you loose on earth shall be loosed in heaven.
                              - Matthew 18:15-19[1]

In the beginning, each church therefore had as a council a consistory of good, honest men, sober and of holy life, who had the authority to correct vices as will be seen below. But experience shows that this state was not for one age only. Therefore it must be held that this office of government is necessary for all time.
                              - Jean Calvin, *L'Institution de la Religion Chrétienne*, Book 4, Chapter 3, Section 8[2]

Out of the evangelist's words, and through the reformer's exegesis, there developed in Calvinist Europe during the sixteenth century a system of church discipline more intensive than any seen since at least the early days of the Christian Church. In Geneva and Huguenot France the *consistoire*, in Scotland the kirk session and/or presbytery, and in Calvinist territories in Germany and the Low Countries the *Kirchenrat* and/or *Presbyterium* sought to ensure that the congregation not only heard the Word, but also made a reasonable effort to live by it. The laymen appointed to these bodies worked with their ministers to chastize and correct, to settle disputes, and were expected themselves to serve as models of piety and godliness. In the process, control over a significant portion of the business of the church was

---

[1] All biblical references come from *The New Oxford Annotated Bible*, (Oxford: Oxford University Press, 1973).

[2] The edition of *L'Institution* used in this study is that published at Geneva in 1955-58, following Calvin's 1560 French edition. All translations are mine, and the passage quoted above appears on page 61 of book 4 in that edition: "Au commencement chaque Eglise a donc eu comme un conseil un consistoire de bons prud'hommes, graves et de sainte vie, qui avaient l'authorité de corriger les vices comme il sera vu ci-apres. Or, que cet état n'ait point été pour un seul âge, l'expérience le démontre. Il faut donc tenir que cet office de gouvernement est nécessaire pour tout temps."

entrusted to these laymen, undercutting the oft-criticized clerical monopoly over the sacraments and salvation which had prevailed in the traditional Catholic Church.[3]

As might be expected, humanity proved unperfectable; there was always business for consistories to do. But the nature of this business differed over time and from one region to another. Such differences may reflect distinct culturally- or environmentally- determined patterns of behavior, the particular interests of church officials, or both. In either case (and it seems likely that the choices of officials had a greater effect on consistorial case-loads than did the behavior of congregations), the study of consistorial records can yield a great deal of information regarding the role of the church in the community and the attitudes and actions of its members, both godly and wayward.

For some, the consistory has seemed the classic institution in the development of puritan behavioral codes, a kind of neighborly "Big Brother." E. William Monter has called the Geneva consistory "the effective motor behind the establishment of the first Puritan society."[4] Steven Ozment has even seen in it and the related spread of Calvinist church ordinances a "new papacy," which simply replaced one brand of ecclesiastical intrusiveness with another.[5] Consistorial investigations certainly seem invasive enough; in an early study of one consistory roll, Oudot de Dainville recounted house-to-house visitations by elders searching for crucifixes or other Catholic images in the southern French village of Ganges, and their spying on a local *sieur* who they suspected was about to meet with a woman for immoral purposes.[6] Robert Kingdon opines that the "moral austerity" characteristic of Calvinism originated with the enforcement of morals by consistory courts.[7] Raymond Mentzer places the

---

[3] The anticlerical literature of the pre-reformation and early Reformation period is voluminous. See, for example, Sebastian Brant's *Ship of Fools*, edited and translated by Edwin Zeydel, (New York: Columbia University Press, 1944); Desiderius Erasmus, "A Pilgrimage for Religion's Sake," in Craig R. Thompson, ed. and trans., *Erasmus: Ten Colloquies*, (New York: Liberal Arts Press, 1957), 56-91; or, for a Scots example, Sir David Lindsay's *Ane Satyre of the Thrie Estaitis*, (Edinburgh: Scottish Text Society, 1931).

[4] E. William Monter, "The Consistory of Geneva, 1559-1569," *Bibliothèque D'Humanisme et Renaissance* 38 (1976), 467-484, at 467.

[5] Steven Ozment, *The Reformation in the Cities: The Appeal of Protestantism to Sixteenth-Century Germany and Switzerland*, (New Haven: Yale University Press, 1975), 153-5 and *ibidem, The Age of Reform: 1250-1550*, (New Haven: Yale University Press, 1980), 372-380.

[6] Oudot de Dainville, "Le Consistoire de Ganges à la fin du XVIe Siècle," *Revue de L'Eglise de France* 18 (1932), 464-485, at 466.

[7] Robert Kingdon, "The Control of Morals in Calvin's Geneva," in Lawrence P. Buck and Jonathan W. Zophy, eds., *The Social History of the Reformation*, (Columbus: Ohio State University Press, 1972), 3-16, at 4. Elsewhere, Kingdon muses on the seeming irony of such

consistory in the vanguard of a process of local "communal reorganization" undertaken by the Huguenots of southern France.[8] Janine Garrisson and Bernard Vogler argue that "of all the lay and ecclesiastical institutions created by Protestantism in the sixteenth century, the consistory is the most original and the most significant in the reformed world of continental Europe, by which it [Protestantism] facilitated solidarity against the Catholic Church and a common faith against nationalisms."[9] Elsewhere, Garrisson has gone so far as to say that the history of French Protestantism *is* the study of consistories.[10]

Such statements, by claiming so much for the consistory, may exaggerate both its historical significance and the real scope of its mission, characterized by Garrisson as nothing short of a complete moral reformation, an essential step in the creation of an earthly commonwealth which would be a "perfect image of the paradise lost."[11] Heinz Schilling makes what is on the surface a more modest claim; in his view, the goal of the consistory was merely, as far as possible, to protect the purity of the Lord's Supper—"Consistorial discipline is the instrument to ensure the worthiness of every Communion participant and with that the purity of the community."[12] The difference between these two views is reflective of the difference between the consistory's theoretical basis and its actual function. The former was an ideal held in common throughout Calvinist Europe, the latter a more reachable goal, influenced by local needs and conditions. As an historian primarily of the early Huguenots, Garrisson puts the consistory's

---

an intense interest in personal morality in a creed which placed such a great emphasis on salvation by faith alone and predestination. See Robert Kingdon, "The Control of Morals by the Earliest Calvinists," in Peter de Klerk, ed., *Renaissance, Reformation, Resurgence*, (Grand Rapids, Michigan: Calvin Theological Seminary, 1976), 95-106, at 96.

[8] Raymond Mentzer, "Ecclesiastical Discipline and Communal Reorganization among the Protestants of Southern France," *European History Quarterly* 21 (1991), 163-83.

[9] J. (Garrisson) Estèbe and Bernard Vogler, "La Genèse d'une société Protestante: Etude comparée de quelques registres consistoriaux Languedociens et Palatins vers 1600," *Annales Economies, Sociétés, Civilisations*, 1976, 362-87, at 362: "De toutes les institutions laïques et ecclesiastiques créées par le protestantisme au XVIe siècle, le Consistoire est bien le plus originale et la plus significative du monde réformé d'Europe occidentale, dont il favorise la solidarité face à l'Eglise Catholique et la foi commune face aux nationalismes."

[10] Janine Garrisson-Estebe, *Les Protestants du Midi, 1559-1598*, (Toulouse: Privat, 1980), 92.

[11] *Ibid*, 114, 227: "image parfait du Paradis perdu."

[12] Heinz Schilling, "Reformierte Kirchenzucht als Sozialdisziplinierung? Die Tätigkeit des Emder Presbyteriums in den Jahren 1557-1562," in Wilfried Ehbrecht and Heinz Schilling, eds., *Niederland und Nordwestdeutschland: Studien zur Regional- und Staatgeschichte Nordwestkontinentaleuropas im Mittelalter und in der Neuzeit*, (Köln: Bohlau, 1983), 261-367, at 274: "Die Kirchenzucht ist das Instrument, die Würdigkeit jedes einzelnen zum Abendmahl und damit die Reinheit der Gemeinde insgesamt sicherzustellen."

work at the forefront of an evangelical crusade aimed at creating the *civitas Dei*. Schilling, concentrating on one particular consistory (that of Emden), over several centuries, prefers to study it against the background of a general "civilizing process"—a metahistorical trend toward a more peaceful and polite society—of which it was but one element.[13]

Heinrich Schmidt, following Schilling in part but downplaying the religious element, posits a "Kolonialismusmodell"—seeing in Reformed church discipline a prime example of elite culture trying to fashion popular culture in its own image.[14] Likewise, Gerhard Oestreich found little of the sacred in the process, and viewed "social discipline" as a facet of Neostoicism, which re-educated the European population for the life of "work, frugality, dutifulness and obedience" which the nascent absolutist state required of its subjects. With this, according to Oestreich, came "a change in the ethos of the individual and his self-perception."[15] Others take such secularization even farther and treat church discipline primarily as an aspect of the history of courts and criminology.[16] Each approach, while

---

[13] John Bossy has suggested that church *disciplina* itself was such a trend, common to Catholic as well as Protestant countries in the sixteenth and seventeenth centuries. See his *Christianity in the West: 1400-1700*, (Oxford: Oxford University Press, 1984), 126-7. Schilling borrows the idea of a "civilizing process" from Norbert Elias, as elucidated in the latter's *Uber den Prozess der Zivilisation. Soziogenetische und psychogenetische Untersuchungen*, (2 Vols) (Bern: 1936).

[14] Heinrich Richard Schmidt, "Die Christianisierung des Sozialverhaltens als permanente Reformation. Aus der Praxis reformierter Sittengerichte in der Schweiz während der frühen Neuzeit," in Peter Blickle and Johannes Kunisch, eds., *Kommunalisierung und Christianisierung: Voraussetzungen und Folgen der Reformation 1400-1600*, (Berlin: Duncker und Humblot, 1989), 113-163, at 121-3. For a discussion of the interplay between "popular" and "elite" culture, see Peter Burke, *Popular Culture in Early Modern Europe*, (London: Maurice Temple Smith, 1978), 205-86.

[15] Gerhard Oestreich, *Neostoicism and the Early Modern State*, (Brigitta Oestreich and H.G. Koenigsberger, eds. and David McLintock, trans.), (Cambridge: Cambridge University Press, 1982), 7, 156-9, 267-70. Oestreich's concentration on discipline as an element of state power makes his theory of dubious value when examining areas (such as Scotland and Huguenot France) where the power to discipline was primarily in ecclesiastical rather than magisterial hands. The same problem exists in R. Po-chia Hsia, *Social Discipline in the Reformation: Central Europe 1550-1750*, (London: Routledge, 1989), e.g. at 122: "One of the consequences of the Reformation and Counter-Reformation was the imposition of social discipline by the early modern state, in a process which displayed a parallel development in Lutheran, Catholic and Calvinist territories." For another criticism of these approaches, see Heinz Schilling, "'History of Crime' or 'History of Sin'? Some Reflections on the Social History of Early Modern Church Discipline," in E.I. Kouri and Tom Scott, eds., *Politics and Society in Reformation Europe: Essays for Sir Geoffrey Elton on his Sixty-Fifth Birthday*, (London: MacMillan, 1987), 289-310, at 290-3.

[16] V.A.C. Gatrell, Bruce Lenman and Geoffrey Parker, eds., *Crime and the Law: The Social History of Crime in Western Europe Since 1500*, (London: Europa, 1980), 11-48 and 120-154 (chapter by Stephen Davies).

illuminating, is extreme; one cannot address the subject without considering its theological elements, but at the same time one must recognize that this was a practical effort, undertaken in many cases for quite secular reasons. Bruce Lenman has noted the effect social disciplining schemes have had in giving legitimation to new political regimes: "puritanical rigour as a means of validating new regimes seems to be a cross-cultural phenomenon, as valid a concept in the Iran of Ayatollah Khomeini as in sixteenth-century Europe."[17] Reformed discipline in the age of the Reformation undoubtedly has a doctrinal history, a social history and a political history, but these threads ought to be woven together, not pulled apart.

Background: The Early Church

Jean Calvin (1509-1564), naturally, looms large in any study of what has come to be viewed as "Calvinist" discipline, mainly because he succeeded in implementing a system at Geneva that was copied elsewhere. But while the system itself may have been original to Geneva, the concept was not, and even those who can be credited with authorship more justly than Calvin did not consider themselves to be originators, but rather re-creators of a system which they believed had operated in the primitive church.

At the root of consistorial discipline was the concept of the ban, or excommunication; this was the ultimate sanction the church possessed. Christ himself has been taken to have spoken of it and its consequences when he gave to the apostle Peter the power of the "keys" in Matthew 16:19: "whatever you bind on earth shall be bound in heaven, and whatever you loose on earth shall be loosed in heaven." Biblical scholars have given the ban a pedigree stretching back to the Garden of Eden, where Adam and Eve transgressed, were cursed by God, and then exiled permanently. At the Dead Sea Essene community of Qumran, exclusion from community meals was apparently the major form of punishment, a significant fact in light of the sacramental Communion "meal" practiced later in Christian churches. Even the disciplinary process described in Matthew 18 (quoted at the beginning of this chapter) was reflective of contemporary Jewish practice.[18]

Excommunication in the early Christian church was not regarded as a sentence of eternal damnation, although it was thought that it could have that effect on an incorrigible sinner. Rather, it was used as a corrective tool, in the hope that the resulting social pressure of being ostracized, as

---

[17] Bruce Lenman, "The Limits of Godly Discipline In the Early Modern Period," in Kaspar von Greyerz, ed., *Religion and Society in Early Modern Europe, 1500-1800*, (London: German Historical Institute, 1984), 124-45, at 130.

[18] Kenneth Hein, *Eucharist and Excommunication: A Study in Early Christian Doctrine and Discipline*, (Bern: Herbert Lang, 1973), 4-5, 11, 17.

well as anxiety over salvation, would lead the sinner to repentance.[19] It was a tool which some communities were reluctant to use, and Paul chastized the church at Corinth in A.D. 57 for its refusal to cast out a member who had committed incest.[20] Sexual sins figure prominently among those mentioned in early church writings; Clement of Alexandria (c. 150-215) mentioned excommunication of sexual sinners along with murderers and heretics.[21] The anthropologist Mary Douglas has used the early Church as an example of a community which sought to hold itself together in a hostile world by placing a high value on chastity and even virginity.[22] Certainly, the practice of discipline and excommunication was important in reinforcing this, and thus in cementing the communal bond.

Naturally, in a society where a particular group is not officially sanctioned, its membership is bound to be fluid, and it is likely to seek a way to define membership through participation in ceremonial rites. Thus Origen (c. 185-254) and other early theologians came to consider participation in Communion and membership in the Church to be one and the same thing. Those who took part were Christians and those who did not, either through lack of interest or exclusion, were not. Communion was a kind of door through which all Christians had to pass, and those responsible for discipline and excommunication were its keepers. The *Didache*, a document of the first-century Church, specified that church members were to confess their sins and settle disputes before participating in Communion, "so that your sacrifice may not be profaned."[23]

As the Church became institutionalized and was given official sanction, first by Roman emperors and later by medieval kings, this exclusivity became more difficult to maintain. Excommunication, imposed by bishops and their deputies, lost much of its spiritual sting as it became a legal formality, often imposed for debt or other secular offenses. One historian of medieval excommunication has called it a "mere relic" of what was once a much more serious penalty.[24] Communion became less of a defining

---

[19] *Ibid*, 70.

[20] 1 Corinthians 5:2, cited in Hein, 92-3.

[21] *Ibid*, 223-4, 273-5.

[22] Mary Douglas, *Purity and Danger: An Analysis of the Concepts of Pollution and Taboo*, (London: Routledge and Kegan Paul, 1966), 158.

[23] Hein, 193, 316-30.

[24] Elisabeth Vodola, *Excommunication in the Middle Ages*, (Berkeley: University of California Press, 1986), 179-80, 192-3. See also Ralph Houlbrooke, *Church Courts and the People During the English Reformation 1520-1570*, (Oxford: Oxford University Press, 1979), 9; Gordon Donaldson, *The Scottish Reformation*, (Cambridge: Cambridge University Press, 1960), 41; Ian Cowan, *The Scottish Reformation*, (New York: St. Martin's Press, 1982), 21; David Smith, "The Spiritual Jurisdiction, 1560-64," *RSCHS* 25 (1993), 1-18, at 3-4. Denis

moment when essentially everyone became a Christian simply by residence
in a Christian territory. Church courts seemed largely unconcerned about
individual behavior.[25] But in the sixteenth century, as central and western
Europe's essential religious unity was shattered, some reformers sought to
rebuild the Church from the ground up and re-create the disciplinary
practice and quest for purity prescribed in the first and second centuries.
This sixteenth-century movement for religious purity coincided with efforts
by laymen throughout Europe to attain more control over the Church. These
two movements were sometimes in harmony (as when reformers sought to
appoint lay elders to the newly-erected consistories) and sometimes in
conflict (as when they clashed with civil authorities over who should
ultimately have the power to excommunicate). The effects—ecclesiastical,
social and political—were to be far-reaching.

Oecolampadius and Bucer

Ulrich Zwingli (1484-1531), Johannes Oecolampadius (1482-1531), Martin
Bucer (1491-1551), Peter Martyr (1500-1562) and Calvin were all keenly
interested in the notion of eldership, and found evidence of it in the North
African churches described by Origen, Cyprian, Optatus, Augustine and
Isidore of Seville.[26] But the first sixteenth-century reformer to argue for an
eldership which would administer discipline independent of civil authority
was Oecolampadius, who insisted on autonomy for the church in the
disciplinary sphere.[27]

Oecolampadius' interest in the reform of individual behavior may have
originated in his short stint as a penitentiary in the diocese of Basel in 1518-
19. In this post, he heard confessions and prescribed penance. But the result
for him was disillusionment; by 1521, having given up his position and
become a monk, he openly criticized Catholic penitential practices. In a

---

McKay cites, for example, Scottish rural deans investigating such seemingly civil cases as the
theft of nails, along with more strictly religious offenses such as absence from Easter
Communion. See his "Parish Life in Scotland, 1500-1560," in David McRoberts, ed., *Essays
on the Scottish Reformation 1513-1625*, (Glasgow: J.S. Burns, 1962), 98.

[25] Noted in the case of Scotland by Patrick Rayner, Bruce Lenman and Geoffrey Parker,
Handlist of Records for the Study of Crime In Early Modern Scotland (to 1747), (London: List
and Index Society, 1982), 144; and Cowan, *Scottish Reformation*, 138.

[26] T.F. Torrance, "The Eldership in the Reformed Church," *Scottish Journal of Theology*
37 (1984), 503-518, at 505.

[27] Akira Demura, *Church Discipline According to Johannes Oecolampadius In the Setting
of His Life and Thought*, (Th.D. Thesis, Princeton Theological Seminary, 1964), 16; Elsie Ann
McKee, *Elders and the Plural Ministry: The Role of Exegetical History in Illuminating John
Calvin's Theology*, (Genève: Libraire Droz, 1988), 18. John Bossy incorrectly credits Bucer
with being the sixteenth-century originator of this concept. See Bossy, 128-9.

tract entitled *Quod Non Sit Onerosa Christianis Confessio*, he charged that the penitentiaries were petty tyrants, and commended the fraternal confession described by St. James (James 5:16) as preferable to the Catholic sacrament of penance. The papal nuncio Aleander, seeing this as a frontal attack on auricular confession, charged that Oecolampadius was "worse than Luther."[28]

Oecolampadius left the cloister and broke with the Catholic Church in 1522. In addition to his concerns about confession, he felt that the old church had abused the sentence of excommunication, imposing it too frequently and for the wrong reasons. In 1525 he wrote a reformed version of the Catholic missal used in Basel up to that time, specifying in what instances excommunication ought to be used:

> We excommunicate [*verbannen*] only those who are to be excommunicated by the Word of God and those who thereby put the body of Christ to shame as unwholesome and rotten members thereof. We should and do make it known that we have no fellowship here in this supper [Communion] with the idolaters, sorcerers, blasphemers, despisers of God's Word and of the holy sacraments of Baptism and the Lord's Supper. May they be excommunicated...who do not hold their father and mother in esteem, who are disobedient to the secular authority and insurgent, who oppose tithe and toll, etc, those who will not let the Word judge in the matter of faith. May these be excommunicated—all murderers and those who do not redress the tendency toward it, all those who fight in wanton sport, fornicator, adulterer, drunkard and reveller, thief, robber, usurer or one who gains improper profit...[29]

Oecolampadius then sought to convert others to his views.

Basel's civic revolution in the spring of 1529 made the city officially protestant, but left unresolved many questions of church polity. The *Reformationsordnung* of April 1529 stipulated that sinners should get two "fraternal admonitions" before being excommunicated, and that the authority to excommunicate was vested solely in parish ministers and deacons.[30] But this latter claim was soon disputed by civic authorities anxious about the prospect of ministerial tyranny. For them, the best reason for reform had been to lessen clerical pretentions and increase lay control over the civic church, not simply to pass power from one type of clergy to another.[31] To counter these concerns, Oecolampadius proposed the appointment of four city councilmen and four other laymen to a twelve-member board of censors

---

[28] Demura, 35, 40-3.

[29] Julius Smerd, ed., *Die evangelischen deutschen Messen bis zu Luthers Deutscher Messe*, (Göttingen: Vandenhoeck and Ruprecht, 1886), 215-6, cited in Demura, 55.

[30] Demura, 71-2.

[31] Ozment, *Reformation in the Cities*, *passim*.

for the town. He saw precedent for this in the *seniores* or *presbyteroi* of the primitive Church. A disciplinary ordinance was passed in June 1530, dividing the city into four consistories, and ordaining three warnings before excommunication.[32] But the Basel magistrates were still hesitant to let the church control the process, and they found allies in other Swiss cities.

The *Ehegericht*, or marriage court, established in Zurich after that city's Reformation in 1525, was a magisterial court, not an ecclesiastical court, and it soon came to handle all sorts of morals cases. Zwingli, the reformer of Zurich, after some wavering on the issue, finally opposed taking ultimate power over excommunication away from the magistrate. To him, the *presbyteroi* of the New Testament were civic officials, responsible more for preventing crime and disorder than for protecting the purity of Communion. He felt that excommunication as practiced by the primitive Church had been an emergency measure, necessitated by the fact that there was as yet no Christian secular government. With the triumph of Christianity in the early middle ages, Zwingli considered Church and society to have become one and the same, whereas Oecolampadius saw a clear, continuing distinction between the two. Indeed, in Zwingli's Zurich, the City Council controlled both excommunication and baptism.[33] Oecolampadius and Zwingli debated the matter in writing, but both died in 1531, leaving the question unsettled, and the ministry of Basel itself divided in opinion. Even before Oecolampadius' death in November, the Basel magistrates had been brought into the excommunication process.[34]

Yet while Oecolampadius' quest for autonomous church discipline through a consistory of ministers and laymen met defeat in Basel and Zurich, it won a significant convert in Martin Bucer, the reformer of Strasbourg. Like Oecolampadius, Bucer was ultimately unsuccessful in getting his own city to adopt the plan, but he brought it to a wider audience including, eventually, Calvin. But Bucer was not simply passing on the ideas of another. Rather, he took the concept of autonomous church discipline with the participation of lay elders, and expanded it into a detailed ecclesiology, with extensive biblical exegesis to back it up. He fully developed the notion of a plural ministry, giving those lay elders a quasi-

---

[32] Demura, 85, 119.

[33] J. Wayne Baker, "Church Discipline or Civil Punishment: On the Origins of the Reformed Schism, 1528-1531," *Andrews University Seminary Studies* 23 (1985), 3-18, at 3-4, 6-11; *ibidem*, "Calvin's Discipline and the Early Reformed Tradition," in Robert Schnucker, ed., *Calviniana*, (Kirksville, Missouri: Sixteenth Century Publishers, 1988), 107-119, at 107-8; Robert Walton, *Zwingli's Theocracy*, (Toronto: University of Toronto Press, 1967), 209-11; John T. McNeill, *The History and Character of Calvinism*, (New York: Oxford University Press, 1954), 78-9.

[34] Demura, 138, 142-3.

clerical vocation. These ideas simmered and developed while he was immersed in the church polity disputes in Strasbourg in the 1530s and 1540s, and during that time he also wrote church ordinances for other cities and territories, leaving behind several descriptions of how he thought the system should work.

Comparing Bucer with Martin Luther, Wilhelm Pauck has observed that whereas Luther saw a distinction between Law and Gospel, Bucer refused to recognize such a barrier and "regarded the Reformation as a movement through which the Christianization of all human life was to be accomplished. The Bible was for him the source and pattern of all legislation required to this end."[35] Nowhere is this more evident than in his disciplinary agenda. In his quest for the reform of individual lives as well as of the church, Bucer was probably influenced by Anabaptist notions of moral purity within the congregation. But Bucer sought a public church, not a gathered one, so he had to find a way to force the less-sanctified into the community of the saints, while at the same time "chase the sinners out of the church."[36] Already, by 1527-28, he was writing that the stubborn sinner must, out of love, be excluded from the community until he saw the error of his ways.[37]

By 1530, Bucer was in correspondence with Oecolampadius on the subject, and in October of that year he visited Basel.[38] From that point on, he became the champion of the need for a powerful church with its own institutions, independent of the civil magistrate.[39] It was also at this time that Bucer was developing his theory of the plural ministry. In his 1530 Gospel commentaries, he argued that Scripture enumerated four types of ministers—doctors (that is, teachers of Theology), pastors, governors (elders) and deacons.[40] All four of these types came to serve on Reformed consistories in various places at various times, but only the participation of the latter three became a requirement. The critical text for Bucer and those who followed him came to be Paul's letter to the Ephesians 4:11-12: "And his gifts were that some should be apostles, some prophets, some evangelists, some pastors and teachers, to equip the saints for the work of

---

[35] From the editor's introduction to *De Regno Christi* in Wilhelm Pauck, ed. and trans., *Melanchthon and Bucer*, (Philadelphia: Westminster Press, 1969), 156.

[36] Jacques Courvoisier, *La Notion d'église Chez Bucer dans son développement historique*, (Paris: Félix Alcan, 1933), 6-8, 13: "[Bucer] veut...chasser les pécheurs de l'église en réintroduisant la discipline de l'église primitive."

[37] *Ibid*, 73.

[38] *Ibid*, 24; H. Strohl, "La Théorie et la Pratique des Quatre Ministères à Strasbourg avant l'Arrivée de Calvin," *BHSPF* 84 (1935), 123-44, at 132-3.

[39] Strohl, 136.

[40] Courvoisier, 88; McKee, 75.

ministry, for building up the body of Christ."[41] And while, from an historical perspective, the appointment of elders seems to mark a move toward increased lay participation in the church, Bucer considered these laymen to be ministers, although not ministers of the word.[42]

Bucer's plural ministry was partially instituted in Strasbourg in 1534, with the passage of ecclesiastical ordinances which mandated the appointment of *Kirchenpfleger*, lay presbyters on a city-wide assembly, who were to seek out those who absented themselves from Communion and find out why. But, much to the frustration of Bucer and his allies, these *Kirchenpfleger* had little power to discipline. All who wished to attend Communion were to be allowed to, leaving it up to God to punish those who did so with guilty consciences. And under no circumstances were sinners, however notorious, to be deprived of civic rights and friendship unless punished by the civil magistrates for a civil offense.[43] For Bucer, to whom the use of excommunication defined the community, this was a critical flaw. Without exclusion from the Communion table, there was, in his eyes, no true spiritual community.[44]

While frustrated at home, Bucer had some success abroad, and in 1538 he was called upon to draft ordinances for the reformation of the Hessian church. These were then approved by the Synod of Ziegenhagen in 1539.[45] In these, the whole system of discipline, including the power of excommunication (*verbannung*), was placed in the hands of ministers, elders and superintendents. All churches in Hesse, however large or small, were to appoint "Presbiteros, das ist Eltesten" to supervise the Christian community.[46] These elders were to ensure that all parish residents came to preaching, but not necessarily to Communion, because those who did so unworthily would endanger not only their own souls, but the whole community (*Gemeyn*). Anyone wishing to participate in Communion had first to be cathechized, and could not be guilty of any major public sin for which they had not performed some sort of repentance. The first type of sinner mentioned as deserving exclusion was one who taught false doctrines, particularly those contrary to the Augsburg Confession. Next came those

---

[41] The importance of this passage is stressed by McKee, 133.

[42] Courvoisier, 101-2.

[43] *Ibid*, 30; Marc Lienhard, "L'Eglise aux mains de l'Etat? Magistrat et Eglise évangélique à Strasbourg de la Réforme à la guerre de Trente Ans," *BSHPF* 130 (1984), 295-318, at 306-7; Amy Nelson Burnett, "Church Discipline and Moral Reformation In the Thought of Martin Bucer," *Sixteenth Century Journal* 22 (1991), 439-56, at 449-50.

[44] Courvoisier, 114.

[45] Ordinances given in Aemilius Ludwig Richter, ed., *Die evangelischen Kirchenordnungen des sechszehnten Jahrhunderts* (2 Vol.), (Nieuwkoop: De Graaf, 1967), 1:290-5.

[46] *Ibid*, 1:290, col. 2.

who blasphemed, either in speech or writing, and then followed a list of other malefactors worthy of the ban: sexual sinners, drunkards, contentious persons, violent quarrellers, murderers and usurers.[47] Here, for the first time in the sixteenth century, was a system involving consistories with lay elders having the power to excommunicate—the type of church polity later established in Geneva, Scotland, the Huguenot churches of France, and other parts of Germany and the Netherlands.

It was at this point (1538-9) in Bucer's Strasbourg career, that he and his fellow ministers welcomed a young Frenchman who had been exiled from his adopted home of Geneva by a city government unwilling either to offend its powerful protector state of Bern, or to place too much power in the hands of the city's new Reformed ministry. This sojourner was Jean Calvin. His stay in Strasbourg came on the heels of Bucer's drafting the Hessian ordinances, and coincided with a renewal of the battle between Strasbourg's ministers and magistrates over the issue of discipline and excommunication.[48] Calvin's views on church discipline, as reflected in his *Institution of the Christian Religion* and his work in Geneva, will be examined later, but one must note here the importance of his residence in Strasbourg in developing these views. When Calvin left Geneva for Strasbourg in 1538, he was interested in church discipline as an antidote to the disorder which he saw as endemic in the world around him, but he had yet to develop (or embrace) the comprehensive theory of discipline, excommunication and the plural ministry which so marked his later career, and which subsequently became so central to "Calvinism." Yet he took just such a theory with him when he returned to Geneva in 1541, and Bucer clearly deserves much of the credit (or blame).[49]

Whatever the effect of Calvin's return on Genevan politics, the Strasbourg he left was no closer to attaining the Bucerian ideal in ecclesiastical polity than it had been upon his arrival. The final conflict between Bucer and his followers and the magistracy came in 1546-7 when the latter blocked Bucer's plan for parish-based elderships which would censure morals in voluntary "little churches within the church."[50] The minister Caspar Hedio, attempting to steer a middle course between Bucer and the magistrates (who were also concerned about the city's position in

---

[47] *Ibid*, 1:291, col. 2, 292, cols. 1-2.

[48] Courvoisier, 34-5, 137; E. William Monter, *Calvin's Geneva*, (New York: John Wiley and Sons, 1967), 67.

[49] Courvoisier probably overstates (or oversimplifies) the case when he claims that Calvin before 1538 was Lutheran and after 1541 "bucérian, ou mieux réformé," but the influence is unmistakable, particularly in the way he adopted Bucer's theory of a plural ministry. See Courvoisier, 143.

[50] "Ecclesiolae in ecclesia." See Lienhard, 309; Burnett, 446-7.

the aftermath of the Imperial victory over the Protestant Schmalkaldic League) reminded Bucer's party that the civil authorities "are also baptized in Jesus Christ," and argued that purely ecclesiastical discipline was impractical:

> We, the preachers and vicars, do not sail alone in the ship, as people say, but rather the authorities, (not the least important part of the church), sail with us and we with them together as subjects; so should we deal with everything for the betterment and necessity of the community of God with the knowledge, will and advice of the authorities.[51]

This was a view Zwingli would have endorsed, as would (later) Thomas Erastus and James VI and I. But to Bucer, it left the church only partly reformed.

Bucer's pleas fell on increasingly deaf ears in the late 1540s, as Strasbourg's magistrates tried to steer a conservative religious course in the interest of peace with the Holy Roman Emperor Charles V. No consistory was ever allowed to take the place of the old church courts. Sins simply became crimes tried in civil courts. The magistrates forbade clergy to name delinquents from the pulpit; they were to restrict themselves to preaching the Gospel.[52]

Bucer himself was exiled from the city, heading for England where he accepted a divinity chair at Cambridge in 1549. There, in the last year of his life, he wrote his major institutional work *De Regno Christi*.[53] This was a prescription for reform of the English church dedicated to the boy king Edward VI, and in it the mature Bucer expounded fully his ecclesiology. Bucer died in March 1551, and the book was not published until 1557, at Basel. Ironically, it never appeared in English during the sixteenth or seventeenth centuries, but a French translation was published at Geneva in 1558.[54]

---

[51] Werner Bellardi, ed., "Ein Bedacht Hedios zur Kirchenzucht in Strassburg aus dem Jahre 1547," in Marijn de Kroon and Friedhelm Krüger, eds., *Bucer und seine Zeit*, (Wiesbaden: Franz Steiner, 1976), 117-132, at 127-8: "sint auch getaufft in Jesum Christum," and "wir, die prediger und pfarrer, nit allein im schiff faren, wie man sagt, sonder die oberkeit, nit der geringer teil der Kirchen, mit vns vnd wir mit ynen sampt den vnterthanen darynnen faren, so solle mann mit wissen, willen vnd radt der Oberkeit furnemmen alles, das Notwendig vnd der Gmein gottes besserlich sein mag."

[52] Lorna Jane Abray, *The People's Reformation: Magistrates, Clergy and Commons in Strasbourg, 1500-1598*, (Ithaca: Cornell University Press, 1985), 46-9.

[53] Available in an abridged English translation by Wilhelm Pauck, ed., *Melanchthon and Bucer*, (Philadelphia: Westminster Press, 1969) and in the original Latin in François Wendel, ed., *De Regno Christi* (*Martini Buceri Opera Latina*, Vol. XV), (Paris: Presses Universitaires de France, 1955).

[54] Pauck, 167; Wendel, lxiv-lxv.

In *De Regno Christi*, Bucer emphasized his view that discipline, properly administered, was an essential aspect of the Christian commonwealth:

> The Kingdom of our saviour Jesus Christ is that administration and care of the eternal life of God's elect, by which this very Lord and King of Heaven, through doctrine and discipline, administered by suitable ministers chosen for this very purpose, gathers to himself his elect, those dispersed throughout the world who are his but whom he nonetheless wills to be subject to worldly powers. He incorporates them into himself and his church and so governs them in it that purged more fully day by day from sins, they live well and happily both here and in the time to come.[55]

Comparing the kingdom of Christ with that of the world, Bucer wrote that both had to "tolerate the wicked while they lie hidden among the good, but when they have done their impious misdeeds openly, and will not change their ways when corrected, it is proper to remove them from the commonwealth...." Any corporal or capital punishment (or exile) was to be left to the worldly powers, however, "for they do not bear the sword in vain," (Romans 13:4). The kingdom of Christ, as represented by the Church, could only use the "chains of repentance" (*vinculis poenitentiae*), and Bucer thought it was enough for the Church to treat notorious sinners as "heathens and publicans." (Matt 16:19)[56]

For evidence of the eldership in the primitive church, Bucer cited Titus 1:5 ("that you might amend what was defective, and appoint elders in every town as I directed you."), Acts 14:23 ("And when they had appointed elders for them in every church, with prayer and fasting...") and 1 Corinthians 12:28 ("And God has appointed in the church first apostles, second prophets, third teachers, then workers of miracles, then healers, helpers, administrators, speakers in various kinds of tongues.")[57] Bucer saw a practical as well as a scriptural justification for the eldership:

> But what single individual would be able to perform so many of the offices of the good shepherd? It has therefore pleased the Holy Spirit from the beginning of the Church to join to the ministers of the word and sacraments, namely, the presiding elders and bishops, other men also from the body of the Church, serious men endowed with a gift for governing, to assist them [the ministers]

---

[55] Pauck, 225; Wendel, 54: "Regnum seruatoris nostri Iesu Christi administratio est et procuratio salutis aeternae electorum Dei, qua hic ipse Dominus et rex coelorum, doctrina et disciplina sua per idoneos et ab ipso delectos ad hoc ipsum ministros administratis, electos suos, quos habet in mundo dispersos et uult nihilominus mundi potestatibus esse subiectos, colligit ad se, sibique et Ecclesiae suae incorporat atque in ea sic gubernat, ut purgati indies plenius peccatis bene beateque uiuant et hic et in futuro."

[56] Pauck, 181; Wendel, 8-9.

[57] Pauck, 230-2; Wendel, 60-1.

in exercising a concern for individuals and in keeping and strengthening the discipline of Christ.[58]

But discipline was not to be the concern of the elders and ministers alone; Bucer argued that every believer ought to assist in correcting the faults of others:

> It is necessary that whoever are really of Christ should have a vigilant concern for their brethren on His authority and power and eagerly exhort whomever they can to their duty, and keep all from sins according to their ability or rescue those who have fallen into them.[59]

Thus discipline was to be a total community effort, and all of the faithful were to assist the elders of the consistory in correcting the faults of their neighbors. It was not enough merely to change forms of worship and beliefs about salvation; true Christians had to reform their behavior, and assist in reforming the behavior of others as well. In Bucer's view, those who committed public crimes "obviously reject and break the yoke of Christ and deny by their deeds the piety that they profess with their lips."[60]

Once such a public sin had been committed, the sinner could only rejoin the Christian community after demonstrating clear, unfeigned repentance, which Bucer felt should begin with the frequenting of sermons, and perhaps fasting as well. Those who are truly penitent, he wrote, "must...expend themselves entirely in all kinds of good works," and those who refuse to show penance "must be reckoned serpents and vipers." Bucer required that the elders stand firm on this, and require *public* signs of repentance; it was not enough for the sinner simply to express sorrow.[61] This requirement for public repentance was to prove difficult to enforce wherever Reformed discipline took root, particularly in cases where the sinner was a prominent and powerful individual. Perhaps anticipating this problem, Bucer cited approvingly the example from Theodoret's *Historia Ecclesiastica* in which

---

[58] Pauck, 232; Wendel, 61: "Haec uero tanta boni pastoris officia quis possit praestare unus multis? Placuit igitur spiritui sancto ab initio Ecclesiae administris uerbi et sacramentorum, primariis scilicet presbyteris et episcopis, adiungi et alios uiros ex Ecclesiae corpore, graues et gubernandi dono praeditos, qui illis adessent in gerenda cura singulorum, et retinenda urgendaque Christi disciplina."

[59] Pauck, 241; Wendel, 71: "necesse est, ut quicumque Christi uere sunt ex ipsius authoritate et magisterio fratrum curam gerant uigilantissimam, atque at officium assidue quoscumque possint exhortentur, a peccatisque omnibus pro uirili sua arceant uel retrahant in ea lapsos."

[60] Pauck, 243; Wendel, 73: "hi sane Christi iugum perfringunt et a se abiiciunt, pietatemque, quam ore professi sunt, factis suis abnegant."

[61] Pauck, 243-4; Wendel, 73-4: "necesse est, ut se bonis operibus omne genus totos impendant," and "serpentes potius et uiperae...habendi sunt."

St. Ambrose (c. 339-397) as Bishop of Milan forbade Emperor Theodosius I from entering the Milanese church after the slaughter of the Thessalonians. Using Theodosius as an *exemplum* for the worldly elite, Bucer noted that the emperor freely accepted Ambrose's criticism, and then abstained from sacred functions for eight months, while he demonstrated his repentance.[62]

De Regno Christi also contains other key elements of what came to be the Reformed disciplinary program. Bucer emphasized the importance of Communion as the central ritual of the Church, and required that unworthy individuals be prevented from polluting it by their participation. He found an example of the type of vigilance required in the writing of St. John Chrysostom (c. 347-407), who reported that deacons patrolled the crowd during the celebration of Communion in the fourth century Greek church to ensure that no unworthy person approached the table.[63] Further, to keep the Sabbath free for religious exercise, Bucer stressed the need to prevent people from working for profit on Sundays, and to prohibit "dissolute games" and "intemperate dining."[64]

In another contention which was to become a common plank in the Reformed disciplinary program (but one which secular magistrates regularly proved hesitant to enforce, as shall be seen), Bucer argued that adultery must be punished by death.[65] For this, Bucer cited Leviticus 20:10 ("If a man commits adultery with the wife of his neighbor, both the adulterer and the adulteress shall be put to death."), Deuteronomy 22:22-4 ("If a man is found lying with the wife of another man, both of them shall die...so you shall purge the evil from Israel..."), and (interestingly) John 8:4-5, in which the scribes and Pharisees asked Christ what to do with the adulteress, reminding him that Mosaic law commanded death by stoning. Bucer seemed to overlook Christ's suggestion in verse 7 "Let him who is without sin...be the first to throw a stone at her," which caused all the would-be executioners to leave, and Christ to tell the woman to go and not sin again. Perhaps sensing that his New Testament evidence did not support the harsh sentence for which he was arguing, Bucer cited several Roman Law precedents for capital punishment in such a case as well.[66] In sum, while Bucer required the creation of the consistory and the appointment of lay elders on New Testament grounds, he saw no New Testament justification for overturning Old Testament law where morality was concerned.

---

[62] Pauck, 187; Wendel, 15.

[63] Pauck, 237; Wendel, 67.

[64] Pauck, 280; Wendel, 114-5: "solutioribus se ludis, intempestiuis commessationibus."

[65] Pauck, 329-30; Wendel, 188-94.

[66] Wendel, 189. (Pauck abridges this section, omitting Bucer's reasoning.)

Calvin

To say that Jean Calvin was remarkably anxious about disorder in the world
around him is hardly to go out on a limb. Such assessments abound in
writings on Calvin, and there is no intention here to break with tradition in
this respect. He certainly saw a world reeling out of control, out of touch
with God and morality. Further, the sins he considered most common were
those which to him attacked the very fabric of the community—sexual sins,
a lack of respect for elders, and an absence of sincere charity.[67] To him, the
syphillis epidemic which struck Europe in the early sixteenth century was
a clear message from God, seeking to chastize man for his promiscuity.[68]
He considered it nearly miraculous that any spirit of justice remained in
mankind, preaching in a sermon on Deuteronomy, "it is certain that all
honesty between men would be gone today were it not for the admirable
providence of God."[69] Calvin was not alone in this view; it was certainly
shared by Bucer and a host of others. But Calvin was perhaps more
optimistic than most that the Church itself could create and manage
institutions which might shepherd mankind back onto the correct path.
Joined with this optimism was determination and the political sensibility
(and luck) which enabled him to succeed in so many of his endeavors. As
William Bouwsma has written, "religious doctrine, for Calvin, was
preeminently a kind of power, and he was at least as concerned as
Machiavelli with the ways in which power could change the world."[70] The
disciplinary apparatus he managed to create at Geneva, which was then
exported to large parts of Europe and the New World, is a prime example
of this.

One could adapt a Reformation cliché and say that, as far as discipline
is concerned, Oecolampadius laid the egg that Calvin hatched, although it
was Bucer who kept it warm in the interim.[71] Calvin was able to take the
Oecoplampadian ideal as developed by Bucer, and put it into practice in
Geneva, eventually to serve as an example for others. Consistorial discipline
independent of the magistracy became a hallmark of the Genevan church,
although it took some time before the issue of ultimate control over
excommunication was settled.

---

[67] William Bouwsma, "The Quest for the Historical Calvin," *ARG* 77 (1986), 47-57, at 52-
3.

[68] André Biéler, *L'Homme et la Femme dans la Morale Calviniste*, (Genève: Labor et
Fides, 1963), 25.

[69] *Opera Calvini* 28:110, cited in Biéler, 55: "Il est certain qu'aujourd'hui toute honnêteté
serait effacée entre les hommes s'il n'y avait une providence admirable de Dieu."

[70] Bouwsma, "Quest for the Historical Calvin," 54.

[71] Or until the Interim.

But before narrating the history of the excommunication battle in Geneva, it would be useful here to explore Calvin's writings on the subject of discipline, particularly as represented in the last French edition of his *Institution of the Christian Religion*, published in 1560, when his power in Geneva was at its highest, and just two years after the French edition of Bucer's *De Regno Christi* was published in that city.

In the *Institution*, Calvin, like Bucer before him, offered both a scriptural justification for the Reformed consistory and a practical explanation of how it was to operate. He argued for the plural ministry (an idea he probably gleaned from Bucer while resident in Strasbourg), comprising those who minister the Word (preachers and pastors) and those who assist the pastors in governing the church.[72] Like Bucer, he took 1 Corinthians 12:28 as a mandate for a plural ministry,[73] and concluded that the injunction of 1 Timothy 5:17 to honor ministers, "especially those who labor in preaching and teaching," implied that there were to be ministers who labored in neither, and "who are assigned to watch over morals, and correct delinquents by excommunication."[74] The process by which they were to do this was explained in Matthew 18:15-19, quoted at the beginning of this chapter.[75] The church was to exercise no civil punishment and excommunication, "la vengeance extreme de l'Eglise," was only to be used "en grande necessité." Calvin also suggested the possibilities of private admonition, or interdiction of Communion "to those who cannot be received without profaning the mystery and sacrament."[76] Elsewhere, he allowed for public admonition, noting St. Paul's advice in 1 Timothy 5:20: "As for those who persist in sin, rebuke them in the presence of all, so that the rest may stand in fear."[77] He was apprehensive that excessive zeal in this effort could damage the Church by driving the weak away, so he stressed that "we [ministers and elders] should begin with ourselves" in the enforcement of discipline.[78]

---

[72] Elsie Anne McKie has found the biblical justification for the eldership to be fully assembled by Calvin by the third (1543) edition of the *Institution* (McKie, 33). This was, of course, after he had returned to Geneva from Strasbourg.

[73] *Institution*, 4:3.8, 61. "Administrators" ("gubernationes" in the Vulgate) were held to be elders.

[74] *Ibid*, 4:11.1, 198-9: "qui étaient députés pour avoir égard sur les moeurs, et corriger les délinquents par l'excommunication."

[75] *Ibid*, 4:11.2, 201.

[76] *Ibid*, 4:11.5, 204-5: "à ceux qu'on n'y peut recevoir sans profaner le mystère et sacrement."

[77] *Ibid*, 4:12.2-3, 217-8.

[78] From his commentary on Galatians 6:1 and sermons on Job, cited by William Bouwsma, *John Calvin: A Sixteenth-Century Portrait*, (Oxford: Oxford University Press, 1988), 218.

Calvin offered three goals for consistorial discipline. First of all, "because the church is the body of Christ [Colossians 1:24], it must not be contaminated by putrid members."[79] If a minister were to admit to Communion someone who could and should be rejected, it would be sacrilege, "as if he gave the body of the Lord to dogs."[80] While Bucer shared this concern, it was one which Calvin had clearly developed before his Strasbourg interlude. In his *Articles sur le Gouvernement de l'Eglise*, proposed to the Genevan magistrates in 1537, he had written:

> The primary order which is required and for which one should have the greatest solicitude is that holy Communion, ordained and instituted to join the followers of our lord Jesus Christ with their chief and among themselves in body and spirit, must not be defiled and contaminated by the communication of those who declare and make manifest by their wicked and iniquitous lives that they do not at all belong to Jesus; for in this profaning of His sacrament our Lord is greatly dishonored.[81]

The second reason for ecclesiastical discipline offered in the *Institution* is to avoid the corruption of the good, a bad example being all too easy for weaker Christians to follow. Thirdly, discipline would inspire repentance in sinners and thus guide them back into Christ's flock.[82] Thus excommunication might not (and, it was hoped, would not) signal a final separation from the church and the elect. In claiming the power of the keys for the church, Calvin walked a tightrope; the Church is God's deputy on earth, but does not encroach into His bailiwick by itself condemning sinners to damnation—"the church binds the one whom it excommunicates: not because it hurls him into ruin and perpetual despair, but because it condemns his life and his morals and now warns him of his condemnation, if he does not return to the way."[83] So the judgment of the Church, pending a change in the sinner, is the sentence of God. In sum, according to Calvin:

---

[79] *Institution*, 4:12.5, 219: "puisque l'Eglise est le corps de Christ, elle ne peut être contaminée par des membres pourris."

[80] *Ibid*: "comme s'il donnait aux chiens le corps du seigneur."

[81] Given in Biéler, 111: "Le principal ordre qui est requis et duquel il convient avoir la plus grande sollicitude, c'est que cette sainte cène, ordonnée et instituée pour conjoindre les membres de notre Seigneur Jésus-Christ avec leur chef et entre eux-mêmes en un corps et un espirit, ne soit souillée et contaminée, si ceux qui se déclarent et manifestent par leur méchante et inique vie n'appartenir nullement à Jésus viennent à y communiquer; car en cette profanation de son sacrement notre Seigneur est grandement déshonoré."

[82] *Institution*, 4:12.5, 219-20.

[83] *Ibid*, 4:11.1, 201-2: "L'Eglise lie celui qu'elle excommunie: non pas qu'elle le jette en ruine et désespoir perpétuels, mais parce qu'elle condamne sa vie et ses moeurs, et déjà l'advertit de sa condamnation, s'il ne retourne en la voie."

> Discipline is therefore like a bridle to restrain and subdue those who are
> rebels against doctrine, and like a spur to pique those who are themselves
> tardy and nonchalant; or even sometimes like a paternal rod, to chastise
> sweetly and with Christian gentleness those who have sinned more seriously.[84]

The ultimate spur and rod in question was, of course, the threat of
excommunication. What excommunication came to amount to for most
people was suspension from Communion until they repented formally, and
in some cases they never did. But the means always existed to have the ban
lifted. The possibility of anathematization, an irrevocable form of
excommunication, was also mentioned by Calvin, but he suggested that it
should be used seldom, if at all.[85] Indeed, Calvin's whole emphasis in his
discussion of discipline was upon its utility in tying the church together, not
in breaking it apart. He even prescribed a ceremony, involving the
imposition of hands, for those readmitted to the sacrament after suspension
or excommunication.[86]

Calvin was ambiguous on how excommunicants ought to be treated. He
maintained that it was unlawful to visit them as friends (de hanter
privement), but in the same breath warned that they must be treated as
brothers, not enemies, and that the congregation must, through exhortation,
teaching, clemency, sweetness and prayer, seek to redirect them.[87] He also
cautioned that too much zeal to use excommunication might lead to schism,
as it had with Donatists and Anabaptists, two favorite targets of his wrath.[88]
Nevertheless, he maintained that the church must reject (debouter)
adulterers, whoremongers (paillards[89]), robbers, abusers, thieves, rapists,
murderers, seditious people, liars, brawlers and those given to quarrels.[90]

The mention of sexual sins before all others seems significant in light of
the obsession with sex subsequently displayed by so many of the Reformed

---

[84] Ibid, 4:12.1, 216: "La discipline est donc comme une bride pour retenir et dompter ceux
qui sont rebelles à la doctrine, et comme un éperon pour piquer ceux qui d'eux-mêmes sont
tardifs et nonchalants; ou bien quelquefois comme une verge paternelle, pour châtier
doucement et avec une mansuétude chrétienne, ceux qui ont failli plus gravement."

[85] Institution, 4:12.10, 224.

[86] Ibid, 4:12.6, 221.

[87] Ibid, 4:12.10, 225.

[88] Ibid, 4:12.12, 226.

[89] Paille meant straw, and paillardise meant "to roll in the hay," in the sexual sense, but
was generally applied to all men accused of promiscuity and their partners. This etymology is
given by Raymond Mentzer in his article "Disciplina nervus ecclesiae: The Calvinist Reform
of Morals at Nîmes," Sixteenth Century Journal 18, (1987), 89-115, at 103.

[90] Institution, 4:12.4, 218. A similar list was included in the Genevan Confession of 1536,
authored by Calvin and Guillaume Farel. See Arthur C. Cochrane, ed., Reformed Confessions
of the 16th Century, (Philadelphia: Westminster Press, 1966), 125.

consistories, particularly in Scotland. Calvin was particularly concerned with the attack on the sacred (albeit non-sacramental) nature of marriage which many sexual sins represented. To him, marriage was indissoluble, except in cases of adultery, and only the innocent party, divorced because of a spouse's infidelity, could ever marry again.[91] Since God unites men and women in marriage, he concluded that sex outside marriage was a grave insult to His dignity. He seemed to recognize that some might find him unreasonable, preaching, "it is true that a man who's taken a roll in the hay can say 'nobody can complain of me, because the two parties agreed together. So what?' Thus is God's temple...profaned. Is this not sacrilege?"[92] Calvin did not follow Bucer in recommending death for adulterers, though.[93]

It is also worth noting that Calvin was not the only Genevan concerned that rampant marital infidelity was tearing away at the fabric of marriage. His ultimate success there was partly due to the fact that so many people agreed with him, and, indeed, the city's prostitutes were targets of the magistrates as well. In March 1536, two months *before* Geneva broke with the Catholic Church, they were ordered out of the city, under the pain of whipping.[94]

There is no intention here to give a history of the Reformation in Geneva,[95] but a few words about the history of the Genevan consistory are in order. Calvin first proposed the creation of a disciplinary court in his 1537 *Ordonnances* for the Genevan church. The court was to be made up of citizens and ministers, and it was to have the power of excommunication, with those who proved stubborn to be handed over to the civil authorities for punishment.[96] But rather than marking the beginning of a new era, the plan only increased tensions between Calvin, his mentor Guillaume Farel, and the Genevan magistrates. The latter were increasingly wary that Calvin and Farel were driving newly-Protestant Geneva, only recently free from Savoyard overlordship, into a religious cleavage with Bern, its much-needed and moderately Protestant protector city. In 1538, the city fathers mandated

---

[91] Biéler, 69-74.

[92] *Opera Calvini*, 28:57, given in Biéler, 41: "Il est vrai qu'un homme qui a paillardé pourra dire: nul ne se plaint de moi; car les deux parties se sont accordées ensemble. Mais quoi? Voilà le temple de Dieu (comme nous avons dit) qui est profané. Est-ce peu de chose que sacrilège?"

[93] *Institution*, 2:8.41-4, 163-6.

[94] Biéler, 108; Kingdon, "The Control of Morals in Calvin's Geneva," 6.

[95] For this, see (among others) E. William Monter, *Calvin's Geneva*, (New York: John Wiley and Sons, 1967).

[96] Harro Höpfl, *The Christian Polity of John Calvin*, (Cambridge: Cambridge University Press, 1982), 64.

that, like the Bernese, the Genevans would use baptismal fonts, celebrate weddings with feasts, have traditional services at Christmas, Easter and Pentecost, and use unleavened bread at Communion. Calvin and Farel refused to accept these practices, and were exiled, with the former heading for Strasbourg.[97]

The pro-Bernese party, known as the *artichauds* (artichokes), had the upper hand in civic affairs for the next three years, but in the autumn of 1541 they were unseated by the *Guillermins* (followers of Farel), and Calvin was invited to return. Ironically, the escort sent by the new council to bring him back was headed by Ami Perrin, who, with his family, was later to become one of the consistory's most famous targets.[98] On November 20, 1541, Geneva's Small Council accepted Calvin's *Ordonnances*, and the Genevan consistory was born.[99] It was headed by a layman, one of the city's four syndics, and included twelve lay elders, selected annually by the Genevan magistrates. While Calvin sought a body able to act independently on the church's behalf, the system of selecting elders ensured that the eldership, at least, would be essentially a committee of magistrates. The *Ordonnances* as adopted specified that two would come from the Small Council, four from the Council of 60, and six from the Council of 200.[100] The rest of the consistory's membership was the city's Venerable Company of Pastors, soon under Calvin's control, and which ranged in number between nine (1542) and nineteen (1564).[101] As a group, elders and ministers were to enforce "the order which must be kept among the leaders in order to observe a good polity in the church."[102]

But, like their earlier counterparts in Basel, Zurich and Strasbourg, the Genevan magistrates remained unwilling to entrust the power of excommunication to the church alone, and the 1541 ordinance left the matter uncertain.[103] Through the 1540s, the magistrates continued to argue that exclusion from Communion was a civil penalty, and the power of excommunication was not firmly settled on the consistory until 1554-5, when Calvin and his followers prevailed in the celebrated case of Philibert

---

[97] Monter, *Calvin's Geneva*, 67; Biéler, 117.

[98] Monter, *Calvin's Geneva*, 70.

[99] The *ordonnances* as passed in 1541 are given in R.M. Kingdon and J.F. Bergier, eds., *Registres de la Compagnie des Pasteurs de Genève au temps de Calvin*, (Genève: Libraire Droz, 1964-), 1:1-13.

[100] *Ibid*, 7.

[101] E. William Monter, "The Consistory of Geneva, 1559-1569," *Bibliothèque d'Humanisme et Renaissance* 38, (1976), 467-484, at 469.

[102] *RCPG*, 1:11: "...l'ordre qu'on doibt tenir envers les grands pour observer bonne pollice en l'eglise."

[103] Monter, *Calvin's Geneva*, 127.

Berthelier, son of the *eidguenot* martyr, whose excommunication the Genevan Council had attempted to overturn.[104]

Obviously, the assumption by the church of authority to try robbers,
murderers, and some of the other malefactors listed above left Calvin open
to the charge that he was trying to usurp civil functions on behalf of the
consistory. Whereas Catholic ecclesiastical courts had confined themselves
to trying churchmen, heretics and debtors, handling marriage cases and
probating wills, Calvin was giving his consistories jurisdiction to try and
punish all evildoers. Here, he distinguished between a civil debt and a
spiritual debt. The Genevan consistory was forbidden to impose a civil
penalty such as a fine, banishment, imprisonment or death. Physical
punishments might be meted out by secular courts, Calvin granted, but the
satisfaction of a debt to civil society did not guarantee that a person had
truly repented his sin. It was up to the consistory to make sure the sinner
was truly remorseful before re-admitting him or her to Communion.

It is in this context that Harro Höpfl's statement that "the distinction
between sin and crime was of little practical significance in early modern
Europe"[105] must be challenged. In theory, many sins were crimes
(particularly in Geneva[106]) and virtually all crimes were sins. But, as shall
be seen, in practice the consistories of Scotland and, to a lesser extent,
France, took it upon themselves to enforce laws which were on the books
but which the civil authorities lacked either the desire or the resources to
enforce. Notes E. William Monter, "the peculiarity of Genevan justice lay
in the fact that the extant laws were fully enforced," even though the laws
in themselves were no more draconian than (unenforced) laws elsewhere.[107]

---

[104] *Ibid*, 84-5; Biéler, 121; Baker, "Calvin's Discipline and...," 114-8; Gillian Lewis,
"Calvinism in Geneva in the Time of Calvin and Beza, 1541-1608," in Menna Prestwich, ed.,
International Calvinism, 1541-1715, (Oxford: Clarendon Press, 1985), 39-70, at 49-50. For
the protest lodged by the Venerable Company of Pastors, see *RCPG* 2:48-51.

[105] Höpfl, 65.

[106] It may be Höpfl's concentration on Geneva which led him to make such a rash
generalization. The city developed a particularly detailed set of laws concerning dancing,
gaming, dress and consumption. See *ibid*, 199. Monter notes that "in the period after Calvin's
death [1564], the consistory was not interested so much in religious orthodoxy as in social
control - down to minute points of behavior." (Monter, "Consistory of Geneva," 483) And,
in that city, political dissent could be sinful, in practice as well as theory. Kingdon cites the
case of the minister Jean-Raymond Merlin, who was deposed by the Venerable Company when
he refused to apologize publicly for a sermon critical of Geneva's *Petit Conseil*. Soon, citizens
who spoke out in support of Merlin were summoned to appear before the consistory. See
Robert Kingdon, *Geneva and the French Protestant Movement, 1564-1572*, (Madison:
University of Wisconsin Press, 1967), 20-22.

[107] Monter, *Calvin's Geneva*, 152-3.

Adulterers were, in some cases, punished with death in Geneva.[108] Engaged couples guilty of fornication were imprisoned for three days on bread and water.[109] The consistory was a major presence, summoning perhaps one in fifteen Genevan adults per year by 1570, and excommunicating one in twenty-five. By the later 1560s, sexual cases accounted for only eight and a half percent of its excommunications, ranking well behind "scandals" and lying (18 percent), domestic quarrels (15.8 percent) and intrafamily quarrels (13.5 percent).[110] Other "Calvinists" were neither as enthusiastic or successful as Calvin himself, and were content if they kept the illegitimacy rate down and patched the occasional dispute. Again, the distinction between Calvin's theory and his followers' practices can lead to misperceptions. The reformer pictured the spiritual and temporal swords punishing sins in unison, both in their own way. But the two rarely worked in such perfect harmony, and the Reformed consistory was a versatile species, changing to adapt to local conditions.

---

[108] Biéler, 125.

[109] Robert Kingdon, "Calvin and the Family: The Work of the Consistory of Geneva," *Pacific Theological Review* 17, (1984), pp. 5-18, at 16. Kingdon calls this punishment "relatively mild," but in fact it appears quite severe relative to the sanctions (if any) which would have been imposed for the same offense elsewhere in Europe at the same time.

[110] Monter, "Consistory of Geneva," 479, 484. Note, however, that what Monter terms "excommunication" (exclusion from at least one Communion) would have been called "suspension" in France or Scotland, with excommunication a more formal process requiring a certain number of summonses, and an official ceremony of reconciliation.

CHAPTER TWO

"THE FACE OF A CHURCH AMANGES US"—THE INSTITUTION
OF REFORMED DISCIPLINE IN SCOTLAND

*And this our weak begynnyng [in 1558] God did so bless, that within few
monethis the hartes of many war so strenthned, that we sought to have the face
of a Church amanges us, and open crymes to be punished without respect of
persone. And for that purpose, by commoun electioun, war eldaris appointed,
to whome the hole brethren promissed obedience...*

- John Knox's *History of
the Reformation in Scotland*[1]

While John Knox (c.1505-1572) probably did not loom as large to his
contemporaries as he does to us (mostly through the pages of his own
History),[2] the erection of a Genevan-style disciplinary system in the
Reformed Kirk of Scotland certainly reflects his influence. Of the nine to
twelve ministers present in December 1560 at the first meeting of the
General Assembly, (the Kirk's legislative body), only Knox and Christopher
Goodman had experienced Calvin's Geneva firsthand.[3] Both had served in
the protestant Church of England during Edward VI's reign and fled to the
continent after the accession of the Catholic Mary Tudor in 1553, eventually
settling in Geneva. Both were ministers in the infant Scottish Kirk from
1559, but, of the two, only Knox had a hand in writing the *Scots Confession*
and *Book of Discipline* of 1560-1, and Goodman, English by birth, returned
south in 1565.[4]

Thus it was largely Knox who, first by correspondence from Geneva,
and then in person, convinced the 'faithful brethren' of his native land to
adopt a scheme for moral reformation seemingly more suited to the crowded
confines of Geneva, with its plentiful opportunities for neighborly oversight,
than to Scotland, a land of hundreds of rural parishes and a few small
burghs. What can be said of the environment to which Knox and his
comrades sought to transplant this urban seedling?

---

[1] Knox, 1:299-300.

[2] Michael Lynch, *Edinburgh and the Reformation*, (Edinburgh: John Donald, 1981), 219-
20.

[3] The *Book of the Universall Kirk* (compiled later from various sources) lists nine ministers.
by name, while John Row (whose father was among those present) claimed that 12 ministers
attended, along with 30 "ruleing-elders." *BUK* 1:3-4; Row 1:5.

[4] G.D. Henderson, ed., *The Scots Confession, 1560 and the Negative Confession, 1581*,
(Edinburgh: Church of Scotland, 1937), 8; Calderwood, 2:41; Knox 6:429, n. 1.

The Social and Political Setting

The Scots population in the late sixteenth century was probably around one million, ninety percent of whom lived in rural areas, often centered upon tiny hamlets or 'farmtouns.' While many settlements had been incorporated over the years, either as royal, ecclesiastical or baronial burghs, few had any size or significance, and those which did were concentrated in the southeast, or clung to the coasts in the northeast and southwest. Price inflation was sharp in Scotland, as it was elsewhere in Europe, and, beset by disease, periodic harvest failures and occasional English invasions or civil strife, much of the population barely scraped by; one survey of the sources for 1550-1600 has found reports of dearth somewhere in the country for 24 out of the 50 years. Population growth was also regularly stymied by outbreaks of plague, which struck southeastern Scotland repeatedly in the period 1560-90, spreading after that to the north of the country as well. One particularly severe spell, 1584-88, saw roughly 1400 die of plague in Edinburgh, 1400 in Perth, 400 in St. Andrews and 300 in Kirkcaldy.[5]

Edinburgh was the largest and most important of the burghs. Its population in 1560 was around 12,000, with perhaps another 4,000 in suburbs, including the Canongate (a separate burgh) and the port of Leith.[6] Between them, Edinburgh and the Canongate contained Edinburgh Castle, Holyrood Palace, the College of Justice (the nation's highest court) and many of Scotland's wealthiest merchants. These two burghs were the center of political and economic influence, despite the fact that neither was graced by a university or an episcopal see. Ranking behind Edinburgh but ahead of all other burghs in size and economic power were Aberdeen, Perth, and Dundee.[7] Aberdeen was an important port, university town, and bishop's

---

[5] *The Chronicle of Perth; A Register of Remarkable Occurrences 1210-1668*, (Edinburgh: Maitland Club, 1831), 4; Michael Flinn, ed., *Scottish Population History From the 17th Century to the 1930s*, (Cambridge: Cambridge University Press, 1977), 109; T.C. Smout, *A History of the Scottish People 1560-1830*, (Glasgow: William Collins, 1969), 100, 111, 143, 152; Jenny Wormald, *Court, Kirk and Community: Scotland 1470-1625*, (Toronto: University of Toronto Press, 1981), 166-7; Gordon Donaldson, *Scotland: James V-James VII*, (Edinburgh: Mercat Press, 1987), 242; L.M. Cullen, T.C. Smout and A. Gibson, "Wages and Comparative Development in Ireland and Scotland, 1565-1780," in Rosalind Mitchison and Peter Roebuck, eds., *Economy and Society in Scotland and Ireland 1500-1939*, (Edinburgh: John Donald, 1988), 105-16, at 106; S.G.E. Lythe, *The Economy of Scotland In Its European Setting, 1550-1625*, (Edinburgh: Oliver and Boyd, 1960), 5-8, 15-23.

[6] Lynch, *Edinburgh and the Reformation*, 3.

[7] Michael Lynch, "Scottish Towns, 1500-1700," in Michael Lynch, ed., *The Early Modern Town in Scotland*, (London: Croom Helm, 1987), 1-35, at 4.

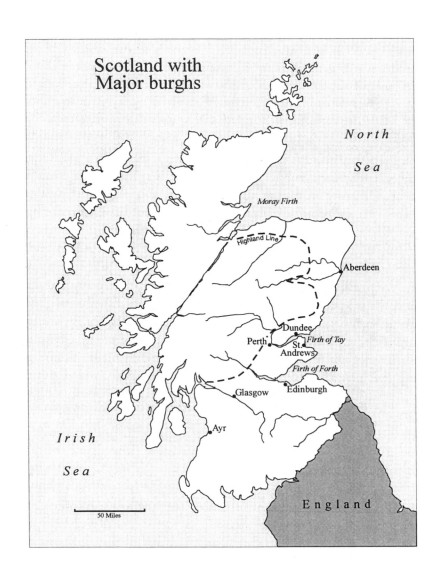

Scotland with
Major burghs

North

Sea

Moray Firth

Highland Line

Aberdeen

Dundee

Perth   Firth of Tay
        St.
      Andrews

Firth of Forth

Glasgow   Edinburgh

Irish

Sea   Ayr

England

50 Miles

seat, with a reputation for political and religious conservatism.[8] Further south, Perth and Dundee sat on the River Tay and the Firth of Tay, respectively. Perth was a craftsmen's town, where merchants were relatively less influential than elsewhere, and Dundee has been termed "the Geneva of Scotland"; both were quick to accept Protestantism, breaking with the Catholic Church before the Scottish Parliament formally outlawed papal authority in 1560.[9] Other burghs worthy of mention were St. Andrews and Glasgow, both influential as archiepiscopal seats and university towns, though not particularly large, and Ayr, on the southwest coast, known—like Perth and Dundee—for its early embrace of protestant ideas.[10]

The rural, or "landwart" expanses in which nine-tenths of the Scots population dwelt, were becoming, in at least one sense, increasingly secularized. While the Catholic Church nominally owned a great deal of land, many of the "kirkmen" who controlled these estates were not clerics at all, but rather lay commendators or titular "abbots," who made no pretence of clerical vocation.[11] They, like many of the bishops, tended to come from the leading families of the land, and some of these, such as the Hamiltons, Gordons, Beatons and Chisholms (not to mention the ubiquitous Stewarts), had established ecclesiastical dynasties alongside their secular lordships.[12] Since the institutional structure of the old church was neither abolished nor taken over by the new church during the Reformation, the influence of many of these ecclesiastical dynasties would last beyond 1560, as their church estates became virtually indistinguishable from other family holdings.

But that was not the only way in which the church as a spiritual institution was losing control of landed wealth. The pressures of inflation and taxation, coupled with the desires of churchmen—both clerical and titular—to realize short-term profits from their estates, had led to

---

[8] Allan White, "The Impact of the Reformation on a Burgh Community: The Case of Aberdeen," in *ibid*, 81-101.

[9] Ian Cowan, *Regional Aspects of the Scottish Reformation*, (London: Historical Assoc., 1978), 14-15, 23-5; Mary Verschuur, "Merchants and Craftsmen in Sixteenth-century Perth," in Lynch, ed., *Early Modern Town in Scotland*, 36-54; Michael Lynch, "The Crown and the Burghs, 1500-1625," in *ibid*, 55-80, at 62; Iain E.F. Flett, *The Conflict of the Reformation and Democracy in the Geneva of Scotland, 1443-1610: An Introduction to Edited Texts of Documents Relating to the Burgh of Dundee*, (St. Andrews University M.Phil. Thesis, 1981), *passim*.

[10] Cowan, *Regional Aspects*, 25.

[11] For a classic example of this, see the discussion of Mark Ker, commendator of Newbattle Abbey, in Margaret H.B. Sanderson, *Mary Stewart's People: Life in Mary Stewart's Scotland*, (Edinburgh: Mercat Press, 1987), 166-77.

[12] Gordon Donaldson, *The Scottish Reformation*, (Cambridge: Cambridge University Press, 1960), 17-19.

widespread feuing of church lands in the sixteenth century. The practice
was not unknown on secular lands as well. Proprietors would offer
customary tenants the opportunity to purchase feu charters, essentially
guaranteeing the tenant families heritable succession in their holdings, in
exchange for a large down payment and limited annual feu-duties. The latter
would become increasingly negligible as inflation took its toll. Tenants who
could not afford the feu charter might lose their holdings to others who
could, but the effect was to make the tenants or whoever took their places
into virtual proprietors.[13] The Scottish laird, traditionally a local bigwig who
was no aristocrat but who could take pride in the fact that he owned his
own estate, was being joined by numerous feuars and portioners who, as
time went on, became in effect lairds themselves. At the parish level, the
dominant influence of one or two landlords, ecclesiastical or secular,
resident or absentee, often splintered into several parts. The kirk sessions
which were eventually established to manage parish affairs and enforce
moral standards would provide a forum in which these local notables, as
elders, could exercise their newfound influence.

While members of local congregations can be divided (albeit not always
neatly) between proprietors and tenants, the nation itself was split
geographically by the distinction between Highland and Lowland. In fact,
Scotland in the sixteenth century was really two nations, roughly divided by
the Highland Geographic Fault. This is a diagonal line running southwest
from Stonehaven, on the east coast south of Aberdeen, to Dumbarton, near
the mouth of the Clyde. Everything north and west of that line—except for
the east coast and the triangle formed in the northeast by Aberdeen,
Fraserburgh and Elgin—was Highland, with a Gaelic-speaking population,
and everything east and south was Lowland, with a population which spoke
"inglis," or, more properly, the Scots dialect thereof.

The history with which we are concerned here is largely that of the
Lowland region. The vastness of the Highland parishes and the shortage of
Reformed clergy with the necessary language skills delayed the evangel-
ization of the Highlands until well into the seventeenth century, although
John Carswell, bishop of the Isles and superintendent of Argyll, did in 1567
oversee a Gaelic translation of the *Book of Common Order*.[14] No sixteenth-

---

[13] *Ibid*, 47-8; Margaret H.B. Sanderson, *Scottish Rural Society in the Sixteenth Century*,
(Edinburgh: John Donald, 1982), 64-83. 135-52; *ibidem*, "Some Aspects of the Church in
Scottish Society in the Era of the Reformation Illustrated from the Sheriffdom of Ayr," *RSCHS*
17, (1970), 81-97; Walter Makey, *The Church of the Covenant, 1637-1651: Revolution and
Social Change in Scotland*, (Edinburgh: John Donald, 1979), 2-6.

[14] Cowan, *Regional Aspects*, 33. Gordon Donaldson, *Scottish Church History*, (Edinburgh:
Scottish Academic Press, 1985), 142-3. James Kirk has sharply dissented from this prevailing
view, however. He argues, based on records of ministerial stipends, that the Reformed Kirk

century kirk session records survive from Gaelic-speaking parishes, and it is quite possible that no sessions were created in these areas until later. Indeed, the Kirk recognized these realities; the Stirling Presbytery as late as 1593 was willing to make a significant exception to policy by licensing William Scot to minister baptism and marriage in four parishes in the northwest of its jurisdiction despite the fact that he was merely a reader, not a minister. This was done because Scot was conversant in "ye ereis langage," the only tongue of the people in that region. Otherwise, it was feared, "thay [the Gaelic-speakers] sould fall in athisme."[15] While almost anyone speaking Scots who appeared in lowland records, whether they came from the locality or elsewhere, was identified by name, a highlander was simply "ane hieland man," regardless of whether the clerk had heard his name. Very occasionally he might get a surname, like the MacGregors whose robberies the previous week kept the parishioners of Kilmadock away from their kirk one Sunday, but he was more often simply a foreign creature, like the "barbarous, bludie and wicket" natives of the Isle of Lewis, who repeatedly drove off lowlanders attempting to settle there in the decade after 1599.[16]

Although Scotland was really two nations, these were united—sometimes rather tenuously—under the one crown of the Stewart dynasty which had reigned since 1371. The idea of the Stewart monarchy was one to which virtually all members of the political nation were committed, but a series of royal minorities in the sixteenth century left the crown chronically weak, prone to factionalism and foreign intrigue, and the sudden policy shifts which accompanied these ailments.[17] The traditional alliance with France spurred the disastrous military expedition against England which culminated in the debacle at Flodden in 1513, and inaugurated the first minority, that of James V. The mistake was repeated 29 years later at Solway Moss, although that loss was less devastating to the nobility and gentry because so many fled rather than be butchered like their forbears in 1513. James V died shortly after he got the news, leaving the crown to his newborn daughter Mary.

The minority of Mary Stewart became a contest for power between her mother Mary of Guise who, allied with Cardinal David Beaton, archbishop

---

made a "sustained assault" on the Gaelic north and west in the 1560s. But even Kirk notes that the vastness of most highland parishes would have minimized contact between clergy and parishioners. See James Kirk, *Patterns of Reform: Continuity and Change in the Reformation Kirk*, (Edinburgh: T&T Clark, 1989), 305-33.

[15] WRH ms CH2/722/2, 21 August 1593.

[16] *Ibid*, 25 September 1593; Smout, *History of the Scottish People*, 105.

[17] The best general account is Gordon Donaldson, *Scotland: James V-James VII*, but also worthwhile is Wormald, *Court, Kirk and Community*.

of St. Andrews, favored a continued French alliance and religious orthodoxy, and a pro-English faction with protestant leanings. The latter triumphed at first, and the governor James Hamilton, earl of Arran, even flirted with official Protestantism in 1543, a spell known later as "Arran's godly fit." Protestant books (most of a Lutheran slant) circulated freely, and there were attacks on religious houses in Perth and Dundee.[18] The Hamiltons were the second family in the realm, but were themselves plagued by weak leadership, and Arran's government soon foundered on objections in the Scottish Parliament and elsewhere to the proposed marriage of the infant Mary to Edward Tudor, Prince of Wales.

Subsequent attempts by the English to force the marriage through military action—the so-called "rough wooing"—caused a reaction in favor of France. Though the English retained possession of several strongholds in the borders and southeastern Scotland, as well as the allegiance of many "assured Scots,"—gentry with protestant leanings and often English pensions—Mary of Guise brought the Hamiltons over to her side. Arran received the French dukedom of Châtelherault, and his brother John became archbishop of St. Andrews after Beaton's assassination in 1546. Beaton was slain in his castle at St. Andrews by a band of Fife lairds shortly after he oversaw the burning of George Wishart for protestant heresy, and his murder took on additional religious significance when Knox joined the Cardinal's enemies in the castle during the subsequent siege, preaching to the group.[19]

But there seems little evidence for widespread popular Protestantism in the country, despite claims to the contrary.[20] The Castle of St. Andrews was recaptured, with French assistance, and Mary of Guise took a number of leading protestant noblemen with her on a 1550 visit to France, where the generosity of King Henri II led to Scottish acceptance of a proposed marriage between the young queen Mary and the dauphin François. In 1554, Mary of Guise was made regent in Arran's place, and the country was clearly back in the orbit of France. In addition, two church councils convened by Archbishop John Hamilton offered some prospect of reform

---

[18] Knox, 1:95-6, 100-106; Donaldson, *Scottish Reformation*, 30-1; Cowan, *Regional Aspects*, 13; Frank Bardgett, *Scotland Reformed: The Reformation in Angus and the Mearns*, (Edinburgh: John Donald, 1989), 25-30.

[19] Knox, 1:174-193; Gordon Donaldson, *All the Queen's Men: Power and Politics in Mary Stewart's Scotland*, (London: Batsford, 1983), 20-2; Michael Lynch, "Calvinism in Scotland, 1559-1638," in Menna Prestwich, ed., *International Calvinism, 1541-1715*, (Oxford: Clarendon Press, 1985), 225-55, at 225-6.

[20] Made most recently by Kirk, *Patterns of Reform*, xi: "Protestantism had secured a firm foundation in the politically assertive and progressive areas of Scotland for over a generation [before 1560]."

of the old church from within.[21]

But just as English heavy-handedness played into French hands in the late 1540s, growing resentment of French interference in Scottish affairs—particularly after the dauphin became François II of France and, (in conjunction with Mary), Scotland—created a fortuitous alliance of xenophobia, anglophilia and Protestantism in the late 1550s. A group of protestant noblemen, the Lords of the Congregation, signed a band to "establish the most blessed word of God" in December 1557. By the time the Queen Regent died, besieged in Edinburgh Castle, in June 1560, the Congregation, with the assistance of an English army, had driven the French faction from power, and confined the French military presence to Leith, which was under siege.[22] Knox himself had returned to Scotland in May 1559, becoming a kind of court preacher to the Lords of the Congregation.

This change was to prove more durable than the "godly fit" of 1543. The advances of the Lords of the Congregation brought anticlerical riots in Perth, Dundee, Stirling, Scone, Linlithgow and Edinburgh in 1559. But these were, at least in some cases, more a reaction by the urban poor against the wealth and hypocrisy of friars than manifestations of committed Protestantism. Burgh councils remained relatively stable, and the Congregation seems to have garnered support more out of hatred of France and envy of "the abundance of salt beef in the friars' kitchens" than love for Calvinism, Anglicanism or any other model of religious reform.[23]

French influence was dealt a crushing blow, however, and the July 1560 Treaty of Edinburgh placed Scotland, despite her French king and queen, in the orbit of Elizabethan England. Mary and François were helpless spectators from afar that August, when a Parliament, of dubious legality, called by the Lords of the Congregation, abolished papal authority and the Mass, and adopted a reformed Confession of Faith.[24] François II died in December 1560, and Mary returned to the Scotland she hardly knew the following August, but both of these events seemed highly unlikely in the summer of 1560. This is the background against which the first steps toward erection of a Reformed disciplinary apparatus took place.

---

[21] Donaldson, *All the Queen's Men*, 25-7; Cowan, *Scottish Reformation*, 81-3.

[22] Knox, 1:273-473; 2:1-72.

[23] Smout, *History of the Scottish People*, 55; Lynch, "Calvinism in Scotland," 227-8, though Lynch does grant extraordinary turnover in the Edinburgh council, where the Protestant council led by Archibald Douglas of Kilspindie replaced that of the Catholic George, Lord Seton. See Lynch, *Edinburgh and the Reformation*, 76-9, 232-5.

[24] *APS*, 2:535; Spottiswoode, 1:327; Knox, 2:121-5.

Kirk Sessions Before 1560

After the 'troubles at Frankfort,' which split the English exile community there in the early 1550s, Knox, Goodman, William Whittingham and their followers moved to Geneva. There, in keeping with local practice under Calvin, they established a consistory to censure misbehavior among the English congregation.[25] Its practices were described in *The Form of Prayers and Ministration of the Sacraments Used in the English Congregation at Geneva*, published in 1556 by the Genevan printer Jean Crespin.[26] Distinguishing the elders, this held "they differ from the ministers in that they preache not the worde, nor minister the sacramentes. In assemblyng the people, nether they withoute the ministers nor the ministers withoute them, may attempt any thing." Both elders and ministers were essential, and were to be nominated by the congregation, examined and chosen by the consistory, and then presented to the congregation for final approval.[27] The *Form of Prayers* gave a traditional reason for policing Communion participation, citing I Corinthians 11: "whosoever shall eate this bread, and drinke the cuppe of the Lorde unworthelye, he shalbe giltie of the bodye and bloud of the Lord...he eateth and drinketh his own damnation, for not havinge due regarde and consideration of the Lordes bodye."[28]

In its discussion of the need for discipline, the *Form of Prayers* was virtually a copy of the relevant sections of Calvin's *Institution*. Church discipline, administered by the eldership, was said to provide the "synewes" holding the body of the Church together. Knox and his fellow exiles used Calvin's metaphors of the bridle, spur and rod, and gave the same three reasons Calvin offered for the necessity of discipline.[29] The *Form of Prayers*, which, as the *Book of Common Order*,[30] was to receive official approval from the Scottish Kirk's General Assembly in 1562, was thus a strictly Calvinist document.[31]

The beginnings of the Scots disciplinary system were already planted before the Parliamentary actions of 1560, and may have been so even

---

[25] Leo F. Solt, *Church and State In Early Modern England, 1509-1640*, (Oxford: Oxford University Press, 1990), 64.

[26] Given in Knox, 4:159-206.

[27] *Ibid*, 4:175-6.

[28] *Ibid*, 4:192.

[29] *Ibid*, 4:203-4. See *Institution*, 4:12.5, 219-20.

[30] *Book of Common Order* given in Knox, 6:275-334.

[31] James Kirk has argued strongly (against Gordon Donaldson) for the "Calvinist" nature of the Scottish Kirk as early as 1560. See James Kirk, "The Influence of Calvinism On the Scottish Reformation," *RSCHS* 18, (1972-4), 157-79.

before Knox's return in May 1559.[32] The passage quoted at the beginning of this chapter suggests that some kirk sessions were functioning at about that time, although exactly where is less clear. The earliest surviving kirk session register is that of St. Andrews, which begins in October 1559 with a passage that reads like a foundation charter.[33] No other kirk session records survive from prior to 1562, but other sources suggest the existence of sessions earlier in some of the major burghs. Dundee apparently had a functioning session from mid-1559, at least, with much overlap between the eldership and town council.[34]

Edinburgh had, according to Knox, a "Privie Kirk," with an elected session, meeting during the 1550s in "secreit and privie conventiounis in Houses, or in the Feilds." Even in this voluntary, secret church, he wrote, "varietie of persones culd not be keipt in gud obedience and honest fame, without oversiers, Elders and Deacones."[35] Its reported leadership included John Willock, an ex-Dominican, James Baron, a merchant and burgh councilor, Michael Christeson, Robert Watson and Alexander Hope, all merchants, Adam Craig, a goldsmith, James Gray, a mason, George Small, a saddler, William Harlaw, a Canongate tailor, and John Cairns, who later served the public kirk as a reader.[36] Knox stressed that this was a group in which godliness mattered more than wealth and social standing. All communicants voted in session elections, he claimed, and the elders and deacons were named in descending order of vote totals, "so that if a puir man exceid the riche man in votes, he preceids him in place." Whether or not this is an idealized portrait, it is certainly true that the elders and deacons listed in the earliest extant *public* kirk session minutes for Edinburgh, those of 1574-5, were much more reflective of the burgh oligarchy than those listed above; the privy kirk may have been a revolutionary cell in more ways than one.[37]

---

[32] Although G.D. Henderson was certainly guilty of partisan exaggeration when he claimed "the eldership had been more or less accepted in Scotland before Knox arrived in 1559...." See his *The Scottish Ruling Elder*, (London: James Clarke, 1935), 30. The possiblity that kirk sessions existed in a few burghs hardly warrants such extrapolation.

[33] David Hay Fleming, ed., *Register of the Minister, Elders and Deacons of the Christian Congregation of St. Andrews*, 2 Vols., (Edinburgh: Scottish History Society, 1889-90), 1:1-2.

[34] Flett, 83-6, 98.

[35] Knox, 2:151-2; James Kirk, "The 'Privy Kirks' and Their Antecedents: The Hidden Face of Scottish Protestantism," in W.J. Sheils and Diana Wood, eds., *Voluntary Religion*, (Oxford: Basil Blackwell, 1986), 155-70, at 167-8.

[36] Calderwood 1:304.

[37] Knox, 2:152-3; SRO ms CH2/450/1, 23v-24v; Lynch, *Edinburgh and the Reformation*, 38-40; *ibidem*, "From Privy Kirk to Burgh Church: An Alternative View of the Process of Protestantisation," in Norman Macdougall, ed., *Church, Politics and Society: Scotland 1408-1929*, (Edinburgh: John Donald, 1983), 85-96, at 86-7, 93.

So the reformers of 1560 already had some local, as well as foreign, examples to go by when they set about prescribing a system of disciplinary oversight for the entire kingdom. It is now time to discuss the commencement of that ambitious program.

Early Prescriptions

In one sense the only 'official' statement of the early Reformed Kirk is the *Scots Confession* of 1560. It received formal approval from Parliament, whereas other elements of the reformed program, most notably the *First Book of Discipline* of 1560-1, did not. And while the General Assembly claimed from the outset the right to legislate for the Kirk, regardless of Parliament, estates or Privy Council,[38] it was limited in what it could accomplish without the support of the traditional political authorities. Parliament's approval of the *Scots Confession* gave the Reformed Kirk a statutory recognition which, while vague in its implications, was ideologically significant. The document remained the official doctrinal statement of the Scottish Kirk until superseded by the Westminster Confession in 1647.[39]

The *Scots Confession* was the work of the 'six Johns'—Knox, Willock, Spottiswoode, Winram, Row and Douglas—who also composed the *First Book of Discipline*. Knox, as mentioned above, had experience in Geneva, and also may have participated in some of the discussions of the protestants of Poitiers, who had drawn up their own Geneva-based *Discipline* in 1557-8.[40] The ex-Dominican Willock had been identified with the protestant cause longer than Knox. He drew the attention of the English authorities while preaching in London in 1540, and in 1553 was implicated in one of the conspiracies aimed at installing Lady Jane Grey on the throne in place of the Catholic Mary Tudor. Fleeing England, he had become preacher to the English congregation at Emden, a northwest German city with several Reformed congregations. He then returned to Scotland, served in Edinburgh's 'Privy Kirk' and preached in Dundee in the late 1550s.[41]

---

[38] Duncan Shaw, *The General Assemblies of the Church of Scotland, 1560-1600*, (Edinburgh: St. Andrew Press, 1964), 20.

[39] Henderson, ed., *Scots Confession*, 19.

[40] W. Stanford Reid, "French Influence on the First Scots Confession and Book of Discipline," *Westminster Theological Journal* 35 (1972), 1-14, at 8-9; James Kirk, *The Development of the Melvillian Movement in Late Sixteenth Century Scotland*, (Edinburgh University Ph.D. Thesis, 1972), 1:64.

[41] Knox, 1:245, 1:388-9; Cowan, *Regional Aspects*, 24-5; Susan Brigden, *London and the Reformation*, (Oxford: Oxford University Press, 1989), 330; Duncan Shaw, "John Willock," in Duncan Shaw, ed., *Reformation and Revolution: Essays Presented to Hugh Watt*, (Edin-

Spottiswoode had also served in the Edwardian Church in England, but the other three authors were Protestants of more recent vintage.[42] Winram, as subprior of St. Andrews, had debated Knox in 1547, and remained Catholic until the eve of the Reformation.[43] Row was working as a papal agent as late as September 1558, and Douglas was rector of St. Andrews University.[44] Given the authors' backgrounds, it seems likely that Knox, and possibly Willock, were the dominant influences on the passages of the confession (and of the *First Book of Discipline*) relating to congregational discipline.[45]

While much of the language of the *Scots Confession* was conventionally Calvinist, in some respects, it went beyond the teachings of Calvin himself. Not only was resistance to tyranny made a duty, but discipline took on more fundamental importance than Calvin ever gave it.[46] Calvin, hesitant to cut off dialogue with other Reformed churches, had refused to make administration of discipline and excommunication a mark of a true church. For him, preaching of the Word and proper administration of the sacraments had been sufficient.[47] But the Scots Confession held "Ecclesiastical discipline uprightlie ministred, as Goddis Worde prescribes, whereby vice is repressed, and vertew nurished" to be the third mark of "the trew Kirk of Christ."[48] This same departure from Calvin was present in the French Reformed Confession (1559), and the Belgic Confession (1561).[49] This suggests that ecclesiastically-administered discipline on the Oecolampadian/Bucerian model, accepted and encouraged by Calvin, was by the 1560s becoming a distinctive feature of a particular strain of Reformed

---

burgh: Saint Andrew Press, 1967), 42-69, at 50-1. For disciplinary practice in the Reformed church at Emden, see Heinz Schilling, "Reformierte Kirchenzucht als Sozialdisziplinierung? Die Tätigkeit des Emder Presbyteriums in den Jahren 1557-1562," in Heinz Schilling and Wilfred Ehbrecht, eds., *Niederlande und Nordwestdeutschland: Studien zur Regional- und Staatgeschichte Nordwestkontinentaleuropas im Mittelalter und in der Neuzeit*, (Köln: Bohlau, 1983), 261-327.

[42] Spottiswoode, 2:336; Lynch, "Calvinism in Scotland," 229-30.

[43] Knox, 1:193-7.

[44] Row, 1:204; Calderwood, 2:41; Spottiswoode, 2:273-4.

[45] Duncan Shaw argued that Willock's contributions to the Scottish Reformation in general have been largely overlooked, perhaps due to the attention focused on Knox. See Shaw, *General Assemblies*, 33.

[46] W. Ian P. Hazlett, "The Scots Confession of 1560: Context, Complexion and Critique," *ARG* 78 (1987), 287-320, at 310-11, 319.

[47] *Institution*, 4:1.9, 21; 4:1.12, 24; Harro Höpfl, *The Christian Polity of John Calvin*, (Cambridge: Cambridge University Press, 1982), 87-8.

[48] Henderson, ed., 75-7.

[49] *Hist. Ecc.*, 1:211-2; Arthur C. Cochrane, ed., *Reformed Confessions of the 16th Century*, (Philadelphia: Westminster Press, 1966), 210.

Protestantism.

Naturally, the framers of the *Scots Confession* were conscious of the danger that a fixation on congregational behavior might carry the scent of works righteousness, condemned by all major anti-Catholic thinkers since Luther. In Article 13, titled "Of the Cause of Gude Warkis," they sought to explain what they felt was the true relationship between faith and works:

> We feir not to affirme, that murtherers, oppressers, cruell persecuters, adulterers, huremongers, filthy persouns, Idolaters, drunkards, thieves, and al workers of iniquity, have nether trew faith, nether ony portion of the Spirit of the Lord Jesus, so long as obstinatlie they continew in their wickednes. For how soone that ever the Spirit of the Lord Jesus, quhilk Gods elect children receive be trew faith, taks possession in the heart of ony man, so soone dois he regenerate and renew the same man.[50]

Thus the 'six Johns' in the *Scots Confession* established the necessity for congregational discipline, and placed it in a soteriological context. This much the secular authorities of Scotland were largely willing to accept. The specifics of the program were left to be enumerated in the *First Book of Discipline*, and this proved harder to sell.

When Knox included the text of the *First Book of Discipline* in his *History*, he wrote that he was doing so "to the end that the Posteriteis to come may juge alsweill quhat the wardlingis refused."[51] But to say they "refused" it is not entirely true. Granted, the Parliament of January 1561 declined to ratify the *First Book* formally, probably due to anxiety over its claims to church revenues, many of which were in the hands of "wardlingis" sitting in Parliament. But many of its provisions were enacted, with the assistance of secular authorities. The Privy Council, for example, appointed five superintendents (among them Winram, Spottiswoode and Willock), as ordained by the book.[52] And while landed interests may have resisted statutory approval for the program of the Reformed Kirk, quite a

---

[50] Henderson, ed., 61-3.

[51] Knox, 2:181-2. Of course, to speak of it in contemporary terms as the *First Book of Discipline* is anachronistic, as it did not acquire that name until there was a *Second Book of Discipline* (1578). The name is used here for convenience's sake. Knox called it the "Buke of Discipline."

[52] James Cameron has suggested that the office of superintendent was grafted on to the "Genevan" polity of other sections of the *First Book of Discipline* to facilitate the reformation of churches in rural areas. In his view, Douglas and Winram, both active in the Catholic reforming councils convened by Archbishop Hamilton in the 1550s, were probably the authors of the section on the office of superintendent. See J.K. Cameron, "The Office of Superintendent in the *First Book of Discipline*," in Bernard Vogler, ed., *L'Institution et les Pouvoirs dans les Eglises de l'Antiquité à nos Jours*, (Bruxelles: Nauwelaerts, 1987), 239-50.

few nobles and leading lairds were willing to endorse the *First Book of Discipline* with their signatures, and did so, in January 1561.[53]

The nascent Reformed Kirk claimed more than the property of the old church; in some passages, the *First Book of Discipline* was a manifesto for a new legal order. Introducing their disciplinary provisions, its authors proclaimed:

> As that no Commonwealth can long flourish or long indure without good lawes and sharpe execution of the same, so neither can the kirk of God be brought to purity neither yet be retained in the same without the order of Ecclesiastical Discipline, which stands in reproving and correcting of the faults, which the civill sword either doth neglect or not punish; Blasphemy, adulterie, murder, perjurie and other crimes capitall, worthy of death, ought not properly to fall under censure of the Kirk, because all such open transgressors of Gods lawes ought to be taken away by the civill sword. But drunkenness, excesse be it in apparel, or be it in eating and drinking, fornication, oppressing of the poore by exactions, deceiving of them in buying and selling by wrang met and measure, wanton words and licentious living tending to slander, doe openly appertaine to the Kirk of God to punish them, as God's word commands.

But, in cases where the civil authorities were slow to act, the Kirk would claim ultimate jurisdiction over all offenses:

> because this accursed Papistrie hath brought in such confusion into the world, that neither was vertue rightly praised neither yet vice severely punished, the Kirk of God is compelled to draw the sword which of God she hath received, against such open and manifest contemnars, cursing and excommunicating all such, as well as those whom the civill sword ought to punish....[54]

This "cursing" or excommunication—the two words had been synonymous in the pre-reformation church and state—was to be in the hands of kirk sessions, staffed by ministers and godly laymen, but independent of civil magistrates. The laymen were to serve as elders and deacons, elected annually (August 1 was suggested as a date for choosing a new session). The manner of election was left up to individual congregations, but the

---

[53] Among them were: Châtelherault, the earl of Arran (his eldest son), Lord James Stewart (the queen's half brother and future earl of Moray), the earls of Argyll, Rothes and Marischal, and Alexander Gordon, bishop of Galloway. There seems to be disagreement as to whether Morton, the future regent, was a signatory. Knox, 2:257-60; Calderwood, 2:50; James Cameron, ed., *The First Book of Discipline*, (Edinburgh: St. Andrew Press, 1972), 70-1, 210-11; George R. Hewitt, *Scotland Under Morton: 1572-80*, (Edinburgh: John Donald, 1982), 4.

[54] Cameron, ed., *First Book*, 165-7.

persons chosen had to be "men of best knowledge in Gods word and cleanest life, men faithfull and of most honest conversation that can be found in the kirk."[55] The book hinted at the later erection of presbyteries when it suggested that, where ministers were scarce, groups of small parishes could join together in one session, "for the pluralitie of kirks without ministers and order, shall rather hurt then edifie."[56] While kirk sessions could handle all sorts of parish business in addition to correction of sins, disciplinary matters were to be of primary concern to the elders, assisted, when necessary, by the deacons.[57]

As might be expected, the *First Book of Discipline* devoted a great deal of attention to marriage and family issues. Children were to consult parents before marrying, but could appeal to the kirk session or civil magistrate if the parents would not agree with their choice, or were trying to force them to marry against their will. If the parents had "na other caus then the commoun sorte of men have; to wit, lack of guidis, or because thei ar nott so hyght-borne as thai requyre," the kirk session was to support the children's wishes. This backing was to be denied to couples who committed fornication, however, although the father of a deflowered virgin could force the man involved to marry her.[58] Innocent parties were allowed divorce on the grounds of adultery, and, if divorced adulterers could not remain continent, it was better to marry than to burn—but they were forbidden to marry anyone except their former spouse as long as the latter was willing to have them back. The authors were in a quandary over the status of adulterers. They argued that such sinners deserved capital punishment, but the secular magistrates were not executing them (and no law had as yet been passed calling for their deaths), so adulterers were bound to continue to live among the faithful. Thus in a concession to hard reality, the *First Book* granted that penitent adulterers could later be reconciled and received at the Communion table.[59]

The *First Book of Discipline* and, indeed, many of the documents of the early Reformed Kirk in Scotland, resound with the notion of collective

---

[55] *Ibid*, 174-5.

[56] *Ibid*, 175. The suggestion that learned ministers and pious laymen also gather weekly in principal towns for "prophecying" seems to point to the "exercise," which became a common feature in the meetings of some presbyteries by the late 1580s. See *ibid*, 187-91; WRH ms CH2/722/1-2, *passim*.

[57] Cameron, ed., *First Book*, 179. It should be noted that the Scottish (and French) diaconate represented a departure from Genevan practice. In Geneva, deacons were civic officials and did not sit on the consistory. See François Méjan, ed., *Discipline de l'Eglise Réformée de France*, (Paris: S.C.E.L., 1947), 228-9.

[58] Cameron, ed., *First Book*, 192-3.

[59] *Ibid*, 196-9.

responsibility. While the practice of fraternal correction was not going to save any souls, that being up to God alone, its neglect could bring God's wrath on the whole community, elect and reprobate. The authors were certain that failure to punish sexual sins in particular would bring divine retribution, and the recurrent visitations of plague, agricultural failure and warfare in sixteenth-century Scotland would have served as a reminder of how terrible that vengeance could be.[60]

Discipline also could provide an opportunity for sinners to prove that they were, despite their faults, among God's chosen. The *Scots Confession* had affirmed that "the sonnes of God...dois fecht against sinne...and gif they fal, they rise againe with earnest and unfained repentance."[61] Repentance, performed publicly if necessary, was to be one of the primary weapons in the reform of popular behavior. The humiliation it brought would serve as a deterrent to sin. Further, by demonstrating remorse openly, the wayward could acknowlege the unacceptability of their actions in a ritual which had the ultimate goal of allowing them to reclaim their place in the community, healing any wounds which might have been opened by their misdeeds.[62]

Not all sins had to be addressed in the public forum of the kirk, though. The *First Book* granted that offenses which were "secret or known to few men" could be privately censured, in keeping with the instructions of Matthew 18. But those which had become widely known required public expiation, to cleanse the kirk of the scandal. In this category were sexual sins, drunkenness, fighting and swearing.[63] Sinners who refused to admit their faults before the session or follow its instructions were to be excommunicated. Excommunication was, theoretically, the ultimate weapon in the kirk's arsenal.

As mentioned earlier, excommunication in the late medieval church had become, in many cases, a legal formality, lacking coercive power. There were laws on the books which imposed disabilities on those who had remained excommunicated without seeking reconciliation with the church,[64] but getting someone excommunicated, like getting them put to the horn (declared an outlaw—the civil equivalent of excommunication) was primarily

---

[60] *Ibid*, 193-4.

[61] Henderson, ed., *Scots Confession*, 63.

[62] This sort of ritual has been common in other, non-western, non-Christian societies as well. See for instance, Mary Douglas' discussion of the role of fines and public sacrifices to atone for offenses among the Nuer in her study *Purity and Danger: An Analysis of the Concepts of Pollution and Taboo*, (London: Routledge and Kegan Paul, 1966), 131-2. Douglas also notes that such rituals can have the effect of "marshalling moral disapproval when it lags."

[63] Cameron, ed., *First Book*, 167-8.

[64] For example, acts of Parliament passed in 1551 and 1552. See *APS*, 2:482, 2:485.

a litigation strategy; secular officials did little to enforce the penalties of excommunication or outlawry *per se*.[65] The authors of the *First Book of Discipline* wanted to restore the sting to the sanction, arguing that excommunication "must be kept with all severity, for lawes made and not kept, engender contempt of virtue, and brings in confusion and liberty to sinne."[66]

This would require not only the aid of the magistrate, but the full weight of societal disapproval. Once a person had been excommunicated, they held:

> may no person (his wife and family onely excepted) have any kind of conversation with him, be it in eating and drinking, buying and selling; yea in saluting or talking with him except that it be at commandement or licence of the Ministrie for his conversion, that he, bu such meanes confounded, seeing himselfe abhorred of the godly and faithfull, may have occasion to repent and so be saved.

Sentences of excommunication, imposed only after a required sequence of three weekly public admonitions, were to be read from pulpits throughout the area, and children of an excommunicant could not be baptized unless presented by some other family member willing to damn the "obstinate contempt of the impenitent."[67] Thus the excommunicant was to be shunned and, if involved in trade, driven out of business. Not surprisingly, many would refuse to participate in such a boycott (or could not, if the excommunicant was their landlord, employer, superior or family head). Such a ban could cut right through the bonds of traditional society; many kirk sessions and, later, presbyteries were forced to treat dealings with excommunicants as sins worthy of censure.

It is unclear how much of the *First Book* its aristocratic signatories might have actually read. It described a ministerially-dominated commonwealth in which the Kirk reclaimed its lands, and adulterers and Catholics were executed by a magistrate whose primary function was to protect the Kirk. Such rhetoric might have inspired those in the vanguard of what was expected to be a religious revolution, but it was hardly a realistic program, given social and political realities. The *First Book* never appeared in print in the sixteenth century.[68] It was certainly known to members of the General

---

[65] Keith M. Brown, *Bloodfeud in Scotland, 1573-1625: Violence, Justice and Politics in an Early Modern Society*, (Edinburgh: John Donald, 1986), 47-8.

[66] Cameron, ed., *First Book*, 167.

[67] *Ibid*, 170. Though the language was masculine, women could be, and were, excommunicated as well.

[68] The first known edition appeared in 1621. See Cameron's introduction to *First Book*, v.

Assembly, however, who treated it as a kind of ecclesiastical constitution.[69]

The General Assembly did commission the publication of The *Book of Common Order* in 1565, however. This was based on the *Form of Prayers and Ministration of the Sacraments* used by Knox and Goodman's congregation during their Genevan exile.[70] In regard to administration and practice of discipline, the two documents were practically the same. But the *Book of Common Order* did include one new passage which must be viewed as a last defense against pollution of the Communion celebration. Where the *Form of Prayers* had invoked I Corinthians 11 against unworthy participants, holding them "giltie of the bodye and bloud of the Lord" and warning that a communicant guilty of serious unconfessed sin "eateth and drinketh his owne damnation," and thus should stay away from the table,[71] the *Book of Common Order* called on God to weed out hypocrites. Before approaching the Communion table, the minister was to issue a general sentence of excommunication against all idolaters, murderers, adulterers, thieves, liars and rebels against parents, princes, magistrates or ministers who attempted to take part in Communion without first repenting.[72] The Kirk clearly viewed the purification of the Communion celebration as one of the ultimate goals of discipline, but one wonders whether such a warning kept anyone away from the table.

Another publication issued by the General Assembly regarding its disciplinary program was the 1569 *Ordoure of Excommunicatioun and of Public Repentance*.[73] This laid out a clear hierarchy of sins, and suggested punishments. Murderers, witches, adulterers, sorcerers, conjurors, "gevars of drinks to destroy children" [i.e. abortionists], and open blasphemers were all said to deserve death by scriptural law, and therefore to warrant excommunication with little delay.[74] Those guilty of fornication, drunkenness, brawling, contempt of the Kirk and Sabbath-breaking could expiate their sins with simple public repentance, and did not merit excommunication unless they refused. Lesser sins, such as absence from kirk, harsh words, pride and vanity were to be dealt with by private admonition and made public only as a last resort.[75] Such guidelines seem simple enough; all that was lacking was a zealous magistrate to act as a

---

[69] *BUK* 1:16; Calderwood, 2:185-6.

[70] *Book of Common Order* given in Knox, 6:287-333. Published in Edinburgh in 1565 by Robert Lekprevik.

[71] Knox, 4:192-3.

[72] *Ibid*, 6:324.

[73] Given in Knox, 6:447-470. Published in Edinburgh in 1569 by Robert Lekprevik.

[74] *Ibid*, 2:449.

[75] *Ibid*, 2:453-4.

'nursing mother' to the infant kirk.

Parliament and the Reform Effort

The Parliament of 1560, having been warned by the absent monarchs not to meddle in religious questions, took the necessary steps to break formally Scotland's ties to Rome and the old church. It outlawed "Idolatrie and superstitioun in the Kirk of God," particularly transubstantiation, salvation by works, pilgrimages and prayers to saints, and forbade the celebration of the Mass or Catholic baptism, with death the recommended penalty for third-time offenders. These negative steps were coupled with an endorsement of the Scots Confession, discussed earlier.[76] Thus 1560 seems to present a clear, though possibly illegal, break with the past. But, like 1492, 1517 and 1534, it marks more the commencement of a process than its completion. Although many sitting in Parliament, particularly those in possession of kirk lands, might have looked back on a job well done, there was, for the more reform-minded, much left to settle. The patrimony of the Kirk was certainly a major concern,[77] but we will concentrate here on the reform of popular behavior and religious practices.

The founding documents of the Reformed Kirk had held that witches, blasphemers and adulterers deserved death for their activities. The General Assembly soon set about seeking statutory endorsement of such severity, petitioning the queen (by now resident in Scotland) in July 1562 to enforce the law of the Old Testament:

> [We] requyre...punischment of horibill vices, sick as ar adultery, fornicatioun, oppin horedome, blasphemy, contempt of God, of his Word and sacraments; quhilks in this Realme, for lack of punischment, do even now sa abound, that sin is reputed to be no sin. And thairfore, as that we see the present signes of Gods wrayth now manifestly appear, so do we forewarne, that he will stryke, or it be long, if his law without punischment be permitted thus manifestly to be contemned. If any object, that punischment cannot be commanded to be executed without a Parliament, we answer that the eternall God in his Parliament hes pronunced death to be the punischment for adulterie and for blasphemie; quhose actis if ye put not to executioun (seeing that Kings ar but his lieutenants, having no power to give lyfe, quhare he commands death) as that he will repute you, and all uthers that foster vice, patrons of impietie, so will he not faill to punisch you for neglecting of his judgements.[78]

---

[76] *APS* 2:535; Spottiswoode, 1:326-7; Knox, 2:121-125.

[77] Knox, 2:92; Donaldson, *Scottish Reformation*, 68-72.

[78] *BUK*, 1:21.

God's Parliament soon got some reinforcement from its Scottish counterpart. In 1563 the latter ordained that "forsamekill as the abominabill and filthy vice and cryme of adulterie hes bene perniciouslie and wickitlie usit within this Realme," all "notoure and manifest committaris of adulterie ...salbe punist with all rigour unto the deid [death] alsweill the woman as the man doar and committar of the samin." The same Parliament mandated death for all users of "witchcraftis sorsarie and necromancie," as well as those who consulted with them.[79] The Parliament of August 1567, meeting after the Queen's defeat at Carberry Hill, extended the death penalty to incest (on the authority of Leviticus 18), and mandated a £40 fine and two hours of public humiliation at the local market cross for fornicators, or a week's imprisonment on bread and water for those unable to pay the fine. Penalties were to increase for second and third offenses.[80]

Parliament was slower to condemn blasphemy (always a nebulous concept, anyway), and the first post-Reformation legislation on that subject did not come until 1581. This merely endorsed a 1551 act, and gave a scale of fines (relatively small and dependent on status) for those guilty of "abhominabill aithis." Those who could not pay at all were to be placed in jougs or stocks for four hours. The General Assembly had sought the death penalty, but the most severe punitive options in this act were banishment or a year's imprisonment, and those only for fourth-time offenders.[81]

Keeping the Sabbath also became a major concern of the reformers, and, here again, Parliament preferred at first merely to reconfirm older legislation. In 1579, noting that "sabbath dayis ar now comounlie violat and brokin alsweill w[i]t[h]in burgh as to landwart," by holding of markets and fairs, by laboring, "be gaming and playing, passing to tavernis & ailhouss and wilfull remaning fra the paroche kirk in tyme of sermone or prayers," Parliament ratified an act passed under James IV against fairs and markets on holy days. In addition, it instituted a scale of fines for those working, playing, or absent from church on the Sabbath.[82] There was no further legislation on the subject until the 1590s.

Parliamentary legislation seemed to tighten prohibitions of Catholic practices as well. Another 1567 act repeated the 1560 ban on the Mass, but

---

[79] *APS*, 2:539.

[80] *Ibid*, 3:25-6.

[81] *Ibid*, 3:212. Parliament did make blasphemy a capital offense in 1661, and there is on record one execution - that of the student Thomas Aikenhead executed after trial in the Justiciary Court in January 1697. He had cursed God and the Trinity. See James Cameron, "Scottish Calvinism and the Principle of Intolerance," in B.A. Gerrish and Robert Benedetto, eds., *Reformatio Perennis: Essays on Calvin and the Reformation in Honor of Ford Lewis Battles*, (Pittsburgh, Pa.: Pickwick Press, 1981), 113-28, at 121-4.

[82] *APS*, 3:138.

extended its penalties to those in attendance, as well as the priest.[83] In 1579 came restrictions on sons of lairds and nobles who went abroad to study in Catholic countries, and in 1581 legislation banned the importation or distribution of books "in the prais and defence of the said paip and his usurpit authoritie or other erroneus doctrine." The 1581 Parliament also legislated specifically against pilgrimages, celebration of saints' days, bonfires and carols, with penalties ranging from a £40 fine for first offenses to death for repeaters.[84] Various other acts against Catholics, particularly those who harbored Jesuits, were passed later in the century.[85]

Because excommunication was the ultimate sanction the Kirk could employ, the success of its disciplinary program was heavily dependent on the pressures exerted on excommunicants, by secular magistrates as well as neighbors. The pre-Reformation acts which attempted to put teeth into the sanction of "cursing" have already been mentioned. Then, in 1572, Parliament held that all those excommunicated "be ordour of the trew reformit kirk" were to be given 40 days to satisfy the Kirk, or else be put to the horn.[86] Of course, horning had in many cases become just as much of an empty formality as excommunication, and Parliament lamented this in 1579, noting that the sanction was so abused that those put to the horn "takkis na feir thairof." Henceforth, the names of those put to the horn were to be read three times a year at the market cross in their district's major burgh, and all their goods and money were to be confiscated.[87]

Thus by the early 1580s Parliament had enacted most of the Kirk's disciplinary program into law, and given its sanctions some legal backing. But in many cases these laws were never enforced. The leading historian of Edinburgh's reformation has argued that "the perils of excommunication—banishment, an inhibition on collecting debts—were enough to ruin even the most prosperous merchant."[88] This may have been so in some cases, but examples are plentiful elsewhere of excommunicants, particularly prominent ones, who seem to have suffered little. Arguably the burghs, as integrated, face-to-face societies, were better able to enforce community standards and, where those standards called for thoroughgoing reform, create something like the godly society imagined by Knox and the other reformers. In what ways did the burghs seek to aid the Kirk's campaign for a behavioral reformation?

---

[83] *Ibid*, 3:22-3.

[84] *Ibid*, 3:138, 3:212-214

[85] In 1587, 1593, 1594 and 1600. See *ibid*, 3:429-30, 4:17, 4:62-3, 4:232.

[86] *APS*, 3:76.

[87] *Ibid*, 3:142-3.

[88] Lynch, *Edinburgh and the Reformation*, 188.

Burgh Governments and Disciplinary Ordinances

The most effective government in sixteenth-century Scotland was local government. Most of the parliamentary legislation discussed earlier was left to local officials to enforce and, in some areas, came on the heels of earlier local ordinances addressing the same problems. Elsewhere, the national effort came first and the local response followed, perhaps with less enthusiasm. This can be illustrated by a comparative discussion of disciplinary ordinances passed in Dundee, Edinburgh and Aberdeen.

The Tayside port of Dundee was, as mentioned earlier, one of the first Scottish burghs to embrace the Reformation. Indeed, Knox claimed it was the first, having officially accepted Protestantism, with Paul Methven as town preacher, in 1558.[89] Dundee's provost, James Haliburton, tutor of Pitcur, was active with the Lords of the Congregation during their military campaigns of 1559.[90] On 10 January 1559 the town council passed a harsh ordinance mandating banishment for those guilty of sexual immorality, and another instituting fines for the sale of ale and wine after ten p.m. By later that year, Dundee evidently had a functioning kirk session.[91]

But banishment of sexual offenders must have been a stronger punishment than the town's magistrates were really willing to enforce, because a new ordinance regarding adultery and fornication was passed in October 1559. Under its provisions, first-time offenders faced public humiliation at the market cross, while recidivists were to be ducked in foul water. Significantly, first-timers were given the option of performing public repentance in church rather than facing the throng at the market cross.[92] Thus in Dundee, well before Parliament outlawed the old church and launched its anti-vice campaign, magistrates were taking steps in the same direction. But they were also already trying to shift sexual cases into the Kirk's jurisdiction, rather than treating them as civil matters, despite their own civic ordinances aimed at combating extramarital sex.

Another phenomenon already visible at Dundee which would be repeated elsewhere was the tendency initially to attack a perceived problem with a draconian regulation, and then retreat to a more enforceable standard, presumably after officials proved reluctant to use the stricter order. There were further adjustments in the ordinances regarding sexual offenders. In 1564, the council ordered that female offenders have their heads shaved,

---

[89] Knox, 1:300.

[90] Bardgett, *Scotland Reformed*, 71-3.

[91] Alexander J. Warden, ed., *Burgh Laws of Dundee*, (London: Longmans Green, 1872), 17; Flett, 83-5, 88, text of sexual offenders' act from council minute book given on 98.

[92] Warden, ed., *Burgh Laws of Dundee*, 18; Flett, 85-6, text of new ordinance on 98.

although this punishment was in 1580 restricted to women who gave birth out of wedlock and then wore their hair uncovered like "ane schameles huir." Also in 1580, a week's imprisonment and possible banishment was added to the ecclesiastical punishment for adultery, though this of course fell far short of the death penalty contained in the 1563 act of Parliament.[93]

In July 1560, Methven (soon to be disgraced by an adultery charge himself) was replaced as Dundee's minister by the ex-friar William Christieson.[94] The town sent two lay representives along with Christieson to the first General Assembly in December 1560, giving it one of the largest delegations there.[95] Three years later, it sent three laymen, including the provost; only the host town of Edinburgh was as well represented.[96] But Dundee's adherence to the cause extended beyond a willingness to legislate against vice and send representatives to Edinburgh; in October 1559 it had also passed an act instituting fines for those guilty of trading during Sunday preaching, and in October 1564 ordered fines or a spell in the "chokis" for those who ignored admonitions to attend services.[97]

As time passed and the local reformation became more widely accepted, Dundee's magistrates took further steps to enforce Sabbath observation, while also extending their regulatory efforts to ensure religious orthodoxy and attack the perceived social dangers of popular pastimes. All of these concerns were displayed in the burgh council meeting of 21 January 1569. First, the council ordered that the burgh's port be closed from ten p.m. Saturday until 4 p.m. Sunday, with exceptions made only for landing fishing boats.[98] Then, it ordered that masters report to the bailies members of their households who "mak argument and disput agains the guid trew religioun and ordour therof and discipline universallye within this realme...."[99] Outdoor performances by minstrels were also targeted; those caught playing after nine p.m. were to be fined 20 shillings and have their instruments destroyed, and anyone seen dancing at such a performance faced a fine.[100] Since these and other spectacles might be accompanied by excessive

---

[93] Flett, 86, 110-11, texts on 99, 120-1.

[94] Knox, 2:87. For Methven's disgrace, which occurred after his removal to Jedburgh and resulted in his flight into England, see Calderwood, 2:207-10; *BUK* 1:29, 32.

[95] *BUK*, 1:3-4. Also sending three were Edinburgh (which hosted the Assembly), St. Andrews, Linlithgow, Leith and Torpichen.

[96] Sederunt, along with a portion of the proceedings, given in Donaldson, *Scottish Church History*, 116-9.

[97] Warden, ed., *Burgh Laws of Dundee*, 19; Flett, 87, texts of acts on 99-100.

[98] Flett, 87.

[99] *Ibid*, 86, text on 99. Warden gives what appears to be the same ordinance, but dates it 21 February. See Warden, ed., *Burgh Laws of Dundee*, 35.

[100] Flett, 88, text on 100.

drinking, in October 1580 the council decided to attack the problem from that angle, passing a graduated scale of fines (from five marks to £10 Scots) for public drunkenness, with chronic offenders subject to banishment.[101]

The calumny spread by quarrelsome neighbors was another social evil which troubled Dundee's magistracy. The prevalence of bloodfeud in Scotland's kin-oriented society provided ample evidence of the need to reconcile disputants before passions escalated.[102] But the Dundee council initially chose to approach neighborly discord as a female problem. The city fathers possibly had neither the confidence in their power nor the sincere desire to quell male violence; doubtless they also found the sight of angry women particularly unseemly. In October 1580, the council ordained that women engaging in "schamefull flyttyng, reproching, sclanderyng, cursyng, bannyng or making ony horrible imprecatiounis, or fearfull blasphemeis of the name of God, betwix thame and ony uther persone" ask publicly for the injured party's forgiveness while on their knees, and pay a fine of 40 shillings. Those unable to pay were to spend three hours on the cuckstool.[103] As the ordinance's wording indicates, blasphemy was often seen as a manifestation of anger toward one's neighbor rather than a conscious attack on God.[104] In October 1581, the council ordered burgh officers to crack down on blasphemy generally, with no distinction made between sexes. This act introduced a scale of fines, and the bailies were to keep their ears tuned for cursing in the public markets. As an incentive to enforcement, they could keep half the fines they collected.[105]

Clearly in Dundee, the "Geneva of Scotland," magistrates were anxious to legislate a local reformation of manners as well as doctrine. Unfortunately, a paucity of records makes it difficult to determine the extent to which these regulations were enforced. But the Kirk clearly received backing in word, and may have in deed as well. Edinburgh, as the leading burgh of the realm, is much better documented, and there too the magistrates displayed early an enthusiasm for a campaign to eradicate both vice and Catholic practices. But Edinburgh's leadership soon demonstrated that it lacked the unity required to maintain such efforts in the face of opposition on several fronts.

In his detailed and sophisticated study of Edinburgh during the reformation era, Michael Lynch has argued against the notion that

---

[101] *Ibid*, 111, text on 121.

[102] For Scottish feuding in general, see Brown, *Bloodfeud in Scotland*. The role of the church courts in attempting to pacify feuds will be discussed later.

[103] Flett, 110, text on 120-1.

[104] An earlier (1559) ordinance had condemned "blasphemy" (sic) against ministers, elders and deacons. See Warden, ed., *Burgh Laws of Dundee*, 18.

[105] Flett, 111, text on 121-2.

Protestantism was an irresistible force there, and suggested that most of the burgh establishment was more concerned with maintaining urban liberties than advancing any particular religious agenda.[106] The reformation crisis of 1559-60 was marked in Edinburgh by a sequence of coup and countercoup between one traditionalist burgh council led by the Catholic George, 5th lord Seton, and another (including some new councilors of lower rank) headed by the Protestant Archibald Douglas of Kilspindie.[107] The Seton council was permanently ousted in April 1560, and the Kilspindie council began its own anti-Catholic and anti-vice campaign that June. On 10 June, it passed an act regarding "the grit number of idolatreris quhoremaisteris [male sexual offenders] and harlottis daylie resortand within this burgh, provokand the indignatioun of God upone the samyn ofttymes furtheschawin be the prechouris...." All such sinners were ordered to "gif testimonie of thair conversioun" before the burgh ministers (Knox and the reader John Cairns) by the following Sunday, or else face six hours of public abuse at the market cross, followed by a carting through the town. Second offenders were to be branded on the cheek and banished, and third-timers put to death.[108] On 20 September the council ordered that the recent act of Parliament against the Mass and Catholic sacraments be proclaimed publicly in Edinburgh.[109]

Like their counterparts in Dundee, the Edinburgh councilors also turned their attention to the proper observance of the Sabbath and the disorderly aspects of popular culture. In October 1560 the council ordered that the Sunday flesh market be moved to Saturday, and that all merchant shops and booths be closed on Sunday. Further, taverns and hostels were to close during morning and afternoon sermons. Another act passed the same day mandated a spell in the branks (an iron bridle and gag) for all who "tak vpone hand to bane, sweir, tak in vane or blasfleme the name of God."[110] This latter act apparently had little effect, however, as in April 1561 the council voted again that some sort of order be established to punish blasphemy.[111] Nor was the move to maintain the Sabbath terribly successful; the council had to issue another proclamation against Sunday markets in July 1563, and in January 1569 introduced a £5 fine for tavernkeepers who

---

[106] Lynch, *Edinburgh and the Reformation*, 8-9. For the traditional view, in which Knox represented the aspirations of a powerful Edinburgh "middle class" firmly committed to Protestantism, see W. Stanford Reid, "The Coming of the Reformation to Edinburgh," *Church History* 42 (1973), 27-44, especially at 44.

[107] Lynch, *Edinburgh and the Reformation*, 76-9.

[108] *Edin. Recs.*, 3:65.

[109] *Ibid*, 3:82-3.

[110] *Ibid*, 3:85-6.

[111] *Ibid*, 3:106-7.

sold refreshments during sermon times.[112]

The Edinburgh magistrates, themselves mainly merchants of some standing, saw connections between popular culture, vagrancy and disorder among the town's craftsmen. The council had tried to oust itinerant beggars before the onset of the Reformation, and this proved a continuing concern.[113] In July 1560, an expulsion order against vagrants was extended to cover "fydlaris pyparis minstrallis, and otheris without maisteris."[114] Street music might foster idleness, drinking and dancing, but these were mild problems compared to the riots engendered by certain craft traditions. A 1555 act of Parliament had forbidden the election of "Robert Hude ...Lytill Johne, Abbot of unressoun, Quenis of Maij" or other customs which mocked the existing social order.[115] On 23 April 1561, on information that some of Edinburgh's craftsmen and servants were planning "to mak convocatioun and assemblie efter the auld wickit maner of Robene Hude, nocht regarding the punisment thretnit in Goddis word vpoun the braikaris of the Saboth, nor having feir of the temporale punischment" contained in the act of Parliament, the town council forbade the planned fête, and threatened participants with banishment.[116] But this failed to prevent the election of the tailor George Dury as "Robert Hude" and the disorderly procession which followed. The council's effort to punish the participants in July led to a riot. Several of the rioters (some of them rather prominent) were eventually tried before the High Court of Justiciary, and had to find "caution" (i.e. a bondsman) that they would submit to the law, although their ultimate fate is unclear.[117] The spring of 1562 seems to have passed peacefully, however, after a 30 April order from the Queen inhibiting the election of Robin Hood.[118] The united front of Catholic queen and protestant burgh council may have been enough to forestall disturbance.

Suppression of traditional rituals was not the only craft grievance, however. For Edinburgh's craftsmen, the transition from passage of ordinances against certain vices to their actual enforcement proved too much to swallow. The city fathers learned about this in November 1560 when they ordered John Sanderson, deacon of the town's fleshers, carted for adultery. His fellow craftsmen protested "that on na wayis thay wald

---

[112] *Ibid*, 3:165, 259. Patrick Porteous was fined 40s by the council on 23 August 1570 for having carted wool to Leith the previous Sunday. See *ibid*, 3:276.

[113] For example, *ibid*, 3:12, 42, 50-1.

[114] *Ibid*, 3:68-9.

[115] *APS* 2:500.

[116] *Edin. Recs.*, 3:107-8.

[117] Some were said to be put to the horn as of August 8. See *Pit. Crim.*, 1:409-10; *Edin. Recs.*, 3:112-3, 118; Knox, 2:157-60; Lynch, *Edinburgh and the Reformation*, 94-5.

[118] *Edin. Recs.*, 3:134.

appreve the samyn ·nor na sic extreme lawis vpoun honest craftismen,
nochtwithstanding it was allegit that thay...had be speciall voit of before
consenttit to the maiking of the said statute vpoun adulteraris contening the
foresaid pane." They broke into the tollbooth, freed him from ward, and
created a riot.[119]

The anti-vice campaign found other targets in addition to unruly craftsmen. Edinburgh's council ordered Grissel Sempill, Lady Stanhouse, to leave
the burgh in 1561 due to her adultery, and was quite pleased to lock up
Katherine Ewin, mistress of the notorious Dominican John Black, in April
1562.[120] But these were special cases. The council minutes give the general
impression that the new vice regulations soon fell into disuse. In May 1562,
noting "the contempt of discipline presentlie execute within this burgh
vpoun fornicatouris," the council ordered three of its members to take a
walk by the loch on the north side of the burgh which also served as a
public sewer, and choose a convenient place "for dowkeing of the saidis
fornicatouris thairin."[121] This was followed six months later by a new
ordinance that the town's bailies round up all adulterers and fornicators,
imprison them for a month on bread and water, and then banish them.
Fornicators were to be given the option of carting through town and public
repentance in the kirk instead. The dean of guild was ordered to prepare the
necessary prison the following month, but in November 1563 (after passage
of the draconian act of Parliament), the ordinance had to be repeated, this
time with the place of incarceration at least specified.[122] At the end of
August 1566, the Queen sent the town council a reminder that all laws
against sexual offenders ought to be enforced, particularly the 1563 act, but
in December it was noted that the space proposed as a prison for Edinburgh's female sinners still lacked a lock.[123] By the end of the 1560s, the
Edinburgh magistrates had relaxed their attitude toward sexual sins, particularly among the prominent.[124]

---

[119] *Edin. Recs.*, 3:89-90. Sanderson claimed he had divorced his wife already. Knox
characterized the rioters as a "raschall multitude, enflambit be some ungodlie craftismen." See
Knox, 2:155-6. The lack of enthusiasm on the part of Edinburgh's craftsmen for a morality
crusade contrasts with Lyndal Roper's findings for the craftsmen of Augsburg. See Lyndal
Roper, *The Holy Household: Women and Morals in Reformation Augsburg*, (Oxford: Oxford
University Press, 1989), *passim*.

[120] *Edin. Recs.*, 3:129, 133.

[121] *Ibid*, 3:135.

[122] *Ibid*, 3:152, 3:154, 3:173-4.

[123] *Ibid*, 3:217, 3:337. W. Stanford Reid has argued that these various regulations were
vigorously enforced, but provides little evidence, and the tone of the council minutes suggests
the opposite conclusion. See Reid, "Coming of the Reformation," 37.

[124] Lynch, *Edinburgh and the Reformation*, 91-3.

The crusade against Edinburgh's Catholics also proceeded by fits and starts. The burgh council intervened to prevent the election of the Catholic smith William Brocas as deacon of the hammermen in May 1562, and on 17 July passed an act that nobody be allowed to hold burgh office save those "as hes adionit thame to the trew kirk of God and congregatioun, and has communicat wity bayth sacramentis, and hes submittit thameselffis vnder discipline." But this ordinance was deleted the following January "at the Quenis Maiesteis command."[125] The united front marshalled by the crown and burgh council against disorderly craftsmen was not up to a religious orthodoxy campaign. But later, after the queen's defeat of 1567-8, the burgh's merchant oligarchy found it easier to prevail, at least in cases where craft privileges in addition to religion were at issue. Thus on 8 May 1568, the hammermen were ordered to elect a new craft deacon in place of the pewterer John Wilson, because Wilson was "ane man of na religioun" who freely admitted he never attended sermons.[126] Not until 1569 is there any evidence of a real campaign against Catholic burgesses. At that time, ten named excommunicants were banished from the town and, it appears, actually forced to leave.[127] In the Canongate, a Catholic burgess was threatened with the loss of his burgess status if he did not join the Reformed Kirk, and he (and his cautioner) promised that he would comply within two weeks.[128] But even in these instances the reasons were probably more political than religious; the country was sliding into an armed conflict between supporters of the exiled queen and those of her infant son, and the councils of Edinburgh and the Canongate had, at first, cast their lots with the latter.[129] It was not until this struggle was over that Edinburgh's council was able to make Protestantism a prerequisite for officeholding, with a new oath instituted in September 1574. Significantly, this required officers, in addition to "renunceand all idolatrie, superstitioun, papisticall erroris quhatsumever..." to pledge loyalty to James VI; the two issues by then seemed inextricably linked.[130] In 1587, the test of religious orthodoxy was

---

[125] *Edin. Recs.*, 3:134-5, 140-1; Lynch, *Edinburgh and the Reformation*, 58.

[126] *Edin. Recs.*, 3:248.

[127] *Ibid*, 3:264; Lynch, *Edinburgh and the Reformation*, 192.

[128] Case of George Harrat, 20 January 1569. See "Extracts From the Records of the Burgh of the Canongate Near Edinburgh," *Maitland Club Miscellany* 2, (Edinburgh: Maitland Club, 1840), 281-359, at 316.

[129] For example, the Edinburgh council ordered on 30 July 1567 that bailies fine all householders who had not set fires the previous day to celebrate the king's coronation. See *Edin. Recs.*, 3:238.

[130] *Edin. Recs.*, 4:26.

added to the burgess oath as well.[131]

There had been scattered cases of prosecutions of individual Catholics earlier, such as the May 1561 case of the advocate Alexander Skene, who admitted to having taken Easter Communion according to the Catholic rite. After a short spell in ward, he was freed on condition that he do public repentance in St. Giles Kirk.[132] Late in 1563, 22 residents of Edinburgh and the Canongate faced a judiciary court trial for having celebrated the Mass at Holyrood on 8 August 1563. While the indictment against them noted that they "aucht to be adiugit and punesit to the deid [with death] with all rigour," nothing seems to have happened, except that three others who did not appear had to forfeit their cautions.[133] The apothecary David Hoppringill, warded by the town bailies in 1566 for marrying "efter the papis fassoun, he being of befoir adionit to the kirk of God and thair [!] disciplyne" was freed on the queen's orders. The woman he married was daughter to the royal macer.[134]

Other prosecutions give evidence of vocal opposition to Edinburgh's new religious regime in addition to the passive Catholicism discussed thus far. William Balfour in Leith was convicted by an assize on 31 December 1561 of a number of offenses against the Reformed Kirk, particularly with having interrupted a pre-Communion examination of parishioners by saying "is yat your communioun? The Devill birst me quhen euir it cumis in my belly! And ye Devill birst yame in quhais belly it cumis, for it is ane verray Devill!"[135] The following April, the Edinburgh council ordered that Ninian McCrechane, a cook, be scourged and placed in the branks for saying "loving to God, my lord Arrane and my lord Bothuile ar aggreit now; Knox quarter is run, he is skurgeit throw the toun."[136] Euphame Dundas, widow of a prominent merchant, was charged by the kirk session in June 1563 with having slandered Knox by saying that the minister had recently been caught with a prostitute. The kirk session appealed to the burgh council, but

---

[131] *Ibid*, 4:496-7. By then there was a significant threat from the protestant left as well as the Catholic right. See Lynch, *Edinburgh and the Reformation*, 191.

[132] *Edin. Recs.*, 3:115, 117.

[133] *Pit. Crim.*, 1:435. Of the 13 men involved, two were merchants and at least six of them craftsmen. Lynch discovered that three of the women charged were wives of men who regularly served on the burgh council in the 1560s. See Lynch, *Edinburgh and the Reformation*, 188-9.

[134] *Edin. Recs.*, 3:215. Margaret Sanderson has suggested that Hoppringill was freed on a technicality; the act of Parliament made attending Mass a crime, but not marriage by Catholic rites. But this overlooks the fact that the burgh ordinances made Catholicism itself a crime. See Margaret H.B. Sanderson, "Catholic Recusancy in Scotland in the Sixteenth Century," *Innes Review* 21 (1970), 87-107, at 101.

[135] Balfour's punishment is not mentioned. See *Pit. Crim.*, 1:416-8.

[136] *Edin. Recs.*, 3:132.

Dundas denied the charge, and it was dropped.[137] At the same council meeting, the draper John Graham, who had shortly before baptized his child as a Catholic, denied that he had publicly endorsed the Mass.[138] It is impossible to quantify opposition based on such scattered cases, but it seems clear that the Reformed Kirk and its program, so closely identified in Edinburgh itself with Knox, were not as popular as has been claimed,[139] and doubts about it extended up to the highest ranks of burgh society.

Like their colleagues in Dundee, Edinburgh's post-Reformation magistrates were concerned to keep peace between neighbors. But their pronouncements on the subject lacked the religious undertones of those of Dundee. An order of 3 October 1567 decreed that all who drew blood in the burgh "with quhatsumeuer kynd of wappin" were to pay a fine of £5. The problem was one of law and order—the profusion of outsiders with "instrumentis bellicall" who used the streets of Edinburgh as a forum for their feuds. There was no mention of the need for Christian brotherhood.[140]

Dundee embraced the Reformation; Edinburgh appears to have grasped it more cautiously. In both cases the town magistrates passed ordinances reflecting a heightened concern for the behavior of individuals. Dundee, less prone to royal and noble interference due to its distance from the political and economic center of the realm, could perhaps more easily adopt the mantle "Geneva of Scotland." Her magistrates may also have simply been more enthusiastic than those of the capital. Of course, the existence of kirk session minutes makes it possible to examine the enforcement of the new order in Edinburgh[141] and the Canongate,[142] and this subject will be treated later. But lest one should conclude that Dundee and Edinburgh were representative of all Scottish burghs in their attitudes toward religious change, it would be worthwhile to investigate the impact of the new thinking in Aberdeen, which neither embraced nor cautiously grasped the Reformation. The burgh councils of both Dundee and Edinburgh in 1558-60 passed religious and social ordinances anticipating the parliamentary legislation of the 1560s. In Aberdeen, the story was the reverse. There, parliamentary statutes, rather than reinforcing steps already taken, served as a tool (of limited effectiveness) to prod a reluctant burgh establishment. One might postulate that Aberdeen, an eastern port and university town,

---

[137] *Ibid*, 3:162, 164.

[138] *Ibid*, 3:152-3, 162. Graham, said to be "excommunicat," was warded at least briefly in 1574, although apparently freed by the Privy Council. See SRO ms CH2/450/1, 12v.

[139] E.g. by W. Stanford Reid. See Reid, "Coming of the Reformation," 33-4.

[140] *Edin. Recs.*, 3:242.

[141] SRO ms CH2/450/1, Edinburgh General Session Register, 1574-5.

[142] A. B. Calderwood, ed., *The Buik of the Kirk of the Canagait, 1564-1567*, (Edinburgh: Scottish Record Society, 1961).

would have been particularly receptive to the intellectual currents of
Protestantism its merchants encountered in their travels throughout the
North and Baltic seas. But this was not the case. Like much of the rest of
non-Gaelic Scotland, it had a brief flirtation with protestant preaching in
1543, but this seems to have had little lasting effect, having been more the
consequence of provost Thomas Menzies' brief alliance with the governor
Arran and the latter's anglophile policy than the result of any popular
clamor.[143] The Menzies were the leading family of burgh society, while the
countryside around Aberdeen was dominated by the earl of Huntly and his
Gordon relatives—including the bishop of Aberdeen—along with their Leslie
allies. There were several attempts by the earls of Huntly to overawe the
burgh in the sixteenth century, but the provost and council were usually able
to keep them at arm's length.[144] Despite their rivalry for control of the
burgh, the Gordons and the Menzies generally agreed on religious questions; both factions were quite conservative in outlook, and viewed reform
sentiment nervously, as a threat to the political balance in Aberdeen and the
northeast.[145] Their view was widely shared; remarkably few of the pre-1560
Catholic clergy in the diocese of Aberdeen ever conformed or served in the
Reformed Kirk, and it was reported as late as November 1572 that the Mass
was still celebrated openly in Old Aberdeen, site of the college. The college
itself remained Catholic until 1569, and the following year the General
Assembly's commissioner for Aberdeen asked to be relieved of his duties
because there "was no obedience in these parts and the ministers were not
answered."[146]

Despite this general religious conservatism, there were some voices on
the burgh council willing to attack the patrimony of the Catholic Church in
1559-60. Whether this was out of an ideological commitment to Protestantism or simply political or material interests is impossible to determine.
On 4 January 1559, upon a report that "certane strangearis" and some
residents of the burgh had attacked the town's monasteries, stealing timber

---

[143] Allan White, "The Impact of the Reformation on a Burgh Community: The Case of
Aberdeen," in Michael Lynch, ed., *The Early Modern Town in Scotland*, (London: Croom
Helm, 1987), 81-101, at 85-6; Bruce McLennan, "The Reformation in the Burgh of
Aberdeen," *Northern Scotland* 2 (1974-7), 119-44, at 125-6.

[144] E.g. *Aber. Recs.*, 2:7, 91-3. See also Allan White, "Queen Mary's Northern Province,"
in Michael Lynch, ed., *Mary Stewart: Queen in Three Kingdoms*, (Oxford: Basil Blackwell,
1988), 53-70, at 63, 66-7.

[145] White, "Impact of the Reformation," 90-3.

[146] Calderwood, 3:228-9; *BUK* 1:190, 254; Sanderson, "Catholic Recusancy," 95; Charles
Haws, "The Diocese of Aberdeen and the Reformation," *Innes Review* 22 (1971), 72-84, at
83-4; White, "Impact of the Reformation," 94-5; *ibidem, Religion, Politics and Society In
Aberdeen, 1543-1593*, (Edinburgh University Ph.D. Thesis, 1985), 281. For religious
conservatism north of the Tay generally, see Donaldson, *Scottish Church History*, 193-7.

and roofing, the bailie and burgh treasurer David Mar moved that the burgh council take over management of the monasteries and their properties, "and the profyttis thairof to be applyit to the commond weill of the toune, and specialy for the furthsettin of Goddis glory, and his trew word and prechours thairof." The motion carried, with one dissent, but the provost and several of his followers were apparently absent, because on 8 January the provost's son Gilbert Menzies appeared, and lodged a protest on behalf of his father, himself, and five other councilors (two of them also named Menzies) against the confiscation, claiming that it was "contrar the mynd of the authorite and manifest tressoune." The provost himself made an appearance on 12 January, condemned the motion of 4 January, and said all preaching should be financed by the bishop (William Gordon). He was joined by 15 others who said they had "for the maist part" been absent on 4 January. Finally, on 23 January, "the counsall concludit...to wphald and menteyine the gray freirs place within this burght, and to suffer no hurt, violence, nor distructioun be don thairto...."[147] The Menzies and their conservative followers thus staved off what seems to have been an attempted protestant coup by a minority faction. While the town may have gained some control over the Greyfriars' property, preaching would remain within the bishop's bailiwick for the time being.[148]

The town did later offer some token support (40 men) to the Lords of the Congregation, but this seems primarily a political move. The motion approved sending the contingent "for defens of the liberty of this realme, and commond weill of this burgh," and carefully noted "that it be nocht to interpryis ony porposs contrar the quenis grace and hir authorite." It also made no mention of the Congregation's religious program.[149] Provost Menzies and nine other councilors vowed in December 1559 to defend the town's religious foundations against iconoclastic attacks "under colour and pretence of godlie reformatioune," threatened by a contingent from the Congregation then in the neighborhood.[150] And, when presented with the *First Book of Discipline* in January 1561, the burgh's representatives

---

[147] *Aber. Recs.*, 1:315-9, 321.

[148] White, "Impact of the Reformation," 91-2. White places these events in January 1559/60, though the published documents in *Aber. Recs.* date the new year from 1 January, which suggests they took place in January 1558/59. White may base his conclusion on unpublished registers he has seen, though he makes no reference to them in discussing these events. The difference is immaterial here, where the purpose is merely to demonstrate the religious and political conservatism of most of the council.

[149] *Aber. Recs.*, 1:322; McLennan, "Reformation in the Burgh of Aberdeen," 127. This was in March 1559 or 1560 - see *caveat* on dating above.

[150] *Ibid*, 325-6.

declined to sign it.[151]

Thus the majority of Aberdeen's magistrates accepted the events of 1559-60 as a political fact (as did the earl of Huntly, their powerful neighbor), but not as a mandate for reform. Like their colleagues in Edinburgh, they were happy to condemn the excesses of unruly craftsmen, as they did in May 1562 and May 1565 after attempts by some of the latter to carry on traditional rituals involving music, processions and elections of mock grandees.[152] They were also willing to try to use the burgh church of St. Nicholas as a forum for the reconciliation of parties who had been at dispute.[153] But the early attack on Catholicism and vice visible in Dundee and, to a lesser extent, Edinburgh, seems to have been absent in Aberdeen.

In its various decrees, ordinances and pronouncements issued in the 1560s, the Aberdeen council avoided the subjects of Catholicism, sex and the Sabbath, all three of which figured prominently in municipal concerns elsewhere. Rather than pass pious ordinances involving civil penalties and then largely leave enforcement up to the kirk session and its ecclesiastical sanctions, these conservative magistrates carried on largely as if nothing had changed from the 1550s. They did hire a protestant preacher, the moderate Adam Heriot, in July 1560, but decided to discontinue his 300-mark annual salary from the burgh coffers in October 1562, on the grounds that paying him was properly the responsibility of the bishop of Aberdeen.[154] Heriot's background (he was not a native of the burgh) must have made it particularly difficult for him to stand up to traditional interests on the Kirk's behalf.[155]

Heriot remained, though, until 1574,[156] and was even given a kirk session with which to consult late in 1562, although this step was probably window-dressing to extricate Aberdeen from a political bind. The burgh was anxious to distance itself from the earl of Huntly's rebellion, which ended in military defeat at Corrichie, just west of Aberdeen, in October 1562.

---

[151] Cameron, ed., *First Book*, 12; White, *Religion, Politics...*, 190.

[152] *Aber. Recs.*, 1:343-4, 459-60.

[153] *Ibid*, 1:331, 352 (cases from March 1561 and November 1562).

[154] *Ibid*, 1:351; Knox, 2:87.

[155] White, *Religion, Politics...*, 172. Heriot had earlier been a canon of St. Andrews. See Charles H. Haws, *Scottish Parish Clergy at the Reformation 1540-1574*, (Edinburgh: Scottish Record Society, 1972), 3. Heriot was also probably seriously overworked - he had the responsibility of ministering in both Aberdeen and Auld Aberdeen (the bishop's seat and university neighborhood) until 1569. See McLennan, "Reformation in the Burgh of Aberdeen," 136.

[156] John Stuart, ed., "The Chronicle of Aberdeen, MCCCCXCI-MDXCV," (written by Walter Cullen, reader at St. Nicholas from 1570), *Spalding Club Miscellany* 2, (Aberdeen: Spalding Club, 1842), 29-70, at 41.

Facing a visit from the firmly protestant earl of Moray, the queen's half-brother and (at that point) leading Scottish advisor, the Aberdeen council established a kirk session to demonstrate its (newfound) commitment to reform.[157]

This session included the Catholic provost Thomas Menzies as well as the protestant bailie David Mar among its 15 elders. Three other elders were councilors who had actively opposed the confiscation of church properties in 1559-60, and several held leases on these properties.[158] Elected in November, the session convened on 10 December to approve a foundation charter. This proclaimed that "[God's] feare, service and honor cheflie stands and consistis in obeying his will, and his hevenlie will to be found and persawit in his most haly ten commandmentis geven to Myses vpone Mont Synai, quhairin is c[on]tenit all quhat he willith his peple to do...." Albeit the session felt that the Gospel was at that time properly preached in Aberdeen, "zit many grewous & haynous crimes & offencis, quhairby ye just vengens of god is p[ro]vokit to fall upoun his peple, is regnant w[ith]in yis toun." Thus, in order that "gud lyfe, c[on]versatioun & maneris may scheyne, & the rottin, poysonit & fylthy flouer of wyce & synn may be wed owt & plukit wp be ye Rutis," the burgh had need of ecclesiastical discipline "albeit yai sall differ in ye punischment, for it pertenis to ye prince to punische w[i]t[h] Dethe."[159]

The new session then endorsed what was essentially the Ten Commandments, with explanations and punishments. Idolatry was defined as the teaching that any being or deity other than God could be the object of prayers, or that any good work of man might "merite or deserue pardon fra the wrath of God for synne bot Criste his merite allanerlie." Those who held such beliefs were to be excommunicated. Further, any person keeping company with an excommunicant would be forced to perform public repentance in the kirk on the Sabbath, and might face fines as well. But the elders, some Catholic themselves, may have already been having second thoughts; this last clause was later struck out. Conspicuously absent is any explicit mention of Catholicism or the Pope.[160]

After this came clauses regarding swearing, keeping the Sabbath, obe-

---

[157] White, *Religion, Politics...*, 169-70.

[158] *Aber. Recs.*, 1:316-9; SRO ms CH2/448/1, 1. This manuscript is paginated rather than foliated, and some excerpts have been published in John Stuart, ed., *Selections From the Records of the Kirk Session, Presbytery and Synod of Aberdeen*, (Aberdeen: Spalding Club, 1846). These should be used with caution, as they contain several significant errors in dating. Since most of the kirk session register remains unpublished, and all of it will be used in this study, all citations are to the manuscript.

[159] SRO ms CH2/448/1, 2.

[160] *Ibid*, 3, although it is impossible to date the retraction.

dience to parents, magistrates, ministers and elders (in that order), and quarrels between parishioners.[161] The Aberdeen elders also expressed their readiness to punish sexual offenders, because "adultery, huyrdom and fornicatioun [are] defendit and forbidden be the expres word off God, and the committaris thairoff to be puneist with dethe, quhilk is negligentlie ouersene, and nocht regardit be all Cristian princis, to quhom in appertenis to puneish the same." Brothel-keepers and prostitutes were to face immediate banishment, and adulterers to be carted through the town and then banished. First-time fornicators could redeem themselves with a public confession, but would be carted and ducked for second offenses and banished for a third.[162]

In addition, beggars not native to Aberdeen were to be expelled, and steps taken against "nychtwalkaris, commone cartaris and dissaris, and dronkartis," with public admonitions from the pulpit and, in recalcitrant cases, excommunication.[163] But these elders, many of them also burgh councilors, again showed their apprehensiveness about religious change when they ordered that "na disputatioun nor ressonyng of the scripturis be at dennar or supper or oppin table, quhairthrow arrysis gryte contentioun and debate." And, ever watchful against ministerial pretentions, the session ordered that Heriot never rebuke publicly "ony notable or particular persoune" without its consent.[164]

Thus the authors of the Aberdonian ecclesiastical ordinances sought to strike a balance, offering the crackdown on vice present in other burghs while avoiding a direct attack on traditions dear to the magistracy, and seeking to curb the dangers of sedition present in the new religious thinking. The earl of Moray may have been impressed enough to forego punishing the town for any role it may have had in Huntly's revolt, but this burst of reforming zeal did not long survive his return southward. The kirk session record for 1562-3 includes only one disciplinary case (a brothel-keeper banished from the burgh in January 1563), but breaks off shortly thereafter, and by all indications, the session ceased to meet.[165] The next leaf carries the heading "the namis of yame yat professis god his haly word and his trew Religioun w[i]t[h]in ye burgh of Aberdene and hes submittit yame self villinglie...to orderlie conver[sa]tion & discipline as it becumis ye childrene of god...," but no names appear underneath![166]

---

[161] *Ibid*, 3-5.

[162] *Ibid*, 5-6.

[163] *Ibid*, 6-7.

[164] *Ibid*, 8.

[165] *Ibid*, 11.

[166] *Ibid*, 12.

The magistrates of Aberdeen took another stab at Reformed discipline in March 1568—again in an atmosphere of political uncertainty—after the deposition and defeat of Queen Mary.[167] They elected a new session and attempted to punish 13 offenders, all sexual cases, but session meetings were again abandoned two months later.[168] Then, in August, provost Menzies was besieged in his house and forced to yield the town to the queen's party, headed in the northeast by the 5th earl of Huntly.[169] The kirk session was not re-created until September 1573, after the final defeat of the queen's supporters.[170] It was not until November 1573 that the session took action against anyone for adherence to Catholicism, and this lone case was not followed by any others until the following April.[171] Keeping the Sabbath did not become a concern of the burgh council until October 1576, when it forbade the sale of fish or flesh during sermon times, though this order had to be repeated in October 1580.[172]

Later Aberdonian ordinances regarding the Sabbath or other aspects of the reformed social program display a sense of civic tardiness, as in 1588 when the council lamented the high incidence of drinking, gaming and merchandising on the Sabbath, "contrar to the custome of reformit kirkis and weill governit commoun weillis of this realme," or a 1592 act against swearing in which the council held that it was "folowing the example of wther reformit congregationis and burghis."[173] In 1591, when ordering an exemplary ritual of humiliation for a baxter guilty of incest with his late wife's niece, the council said it did so because "be the lawis estableschit within this realme thair hes not bene ane ordour of punischment for the samen sa speciallie devysit."[174] Aberdeen's magistrates were apparently ignorant (perhaps willfully so) of the 1567 act of Parliament which made incest a capital offense. Indeed, while the council occasionally took notice of sexual offenders who presumably had refused to submit to the discipline of the local kirk, its published records from the sixteenth century do not yield a single ordinance against sexual offenses; these were held to fall

---

[167] She lost the battle of Carberry in June 1567, was forced to abdicate at Lochleven the following month, was defeated at Langside and fled into England in May 1568. See Donaldson, *All the Queen's Men*, 83-110.

[168] SRO ms CH2/448/1, 13-18.

[169] White, "Queen Mary's Northern Province," 66-7.

[170] SRO ms CH2/448/1, 19-20.

[171] *Ibid*, 25, 34.

[172] *Aber. Recs.*, 2:27-8, 38.

[173] *Ibid*, 2:62, 73-4. The act against swearing mentioned an act of Parliament passed 11 years earlier, and noted that Aberdeen had never addressed the subject in its civic ordinances.

[174] *Ibid*, 2:71-2.

within the kirk's bailiwick alone in this northern burgh.[175]

Thus the institution of a reformed social regime followed significantly different paths in Dundee, Edinburgh and Aberdeen. Dundee had a zealous magistracy quick to support its kirk session with stern civic ordinances. Edinburgh's "privy kirk" received similar support as it became a public kirk, although the initial zeal turned to caution as enforcement of moral and religious standards fell increasingly to the kirk session. In Aberdeen, ecclesiastical discipline was a political football for at least a dozen years after 1560, and the magistrates were slow to take an active role in the construction of any new Jerusalem. Such differences in local polities will be important considerations later, when we examine the actual operation of the kirk sessions and presbyteries in different localities. As Michael Lynch has pointed out, there was no single Scottish Reformation, but rather a series of local reformations, each progressing at its own pace.[176] The institution and practice of Reformed discipline provides one yardstick with which to chart their growth as well as their idiosyncracies.

The General Assembly and Discipline, 1560-81

Despite such localism, there was one central institution of the Kirk working to implement its program at the national level. This was the General Assembly. Jenny Wormald has argued that through their participation in this body and in regional synods the ministers and elders of the Reformed Kirk forged links between the center and the localities stronger than any Scotland, with its relatively weak central governmental institutions, had previously experienced.[177] The proof of such an assertion would have to rest on more attendance lists than have survived. Through reconstruction of records lost in the London Parliament fire of 1834, it has become possible to determine what business was conducted at most of the meetings of the General Assembly during the sixteenth century, but it is still impossible in most cases to say who was conducting it.[178] One thing which does seem clear is that the more conservative north, despite its rough parity in population with the south, was under-represented. This tendency was established from the start; Montrose was the northernmost locality sending representatives to the first General Assembly in December 1560, and it

---

[175] *Ibid*, 2:29, 203. In the latter case, that of the flesher John Hutcheon, accused in 1599 of adultery, absence from the kirk for seven years, and assault on his wife, an assize refused to rule on the first two charges on the grounds that they were "meir spirituall and ecclesiastic" than civil, and should have been tried by the kirk session. The third charge was dropped.

[176] Lynch, "Calvinism in Scotland," 229.

[177] Wormald, *Court, Kirk and Community*, 40.

[178] Shaw, *General Assemblies*, 1-12.

probably only had people there because its provost (and one of its two representatives), John Erskine of Dun, was so active in national politics, both civil and ecclesiastical.[179] The northern burghs of Aberdeen and Elgin, for instance, were not represented at the General Assemblies of December 1560, June 1562, or December 1563 (the only early General Assemblies for which attendance lists have survived), and even as late as August 1590, only six out of the 163 representatives came from north of Angus and the Mearns.[180] This is mostly explained by geography; the General Assembly usually met in the south, particularly at Edinburgh, and it was difficult for ministers and lay elders from more distant parts to attend.[181] This attendance problem both contributed to, and was exacerbated by, the lukewarm attitude toward reform demonstrated in Aberdeen and other northern communities. Lack of northern representation at the General Assembly allowed a clique of more radical southern ministers to exercise inordinate influence over the Kirk, a tendency James VI sought to overcome in the 1590s and after 1600 when he pressured the General Assembly to meet further north. The point of all this for present purposes is that, through the late sixteenth century, the General Assembly was largely a regional, not a national body, and its disciplinary agenda was likely to make headway only in those regions which sent representatives to its meetings.

Ambitious goals had been set in the *First Book of Discipline* and elsewhere, but the process of erecting the new order was only just beginning in 1560. The General Assembly was the central authority largely responsible for the erection of that system. Much of its time was spent drawing up petitions and appointing delegations to lobby the crown or nobility on behalf of the Kirk, with an eye either to enforcement of laws, or recovery of kirk lands in the control of laymen. But it also had to concern itself with creating policy guidelines for the Kirk itself, and these often concerned its disciplinary functions in one way or another.

Perhaps the first policy established by the General Assembly at its inaugural meeting in 1560 regarding the new disciplinary regime was the stipulation that the names of all prospective elders, deacons and ministers be read aloud in parochial kirks a week before their formal admissions, so

---

[179] *BUK* 1:3-4. For a recent study of Erskine of Dun, see Frank Bardgett, "John Erskine of Dun: A Theological Reassessment," *Scottish Journal of Theology* 43, (1990), 59-85.

[180] *BUK*, 1:13; Donaldson, *Scottish Church History*, 116-7, 196. Only 17 percent of the representatives at the August 1590 assembly came from north of the Tay, although roughly half of Scotland's population dwelt in that region. See James Kirk, *The Development of the Melvillian Movement in Late Sixteenth Century Scotland*, (Edinburgh University Ph.D. Thesis, 1972), 1:393.

[181] For a more detailed discussion of this point, see Shaw, *General Assemblies*, 116-7.

that objections could be raised.[182] It is difficult to determine how faithfully this injunction was followed; elections to sessions in many burghs seem to have been controlled by burgh councils, and in rural parishes they became so infrequent that congregations likely did not have the participatory role imagined by the General Assembly. Where this nomination policy was followed, it was largely a formality.[183] By 1578, the crown and the General Assembly agreed that the office of lay elder ought to become perpetual, and this proposal was written into the *Second Book of Discipline*, adopted by the assembly in 1581.[184]

Another problem regarding the eldership was apathy. Elders were supposed to be chosen for their godliness and zeal, but many were in fact chosen because of their power and prominence in the community. The General Assembly of June/July 1562 had to address "the disobedience and negligence of elders in assisting ministers to correct offenses...." It recommended that such people be reported to superintendents and that processes of excommunication be commenced against them.[185] The Canongate Kirk Session found itself faced with this problem when the bailie James Wilkie refused to accept the office of elder to which he had been elected in September 1564. The threat of public admonition from the pulpit must have worked in his case, because he did at least attend later meetings.[186] But if the elders in question were prominent enough, or general disobedience widespread enough, such steps were likely to be futile. Procedural questions regarding public admonition and other disciplinary procedures also had to be resolved by the General Assembly. The "flatterers of the court" reviled by John Knox opposed the naming of names in public admonitions in 1563-4, but the assembly held to the stricter standard that all serious sinners should be censured publicly.[187] Public admonitions were to be used when an offender refused a private summons to appear before a kirk session. Those who appeared and were found guilty would be privately admonished and often given some ritual of public repentance to perform; excommunication was usually reserved for those who refused to answer charges or to perform the required repentance. It was less clear whether sinners who allowed themselves to be excommunicated required any extra

---

[182] Calderwood, 2:44-5.

[183] For a gross exaggeration of the democratic nature of elections to kirk sessions, and disciplinary proceedings in general, see Ivo MacNaughton Clark, *A History of Church Discipline in Scotland*, (Aberdeen: Lindsay, 1929), 82-3.

[184] Calderwood, 3:413; James Kirk, ed., *The Second Book of Discipline*, (Edinburgh: St. Andrew Press, 1980), 192.

[185] Calderwood, 2:185-6; *BUK*, 1:16.

[186] *BKC*, 6, 9.

[187] Knox, 2:419.

reparation when later seeking readmission to the congregation. A group of adulterers and incestuous persons appeared barefoot, bareheaded and in linen before the General Assembly meeting in Edinburgh in March 1570, prompting the body to determine that such pilgrimages were unnecessary, and that the offenders could be reconciled in their own parish kirks. Penitent excommunicants were to wait outside the kirk door in sackcloth while the congregation filed in, and then move to a "stool of repentance" to listen to the sermon. Those who had not been excommunicated could simply pass the service bareheaded, sitting on the stool to recall their sin.[188]

Many of the conflicts in the early Scottish Reformed Kirk centered on the issue of structure and authority within the Kirk, particularly the roles to be played by superintendents and bishops. This ground has been covered extensively by historians,[189] and there is no need to tread well-worn paths here, save to discuss the question as it relates to the creation and operation of the disciplinary system. The Privy Council had appointed five regional superindendents at the Kirk's request in 1560, although only certain geographical areas were covered, and no new superintendents were ever appointed after that.[190] In addition, two pre-Reformation bishops supported, at least nominally, the Reformation, and continued to serve in the new Kirk.[191] Appointments to bishoprics continued afterward, but relations

---

[188] Calderwood, 2:539.

[189] The pro-episcopal line, which holds that the early Scottish reformers favored giving bishops a leading role, has a pedigree stretching from John Spottiswoode to Gordon Donaldson. The opposing view, which sees the initial acceptance of bishops as a tactical concession by the Kirk to the government, not intended to be permanent, and superintendents as a temporary measure occasioned by the need to plant Reformed kirks with ministers throughout the country, has been taken by "presbyterian" historians from Calderwood to James Kirk. Also tied in with this discussion is the question of how soon the "two kingdoms" theory, which opposed government intervention in Kirk affairs, became widespread among ministers. Kirk sees it as present in Knox himself, and common among early reformers, while Donaldson traces it to the return of Andrew Melville, a disciple of Pierre Ramus and Theodore Beza, to Scotland from Geneva in 1574. James Cameron has studied the office of the superintendency. See bibliography for selections by all of these authors, or, for a general synthesis, see David George Mullan, *Episcopacy in Scotland: The History of an Idea, 1560-1638*, (Edinburgh: John Donald, 1986), passim.

[190] The five were: John Carswell (Argyll and the Isles), John Erskine of Dun (Angus and the Mearns), John Spottiswoode (Lothian), John Willock (Glasgow and the west) and John Winram (Fife). See Knox, 2:87.

[191] These were Alexander Gordon of Galloway (brother of the 4th earl of Huntly and also titular archbishop of Athens) and Adam Bothwell of Orkney. John Campbell, bishop-elect of the Isles, supported the Reformation, but after having done so was unable to take control of his diocese. Robert Stewart (brother of Matthew, 4th earl of Lennox), was lay administrator of the bishopric of Caithness before the Reformation, and likewise backed the new Kirk. James Hamilton of Argyll, (half-brother of the duke of Châtelherault) who had also never been consecrated, voted with the reformers at the 1560 Parliament, but played no significant role

between these bishops (usually appointed by the crown for political reasons)
and the General Assembly proved troubled.

The superindendents were built into the disciplinary system by December
1564, when the General Assembly ruled that certain kinds of trilapse sinners
had to be referred by their kirk sessions to the regional superindendent
before they would be allowed to do public repentance and be readmitted to
Communion.[192] Later, in March 1571, the assembly reminded superintendents that they were to "tak up particular delations [accusations] in cheefe
and metropolitane kirks" within their bailiwicks on a weekly basis. The
superintendents were also urged to prod ministers who were reluctant to
excommunicate notorious sinners.[193] The paucity of kirk session records
from the period in which the superintendents were active makes it difficult
to assess their activities as disciplinary judges, but John Winram,
superintendent of Fife, did sit quite often with the St. Andrews Kirk Session
during the 1560s and early 1570s, while John Spottiswoode (Lothian) almost
never appeared with the Canongate session during the period 1564-7, for
which the register survives, though he may have sat with the Edinburgh
Session, for which there are no records before 1574.[194] The latter take note
of offenders who were referred to Spottiswoode and the Synod of Lothian
in September 1574, but by then it appears he no longer attended the
Edinburgh Session, if he ever had.[195]

The bishops were more problematic. By an agreement reached at Leith
in 1572 with the regency of the earl of Mar, the Kirk accepted the
appointment of bishops during the king's minority (James was then six).[196]
In theory, these were to be preaching bishops, somehow answerable to the
General Assembly. Insofar as they were to help oversee the Kirk's
disciplinary apparatus, they seem to have been generally remiss, at least
during the early years of the system. In August 1573 the assembly ordered
that bishops, along with superintendents and commissioners appointed by
the Kirk, broadcast the names of excommunicants. They were also to
conduct regular visitations, handling more serious disciplinary cases such

---

thereafter. See Donaldson, *Scottish Reformation*, 58-60; *ibidem, All the Queen's Men*, 37.

[192] Calderwood, 2:287.

[193] *Ibid*, 3:36-7.

[194] E.g. *StAKS* 1:81-6, 104-7, 133-9, 143-6, 151-6, 168-9, 172-4, 180-94, 207-12, 338,
361 (Winram, who sometimes styled himself "episcopus fifanorum" last convened the St.
Andrews session as his own disciplinary court in February 1572, though he lived until 1582).
Spottiswoode is recorded as present with the Canongate Session only once - in December 1565
when it considered the case of Marjorie Brisson, charged with murder. See *BKC*, 30.

[195] SRO ms CH2/450/1, 19r, 22r.

[196] *BUK* 1:204-5; Calderwood, 3:168-70; Donaldson, *Scottish Reformation*, 163-5.

as witchcraft during these circuits.[197] The following March, James Patoun, bishop of Dunkeld, was censured for his refusal to excommunicate the earl and countess of Atholl, Catholics and supporters of the queen's party in the recent civil war.[198] Despite repeated prodding, he still had not done so as of March 1575.[199] James Boyd, archbishop of Glasgow, was attacked for general laxity, including refusal to preach or take action against adulterers referred to him, in April 1576, and George Douglas, bishop of Moray, was himself accused of fornication in March 1574.[200]

There is at least one example of a bishop who assisted a kirk session regularly. John Douglas, co-author of the *First Book of Discipline*, Rector of the university and longtime elder of the St. Andrews Kirk Session, was appointed archbishop of St. Andrews in 1571, continued to serve as an elder, and lent the authority of his position to summonses issued by the session.[201] But he was already a reformer and activist before his episcopal appointment. He died in 1572, succeeded by Patrick Adamson, the Judas Iscariot of Presbyterian historiography, who referred one alleged witch to the session, but otherwise took little interest in its disciplinary activities.[202]

So the Kirk's disciplinary structure was weak at the intermediate levels, between the individual sessions and the General Assembly. The latter could pass countless resolutions and orders, but these might never become known beyond the relatively few ministers and elders in attendance. And even those present might ignore policies with impunity; there was usually no effective regional authority to make them toe the line. The superintendents retired or died without replacements, and the bishops proved uncooperative. These problems led in large measure to the eventual drafting of the *Second Book of Discipline*, and the creation in 1581 of 13 model presbyteries, innovations which will be discussed later.

During the first decade or so of its existence, the General Assembly devoted a great deal of attention to questions involving sexuality and marriage: how certain kinds of offenses should be treated, what punishments should be employed and who should be allowed to marry. Over time, however, this concern with cataloguing and categorizing all sorts of sexual pairings declined a bit. Marriage without public reading of banns was still

---

[197] Calderwood, 3:299. Witches were to be ordered to perform public repentance in sackcloth or else be excommunicated, although Parliament in 1563 had made witchcraft a capital crime.

[198] *Ibid*, 3:303.

[199] *Ibid*, 3:330-1, 341.

[200] *Ibid*, 3:302, 304, 358.

[201] *StAKS*, 1:350, 366.

[202] *Ibid*, 2:508-9. Case of Alison Pearson, 28 August 1583.

an issue in August 1575,[203] but an increasing proportion of the disciplinary questions taken up by the assembly concerned matters outside sex and marriage. By the late 1570s, concern was shifting toward the observation of public fasts (unknown a decade earlier) and the Sabbath.[204] This pattern, of near-exclusive concern with sex followed by diversification into other (and more controversial) areas of misbehavior, was to prove common among individual kirk sessions also, as will be seen below. Ministers and elders who could agree on little else at first could all accept the need for a campaign against sexual irregularity. Illegitimacy, particularly among the lower orders, contributed to pauperism and vagrancy; such logic could appeal to committed reformers and closet (or overt) Catholics alike. Other elements of the reform program might have to wait a decade or two.

Another role played by the General Assembly in the newly-erected disciplinary system was that of court of final appeal. It was, in this sense, the ultimate kirk session. Sometimes the assembly would discipline churchmen, such as Paul Methven or the bishop of Moray, for behavioral lapses (as opposed to heresy or dereliction of duty).[205] The lay cases it handled usually involved eminent people unmoved by the pressure of their own kirk sessions or regional synods, or complex cases referred from the lower courts for adjudication. Among the former was the case of the countess of Argyll, half sister to the queen, censured in December 1567 for separating herself from her husband (a leading protestant nobleman) and for having assisted at the Catholic baptism of prince Charles James, (by then crowned as James VI by the queen's opponents) the previous December.[206] One Captain Anstruther, who admitted participating in the Mass while in France "albeit in his conscience he haittit the same as idolatrie" might have been referred to the General Assembly of July 1580 out of uncertainty as to appropriate punishment. His case was remitted back to the Synod of Fife.[207]

---

[203] Calderwood, 3:356-7.

[204] For example, *ibid*, 3:384, 399-400, 405; *BUK* 2:411. The General Assembly first allowed for the possibility of public fasts in March 1571. See *BUK* 1:193-4. The growing tendency by the Kirk in the period 1575-1600 to order public fasting seems a good example of the "new papist" tendencies in Calvinism discussed by Steven Ozment. See Steven Ozment, *The Reformation in the Cities: The Appeal of Protestantism to Sixteenth-Century Germany and Switzerland*, (New Haven: Yale University Press, 1975), 151-60.

[205] *BUK* 1:29, 32; Calderwood, 2:207-10, 3:302-4. I make the distinction because actions taken against clergy for heresy or malfeasance in their *official* duties do not fall within the purview of this study.

[206] Calderwood, 2:397. The countess and earl of Argyll were eventually divorced in June 1573. See George Hewitt, *Scotland Under Morton: 1572-80*, (Edinburgh: John Donald, 1982), 25.

[207] *BUK* 2:458-9.

The lack of any clean break with the structure of the old church in the Scottish Reformation required a redrawing of jurisdictional boundaries. The reformers certainly felt that the new kirk, with its court structure, should replace the old, but the powers and duties of the pre-Reformation bishops were not abolished in any constitutional sense. The old episcopal consistories had heard cases concerning adherence to oaths (including marriage), as well as cases of slander, theft, or absence from Easter Communion.[208] While such breadth covered (literally) a wide variety of sins, in fact well over half of the cases considered involved the execution of testaments or fulfillment of contracts involving goods or money. Non-payment of teinds (tithes) was a major concern as well, while marriage questions, slander and the rest lagged well behind.[209] It certainly appears that money questions mattered more than behavioral ones. What happened after 1560 was that the latter became the more or less exclusive preserve of the new church courts, and the former gravitated elsewhere. Neither Oecoplampadius, Bucer, Calvin or the authors of the *First Book of Discipline* had envisioned a consistory which would adjudicate wills or enforce business contracts; these seemed clearly a civil concern.

Less clear in its categorization was divorce. On the one hand it broke a spiritual bond which had, in the Catholic Church, enjoyed the status of a sacrament. But among those with property, it was also a contractual arrangement, bringing with it financial obligations. Technically, the old bishops had never granted divorces, only annulments. The new Kirk was willing to accept divorces, but was not certain they should be granted by its own courts. During 1560-3, the General Assembly heard appeals on actions taken by the conforming bishops concerning adherence and annulment, but in June 1562 it requested that the Privy Council establish a divorce policy, either by giving authority to kirk sessions, or establishing a new type of court to handle divorces.[210] The result was the establishment early in 1564 of a commissary court in Edinburgh with (eventually) a subsidiary system of regional commissaries, set up on the old diocesan structure. These granted divorces and heard cases involving teinds, testaments and defamation, and their judges were nominated by the College of Justice in

---

[208] Gordon Donaldson, "The Church Courts," in *An Introduction to Scottish Legal History*, (Edinburgh: Stair Society, 1958), 363-373, at 363; Denis McKay, "Parish Life in Scotland, 1500-1560," in David McRoberts, ed., *Essays on the Scottish Reformation, 1513-1625*, (Glasgow: J.S. Burns, 1962), 85-115, at 98, 113.

[209] Donaldson, "Church Courts," 366.

[210] *BUK* 1:19, 31, 35; Calderwood, 2:191-3; David Smith, "The Spiritual Jurisdiction, 1560-64," *RSCHS* 25 (1993), 1-18; Donaldson, "Church Courts," 367.

Edinburgh, essentially the juridical wing of the Privy Council.[211] Thus they took over what had in practice been the main business of the old episcopal courts, while discipline, hitherto a relatively small concern, became the *raison d'être* of the courts of the Reformed Kirk.

There remained the eternal problem of the boundary between civil and ecclesiastical jurisdiction. The Kirk saw its sanctions as independent of any civil penalties, corporal or pecunial, which the state might impose. This was underlined by the General Assembly in March 1573, when it held:

> It is nather agreeable to the Word of God, nor to the practise of the primitive
> Kirk, that the administratioun of the word and sacraments, and ministration
> of criminall and civill justice, be so confounded, that one person beare both
> the charges.[212]

Such distinctions could not flourish, however, in a society where burgh bailies and barons or their officials would sit as elders on ecclesiastical courts. The assembly had wrung its hands in 1572 when Robert Pont, minister of St. Cuthberts, (on the outskirts of Edinburgh), was made a Lord of Session.[213] But Pont, whose credentials as a reformer were impeccable, accepted the position, and remained active in the Kirk's affairs for the rest of the century and into the next.[214]

In fact, the Kirk needed the support of the civil authorities, both to protect and augment its revenues, and to lend sting to its sanctions. Certainly, excommunication was to remain a spiritual punishment, outwith the control of civil judges. But in the vast majority of disciplinary cases which did not lead to excommunication, the lines were not so clear. Local miscreants were likely to encounter many of the same faces in the kirk session they regularly met in the burgh or baronial court. With that qualification in mind, it is time to move from examining the institution of discipline, from above, and shed some light on its enforcement, from below.

---

[211] Smith, "Spiritual Jurisdiction," 17; Donaldson, "Church Courts," 368-70. In 1609, the right to appoint commissary judges was given back to the bishops, and appeals from local commissaries were channelled directly to the Lords of Session (College of Justice), bypassing the Edinburgh Commissary.

[212] Calderwood, 3:281.

[213] *Ibid*, 3:168-9, 277.

[214] Although he was disqualified as a Lord of Session due to his status as a clergyman by an act of Parliament in 1584. He moderated several General Assemblies and was appointed Bishop of Caithness by the king in 1587, but declined the position. See Mullan, *Episcopacy in Scotland*, 65.

CHAPTER THREE

THE PRACTICE OF REFORMED SOCIAL DISCIPLINE
IN SCOTLAND, 1559-1581

The quhilk daye [10 May 1564], Johane Bycartoun, saidlar, citiner of Sanctandrois, delated for contempt of the establesched ordor of the Reformed Kyrk wythin the citie of Sanctandrois, in procuryng of his barne [child]...to be presented to baptisme be Mr. Dauid Meldrum, his self being present for the tym wythin the cite wald nocht present his awyn child to baptisme.... Johane, called befoyr the ministerie [session]...all reverence set asyd, stubburnly, wyth pertinacite, affirmit and mantenit his contempt of the said ordor, saying...I never presented ane of my awyn barnis to baptism nor never wyll! I hav nothing to do wyth yow nor yowr ordor, it is nocht grundit upon the Scriptur, it is bot idolatre inventit be the braen of man!
                                              - St Andrews Kirk Session Register[1]

[On 22 April 1574] Comperd Jonet Knowis and, desyred to give co[n]fession of hir fayt[h] and renownce papistrie, sayd, she wald co[n]fesse all good things and refuse all ewill things, but wold not deny the Mes [Mass] in especiall.
                                              - Aberdeen Kirk Session Register[2]

Sources which echo the voices of more or less anonymous people of four centuries ago speaking their minds on the topics of religion and social ethics are rare and valuable indeed. The theologians, writers, princes and political figures of sixteenth century Europe been examined, praised, condemned, spiritually and intellectually dissected and even psychoanalyzed by generations of historians. Attention has finally shifted in the last twenty-five years or so to those forming the rest of the population, but they have still generally received only bit parts as authors (if not writers) of wills, tenants or freeholders, indigents or bread rioters.[3] While Scotland has its social

---

[1] *StAKS*, 1:194-5.

[2] SRO ms CH2/448/1, 34. (Manuscript paginated rather than foliated). Knowis did submit to the Reformed Kirk on 17 June 1574, however. See *ibid*, 40.

[3] For some examples which buck this trend, see Natalie Davis, *The Return of Martin Guerre*, (Cambridge, Mass: Harvard University Press, 1983); Paul Seaver, *Wallington's World: The Life of a Puritan Artisan in Seventeenth-Century London*, (Stanford: Stanford University Press, 1985); Christopher Hill, *The World Turned Upside Down*, (London: Maurice Temple Smith, 1972); Alan MacFarlane, *The Family Life of Ralph Josselin*, (Cambridge: Cambridge University Press, 1970); Carlo Ginzburg, *The Cheese and the Worms*, (Baltimore: Johns Hopkins University Press, 1980); Michael Kunze, *Highroad to the Stake*, (Chicago:

historians, sixteenth-century Scotland, so beloved by devotees of religion and politics, has not been particularly well served in this respect.[4]

The records of kirk sessions and (after 1581) presbyteries give us an opportunity to correct this oversight. A group of historians assembling sources for the history of Scottish criminality wrote that kirk session registers are "without doubt the most interesting, most amusing, and most human of all the sources for the study of crime in early modern Scotland."[5] Their interest and usefulness extends beyond the history of crime as well. First of all, crime and sin were not always the same thing in early modern Europe, though the categories often overlapped.[6] In addition to crime and sin, kirk session records can tell us a great deal about social (including gender) relations, marriage, charity and (as the examples above demonstrate), religious belief and practice. Granted, much of the language used in the registers is formulaic—a kind of sixteenth-century ecclesiastical bureaucratese. But this language barrier does not wholly obscure the attitudes and behavior described. Further, sometimes the outbursts of those called before the courts appear to have so moved the clerks that they broke custom and rendered them more or less exactly as spoken, thus providing us with a true nugget in what is already a rich vein. One aim of this chapter is to tune our ears to these voices, and come to understand what they were talking about, as we examine the actual practice of Reformed social discipline in the first twenty years of the Scottish Reformation, before the creation of the presbytery courts in 1581.

Relatively few kirk session records from prior to 1581 have survived.[7]

University of Chicago Press, 1987); David Sabean, *Power in the Blood*, (Cambridge: Cambridge University Press, 1984).

[4] Although Margaret H.B. Sanderson has made major contributions, particularly in her *Scottish Rural Society in the Sixteenth Century*, (Edinburgh: John Donald, 1982).

[5] Patrick Rayner, Bruce Lenman and Geoffrey Parker, eds., *Handlist of Records for the Study of Crime in Early Modern Scotland (to 1747)*, (London: List and Index Society, 1977), 147.

[6] Heinz Schilling, "'History of Crime' or 'History of Sin'? Some Reflections on the Social History of Early Modern Church Discipline," in E.I. Kouri and Tom Scott, eds., *Politics and Society in Reformation Europe: Essays for Sir Geoffrey Elton on His Sixty-fifth Birthday*, (London: MacMillan, 1987), 289-310, at 290-3, 302-4. Schilling categorizes Scotland along with parts of Germany where submission to ecclesiastical discipline was not voluntary, but the case is really not so clear-cut. Submission to discipline was often a voluntary matter, at least in some Scottish communities in the first few decades of the Reformation.

[7] Those that have, and the sources in which they may be found are St. Andrews, 1559-1600: David Hay Fleming, ed., *Register of the Minister, Elders and Deacons of the Christian Congregation of St Andrews, 1559-1600*, (2 vol.) (Edinburgh: Scottish History Society, 1889-90); The Canongate, 1564-7: Alma B. Calderwood, ed., *The Buik of the Kirk of the Canagait, 1564-1567*, (Edinburgh: Scottish Record Society, 1961); Monifieth, 1562-1620, with gaps: NRH ms OPR 310/1; Aberdeen St. Nicholas, 1562-3, 1568, 1573-8: SRO ms CH2/448/1;

Perhaps in part due to this paucity, few historians have made significant use of them (or indeed of any of the kirk session or presbytery records from before around 1610), beyond mining them for the occasional anecdote. The only exceptions to this are a handful of local or regional studies which have cited kirk session material to illustrate particular points,[8] and one attempt at a statistically-based study of the most complete published sixteenth-century register we have.[9] As yet, nobody has sought to examine the implementation of kirk-based social discipline across the nation as a whole during this period. Any attempt to do so must take into account the compositions of the sessions themselves, their places in local power structures, the disciplinary interests of the ministers and elders and the reactions of parishioners, men and women, to the new order. Such an approach may, in tracing the evolution of the system, uncover regional differences, as well as divergences between urban and rural communities. Further, men and women may prove to have had, in the Kirk's eyes, differing sin habits, and certain sins may have been particularly difficult to root out or, at least, to punish. Over time, one or several sessions may have shown increased interest in particular sins, perhaps in reaction to social or political forces. All of these variations ought to be explained where possible, and the answers should reveal a great deal about Reformed ideology as a social force.

This chapter will offer a survey of the operations of most of the pre-1582 kirk sessions for which records have survived. Particular issues, such as sexuality, conflict resolution, witchcraft, and the degree to which social discipline may have been a levelling or even revolutionary force will be taken up later, on a nationwide basis. For now, the aim is to examine the

---

Edinburgh General Session, 1574-5: SRO ms CH2/450/1 (mostly transcribed in RH2/1/35); Perth St. John's, 1577-86: SRO ms CH2/521/1; Anstruther Wester, 1577-1601: NRH ms OPR 403/1.

[8] Michael Lynch, *Edinburgh and the Reformation*, (Edinburgh: John Donald, 1981); Frank Bardgett, *Scotland Reformed: The Reformation In Angus and the Mearns*, (Edinburgh: John Donald, 1989); *ibidem*, "The Monifieth Kirk Register," *RSCHS* 23 (1987-89), 175-95; Allan White, *Religion, Politics and Society in Aberdeen: 1543-1593*, (Edinburgh University Ph.D. Thesis, 1985). Walter Roland Foster makes limited use of some early 17th century session and presbytery material in his *The Church Before the Covenants: The Church of Scotland 1596-1638*, (Edinburgh: Scottish Academic Press, 1975).

[9] Geoffrey Parker, "'The Kirk By Law Established' and the Origins of the 'Taming of Scotland': St Andrews 1559-1600," in Leah Leneman, ed., *Perspectives in Scottish Social History: Essays in Honour of Rosalind Mitchison*, (Aberdeen: Aberdeen University Press, 1988), 1-32. This was republished, with a few changes, in Raymond Mentzer, ed., *Sin and the Calvinists: Morals Control and the Consistory in the Reformed Tradition*, (Kirksville, Mo.: Sixteenth Century Publishers, 1994), 159-97, but references here are to the original essay. Parker's approach is sound, but his study is marred by errors of fact and dubious interpretations, some of which I will discuss later.

Scotland with
Communities Featured
in this Study

North

Sea

Moray Firth

Highland Line   •Rothiemay

                              •Aberdeen

                      •Monifieth
                              Firth of Tay
                  •St. Andrews
                              •Anstruther Wester
                              Firth of Forth
      Stirling•
            Edinburgh•
                    Canongate

      •Dundonald

Irish

Sea

• Indicates Community Included
   in this Study   England

━━━━
50 Miles

early kirk session in its local context, starting with the session for which the earliest records survive, that of St. Andrews.

St. Andrews

The magistrates of St. Andrews, led by the provost Patrick Lermonth of Dairsie, officially adopted the Reformation in June 1559, during a visit by the Lords of the Congregation which included public preaching by John Knox himself.[10] From that point on, St. Andrews was firmly in the protestant camp, sending its minister Christopher Goodman and two laymen to represent it at the first General Assembly in December 1560.[11] The town was regionally important based on its size and location alone; situated on a bay in the North Sea, it was a gateway into the fertile countryside of Fife, blessed with a relatively mild climate. In addition to the merchants, tailors, fleshers, maltmen, weavers and cutlers serving the local populace, a sizeable number of residents were fishermen or mariners, albeit the latter were often absent on long voyages. The presence of the university gave the town a sizeable cohort of students and teachers as well. A population estimate for the later sixteenth century seems hazardous, but a figure of 3-4,000 for St. Andrews and its immediate environs may be reasonable.[12] Most importantly, the presence of a university, coupled with the town's status as an archiepiscopal see, greatly enhanced its importance.[13]

The register for the St. Andrews Kirk Session is not only the earliest extant session record in Scotland, it is also the most complete for the sixteenth century,[14] including the details of 2156 actions against individuals for various lapses ranging from failure to attend church on Sunday to murder and witchcraft, between 1559 and 1600.[15] Because disciplinary

---

[10] Knox, 1:349-50, 6:680; Jane E.A. Dawson, "'The Face of Ane Perfyt Reformed Kyrk': St Andrews and the Early Scottish Reformation," in James Kirk, ed., *Humanism and Reform: The Church in Europe, England and Scotland, 1400-1643*, (Oxford: Blackwell, 1991), 413-36, protestant takeover described at 415-6.

[11] *BUK*, 1:3-4.

[12] Parker, "Kirk By Law Established," 1.

[13] Jane Dawson has argued that St. Andrews remained Scotland's ecclesiastical capital after the Reformation "because it achieved the most successful Reformation in the country." See Dawson, 414-5. Such a judgement may be premature, given how little is known about the Reformation in most Scots burghs.

[14] Although there is a one-year gap in the record between February 1566/7 and February 1567/8. See *StAKS*, 1:292-3.

[15] All calculations in this study, unless noted otherwise, are my own. A "case" is defined as any instance in which an individual, almost always named, is charged with a particular sin of commission or omission. Thus for example if five people are charged with participating in one act, it is treated here as five cases. Likewise, if one person is simultaneously charged with

practice became more intensive (in numbers of prosecutions) late in the century, most of those cases date from 1582 and after, but 751 of them were initiated before then.[16]

The session held its first recorded meeting on July 25, 1559, with no further known activities until October, when the election of a new set of elders and deacons took place.[17] Before listing the names of those elected, the clerk recorded the protocol for electing them, approved by the provost, bailies, burgh council and university officials. The procedure established was specifically tailored to the needs of the town and its oligarchy.[18] Elections were to take place annually on the second Friday after council elections, usually held in October. The provost and university rector had the right to nominate all candidates from the burgh and colleges, respectively, giving the names to the minister who would read them from the pulpit. Thereafter, the council, free burgesses and university regents would meet to elect elders and deacons from among those nominated.[19] Thus the eldership would, in effect, be a civic commission appointed by the burgh council and university leadership, reflecting both the solidarity and tensions within those groups. Only in times of local political upheaval (relatively rare between 1559 and 1582) was the session likely to confront the council or display clear signs of partisanship.[20]

The rural lairds from around St. Andrews came eventually to comprise a third element in the eldership, although they were largely absent before

---

two distinct offenses, it counts as two. A fornicating couple would be treated as two cases, unless the session makes no apparent effort to discipline one partner. Disciplinary actions against clergy for lapses in their official duties, such as accepting money for performing baptisms or marriages, are not counted, because I consider such processes to be administrative rather than pastoral.

[16] A case is dated from its first mention in the register. Thus a person first summoned in December 1566 who did not actually appear or accept a sentence of repentance until the following March would be treated as a 1566 case.

[17] *StAKS*, 1:1-3.

[18] It ought to be noted that the St. Andrews Burgh Council had some influence over local church affairs even before the Reformation. By 1538, for example, the council held patronage rights over at least 12 altars in the burgh church of Holy Trinity. See W.E.K. Rankin, *The Parish Church of the Holy Trinity, St Andrews*, (Edinburgh: Oliver and Boyd, 1955), 7.

[19] *StAKS*, 1:1-2. The last published full-length study of Scottish church discipline made the rather absurd claim that ministers and elders were "popularly elected." This statement was apparently based on the St. Andrews register, as it is the only kirk session material from prior to 1631 cited by the author. See Ivo MacNaughton Clark, *A History of Church Discipline in Scotland*, (Aberdeen: Lindsay, 1929), 82.

[20] Dawson concluded that burgh authorities were generally enthusiastic backers of the decrees of the kirk session. See Dawson, 429-30.

1570.[21] In all, 231 individuals served as elders or deacons at least once during the period 1559-1600, 88 of them before 1582.[22] Of the 231, 18 were clearly university representatives, and 48 were identified by their rural domicile, leaving 165, the vast majority of whom were probably burgh representatives. While the figure of 231 seems impressively high, one should bear in mind the time span (40 years), and the greater exclusivity of the eldership as opposed to the diaconate. While the average session included fewer deacons than elders (typically there would be 10-14 elders and 8-12 deacons), many more men passed through the ranks of the diaconate than the eldership. The deacons, faced with the cumbersome duties of alms collection and distribution, were usually of lower status than the elders, and the *First Book of Discipline* had recommended that while elders could be re-elected, deacons should not have to serve again for three years.[23] The eldership at St. Andrews was highly oligarchic, and death, rather than any ideal of broader participation, was the usual agent of turnover.

The oligarchic nature of the eldership is most clearly evident in the surnames of those chosen. The session elected in 1559 included, among its 12 elders, two Lermonths (relatives of the provost), two Martins and two Geddys, with a third Geddy serving as deacon. Never again were so many families doubly represented in the eldership, but members of certain families were almost constantly present. In all, five Lermonths served as elders between 1559 and 1600 (two of them provosts and two of them bailies). These were joined by five Woods, four Welwoods, four Wemysses, four Ramsays, four Martins, three Geddys and three Russells.

Of course, not all those elected to the eldership took active roles. Without sederunts (attendance lists), it is difficult to gauge the diligence of individual elders, although general complaints of poor attendance and

---

[21] While a number of burgesses (and the provost) were also lairds in the region, the first elder identified primarily by his rural domicile was James Forret of Polduff, who first appeared on the session list of 1569, although he was listed as "in Polduff" rather than "of Polduff" ("of" being an indication of lairdly or at least feuar status) until 1572. He was not joined by any other rural elders until the latter date, either. See *StAKS*, 1:323, 342, 368.

[22] Since so many relatives (fathers and sons or uncles and nephews) shared the same first and last names, distinguishing between individuals was sometimes (in perhaps four or five cases) difficult. For consistency's sake, I adopted the requirement of a ten-year absence of a name from session lists before assuming that, rather than an old elder or deacon returning, a new holder of the same name had been elected. Thus the figure of 231 serving on the session should be regarded as a conservative estimate, particularly since several session lists from the late 1560s are missing.

[23] James Cameron, ed., *The First Book of Discipline*, (Edinburgh: Saint Andrew Press, 1972), 175.

tardiness are common in the session register.[24] But certain elders (and deacons) became fixtures, serving lengthy terms, and these are likely to have been the most active and influential within the session. Sometime bailie and burgh councilor Thomas Balfour was an elder on every recorded session until 1582, when he died.[25] Another occasional bailie, William Cook, was first elected elder in 1560 and served continuously until 1590. Martin Geddy, elder on the first session, did not sit on his final session until 1591, although he had taken a few scattered years off. Burgh clerk John Motto, likewise a 1559 elder, served on almost every session until 1581. James Wilkie, provost of St. Leonard's College and, after 1577, rector of the university, joined the eldership in 1561 and sat on his last session in 1581. Only a couple deacons displayed such stamina—George Black, who also served the parish as reader and was a deacon from 1559 to 1583, and the merchant William Yule, deacon from 1561 to 1591 (with few breaks), and briefly an elder thereafter.

What was the occupational status of these elders? The university representatives, such as Wilkie, John Rutherford, John Douglas, and, later, Andrew Melville, were college principals, regents or university rectors. Burgh representatives would certainly all have been burgesses. The bailies and burgh clerk generally sat on the session. While the larger elderships elected in the 1590s included advocates, skippers, maltmen and even a smith,[26] the smaller groups elected earlier were more exclusive, generally consisting of substantial merchants who took turns as bailies and would have regularly sat on the burgh council as well. The rural elders were all landholders, usually lairds, but occasionally feuars or portioners. It was not unusual for an urban craftsman or rural tenant to join the diaconate, but he would have had little prospect of becoming an elder.

Thus the eldership, at least, was a closed corporation, and generally recognized as such. It could be accused of favoritism; in February 1571 parishioner Alexander Laing allegedly told minister Robert Hamilton, "William Geddye aucht to sit on the stuil [of repentance] als weil as I; and gyf ye do it nocht [i.e., force him to] ye wil be accusat of parcialite." Called before the session, which at that point included one Geddy elder, and included two in both the previous and following years, Laing denied the statement.[27] The session in 1559-61, with two Geddys as elders and one as deacon, also seemed to defend family interests. William Rantoun, having

---

[24] E.g. *StAKS* 1:72, 362, 396.

[25] His tombstone, one of a handful of sixteeth-century St. Andrews tombstones which has survived, gives 1582 as the year of his death, and praises him for his service to the burgh council.

[26] *StAKS* 2:788-90, 831, 871, 893.

[27] *Ibid*, 1:346.

done public repentance for adultery in November 1559, appeared on 1 February 1560, seeking to divorce his wife Elizabeth Geddy on the grounds of her adultery. Despite the testimony of a number of witnesses that her adultery had predated his, she was allowed to purge herself under oath, and John Knox, temporarily minister in St. Andrews, was ordered to declare her innocence from the pulpit. Then in January 1561, the session granted her a divorce on the grounds of his adultery, thus allowing her to recover her tocher (dowry) of 200 marks.[28]

Bailie and elder John Martin safeguarded his own family in December 1570, when Jonet Smith, daughter of a local maltman, complained that she had been violently abducted by Steven Martin, son of an area laird. Under questioning from John Martin, she granted that she had not been raped, and remained a virgin, "and heirupon the said Johne Martine, in name and behalf of the said Stevin Martine, askit act and instrument," thus gaining an affidavit to help his relative defend himself from any future accusation arising from the matter.[29] Henry Lermonth, son of a bailie and elder, and kinsman of the provost, was allowed to purge himself of a charge of incestuous adultery in November 1574, three years after the matter was first brought up, despite the testimony of witnesses (many of them apparently reluctant to appear) against him. Although he had ignored repeated summonses, the minister was told not to warn him from the pulpit, and his father told his fellow elders that he had no knowledge of any wrongdoing on his son's part.[30]

In addition to its status as a civic body, seeking to bring about a reformation of manners and defend the interests of the local oligarchy, the kirk session of St. Andrews took on a regional role when it acted as the court of John Winram, superindendent of Fife.[31] The superintendent's court heard cases from all over Fife, particularly from parishes which did not have kirk sessions, or in instances when the local session was having

---

[28] *Ibid*, 1:18-27, 37-8, 59-60.

[29] *Ibid*, 1:343-4.

[30] *Ibid*, 1:350-60, 362, 401-2. The general issue of disciplinary treatment of the prominent vs. treatment of the general population will be discussed on a nationwide scale in a later chapter.

[31] Superindendents were to convene with the session in their town of residence. See Cameron, ed., *First Book of Discipline*, 115-28; *ibidem*, "The Office of Superidendent in the First Book of Discipline," in Bernard Vogler, ed., *L'Institution et les Pouvoirs dans les Eglises de l'Antiquité à nos Jours (Miscellanea Historiae Ecclesiasticae* 8), (Bruxelles: Nauwelaerts, 1987), 239-50; Gordon Donaldson, *The Scottish Reformation*, (Cambridge: Cambridge University Press, 1960), 123; *ibidem*, "The Church Courts," in *An Introduction to Scottish Legal History*, (Edinburgh: Stair Society, 1958), 363-73, at 367; James Kirk, "The Polities of the Best Reformed Kirks: Scottish Achievements and English Aspirations in Church Government After the Reformation," *Scottish Historical Review* 59 (1980), 22-53, at 29.

difficulty. Thus, for instance, it heard charges in July 1561 against Mr. Alexander Wardlaw, "pretendit parson of Balingry," and brother to the laird of Torrie, who had allegedly slandered Winram and tried to prevent his appointee as minister of Ballingry from preaching there.[32] A similar case originated in Crail several months later, when William Morton, laird of Cambo and member of the "Reformation Parliament" of 1560, interrupted minister John Melville while the latter was preaching, proclaiming "my brother is and salbe vicar of Crayll quhen thow sal thyg [beg] thy mayt, fals smayk; I sall pul ye owt of the pulpot be the luggis [ears], and chais ye owt of this town!"[33] In addition to cases of lairdly resentment over ministerial provision, the session acting as Winram's court considered simpler disciplinary matters from the region, such as the case of Begis Calwart in Kingsbarns, who had refused to do public repentance for slander in the kirk of Crail, and William Bowsie in Crail, who had ignored several summonses by the local session to answer charges of adultery, but did appear in St. Andrews when summoned by the superintendent.[34]

Winram was active as superintendent from 1560 to 1572. In April 1571, he presented a "chartour of reces" to the session, but the elders refused his resignation on the grounds that without him, they could only consider matters originating within the parish of St. Andrews.[35] Despite this refusal, the session heard only one more case as Winram's court after that. All told, the session heard 433 cases in the period 1559-72, and in 138 of these, the clerk reported that Winram was present, or that the session was acting in his name. Table 3.1 gives a breakdown, according to gender and two other factors, of the caseload of the session as a whole for the period 1559-72, and those times when it was acting either on Winram's behalf (roughly one third of the time), or solely as the kirk session of St. Andrews. The most significant differences between the powers of the session in its two capacities appear in the last two rows, which enumerate "no-shows" and cases involving prominent sinners. A "no-show" is an instance in which a person summoned one or more times to answer for an offense never appeared before the session. As table 3.1 indicates, nearly a third of those summoned by Winram's court failed to appear, while the St. Andrews session working on its own was much more successful in this regard.

Winram, in his pseudo-episcopal role, may have been more personally prominent than the elders of St. Andrews, but respect for his position was often insufficient to overcome the difficulties presented by poor communica-

---

[32] *StAKS*, 1:82-8.

[33] *Ibid*, 1:105-7.

[34] *Ibid*, 1:104-6, 143.

[35] *Ibid*, 1:346-7.

tion, difficult travel, and probable chastisement in getting a distant sinner to appear. This problem may have contributed to the abandonment of the superintendencies, and it resurfaced later under the presbyterian system.

TABLE 3.1—DISCIPLINARY ACTIVITIES,
ST. ANDREWS KIRK SESSION, 1559-72

	Session as superintendent court	Session acting on its own	Total cases, 1559-72
Cases	138	295	433
Male	85 (62%)	201 (68%)	286 (66%)
Female	53 (38%)	94 (32%)	147 (34%)
No-shows	45 (33%)	22 (7%)	67 (15%)
Elite	22 (16%)	27 (9%)	49 (11%)

The disciplinary courts of the Scottish Kirk simply were not effective over long distances, unless assisted by local authorities who would help to ensure compliance. The elders of St. Andrews knew their neighbors, and, tied as they were to the local oligarchy, could nearly always ensure that malefactors would at least appear to answer charges. While they, as well as Winram, sometimes summoned people from outside the burgh, the vast majority of cases handled by the St. Andrews session on its own involved local residents.

The other major difference between the caseload of Winram's court and the session acting on its own as revealed in table 3.1 is the higher percentage of cases involving prominent individuals in the superintendent's court (16 percent as opposed to nine percent for the session on its own). This is not so surprising, since cases involving prominent people were usually the most difficult for local sessions to handle, and thus more likely to require intervention from the superintendent. He may not have had much better luck, either; the high rate of refusals to appear in his caseload is doubtless in part a reflection of the higher proportion of cases involving notables he had to handle.

The most difficult cases of all sometimes resulted in excommunication, in theory the ultimate sanction at the Kirk's disposal. Once a sinner had been excommunicated, he or she was to receive no "benefits of the

Kirk"—Communion, marriage or baptism of children—and was to be shunned by neighbors, who could neither speak with, entertain, or do business with the offender until he or she made amends. The effectiveness of this sanction differed greatly from one community to another, depending on local authorities and attitudes, and also on the prominence of the individual involved; some people were simply too important to ignore. The St. Andrews sadler John Bicarton, whose attitude toward the new religious regime is described in the quotation at the beginning of this chapter, was excommunicated for his religious dissent on 9 July 1564. This came after he proved just as stubborn before the burgh council as he had been earlier in the session. The minister Christopher Goodman read the sentence from the pulpit, ordering that "nane of the faythfull fearyng God, fra this hour furth, accumpany wyth hym in commonyng, talkyn, bying, selling eating, drynkyn or other way quhatsoever, except thai be apoynted of the Kyrk for his amendment." The sentence was apparently effective, as Bicarton applied for reinstatement the following February, and the session clerk noted that he had "sustenit gret dampneg and disays in guddis and body, throw his awyn wyckednes and adheryng to the consall of the ongodlye." But this was also used as justification for mitigating his repentance; he only had to make a public confession, and was spared sitting on the stool of repentance in sackcloth.[36]

Thus in this case, excommunication was an effective weapon in getting a sinner to submit, although Bicarton's stubbornness may have earned him a lighter repentance ritual than otherwise would have been required. Local authorities such as the burgh council were willing to add their authority to the Kirk's sanctions, and Bicarton's neighbors and business associates made life difficult enough for him that he had to give in. Christine Yule, daughter of a baxter, was twice charged with adultery (in 1575 and 1578), and refused to do public repentance in either case. She was excommunicated after the second charge, but this apparently had little effect; she never even appeared to answer charges.[37] Not having a business to maintain, she may have been able to bear life outside the pale of the Kirk more easily than Bicarton.

In any case, one should beware of overestimating the effectiveness of excommunication.[38] Even in St. Andrews, with its relatively cooperative magistrates, Yule's case was much more typical than Bicarton's. Of 23

---

[36] *Ibid*, 1:194-206.

[37] *Ibid*, 1:407-8, 413, 429, 448, 456.

[38] Michael Lynch has argued for its effectiveness in Edinburgh and Robert Kingdon has made the same claim for Geneva. See Lynch, *Edinburgh and the Reformation*, (Edinburgh: John Donald, 1981), 188; Kingdon, "Calvin and the Family: The Work of the Consistory in Geneva," *Pacific Theological Review* 17 (1984), 5-18, at 8-9.

people excommunicated by the St. Andrews session (both on its own and acting with Winram) between 1559 and 1581, 17 of them never bothered to appear, thus in effect thumbing their noses at the Kirk and its disciplinary system.[39] Excommunication was a last resort and, usually, an admission of failure. The St. Andrews session seemed to recognize this, and showed an increasing reluctance to excommunicate as time went on. Of the 23 excommunications, 20 of them were for charges first lodged before 1569, 12 of them from 1564 alone.

While excommunication was the ultimate sanction, one did not necessarily have to commit the ultimate sin to warrant it. Indeed, simple fornication was the original charge in nine of the cases leading to excommunication. Sixteen of the original charges were sexual in nature, six involved religious dissent, and the other involved spousal desertion. Generally, a person's refusal to answer charges or perform repentance was more significant in getting him or her excommunicated than the gravity of the original charge. This underscores the restorative principle upon which the disciplinary system was based. Anyone willing to demonstrate remorse (albeit often in a humiliating way) would be welcomed back into the arms of the Kirk, no matter how serious the offense.

Having raised the subject of types of sin, it seems worthwhile to explore the disciplinary interests of the St. Andrews session. In compiling the database for this study, I have sought to assign every offense to one of 20 different categories.[40] Thus all sexual cases are placed in one category. Disputes within families form another category, as do Sabbath breaches, violent attacks, cases of religious dissent, and so on. Needless to say, some sins proved much more common than others. This does not necessarily mean that they were the most frequently committed sins; it would be extremely hazardous to attempt to profile early modern criminality through kirk session registers.[41] The offenses which appear the most frequently in

---

[39] Excommunications were much more likely to be issued under Winram's authority; of the 23 (only 3 of which came after 1572), 17 of them were issued by the session as the court of the superintendent of Fife.

[40] Since some offenses proved rather rare, or were entirely nonexistent in certain localities, the tables which follow never list all 20 sin classes, but only those most common for the community in question.

[41] This warning has been issued elsewhere about early modern court records in general. See Bruce Lenman and Geoffrey Parker, "The State, the Community and the Criminal Law in Early Modern Europe," in V.A.C. Gatrell, Bruce Lenman and Geoffrey Parker, eds., *Crime and the Law: The Social History of Crime in Western Europe Since 1500*, (London: Europa, 1980), 11-48, at 46-7.

TABLE 3.2—BREAKDOWN OF CASES FOR ST. ANDREWS KIRK
SESSION AS SUPERINTENDENT'S COURT OF FIFE, 1559-72

Offense category	Cases	Males	Females	No-shows
Sexuality	71 (51%)	41	30	25 (35%)
Marriage questions	18 (13%)	10	8	2 (11%)
Disputes w/in fam.	14 (10%)	6	8	4 (28%)
Relig. diss/practice	11 (8%)	11	0	8 (73%)
Sabbath breach	6 (4%)	6	0	0 (-)
Slander/bickering	4 (3%)	2	2	3 (75%)
Dealing w/outcasts	4 (3%)	3	1	1 (25%)
Totals	138	85	53	45 (33%)

TABLE 3.3—BREAKDOWN OF CASES FOR ST. ANDREWS KIRK
SESSION WORKING ON ITS OWN, 1559-72

Offense category	Cases	Males	Females	No-shows
Sexuality	169 (57%)	91	78	17 (10%)
Relig. diss/practice	45 (15%)	41	4	2 (4%)
Sabbath breach	29 (10%)	28	1	0 (-)
Communion absence	15 (5%)	15	0	0 (-)
Disputes w/in fam.	9 (3%)	4	5	1 (11%)
Marriage questions	6 (2%)	5	1	0 (-)
Slander/bickering	6 (2%)	3	3	1 (17%)
Totals	295	201	94	22 (7.5%)

TABLE 3.4—BREAKDOWN OF ALL DISCIPLINARY CASES FOR ST. ANDREWS KIRK SESSION, 1559-81

Offense category	Cases	Males	Females	No-shows
Sexuality	437 (58%)	231	205	93 (21%)
Relig. diss/practice	89 (12%)	82	7	15 (17%)
Sabbath breach	66 (9%)	62	4	1 (2%)
Disputes w/in fam.	34 (5%)	16	18	7 (21%)
Marriage questions	29 (4%)	18	11	2 (7%)
Communion absence	27 (4%)	23	4	9 (33%)
Slander/bickering	16 (2%)	7	9	6 (38%)
Totals	751	479	271	145 (19%)

the register were probably those which were easiest to detect, and which the ministers and elders were most interested in punishing. The three tables above offer a breakdown of cases by offense classification for the St. Andrews session when acting with superintendent John Winram, 1559-72 (table 3.2), the session acting on its own, 1559-72 (table 3.3), and all cases handled by the session, 1559-1581 (table 3.4). Within each table, offense categories are listed in descending order of prevalence. The sums of numbers in the columns do not equal the totals because only the most common offense categories are listed. The "no-show" percentages are calculated for within each offense category.

Differentiating among types of sin can lead to hairsplitting among historians as well as philosophers; obviously, some distinctions are clearer than others. Thus while absence from Communion (one offense category) might in some instances have been an indication of Catholicism or other religious dissent (a different offense category), or enmity with neighbors (yet a third offense category), a charge of Communion absence can only be classified as Communion absence unless more fully explained. Likewise, marriage questions usually involved the claim that one partner was trying to back out, or "resile," from a betrothal, while unmarried pregnant women often alleged promise of marriage, either to excuse themselves or force their partners to legitimize their unions. The standard used here has been to classify such claims as marriage questions only when the technical verb "to resile" or some form thereof was employed. Such problems highlight the necessity, in assessing figures such as these, of bearing in mind the degree to which certain offenses could be related.

As tables 3.2-3.4 indicate, sexuality was the major concern of the St. Andrews Kirk Session, in all its disciplinary capacities, during the period under consideration. The proportion of cases involving sexual misbehavior ranged from 51 to 58 percent, while no other class of sin ever topped 15 percent. Significantly, neither gender seems to have been singled out as primarily guilty. Male sexual offenders were a little more numerous, but this may have been due to the fact that pregnancy out of wedlock was usually the major piece of evidence in these cases, and a significant number of women died in childbirth. Those who died had escaped the Kirk's jurisdiction, but their paramours, if known, had not. The session when acting on its own in 1559-72 was particularly successful in persuading sexual offenders to appear, with a refusal to appear rate of only 10 percent, compared with a rate of 35 percent when acting as Winram's court.

It is in the ranking of offense types other than sexuality that real differences appear in the disciplinary concerns of the session in its various guises. As the superintendent's court, the session spent much time considering marriage questions and disputes within families (often between husbands and wives), while these issues did not attract so much attention from the session acting on its own. This is probably a reflection of Winram's pseudo-episcopal function. As explained earlier, the pre-Reformation bishops' courts had heard suits of marriage annulment, as well as any case in which a breach of contract was alleged.[42] Couples, particularly prominent couples whose marriages involved significant property settlements, brought their disputes and alleged betrothals before Winram just as they would have brought them to a bishop earlier. The numbers of these cases did decline after 1564, however, as commissary courts were established to hear divorce suits.

While Winram maintained something like a traditional bishop's court, the session turned its own disciplinary concerns toward questions of doctrine

---

[42] See chapter two for a discussion of the evolution of Scottish ecclesiastical jurisdictions before and after the Reformation.

and religious observance. Religious dissent, Sabbath breach and Communion absence were its major disciplinary worries after sexuality, and its targets were almost all males. This is explained by several factors. First, quite a few Catholic priests and ex-priests lived in the burgh, due to its educational and ecclesiastical importance. Most of the old clergy here, as elsewhere in Scotland, never served in the Reformed Kirk,[43] leaving a large number of unreformed benefice holders resident in the burgh and surrounding area. Many of these were compelled to appear before the session in 1560-1 and swear allegiance to the *Scots Confession*. In contrast, Sabbath breach was typically a lay, rather than a clerical, sin. In St. Andrews during these years it often involved the merchandising of goods, generally a male activity. Finally, in cases of Communion absence, males as heads of households were usually targeted, even though their whole families may have been guilty of the offense. The session sought to bring wives, adult children and servants into conformity by first pressuring the household head, on the thinking that the others would follow suit once he had been brought around.

Table 3.4, by lumping together all the session's disciplinary activities between 1559 and 1581, masked significant differences in these interests over time. While St. Andrews was spared much of the political upheaval which racked other Scottish burghs and regions, particularly during the civil war period of 1567-73, there were still changes afoot. Many of these were associated with the creation and enforcement of the new religious order: the overthrow of the Catholic Church, the effort to eliminate traditional Catholic beliefs and practices among the populace, and the replacement of these with behaviors reflective of the Reformed attitude toward life and worship. Any attempt to instill such changes in *mentalité* was bound to take several decades at least, and table 3.5 attempts to demonstrate how the St. Andrews session directed its efforts in this regard during roughly the first two decades of the process.

Table 3.4 revealed that religious dissent was the second leading disciplinary concern of the St. Andrews Kirk Session during the period, but, as table 3.5 shows, this concern was highly episodic, with 61 of the 89 cases occurring in two years, 1560 and 1574. In fact, there were so many cases of religious dissent in those two years that they outnumbered sexual cases (and by a wide margin in 1560). Of the 35 cases of religious dissent from 1560, 28 were men identified as Catholic priests, who were thus religiously suspect. Just over 300 local householders had signed the band of the Lords of the Congregation between November 1559 and February 1560, but, in the cases of Catholic clergy, special pledges were demanded. Thus

---

[43] Charles H. Haws, "The Diocese of St. Andrews at the Reformation," *RSCHS* 18 (1972-4), 115-32, at 118-27.

John Wilson, "umquhile" [former] canon of Holyrood Abbey, was forced on February 1 to make a public repudiation of Catholicism in general and of "that lecherouss swyne the Byschop of Rome" in particular. Other priests had to renounce any former vows, or future pledges they might make, to uphold the Catholic faith.[44] Significantly, these actions were taken before the meeting of the "Reformation Parliament" and the official break with Rome that summer; they were part of a local reformation which partially predated its national counterpart.

The importance of public recantation should not be overlooked. At least some of these clergy (e.g. those who had preached and publicly ministered

TABLE 3.5—BREAKDOWN OF CASES BY YEAR FOR ST.
ANDREWS KIRK SESSION, 1559-81

Column Headings:
    1 - Sexuality
    2 - Religious dissent or unorthodox practices
    3 - Sabbath breach
    4 - Disputes within the family
    5 - Marriage questions
    6 - Communion Absence
    7 - Slander/bickering
    8 - Rebellion against kirk/disobedience
    9 - Dealings with excommunicants/outcasts

Year	Total	1	2	3	4	5	6	7	8	9
1559	4	3	-	-	-	-	-	-	-	1
1560	43	5	35	-	1	2	-	-	-	-
1561	11	1	2	-	2	-	-	3	1	-
1562	33	27	-	-	1	2	-	-	-	-
1563	24	17	1	-	1	4	-	-	-	-
1564	51	37	8	-	4	-	1	-	-	-
1565	52	44	-	-	2	4	-	1	-	-

---

[44] *StAKS*, 1:6-15.

Year	Total	1	2	3	4	5	6	7	8	9
1566	26	20	3	-	-	3	-	-	-	-
1567*	3	-	2	-	1	-	-	-	-	-
1568*	49	23	2	6	3	6	-	4	-	2
1569	29	15	2	1	2	2	3	-	2	1
1570	26	11	1	1	5	-	-	2	-	1
1571	29	12	-	13	-	-	1	-	2	-
1572	53	25	-	14	1	1	11	-	-	-
1573	42	26	5	3	1	-	5	1	-	-
1574	63	24	26	3	-	1	-	1	1	-
1575	26	18	2	-	-	1	3	2	-	-
1576	35	7	-	24	1	-	-	-	-	-
1577	34	24	-	1	2	2	-	-	-	-
1578	23	19	-	-	2	-	-	-	-	-
1579	31	25	-	-	2	1	-	-	-	-
1580	40	36	-	-	1	-	1	1	1	-
1581	24	18	-	-	2	-	2	1	-	-

*There is a gap in the session register between February 1567 and February 1568. (Note: numbers within years may not add up to the listed annual totals due to leftover cases which do not fit the listed categories.)

the sacraments), would have had, by virtue of their office, a special relationship with God in the eyes of the faithful. Now they were required to declare in the presence of their former spiritual charges that it was all a fraud. It is hard to gauge the support Catholicism had among the lay population, but there were examples of discontent with the new order in 1560, such as Walter Adie, who asked a deacon passing out Communion tokens, "will ye give me ane techet to be served the Divellis dirt? I sall by ane poynt of wyne and ane laif, and I sall haif als gude ane sacrament as the best of them all sall haif." On the same day, one John Law was charged with having declared: "the Divell knok owt John Knox barnes [brains], for, quhen he [Law] wald see him hanget, he wald gett his sacrament."[45] Although it has been claimed otherwise, there is evidence within the register that all residents of the burgh were subject to discipline from the beginning, whether they claimed to be members of the Reformed Kirk or not.[46]

Lay Catholics were spared the public recantation forced upon Catholic clergy, but even they sometimes feared humiliation. The lawyer James Dischington requested and received several delays when asked to sign the *Scots Confession* in 1568. On 23 July he appeared and explained that if he signed, "it wald be blaudit [bragged] upon every mannis teitht, and forther he wald be blawdid in the pulpet quhair the preacheris ralis by thair text; and sa [he] departit wytht fume and anger, nochtwythstanding the seat [session] promist that his writting sould nocht be blawdit...." He did eventually sign, although not before nearly another year had passed.[47]

As the Reformation slowly took hold in St. Andrews, the session summoned fewer people for Catholicism *per se*, taking aim instead at traditional religious practices associated with the old religion. The apparent dragnet against dissent in 1574 was due to a crackdown on the observance of Christmas. Twenty-six people, all male and most if not all of them craftsmen, were charged in January and February with having observed the traditional feast, now officially regarded as superstitious. Most were punished only with private admonitions; the session may have feared unrest after Walter Younger, one of the first charged, reportedly opined that "it becam nocht honest men to sit upon the penitent stule," and that he was "ane yowng man and saw Zwil [Yule] day kepit halyday, and that the tyme may cum that he may see the like yit."[48] A mason charged with the same offense the following year was made to promise that in the future, even if nobody gave him any work on Christmas, "he sal wirk som riggen stanis of his awin."[49]

Intolerance of Yule observance was becoming a litmus test of reform elsewhere in Scotland as well. The Regent Morton admonished the politically suspect Aberdeen Burgh Council against "the superstitious keping of festivall days usit of befor in tyme of ignorance & papistrie" in August 1574, and the council and kirk session there responded by summoning a

---

[45] *Ibid*, 1:34-6. For dissent which is clearly non-Catholic, see *ibid*, 1:43-4.

[46] *Ibid*, 1:135-9, for case of Mr. Thomas Methven, who claimed he was immune from the session's jurisdiction, but was told that all residents of the burgh were subject to it. Geoffrey Parker has claimed that Catholics were not subject to the session before 1567. See Parker, "Kirk by Law Established," 8.

[47] *StAKS*, 1:296-7, 319-20.

[48] *Ibid*, 1:389.

[49] *Ibid*, 1:404.

number of offenders the following December and January.[50] Catholic practices lingered in Aberdeen, but in St. Andrews the effort to stamp them out may have been more successful. After 1574-5, cases of religious dissent or "superstition" virtually disappear until the mid-1590s, when the Kirk at the national level became obsessed by fears of Catholic conspiracy.

Whereas simple denial of Catholicism had been acceptable to the St. Andrews elders in the 1560s, they were enforcing a more difficult standard by the mid-1570s. As table 3.5 shows, nobody was even charged with breaking the Sabbath before 1568. But this offense became a major concern in 1571-2, and cases of Sabbath breach outnumbered sexual cases in 1576. Likewise cases of Communion absence, while never plentiful, are mostly clustered in the early 1570s. Communion was becoming, in the local kirk's eyes, a communal love feast, and all who were not infirm or suspended for disciplinary reasons were expected to partake. In 1575, James Gilrith faced the accusation that he had refused to take the hand of John Cook's wife during Communion, and Thomas Hudson was charged with taking Communion while at enmity with Andrew Colyne, though he denied it.[51] Parishioners could no longer simply avoid that which was considered evil; they had to embrace the good as well.

Just as the residents of St. Andrews were being pressed to demonstrate more godly zeal in the mid-1570s, their minister and elders were facing external pressures to enforce higher standards. Although it had been one of the first burghs to adopt reform, by 1575 St. Andrews had lagged behind, in the opinion of the General Assembly. The latter deputized several Edinburgh-area ministers and the Edinburgh Kirk Session to investigate charges against the St. Andrews elders and their minister, Robert Hamilton. Hamilton and company had allegedly tolerated the performance of Robin Hood plays during a fast ordered by the General Assembly, regularly allowed "p[ro]phane playis and sic uyer thingis" on the Sabbath, winked at the performance of a clerk play during the wedding of the daughter of the elder Thomas Balfour, and held neither exercises (communal study by ministry and elders of biblical texts), nor preaching on Friday or Sunday afternoons. Hamilton himself had allegedly shot at the "papingo" (a parrot-shaped archery target) during the fast.[52]

Hamilton appeared before the Edinburgh session on 24 February 1575, and claimed ignorance of the fast. He said the Robin Hood plays were performed privately by servants and children, and that the session had asked the local magistrates to forbid them. He granted that the clerk play had

---

[50] SRO ms CH2/448/1, 58-9, 61; *Aber. Recs.*, 2:25-6.

[51] *StAKS*, 1:409-10.

[52] SRO ms CH2/450/1, 43r-44v.

taken place, but excused it on the grounds that it was not performed during preaching hours. He said shooting at the papingo occurred regularly on Monday afternoons, and that he and the elders had enough to do already, without the exercise. As for preaching on Friday and Sunday afternoons, Hamilton argued that even his predecessor Christopher Goodman, so noted for his zeal, had refused orders from the General Assembly to preach at those times.[53]

There is no record of this matter in the session register, but the complaints may have had local roots, perhaps in a generational conflict within the leadership of the parish kirk. James Melville, diarist, enthusiastic presbyterian and nephew of the scholar and controversialist Andrew Melville, had been a student at St. Leonard's College in St. Andrews in the early 1570s. He praised the early reform (under Goodman's ministry) there, but criticized Hamilton, who was also provost of St. Mary's College, for his "cauldness."[54] Balfour, as noted earlier, had been an elder since 1559, and was from one of the burgh's most prominent families. Two college regents, Archibald and John Hamilton, both of whom served on sessions in the early 1570s, afterward became Catholics. Melville characterized John Rutherford, provost of St. Salvator's, and another fixture on the session until 1576, as "evill myndit."[55] Ten new elders joined the session during the period 1573-8 and, although one of these was John Hamilton, many of the rest may have represented new thinking more to the liking of James Melville. The February 1576 crackdown on those who worked or sold merchandise on the Sabbath probably reflects a combination of this new thinking and of the pressure put on Hamilton (who remained as minister until his death in April 1581) by the General Assembly.[56] It is certain that the impetus came from ecclesiastical rather than secular sources; the first post-1560 act of Parliament regarding Sabbath observance was not passed until 1579.[57] The Sabbath-breakers of 1576 were admonished and passed on to the local bailies for civil punishment, but the fact that Sabbath-breach then practically disappears from the record until another cluster of charges in February 1582 suggests that the magistrates were as yet unwilling to do much about it. So after 1576, having largely vanquished local Catholicism, and as yet unable to do more than warn people against Sabbath breach, or attack the quarrels and violent feuds endemic to Scottish society, the St. Andrews elders focused even more exclusively on what had usually been

---

[53] *Ibid*, 45r.
[54] *JMD*, 124.
[55] *Ibid*, 26-7.
[56] *StAKS*, 1:416-7.
[57] *APS*, 3:138.

their leading concern all along: sexual misbehavior. Although the authors of the *First Book of Discipline* had placed drunkenness, fighting and swearing on an equal footing with sexual misbehavior among sins the kirk session ought to punish,[58] the St. Andrews elders settled upon sexuality. This, it would seem, was an issue on which all local powers could agree.

Sexuality had figured heavily in the kirk session's caseload since early in the 1560s. The first year with a high number of sexual cases was 1562, when 27 out of 33 cases involved illicit sexual relations. Sex then became the session's main disciplinary priority in 28 of the next 31 years for which the records are reasonably complete. In fact, sexuality became its nearly exclusive concern in the 1580s, with no other offense category becoming prominent again until the 1590s. The reasons for this seeming obsession with sex, common to many kirk sessions, and to the Scots Reformed Kirk generally, were both economic and religious, and will be discussed later in the national context.

Women were not singled out as temptresses in St. Andrews. In fact, men outnumbered women among those charged with sexual offenses, 231-205. Usually, the session named and summoned both parties in any illicit sexual liason. This would not prove to be the case everywhere, as we will see later.

Most sexual cases involved fornication. Those who admitted guilt were almost always required to perform public repentance—sitting through a Sunday church service while seated on a "stool of repentance" in plain view of the congregation. Repeat offenders might have their penalties doubled or tripled. Adultery and incest were regarded as more serious sins. Charges arising from incest between blood relatives were quite rare, but cases of sexual relationships between those related by marriage were more common. Thus when Andrew Duncan had a child by his nephew's widow, the session ordered both to perform public repentance six times for "horribill incest."[59] Adulterers were also required to perform public repentance several times, sometimes in sackcloth.

In addition to ecclesiastical penalties, the session often ordered civil penalties against sexual offenders. The burgh council was accustomed to some jurisdiction over those who dwelled within burgh walls, and elders who were also councilors may have seen little distinction between the two roles. But the register is often vague as to what civil punishment might entail. Fines were only mentioned in 11 of the 437 sexual cases pursued before 1582. Imprisonment for up to a week may have been more common; Thomas Wood confessed to fornication (while engaged) to Catherine Wilson

---

[58] Cameron, ed., *First Book of Discipline*, 168.
[59] *StAKS*, 1:233.

on 26 March 1572, but was given only public repentance, with no incarceration, "becaus he is nocht nor was indwellar in this towne...."[60] But even
offenders who were burgh residents must have been imprisoned only
irregularly. The session was forever restating its view that adulterers and
fornicators ought to be locked up, an indication that such penalties were not
being carried out.[61] Imprisonment does not seem to have become a matter
of course until the 1580s.

Incarceration was relatively rare throughout the Scottish legal system in
the sixteenth century. Authorities had traditionally used other means to
ensure compliance and, particularly during the first few years of its
activities, the St. Andrews session resorted to these. The most common was
the requirement that someone found guilty of a sin requiring public
repentance find "caution" (i.e., a bondsman) that they would follow the
session's directions. By 1568, £40 Scots had become the usual cautionary
sum.[62] If the sinner failed to perform his or her repentance, the cautioner
would forfeit the £40. The cautioner was presumed to be a person with
some influence over the offender, often a kinsman, landlord or employer.
This practice was common in the civil as well as ecclesiastical court
system,[63] but the St. Andrews session eventually gave up on it, perhaps
because the elders lacked the power to force cautioners to pay up when their
charges failed to perform repentance. In 1576 the session ruled that it would
no longer accept cautions from adulterers and fornicators, and would instead
require them to give satisfaction immediately.[64] It then renewed its efforts
to impose terms of imprisonment.

There was one class of sinner which Scottish magistrates in general
displayed little hesitation in punishing—those considered guilty of witchcraft
and sorcery. Witchcraft had received some attention from the Kirk and
Parliament at the national level, the latter in 1563 having mandated capital
punishment for its practitioners.[65] Christina Larner, in her study of the
Scottish witch-hunt, suggested that most cases originated in kirk sessions,

---

[60] *StAKS*, 1:363.

[61] *StAKS*, 1:373-4, 417, 427.

[62] *StAKS*, 1:295, 303. The value of the Scots pound was falling rapidly relative to sterling
at this time. In the late 1560s, £1 Sterling was worth roughly £6 Scots, and the Scots pound
sunk to a 12:1 ratio by 1600. See L.M. Cullen, T.C. Smout and A. Gibson, "Wages and
Comparative Development in Ireland and Scotland, 1565-1780," in Rosalind Mitchison and
Peter Roebuck, eds., *Economy and Society in Scotland and Ireland, 1500-1939*, (Edinburgh:
John Donald, 1988), 105-16, at 105, 115; S.G.E. Lythe, *The Economy of Scotland In Its
European Setting, 1550-1625*, (Edinburgh: Oliver and Boyd, 1960), 101-2.

[63] For a few examples, see *Pit. Crim.*, 1(part 2):2, 5, 12-3, 20, 33.

[64] *StAKS*, 1:419.

[65] *APS*, 2:539; Calderwood, 2:289.

but the St. Andrews register shows little evidence of this for the period 1559-81.[66] James Melville reported that he had seen John Knox preach in St. Andrews at the execution of a witch, an event which likely would have taken place in 1570 or 1571, but there is no evidence that the kirk session had any role in the prosecution.[67] The first witchcraft case in the St. Andrews register dates from January 1576, and it involved Marjorie Smith, apparently known as a practicing witch and healer in and around St. Andrews for at least four years. She and her husband fled the area before the case could be concluded, however.[68] Bessie Robertson was charged with witchcraft in October 1581, but she never appeared before the session, and her ultimate fate is unknown.[69] These are the only witchcraft cases in the register for the period in question. While large-scale witchhunting did not occur in Scotland until the 1590s,[70] it is nevertheless noteworthy that the sin of witchcraft so rarely came to the attention of the St. Andrews elders during this earlier period.

By 1581 the elders of St. Andrews were concentrating on sexual sins to the near exclusion of all others, and had yet to make a concerted effort regarding Sabbath observance, peacemaking, church attendance or magic—all issues which figured prominently among the national Kirk's concerns. Taking the 1570s as reflective of the system in full operation, cases averaged 36 per year. If one supposes that 2,000 of the 3-4,000 residents of the burgh and immediate neighborhood were communicants, the parish of St. Andrews would have had one disciplinary case annually for every 56 residents.

But as valuable as the St. Andrews register is, particularly for its time span, we should not take it as representative of all Scotland during the period, particularly since other early registers do exist.[71] There are kirk session records for Aberdeen and Monifieth (a rural parish on the Angus coast) dating from 1562, but these are fragmentary until the 1570s.[72] The only register from the 1560s besides St. Andrews which records complete years, allowing quantitative study of the caseload, is that of the Canongate from 1564 to 1567, and it is to that parish that we will now turn.

---

[66] Christina Larner, *Enemies of God: The Witch-hunt in Scotland*, (London: Chatto and Windus, 1981), 58, 62, 104.

[67] *JMD*, 58.

[68] *StAKS*, 1:414-6.

[69] *Ibid*, 1:455.

[70] Larner, *Enemies of God*, 60-1.

[71] As has Geoffrey Parker, who is also mistaken on the number of registers from the period which have survived. See his "The Kirk by Law Established," 7.

[72] Aberdeen is SRO ms CH2/448/1; Monifieth is NRH ms OPR 310/1.

The Canongate

The Canongate in the mid-1560s was a burgh of regality belonging to Lord
Robert Stewart, commendator of Holyrood Abbey, a natural son of James
V.[73] The burgh was on the doorstep of Edinburgh, the nation's capital,
straddling the bottom half of the ridge which slopes down from Edinburgh
Castle to the royal palace of Holyrood. Although the Canongate today has
its own kirk, this was not constructed until the seventeenth century, and the
sixteenth-century congregation gathered in the kirk in Holyrood Abbey. Its
first Reformed minister was John Craig, formerly a Dominican friar in
Bologna. By 1564 Craig had become John Knox's fellow minister in
Edinburgh, and the Canongate's minister was John Brand, a former canon
of Holyrood.[74]

While its population was much smaller than Edinburgh's, the Canongate
still had a considerable number of residents; Brand (who doubled as session
clerk) recorded Communion participation totals of between 900 and 1250
parishioners, with the lowest figures in 1564-5 and the highest in 1567.[75]
These numbers suggest a total burgh population of around 2,000, taking into
consideration children and those who, for whatever reason, did not attend
Communion. The presence of the royal court at Holyrood drew wealth and
nobility into the burgh, giving it some very prominent residents. For
example, Harry Burrel, Edinburgh's wealthiest flesher, was a member of
the Canongate congregation, and served as an elder in 1566-7.[76] So was Sir
John Bellenden of Auchnoule, justice clerk of the realm. And it was in the
Canongate kirk in the summer of 1565 that the marriage banns of Queen
Mary Stewart and Henry, Lord Darnley, were proclaimed.[77] But the
Canongate parish was not simply that of an exclusive suburb; it also
included parts of the port of Leith and the notorious red light district in and
around the Cowgate, which occupied much of the kirk session's attention.

Like the kirk session of St. Andrews, the session of the Canongate was
staffed by leading members of the burgh establishment. Of the eight
Canongate elders elected in August 1564, five were certainly burgh
councilors and bailies at various times in the 1560s. In addition, two of the

---

[73] Marguerite Wood, ed., *Book of Records of the Ancient Privileges of the Canongate*,
(Edinburgh: Scottish Record Society, 1956), 3, 27.

[74] Charles H. Haws, *Scottish Parish Clergy at the Reformation 1540-1574*, (Edinburgh:
Scottish Record Society, 1972), 36; Ronald Selby Wright, *The Kirk in the Canongate: A Short
History from 1128 to the Present Day*, (Edinburgh: Oliver and Boyd, 1956), 31-3.

[75] *BKC*, 6, 18, 25, 43, 51, 63, 71.

[76] *Ibid*, 51. He was worth £2,022 when he died. See Michael Lynch, *Edinburgh and the
Reformation*, (Edinburgh: John Donald, 1981), 53.

[77] *BKC*, 25.

eight deacons can be identified positively as burgh councilors late in the decade.[78] A system of rotation was practiced within the eldership (unlike at St. Andrews), so that none of the elders from the Canongate proper were re-elected in 1565, although two elders each from Leith and the Cowgate were. Among the eight Canongate elders of 1565, six were certainly councilors and/or bailies in the 1560s, as were three of the eight deacons.[79] Members of the session elected the following year were said to be named "as thay war lyttit with moniest wottis," although just who was voting is unclear. Significantly, the list included a number of new names, although two of the elders named had served on the session two years before.

This seeming democratization was followed in 1567 by something of a return to form; five of the eight Canongate elders chosen that year also appear as councilors and/or bailies.[80] As with previous years, there were no repeaters among the Canongate elders or deacons. Thus the Canongate elders, while generally just as well-connected with the burgh government as their counterparts in St. Andrews, did not remain on the session year after year as those in St. Andrews did. What is more, the evidence from 1566 suggests that session elections could be open to conflicting influences; one of the elders and one of the deacons elected in 1566 refused to serve. The extant session register begins in August 1564 and leaves off almost exactly three years later. It records 287 individual disciplinary cases, an average of just under 96 per year. This means that there was roughly one case annually for every ten Communion participants, a figure which St. Andrews never approached. Such a high ratio suggests that the enforcement of social discipline was a much more intensive process in the Canongate than at St. Andrews. Table 3.6 details the distribution of the session's disciplinary efforts. Like their peers in St. Andrews, the Canongate elders spent much more time attacking sexual sins than any other type. But they did not take the gender-neutral approach favored in St. Andrews. Granted, many men were charged with sexual sins in the Canongate, but more women were, by a margin of 94-55. And, even when both partners were summoned, they might be treated differently, as were David Pearson and Isobel Mowtray in October 1564. The couple admitted to having a child out of wedlock. She was ordered to leave the burgh within 48 hours "wnder the pane of schorging," while he was given four hours in the branks [stocks], which he avoided by promising to pay a fine of 40 shillings instead.[81] A month later the session drew up a list of sexual sinners "within this reformit

---

[78] *Ibid*, 5; *Canon. Recs.*, 285-6, 301, 312, 323.

[79] *BKC*, 26.

[80] *Ibid*, 72.

[81] *BKC*, 8-9.

TABLE 3.6—BREAKDOWN OF DISCIPLINARY CASES FOR CANONGATE KIRK SESSION, 1564-67

Offense category	Cases	Males	Females	No-shows
Sexuality	149 (52%)	55	94	25 (17%)
Slander, bickering	65 (23%)	39	26	3 (5%)
Dealings with outcasts	24 (8%)	17	7	5 (21%)
Violence, assault	12 (4%)	9	3	1 (8%)
Religious diss/practice	9 (3%)	8	1	4 (44%)
Marriage questions	7 (2%)	7	0	3 (43%)
Communion absence	5 (2%)	5	0	3 (60%)
Totals	287	149	138	49 (17%)

(Note: numbers within listed categories do not equal the totals due to other cases scattered throughout less common categories. "No-show" percentages calculated for within each sin category.)

TABLE 3.7—DISCIPLINARY TRENDS IN THE CANONGATE, 1564-67

	1564*	1565	1566	1567*
Total cases	47	90	83	67
Total: Sexuality	39 (83%)	60 (67%)	33 (40%)	17 (25%)
Sexuality: males	11	23	14	7
Sexuality: females	28	37	19	10
Verbal conflicts	0	17 (19%)	19 (23%)	29 (43%)
Violent conflicts	0	2 (2%)	0	10 (15%)

*indicates incomplete year

gait," for action by the civil magistrates. Twelve women were named, as were their partners, but the session was clearly only after the women, some of whom were rounded up and brought before the session on 2 December 1564.[82] A group trial of sexual sinners convened with the session, bailies and Justice Clerk Bellenden in December 1565 considered the cases of sixteen women but no men, although one male did appear before the session the next day because he wished to marry one of the defendants.[83]

But the double standard was much more pronounced in 1564-5 than it was later, as table 3.7 (above) shows. This adjustment was coupled with other changes in the session's disciplinary interests, also visible in table 3.7. In this table, cases are broken down within calendar years, but it should be noted that 1564 and 1567 are not complete years, since the register begins and ends in August.

One should be hesitant to suggest trends based on records from only four consecutive years, but the figures in the table above are striking. First all, while the gender disparity among sexual sinners remained at the end, it was reduced from the level of 1564. In 1564, 72 percent of those charged with sexual offenses were female, while in 1567 only 59 percent were. More importantly, the overall proportion of sexual cases plummeted from 83 percent to 25 percent, although the total number of cases of all types did not change a great deal.[84] Clearly, this was not simply a matter of the session adding new offenses to an existing, steady workload. Rather, the elders were redirecting their efforts away from sexuality and into conflict resolution.

Faced with such evidence, one might ask whether the elders thought they had mostly solved the problem of illicit sexuality between 1564 and 1567. Focusing on women from the outset, they undertook a campaign of banishment against offenders such as Isobel Mowtray, mentioned above, or a servant woman banished in September 1564 by the bailies "assistane the assemble of the kirke," who was told that she would be scourged and branded on the cheek if she did not depart.[85] By the end of the year, female offenders who were banished were also threatened with having their heads shaved should they remain.[86] But such severe punishments were modified—or perhaps simply clarified—by April 1565, when a female fornicator was put in the branks for two hours and then "baniest the gait

---

[82] *Ibid*, 11-12.

[83] *Ibid*, 34-5.

[84] Keeping in mind that the 1564 figures are for only four and a half months, while the 1567 totals are for seven and a half.

[85] *BKC*, 7.

[86] *Ibid*, 15.

unto scho satisfie to the kirk be repentance and satisfie the siweill maiestract."[87] Thus a sentence of banishment might not really be enforced unless an offender refused to perform public repentance and/or pay a fine.

So while the elders in the session, perhaps encouraged by the minister and the more zealous members of the congregation, were quick to pass harsh regulations, the bailies and councilors (some of whom were, of course, elders as well) were more reluctant to put civil authority behind these pronouncements.[88] In 1566-7, the session complained repeatedly that the bailies were far too tolerant, and were neglecting to pursue sexual offenders.[89] Thus it would seem that by 1567 the minister and elders, rather than reflecting with satisfaction on their near eradication of sexual vice in the burgh, were instead disappointed that their early enthusiasm had been rewarded with so little cooperation from burgh authorities. This may have led them to redirect their efforts toward the fostering of Christian love through conflict resolution.

The session considered relatively few cases of conflict within families, although it did seek, for instance, to restore harmony to the household of the baxter George Stene and his wife, Jonet Murdo. Stene complained to the elders that he could no longer live with his wife because of her "wickitnes of toung and casting at him with hir handis, stannis [stones] and dirt...." She pled self-defense, charging, "I have gretter caus to complan upone him, for I dred bodelye harme of him." The session found them both guilty, "bot specialle the said Jonet," and ordered her to ask her husband for forgiveness. The pair were warned to behave in the future or else be "put out of the kirk as wicket doars."[90]

Mostly, however, the session sought to bring reconciliation between quarrelsome neighbors. Such mediation had occasionally taken place before the burgh council in the past, so the concept was not entirely new.[91] But the pastoral element of the session's mission gave it a new meaning, as well as bringing more women into the process. The session hosted a number of mass reconciliations, usually on the eve of Communion celebrations, in order to ensure that those gathered around the Communion table would at least outwardly be in harmony. One such meeting in January 1567 involved twenty-four parishioners. Usually all parties were found equally guilty, though there were exceptions, such as Bessie Rokart and her daughter

---

[87] *Ibid*, 20.

[88] The (fragmentary) council records from the 1560s show little evidence of morality regulation by the bailies and council. See *Canon. Recs.*, *passim*.

[89] *BKC*, 39, 43, 46, 54, 68.

[90] *Ibid*, 38.

[91] See, for example, *Canon. Recs.*, 290-301.

Ellen, who were told to apologize to the widow Jonat Cuthbert for having called Cuthbert's late husband a thief while he lay on his deathbed.[92] Other conflicts carried the potential for bloodshed, as in August 1566 when the bailie James Wilkie complained that John Mosman was harboring a man in his house who had killed one of Wilkie's kinsmen. Such a charge threatened to draw Mosman into what was apparently a bloodfeud, and the session admonished him to remove the man from his house.[93]

Conflicts were sometimes mediated when there was no Communion celebration in the near future as well. They might be referred to arbitration, such as a dispute in June 1566 between the elders James Hart and Robert Muir. Hart charged that Muir had called him a "bangester" (bully), and the arbiters found Muir to be at fault, ordering that he apologize and be removed from the session.[94]

Some conflicts had already escalated into violence and, in the extraordinary case of Marjorie Brisone, reconciliation had to be with the congregation, rather than with the individual. She was charged with murder but, having paid an assythement to the victim's kin and purchased a remission from the crown, needed only to satisfy the Kirk. In order to do so, she was told to perform public repentance for three consecutive Sundays clad in white, barefoot, bare-legged, with her head uncovered, while holding a knife dipped in blood. On each Sunday she was to request the congregation's forgiveness, and, on the third, an elder would receive her by the hand and take the knife from her, signifying her readmittance into the Kirk.[95]

Thus, after an initial crackdown on sexual vice, the Canongate elders returned to what was in some respects a traditional responsibility for them, that of mediation. But, with the need to sanctify the Reformed Communion rite through neighborly harmony, coupled with the significance of the ritual of public repentance in church, this role took on a new and expanded meaning. This provides a good example of a way in which the ideology of Reformed Christianity adapted to local conditions.

In other respects the elders of the Canongate proved remarkably uninterested in the new religious currents. They had no qualms about baptizing the child of "John Ackman, papest" in June 1566, and the

---

[92] *BKC*, 60-3, Rokart-Cuthbert dispute on 62.

[93] *Ibid*, 50.

[94] *Ibid*, 45-6.

[95] *Ibid*, 36. An assythement or kinbuit was a compensatory sum paid to victims of violence or their relatives by the perpetrator. It enabled the parties to settle out of court, thus sparing the guilty party from a criminal process. Purchasing a letter of remission from the crown was supposed to grant the guilty party a delay in criminal proceedings while he (or she) negotiated compensation. See Brown, *Bloodfeud in Scotland*, 52-4, 56.

sometime elder John Oswald acted as a witness to the ceremony.[96] Their register used—with no hint of disapproval—the "feist of Yule" to identify the due date of a required payment, and as late as 1586 the Canongate session was censured by the Edinburgh Presbytery for having allowed burial within the kirk building in violation of orders from the General Assembly.[97]

But the proximity of the royal court is one factor to consider before branding the Canongate elders as religious backsliders or crypto-Catholics. The monarch was Catholic until 1567, and this certainly had an effect on the burgh closest to her primary residence. On 7 October 1564, the Catholic priest John Scot appeared before the session, charged with operating an unauthorized school. Rather than submitting to judgment, he told the session: "I have no thing to do with yow for ye have no power ower me." He then produced a letter purportedly from the queen stating, "becaus he wes of the quene gracis religioun he was persewit," and forbidding the magistrates of the Canongate or Edinburgh from molesting him. The elders were suspicious because the letter was unsealed, but seemed to conclude that if it were proven authentic, they could do nothing about Scot or his school.[98] A couple charged with fornication in September 1566 replied that they had been married "in the quenis chappell at the mes," which the session was prepared to accept if a testimonial were produced.[99] The session had to recognize that Catholicism was practiced by many in the area, and reach a *modus vivendi* with the traditional faith. Significantly, it did not hear many cases involving religious dissent in the period 1564-7. Nor was anyone officially excommunicated for any reason, although a number of individuals were "suspended" from Communion pending public repentance.

The Canongate elders were quite willing to display zeal for reform where the burgh's craftsmen were concerned, however. On 3 September 1564 they proclaimed:

> The kirk haifand knawlege how syndre brither of craiftis biand once at the commonioun, and sum oderis under promis, hes absentit thame selfis frome the last commonioun, sum oderis that hes bene at it frequentis nocht the sermonis bot rether to pastyme, playand and drinking, quha suld gif gude exampill wnto uthairis, thairfor the kirke maist hartfullie exhortis the diakins of the craftis with the rest of the faythfull to resone with thair bretherin the occatioun of the formar faltis, and to exhort thair bredering to amend in tyme cuming, quhilk gif thai do, the formar faltis sall nocht be rememberit.

---

[96] *BKC*, 91.

[97] *Ibid*, 29, SRO ms CH2/121/1, 7r-8r.

[98] *BKC*, 8.

[99] *Ibid*, 55-6. In this case, no testimonial was forthcoming, so the male in the pair was warded until they ratified their marriage before the Reformed congregation.

Those who remained "stubborn," however, would have other measures taken against them "as Godis word dois requyr."[100]

In the eyes of the Canongate elders, the fact that the burgh's craftsmen had attended, or promised to attend, the Reformed Communion ceremony, made them subject to the session's authority. That authority would be used to curb the riot and sedition likely to arise from the craftsmen's Sunday pastimes. The session never issued a single charge of Sabbath breach *per se* against any individual in the congregation, and the burgh council did not seek to close taverns during Sunday preaching until 1569, but in August 1566, the session issued an order forbidding the crafts to convene on Sundays, as they still regularly did.[101] Nearly a year later, it ordered some of the burgh's tailors to perform public repentance for having, "of malice and set purpois," chosen James Galbraith as their craft deacon although he had been debarred (by whom is unclear) "from all office in ane common weill."[102] Here, Reformed discipline gave the burgh authorities, in their alternative guise as session elders, a new weapon in the old struggle against craft liberties.

The cessation of the Canongate register in 1567 makes it impossible to trace further the session's disciplinary activities in the sixteenth century. But the evidence of 1564-7 suggests that, after an initial crusade against sexual irregularity, the elders chose a course very much in keeping with burgh traditions, albeit somewhat modified by Reformed ideals. They did not hesitate to use their powers to meddle in craft elections but, unlike the elders of St. Andrews, they were generally tolerant of local Catholicism. Most importantly, they devoted a great deal of attention to healing the rifts within burgh society. It would be interesting to trace the session's activities during the civil war period of 1567-73, but the records for this do not exist. Session records for nearby Edinburgh do begin in April 1574, however, and demonstrate that, by that time, Reformed discipline in the nation's capital had become highly politicized.

Edinburgh

Edinburgh, the wealthiest and most populous burgh in Scotland, home of the nation's highest legal court as well as customary meeting site for Parliament and the Kirk's General Assembly, was the stage upon which many of the leading political dramas of the late sixteenth century were performed. It was also a densely-packed city, housing all strata of people.

---

[100] *BKC*, 6-7.

[101] *Canon. Recs.*, 317; *BKC*, 54.

[102] *BKC*, 71

Constricted by its walls and by the loch to the north which served as a public sewer (later drained, the site of Waverly Railway Station and the Prince's Street Gardens today), the burgh had generally been forced to expand its buildings upward rather than outward in order to house its population of around 12,000.[103]

In April 1574, when its earliest surviving kirk session register begins, Edinburgh was still recovering from the strife of the recent civil war between the supporters of the exiled Mary, Queen of Scots and her infant son James VI. This conflict had exacted a particularly heavy toll locally. The queen's party had ruled the burgh from spring 1571 until summer 1572, driving many leading burgesses who supported the king to take up temporary residence in the nearby port of Leith. Meanwhile, the queen's supporters punished some of these exiles by demolishing their homes, thereby ensuring that bitterness would linger long after the conflict was over. Even after the king's party returned to power in the burgh, the town was still subject to harassment (and occasional bombardment) from Edinburgh Castle, whose captain, Sir William Kirkcaldy of Grange, continued to support the queen until forced to surrender in May 1573.[104]

In such an atmosphere, the burgh's kirk session was no stranger to political conflicts. Just as the various takeovers of the city during the civil war had been accompanied by the naming of new burgh councils, supporters of the two sides had each nominated their own kirk sessions. While the queen's party held a parliament in Edinburgh in June 1571, it ordered minister John Craig to convene the session and read to it a proclamation nullifying James VI's coronation. When Craig refused to pray for the queen's cause, he was declared deposed, John Knox having already fled to St. Andrews.[105] Earlier, when Knox had denounced Kirkcaldy of Grange from the pulpit as "a cruell murtherer, and open throat-cutter" due to a killing by some of Grange's men and his complicity in rescuing one of the murderers from the Edinburgh's tollbooth, Grange complained to the session that Knox had slandered him. Knox responded that Grange himself should be admonished for his "offence committed against God, against the partie, against the Kirk, and cheeflie against the magistrat."[106]

After the king's party returned to power in the burgh and on the kirk session, it immediately began requiring that those who had supported the

---

[103] Population figure for Edinburgh proper, not counting suburbs. See Lynch, *Edinburgh and the Reformation*, 2-3.

[104] *Ibid*, 131-43; George R. Hewitt, *Scotland Under Morton, 1572-80*, (Edinburgh: John Donald, 1982), 26-9.

[105] Calderwood, 3:97.

[106] *Ibid*, 3:20-9.

queen express repentance before the session.[107] When the extant register begins, on 1 April 1574, this process of political cleansing was in full swing. On that very day, 30 men appeared before the session, two of them for active rebellion "in ye laitt trabills rasit...not onlie aganis our mr. and salvator Christ bot als[o] aganis o[u]r sov[er]ane lord his grace," and the others merely for having remained in town while the queen's party held sway. They were told to go to the kirk (St. Giles) on the following Wednesday and stand bareheaded in black clothes by the door, while people filed in for the afternoon preaching. Then they were to sit in the place set aside for repentance within the kirk for the length of the sermon.[108] When the register ends in November 1575, the burghal purging was still incomplete, with scattered cases continuing.

The new, godly town was cleaning out the vestiges of sedition from the old. In all, 94 residents of the burgh were forced to expiate their past political allegiance between April 1574 and November 1575. The session ruled on 29 April 1574 that nobody who had remained in town or rebelled during the recent troubles could receive a token admitting them to Communion until they had performed public repentance, and this order was repeated the following December.[109] Some were treated more harshly than others: four men who confessed on 20 May 1574 to having remained in the castle while it was under siege,

> during ye q[uhi]lk tyme yai tuik plane p[ar]te w[i]t[h] ye declarit trators being yairin for ye tyme, assistit all yair maist veikit factis and int[er]prys[e]s, as weill in ye demolising and casting downe of sayt biggyis [buildings] and hous[e]s of ye said burgh as rasing of fyir w[i]t[h]in ye same w[i]t[h] schowting of greit and small pes[e]s indefferentlie in ye faces of all w[i]t[h]out ye feir of god...

were ordered to perform their repentance on a Wednesday, Friday and Sunday.[110] In some cases, ex-rebels were told to donate a gown or contribute 40 shillings to the poor in addition to multiple appearances on the penitents' stool.[111] Those whose fault had been merely to remain in town were generally given only one day of public repentance, and a few were excused altogether, such as the servant girl Jonet Aikenhead who, although she had remained in the castle while it was under siege, was forgiven

---

[107] *Ibid*, 3:225.

[108] SRO ms CH2/450/1, 1r-v.

[109] *Ibid*, 3v-4r, 32v.

[110] *Ibid*, 7v.

[111] *Ibid*, 30v, cases of John Stevenson and Thomas Ballantyne.

because she had been just ten years old at the time.[112] While an act of Parliament passed in the wake of the civil war had ordered that all former rebels be "admonischit be the pastouris and ministeris of the kirk to acknawledge thair offence and returne to thair detfull obedience," there is no evidence of such a process taking place anywhere but in the capital; all other contemporary session registers are silent on the subject.[113]

Not surprisingly, several of those summoned on such charges questioned whether political loyalty fell within the kirk session's bailiwick. Notable among these were Thomas MacCalzean of Cliftonhall, a senator of the College of Justice, and the advocate John Moscrope.[114] The latter protested in November 1574 that he could not be held accountable before the Kirk because he had already obtained a royal pardon for his activities during the civil war. He still had not submitted by the following September, when a public admonition and threat of excommunication finally induced him to perform repentance.[115] Resentment over activities during the late troubles could be targeted against elders as well, as in December 1574 when the merchant William Fairlie appeared in the session and charged Adam Fullarton, merchant and elder, with corrupt dealings during the conflict. The session considered the matter, ruled that Fullarton had done nothing wrong, and ordered the two to shake hands. Fullarton offered Fairlie his hand, "bot ye said Williame obstenatlie refusit to do ye same, saying y[a]t he [Fullarton] had wantit his geir and yrfoir [Fairlie] could not remit ye gurge of his hart." In response, the session suspended Fairlie from Communion.[116]

Fairlie's charge may have been motivated in part by a sense of disenfranchisement, because by the mid-1570s the Edinburgh Kirk Session, particularly the eldership, had become a rather select fraternity.[117] Fullarton, a leader among local protestants since 1559, was quite rich, and had taken legal action to confiscate goods and mulct erstwhile supporters of the queen in the aftermath of the civil war.[118] He was distinguished both by wealth and by a long and unwavering public commitment to protestantism. By 1574 it was impossible to become an elder without at least one, and preferably both, of these marks.

---

[112] *Ibid*, 56v.

[113] *APS*, 3:72-3. Along with St. Andrews (*StAKS*), there are contemporary registers for Aberdeen (SRO ms CH2/450/1) and Monifieth (NRH ms OPR 310/1).

[114] SRO ms CH2/450/1, 5v-6r, 28r-v, 31r-v, 46r-48r, 52v-54v, 60r-61r, 65r-v, 68v, 69v, 71v-72v.

[115] SRO ms CH2/450/1, 73r.

[116] *Ibid*, 32r.

[117] A point made previously by Michael Lynch in *Edinburgh and the Reformation*, 40-1.

[118] Lynch, *Edinburgh and the Reformation*, 282, 300.

The first session election for which records exist is that of October 1574. The leet, or list of candidates, was read from the pulpit early in the month. It contained 49 nominations for elder and only six for deacon. Of the 49, 22 were identified as merchants, and two as bailies, both of the latter being merchants as well. Eighteen were craftsmen, and four were lawyers. All six of the candidates for deacon were merchants.[119] But when the actual election took place late in the month (with no mention of who actually voted), only one of the eighteen craftsmen listed as candidates actually made it into the eldership. Seven of the rest dropped down and were elected as deacons, but even on the diaconate they were outnumbered by the nine merchants named. The twelve elders elected included six merchants (the two bailies among them), three lawyers, two clerks (including James McGill, clerk of register) and the lone craftsman, baxter David Kinloch.[120] The leet for the 1575 election is not given in the register, but the final list of elders and deacons displays similar characteristics to that of the previous year. Nobody was re-elected, but the twelve elders included only two craftsmen—a surgeon and a wealthy skinner. The others were five merchants (including a bailie), three lawyers, a senator of the College of Justice and the brother of an aristocrat. The sixteen deacons included seven merchants, six craftsmen, two lawyers and an apothecary.[121]

It was elections like these that led the craft deacons to complain in December 1574 that the merchants were shutting them out of burgh government, trying to raise the prices of burgess-ship and guildry, and electing officials without consulting the crafts.[122] Cuthbert Thompson, deacon of the fleshers, took this complaint to the regent two months later, leading burgh treasurer James Ross to charge that Thompson was "trubling...his lauchfull maiestratis contrair his aith."[123] The merchant oligarchy was determined to keep control of all civic institutions, the kirk session included.

Obviously, the town's ministry was also important in determining what actions the local kirk would take. With Knox dead and Craig departed for Montrose and, eventually, Aberdeen, Edinburgh hired a new corps of ministers, all of whom were involved with presbyterian radicalism by the 1580s. James Lawson, Walter Balcanquhal and John Durie can each be

---

[119] SRO ms CH2/450/1, 21r.

[120] Ibid, 23v-24v; Lynch provides some biographical details on those elected in Edinburgh and the Reformation, appendix iii, 269-71.

[121] SRO ms CH2/450/1, 75v; Lynch, Edinburgh and the Reformation, 271-3.

[122] Edin. Recs., 4:32-4.

[123] Ibid, 4:36.

identified as ministers in Edinburgh by 1574.[124] James Melville, whose ideological standards were high, reported "God glorified him self notablie with that ministerie of Edinbruche in these dayes," praising Durie in particular for his "continuall walking with God in meditation and prayer," although he was "of small literature." One report of Durie's triumphant return to Edinburgh after a short exile from the burgh in 1582 suggests that he was quite popular among the city's residents.[125] Lawson was to become prominent in the Kirk at the national level, serving on the executive committees of several general assemblies and on the committee which wrote the *Second Book of Discipline*.[126] He died in London, while in exile with the rest of Edinburgh's Melvillian ministers, in 1584.[127]

Thus Scotland's capital had a ministry with impeccable reformist credentials and a kirk session of high status. Table 3.8 details their disciplinary activities between April 1574 and November 1575. The Edinburgh Kirk Session's disciplinary caseload during this period was dom-

TABLE 3.8—BREAKDOWN OF CASES BY OFFENSE
CATEGORY, EDINBURGH KIRK SESSION, 1574-75

Offense category	Cases	Males	Females	No-shows
Sexuality	172(54%)	69	103	14 (8%)
Political disloyalty	94 (29%)	92	2	0
Quarrels within family	7 (2%)	4	3	0
Relig. diss./practice	7 (2%)	7	0	1 (14%)
Dress/consumption	6 (2%)	4	2	3 (50%)
Disobedient to kirk	5 (1.5%)	5	0	0
Total	321	202	119	28 (9%)

(Note: numbers within listed categories do not equal the totals due to other cases scattered throughout less common categories. "No-show" percentages calculated for within each sin category, but since session register does not record all summonses, real no-show rates were probably higher.)

---

124 Haws, *Scottish Parish Clergy*, 214.

125 *JMD*, 78; Calderwood 8:226.

126 *BUK* 1:362, 2:407, 469-70, 548; Calderwood 3:398, 410, 433-42.

127 Calderwood, 4:76, 167-9; *Wodrow Miscellany* 1, 449-51.

inated by sex and politics. It appears that the overtaxed disciplinary system had little time for anything else. With 12,000 residents, the burgh likely had roughly 7,000 communicants during this period. This unwieldy congregation was later split into four parishes, each with its own session, but in 1574-5, one session still had responsibility over all. Multiplying 321 cases by two-thirds, to get something like a one-year caseload (214), and then comparing it to 7,000 yields a ratio of approximately one annual case for every 33 communicants, far below the one to ten ratio displayed by the Canongate in the mid-1560s. Edinburgh's disciplinary apparatus did not touch many of the burgh's residents directly, and those who fell into its net could only have been the most obvious offenders. Naturally, pregnant women without husbands were the easiest targets, and many more women (103) than men (69) were charged with sexual offenses. Typical was Marion Kirk who on 7 April 1575 admitted that she had "sundry tymes...partlie throw ye fregillitie of ye fleche and partlie be ye instigatioun of Sathane...geven ye use of hir body...in ye fylthe syne and vise of fornicatioun."[128] Such language was common in the session register. Offenders were invariably told to perform public repentance, and, in some cases, fines were mentioned.[129] The bailies present in the session would often try to collect the fine on the spot, and those told to "satisfy" the magistrate in addition to public repentance probably had the choice of a fine or some form of ritual humiliation at the burgh's market cross. Even couples who committed fornication while engaged did not escape the session's attention; no sexual relationship unsanctified by an official church ceremony was acceptable.[130] Adultery was of course viewed as a more serious offense. Adulterers were referred to the superintendent and Synod of Lothian, and there told to perform public repentance on every preaching day until the next meeting of the General Assembly, which could be a period of several months.[131]

The session was also generally eager to determine where the children produced by illicit unions had been baptized, if at all. The record suggests that those who sought to avoid the censures of the Kirk by leaving the child unbaptized for any length of time were more harshly punished.[132] The Kirk was concerned to police baptism in part because it was often in seeking to have their children baptized that illicit couples came to the Kirk's attention;

---

[128] SRO ms CH2/450/1, 51r.

[129] Such as that of James Marjoriebanks, fined £3 in addition to his public repentance on 22 July 1574. See *ibid*, 13r.

[130] *Ibid*, 19v, 21v.

[131] *Ibid*, 19r, 22r.

[132] For example, Alexander Frier, whose child died unbaptized, Robert Cowan, whose child was still alive but unbaptized, and Ellen Borthwick, who said she no longer knew the whereabouts of her three-year-old child. *Ibid*, 18r, 19v.

baptism of the child could be made contingent on performance of public
repentance by the parents.

With 83 percent of its disciplinary attention taken up by sexual and
political offenses, the Edinburgh Kirk Session had time for little else when
it came to imposing new standards of behavior. There are no cases of
Sabbath breach, although observance of the Sabbath may have already been
enforced by the burgh's magistrates. Nor was the session much of a dispute
mediator. There are a few other scattered cases, however, which point to
a broader range of concerns. The session was willing to order that
consensual marriages proceed despite parental objections, and considered
two cases involving charges of usury.[133] The register also contains hints of
the increasing disapproval displayed by authorities throughout western
Europe of many aspects of popular culture.[134] Patrick Bell was hauled
before the session on 9 December 1574 and attacked "as ane blasphemer of
godis name and playar at kartis and dyce." He agreed to accept banishment
from the burgh if he again fell into these habits.[135] Janet Cady had fallen
afoul of the Kirk the previous August for dancing while dressed in men's
clothing.[136] The bailies who served on the session were told in January 1575
to speak to the burgh council about the problem of "colmone drinking and
dansing in hous[e]s fra aucht or nyne houris at ewin past."[137]

But the session did not simply operate through prohibitions. Its members
took seriously the obligation to care for the (godly) poor and catechize the
ignorant. Parishioners were examined on points of doctrine before being
given Communion tokens, although there is evidence that many skipped the
procedure altogether.[138] In October 1574 the session had to begin scheduling
Sunday preaching in the tollbooth due to the happy problem of overcrowd-
ing in St. Giles.[139] An attempt by burgh authorities in 1575 to replace the
old system of alms collection with a municipal poor tax was a disaster, and

---

[133] SRO ms CH2/450/1, 23r, 34r, 52r-v. Both usury charges were against women. Both
were ruled guilty, although in neither case was public repentance ordered. Marion Robertson,
who admitted receiving 6 pence weekly per pound, which would add up to an astounding 130
percent annually, was turned over the the magistrates for civil punishment. No punishment was
mentioned in the case of Issobel Clark, who admitted that she loaned Robert Ferguson 20s at
the even higher interest rate of 4s per week.

[134] Peter Burke, *Popular Culture in Early Modern Europe*, (London: Maurice Temple
Smith, 1978), 207-34.

[135] SRO ms CH2/450/1, 33v.

[136] *Ibid*, 15v.

[137] *Ibid*, 38v.

[138] *Ibid*, 4r, 55r.

[139] *Ibid*, 22r.

charity was back in the session deacons' hands by the following spring.[140]

Of course the Edinburgh session still faced the problem of dissent. Some dissenters were brought into the fold, such as the Catholics James Marjoriebanks and Alexander Purves, excommunicated for six years, who joined the Reformed congregation in July 1574. Both had to perform public repentance in sackcloth two Sundays and two weekdays before they were accepted, but they apparently complied.[141] Neill Lang was less contrite. Charged with orchestrating "pompous convoy and supperflowis banketting" at his sister's wedding in violation of kirk ordinances, he refused to perform repentance when ordered, and reportedly proclaimed

> in grit disdane and disspyt yat he rather wald be of the devillis kirk [than] be of ye kirk of this burgh and that he sould nevir be ane member tharof and wald nocht knaw the same as ye kirk and that ye elderis and deaconis wer bot fallowis, w[i]t[h] sic other mast opprobrius and dispytfull words....[142]

Lang's dissent may have been fueled more by anger than theological reflection and later, probably in a calmer mood, he denied the statement.[143] But the outburst demonstrates how the legitimacy of the session—still a relatively new institution—was vulnerable to attack.

The working people of Edinburgh were not too busy (or illiterate) for religious musing, either. The minister John Durie reported hearing Walter Thomson, a messenger, tell John Seton, a dyer, that prayers for the dead were necessary for their salvation. Thomson said such a view was confirmed by Judas Maccabeus, to which Seton replied that the First Book of Maccabees "wes apographa and sua wes not in ye can[on]s of the ebrewis and it wes not the ditement of the spreit of god and sua na cradeit aucht to be gevin yairto." Brought before the session, Thomson said he had merely posed the question, but did not himself believe in Purgatory.[144] One wonders how many other such conversations passed unheard by the ministry or session members.

Obviously, the Edinburgh session had more business than it could handle. It had a clear program for reform, and was willing, on occasion, to hear cases involving a wide range of offenses. Some of these, like usury, loomed large in ministerial denunciations, but rarely received much

---

[140] *Ibid*, 27v, 57r. The register lists weekly alms collection (and sometimes distribution) totals. Collections fell drastically during the experiment with the poor tax. See also *Edin. Recs.*, 4:39-40, 48-9; Lynch, *Edinburgh and the Reformation*, 20.

[141] SRO ms CH2/450/1, 10v, 11v, 12v-13r.

[142] *Ibid*, 42r, 50v.

[143] *Ibid*, 51v.

[144] *Ibid*, 37v.

attention from the post-Reformation church courts.[145] Others, like gambling and dancing, were later to become targets of puritans everywhere. But for the time being, it was all the session could do to try to keep the illegitimacy rate down, feed the worthy poor, and force former rebels to display remorse. This last concern looms unnaturally large in this snapshot because of the moment at which it was taken—just after the civil war. But Edinburgh had been divided against itself, and some of that division would spill into the disciplinary proceedings of the burgh church. Aberdeen, far to the north and removed from the center of conflict, played a more ambivalent role in the civil war. There, the kirk session had fewer issues and fewer parishioners to concern itself with, and not much of a program at all.

Aberdeen

The city fathers of Aberdeen accepted the Reformation with great hesitation, as described earlier.[146] Many of the steps they took toward reform came only under outside pressure. The early history of Aberdeen's kirk session provides a good example of this reluctance. Created in 1562 in response to a visit from the earl of Moray, and in order to distance the burgh from the rebellion of the Catholic earl of Huntly, the session ceased to function as soon as the political crisis had passed. It was briefly resurrected in 1568, just after the deposition of Mary Stewart, only to be abandoned two months later when the the queen's supporters took control of the burgh. It was not until September 1573, with the civil war settled, that a lasting kirk session was established, its foundation coinciding with the arrival of John Craig—formerly minister in the Canongate, Edinburgh and Montrose—to take the parochial charge.[147]

It is reflective of the peculiar religious *status quo* in Aberdeen that Catholicism was considered no impediment to membership on the session, provided one was of sufficient local importance. The leading Catholic elected in September 1573 was also the first elder listed: the burgh's provost, Thomas Menzies of Pitfodels. In all, five of the thirteen elders

---

[145] T.C. Smout, *A History of the Scottish People, 1560-1830*, (Glasgow: William Collins, 1969), 150.

[146] See chapter two, above.

[147] SRO ms CH2/448/1, 19 (manuscript paginated rather than foliated); John Stuart, ed., "The Chronicle of Aberdeen, MCCCCXCI-MDXCV," *Spalding Club Miscellany* 2, (Aberdeen: Spalding Club, 1842), 29-70, at 40. For a biographical sketch of Craig, in all respects a moderate, see T. Angus Kerr, "John Craig, Minister of Aberdeen and King's Chaplain," in Duncan Shaw, ed., *Reformation and Revolution, Essays Presented to Hugh Watt*, (Edinburgh: Saint Andrew Press, 1967), 100-23.

listed can be identified as men who had actively opposed the Reformation in 1559-60, and only one as a supporter.[148] While the opinions of some may have changed in the intervening thirteen years, it is certain that several of these men's wives were still avowedly Catholic in 1574; the old faith still ruled their hearths if not their hearts.[149]

The Menzies family in particular was associated with Catholicism. Provost Thomas Menzies kept a family priest until his death in 1576. His son Gilbert, who succeeded him as provost that year, declined to participate in the Reformed Communion ceremony, and never served on the session.[150] In all, eight members of the Menzies family were mentioned as Catholics in the session register, and only two of them were ever induced to sign the *Scots Confession*.[151] The main family line, Menzies of Pitfodels, remained Catholic until it died out in 1843.[152] Nevertheless, there were multiple elders from the Menzies family on all but one of the seven sessions elected from 1573 to 1580, and the name was never entirely absent from the eldership.[153]

No other family was constantly present on the session in such high numbers as the Menzies. But the session was nevertheless largely a closed preserve of Aberdeen's leading families. The Grays were represented, at least as deacons, on all seven sessions elected from 1573-80. The Chalmers had members on five, as did the Knowles, Lumisdens, Johnstons and Hunters. Next came the Cullens (who supplied the kirk's reader during the period), Rutherfords, Middletons and Forbes, with members on four of the seven sessions. This oligarchy held itself together through ties of marriage and baptism; the Cullens, for example, were connected through baptismal sponsorship with the Menzies, Rutherford, Forbes and Gray families. These ties, visible through the carefully-recorded witnessing of baptisms, were of considerable social importance. In addition, Walter Cullen, reader in the burgh church of St. Nicholas, inherited the vicarage there from an uncle, John Collison, who was a Catholic priest, and the grant was confirmed in

---

[148] The supporter was David Mar. Opponents were: Provost Menzies, Gilbert Menzies Sr., Alexander Chalmer Sr., George Middleton (bailie in 1573-4) and Andrew Hunter. See SRO ms CH2/448/1, 19; *Aber. Recs.*, 1:315-9. For a discussion of lingering Catholicism in the burgh, see Allan White, "The Impact of the Reformation on a Burgh Community: The Case of Aberdeen," in Michael Lynch, ed., *The Early Modern Town in Scotland*, (London: Croom Helm, 1987), 81-101, at 96-7.

[149] SRO ms CH2/448/1, 34, 38, 40, 47, 50-1.

[150] *Ibid*, 46; Bruce McLennan, "The Reformation in the Burgh of Aberdeen," *Northern Scotland* 2 (1974-7), 119-44, at 137.

[151] SRO ms CH2/448/1, 34, 40, 46, 47, 50-1.

[152] McLennan, "Reformation in Aberdeen," 133.

[153] SRO ms CH2/448/1, 19, 53, 77, 99, 121, 133; "Chronicle of Aberdeen," 52.

1577 by the court of William Gordon, Catholic bishop of Aberdeen.[154] Such family connections were too strong to be broken by religious differences, and religious ambivalence was to color the session's attitude toward recusancy, as will be seen.

Despite the dominance of the session by a few families, elders and deacons did not serve in near perpetuity, as in St. Andrews. In preparation for the election of October 1574, leets were drawn up with twice as many names as there were available offices, and read aloud to the congregation.[155] An election followed, but no mention is made of who voted. Nevertheless, not a single elder or deacon was re-elected from the previous session, although several fathers were replaced by sons or nephews, and vice-versa.[156] Such openness did not become habitual, however. In October 1575, four elders from the 1574-5 session were named again, and seven of the 1573-4 elders were brought back. Only two elders were chosen who had not served on one of the two previous sessions, and they came from the safely prominent families of Menzies and Rutherford.[157] A rotation system became so common that the session elected in October 1577 did not contain a single elder who had not served on at least one of the previous two sessions.[158] Also reflective of the religious, political and social conservatism of Aberdeen is the fact that this last session was "inauguraitt" by the new bishop of Aberdeen, David Cunningham, who had himself just been consecrated by Patrick Adamson, the Erastian and strongly anti-presbyterian archbishop of St. Andrews. Episcopal inauguration of the session was repeated two years later.[159]

The most obvious effect this conservatism had on the session's disciplinary activities was in its mild treatment of Catholics. Men who were themselves Catholics, crypto-Catholics or who had Catholic wives could hardly spearhead an orthodoxy crusade which might find a target too close to home. The session chose to proceed delicately, ruling on 12 November 1573 that those "transgressors againis ye Religion" who did not attend sermons "be first handillit & travellit w[i]t[h] gentilly, gif be ony meanis possiblie yai may be von."[160] Marjorie Urquhart, examined on her religious beliefs in March 1575, refused to promise she would attend the Reformed Communion, saying she "had sic ane pyk on hir c[on]science yat show culd

---

[154] "Chronicle of Aberdeen," 36-40, 45.

[155] SRO ms CH2/448/1, 51.

[156] *Ibid*, 53.

[157] *Ibid*, 77.

[158] *Ibid*, 121.

[159] "Chronicle of Aberdeen," 46, 52.

[160] SRO ms CH2/448/1, 25.

not be fulle of yis p[rese]nt religione now in Scotland." No action was taken against her, and several months later she did sign the confession of faith.[161] Thomas Menzies, son of the provost, was certainly treated gently; first summoned in April 1574, he declined to appear before the session until June, and then simply declined to say whether he would join the Reformed congregation. Nothing more was said on the matter.[162]

Under such circumstances, it might be asked why the session bothered with Catholics at all. In fact, it was clearly reluctant to take up the issue. From its refoundation in September 1573 until the following April it handled only one case of religious dissent.[163] But by that time the minister Craig, who, although no radical, was unwilling to tolerate open recusancy, was unhappy with this inactivity. On 15 April, he presented a bill of complaint to the session, which the session referred to the burgh council.[164] The nature of the grievance was not specified, but it probably concerned laxity in pursuing dissenters, because a number of prominent Catholics were summoned before the session in the following ten days. All were asked to join the Reformed congregation, and some did, but none who refused were punished.[165] In addition to Craig, there may have been elders pressing for action as well. David Mar, Aberdeen's leading protestant in 1559-60, was a session elder, and a true believer such as he would have been more likely to play an active part in session meetings than the Catholic provost.[166] And, as it had on previous occasions, Aberdeen soon felt external pressure to show more commitment to reform.

The earl of Huntly had coerced the burgh into supporting the exiled queen during the civil war, and, in October 1572, with the fortunes of the queen's party on the wane, the council had voted him a gift of 600 marks to get him to remove his soldiers from the burgh.[167] Although whatever support the burgh gave to him had been lukewarm and forced, its officials were nevertheless tainted by it. The earl of Morton, regent for James VI, paid a visit in August 1574, and the town offered him a contribution of 4000 marks to help him overlook its past associations.[168]

---

[161] *Ibid*, 66, 71.

[162] *Ibid*, 34, 40.

[163] *Ibid*, 25-6, case of Mr. Robert Rowst, who was told to perform public repentance three times.

[164] *Ibid*, 34.

[165] *Ibid*, 34-5, 40. See also Allan White, *Religion, Politics and Society In Aberdeen, 1543-1593*, (Edinburgh University Ph.D. Thesis, 1985), 294-5.

[166] *Aber. Recs.*, 1:315-6.

[167] *Ibid*, 2:7.

[168] *Ibid*, 2:11-3, 18; "Chronicle of Aberdeen, 41; Hewitt, *Scotland Under Morton*, 39-40. Of the 4,000 marks, 1,000 was later forgiven.

But because the Marian cause, as well as that of the Gordon earls of
Huntly, had been identified with Catholicism, Morton insisted that the burgh
government distance itself from the old faith. He summoned the four bailies
(all of them session elders) and ordered them to forbid "the superstitious
keping of festvall days usit of befor in tyme of ignorance & papistrie." He
also told them to enforce Sabbath observance, redesign the kirk for
Reformed worship by removing the organ and priests' stalls, and take order
with those who kept images "or utheris monumentis of ydolatrie" in their
homes.[169] He also extracted promises from Gilbert Menzies, younger, (son
of the provost) to join the congregation, and from his uncle Gilbert Menzies
(a bailie and elder) to get his own Catholic wife and children to do
likewise.[170]

While there were a few scattered instances of Catholics being called
before the session and urged to join the congregation after Morton's visit,
its most tangible result in terms of the burgh kirk's disciplinary agenda was
a mild crackdown on the celebration of Christmas. Fifteen people, fourteen
of them women, appeared before the session on 30 December 1574, and
granted that they were guilty of "plaing, dansink & singin off fylthy
karrells" on Yule Day. The lone male, a cordiner who apparently was
summoned as a representative of the town's craftsmen, admitted merely to
"kepin halyday on youlday," and displayed little remorse.[171] All of the
group were given private admonitions and sent home. Such leniency may
have been too much for the burgh council, which was more anxious to keep
Morton happy, and on 25 January, several craft deacons were summoned
before the council. They were charged with abstaining from labor on
Christmas, and celebrating the occasion instead. The craftsmen replied that
the session had already dealt with the matter, but nevertheless denied that
they had observed the traditional holy day in any particular fashion.[172]

There are no further examples of the session charging anyone with Yule
observance in the extant register, which ends in November 1578. It appears
that the matter was simply delegated to the craft deacons; the session
ordered them in January 1577 to investigate whether any craftsmen had
been guilty of "sitting ydill" the previous Christmas.[173] Such vigilance was
unlikely to deter any of the traditionally-minded, but since the feast only
occured once a year and there were no more visits from the regent in the
offing, the issue got little further attention. Not surprisingly, other aspects

---

[169] SRO ms CH2/448/1, 61.

[170] *Ibid*, 46-7.

[171] *Ibid*, 58-9.

[172] *Aber. Recs.*, 2:25-6.

[173] SRO ms CH2/448/1, 107.

of Aberdonian zeal flagged as the regent's visit faded into memory as well; the session (or perhaps the minister and some of the more committed elders) complained to the council in February 1575 that the acts passed in the regent's presence the previous August were not being enforced.[174]

In fact, when left to their own devices, the elders of Aberdeen confined their disciplinary concerns largely to sexual matters and the regularization of marriage. The few cases (14 in all) handled during the session's brief incarnations in 1562-3 and 1568 had all been sexual, and this trend continued after its 1573 refoundation, as table 3.9 demonstrates. The session devoted 85 percent of its caseload to combatting sexual sin and ensuring that marriage would be a legal state sanctified by a church ceremony. Of the remaining cases, more than half related to open Catholicism or lingering

TABLE 3.9—DISCIPLINARY CASES HANDLED BY ABERDEEN
KIRK SESSION, 1573-78

Offense category	Cases	Males	Females	No-shows
Sexuality	291 (65%)	130	161	19 (7%)
Marriage	88 (20%)	67	21	3 (3.5%)
Relig. diss./practice	37 (8%)	12	25	5 (14%)
Sabbath breach	6 (1.5%)	6	0	0
Popular culture	5 (1%)	0	5	0
Total	446	229	217	30 (7%)

(Note: numbers within listed categories do not equal the totals due to other cases scattered throughout less common categories. "No-show" percentages calculated for within each sin category. Due to irregularity in recording summonses, no-show figures should be regarded as minimum estimates.)

Catholic practices, and both of these were local phenomena which the session addressed reluctantly, as we have seen. There is little trace of the concern for political correctness shown in Edinburgh, or resolution of quarrels, as in the Canongate. And although the five years comprised a relatively short period, they were, in effect, the first five years in which Reformed social discipline was enforced in Aberdeen. This makes a year-by-year breakdown, such as that given below in table 3.10, useful. The

---

[174] *Ibid*, 65.

most obvious trend visible in table 3.10 is the diminishing enthusiasm of the session. From a peak caseload of 207 in 1574, its first full year of existence, its case numbers dwindled to 41 in 1577 (the last full year for the register) and a mere 14 for the first ten and a half months of 1578. One estimate places the total population for Aberdeen and Auld Aberdeen, its smaller northern neighbor, at 4,000 during this period.[175] Assigning 1,000 of those to Auld Aberdeen would leave 3,000 in Aberdeen proper, of which perhaps 1,800 were adults. This would mean that more than one in ten adults fell afoul of the session in 1574, a level of disciplinary intensity comparable to that shown in the Canongate in the mid-1560s. But by 1577 the ratio would have sunk to a far milder one in forty-four.

It is hard to believe that the residents of Aberdeen would have changed their behavior in such a short time, and the May 1577 threat by Craig to

TABLE 3.10—CASELOAD BREAKDOWN BY YEAR, ABERDEEN
KIRK SESSION, 1573-78

Year	Total cases	Sexuality	Marriage	Religion	Other
1573*	31	26 (84%)	2 (6%)	1 (3%)	2 (6%)
1574	207	102 (49%)	61 (29%)	33 (16%)	11 (5%)
1575	87	60 (70%)	21 (24%)	3 (3.5%)	3 (3.5%)
1576	66	55 (83%)	4 (6%)	0	7 (11%)
1577	41	37 (90%)	0	0	4 (10%)
1578*	14	11 (79%)	0	0	3 (21%)

*partial years—register begins in September 1573, ends in November 1578

resign unless the session enforced its own statutes suggests they had not.[176] The elders had probably decided that the sort of scrutiny practiced in 1574 was no longer necessary (lacking external political pressure) nor in keeping with local needs and traditions. In November 1577, Craig requested that the bailies and session enforce the acts of Parliament regarding fornication. The bailies replied that such a policy could only be enacted by order of the burgh council, and the unfilled blank space left in the register for the

---

[175] McLennan, "Reformation in Burgh of Aberdeen," 129.

[176] SRO ms CH2/448/1, 114. The entry in the register indicates that Craig complained to the General Assembly as well.

council's reply speaks volumes.[177] These philosophical disagreements may explain Craig's abrupt departure from the burgh and his charge in September 1579, as well as the disapproving tone in which it was described by the reader Walter Cullen, member of an old Aberdonian family.[178]

The session had certainly begun its activities with pious resolve, declaring on 8 October 1573 that no children "born in huirdom" would be baptized until their parents had performed public repentance.[179] But this policy was almost immediately abandoned. Perhaps it seemed too draconian, when newborn mortality was so high, to force children to wait unbaptized for their parents to perform a ritual that most were in no hurry to undertake. The elders may simply have been too attached to legal custom to imagine using different procedures in the session than they did in any other local court, despite the fact that, in theory at least, the session was unique. For whatever reason, by late October 1573 they were regularly ordering the baptism of children born out of wedlock, provided the parents were able to find a cautioner to pledge that they would perform the required repentance.[180] This had the effect of postponing the latter indefinitely, and there only seem to have been sporadic efforts to enforce the cautionary agreements later on. In July 1574, the session found it necessary to remind people that public repentance was to take place in the kirk on Sunday during preaching, and listed 29 fornicators who had not yet performed it, some of whom had found caution to do so months before. A similar reminder was issued the following June.[181]

Sexual sinners were obviously reluctant to undergo new and humiliating punishments for offenses which had been winked at in the recent past. Public repentance could injure honor, both for offenders and their families. Thus on 11 November 1574, the session gave William Davidson (possibly the elder of that name) "many exhortationeis," to "suffer" his wife to do public repentance for her adultery, but "he answured stuburnely, that in no wayes wold he suffer hir to do any more then she had done." Public admonitions were ordered against him, with no clear result.[182]

While public repentances may have been performed only sporadically,

---

[177] *Ibid*, 125. There is one example of civil punishment in the council register; on 9 August 1577, two women and another person whose sex is unclear were banished for fornication committed "in sic abhominabill sort nocht worthie to be rehersit." See *Aber. Recs.*, 2:29. It should also be noted that many sexual offenders were fined, as will be discussed below.

[178] "Chronicle of Aberdeen," 51, which states he "left his floik on prowyditt of ane minister, to be preschour to the kingis grace, as he allegit."

[179] SRO ms CH2/448/1, 22.

[180] *Ibid*, 22-6.

[181] *Ibid*, 43-4, 72.

[182] *Ibid*, 56.

the session showed increasing willingness to order fines against sexual offenders. Rare before 1575, fines soon became common; of 55 sexual offenders in 1576, 47 were stated explicitly to have been fined. Amounts could vary, depending on the wealth of the individual and his or her past behavioral record.[183] While it was never stated for what purpose the money raised through fines was used, support of the poor and payment of the minister, reader, kirk officer and session clerk seem likely uses for this form of "sin tax." By the end of the period, offenders were generally told either to pay a stated fine or stand several hours at the market cross with paper crowns on their heads emblazoned with their offenses.[184] Doubtless, all who could afford the fine paid it rather than endure the humiliation. This procedure, coupled with the haphazard enforcement of public repentance, would have allowed sexual sinners of any substance to avoid entirely the public acknowledgement of their offenses.

One behavioral concern the Aberdeen elders did apparently take seriously was irregular marriage. This issue received much more attention in Aberdeen than in any other community examined in this study.[185] The Church throughout western Europe had been trying to gain control over the institution of marriage since the eleventh century,[186] and northern Scotland was one of the final frontiers in this effort. There is some debate on how widespread the custom of "handfast" marriage—in which couples would seal their alliance outdoors or at home, before witnesses but not necessarily clergy—was in sixteenth-century Scotland. The authors of one recent study have opined that it was certainly dead by the mid-seventeenth century, except perhaps in the Highlands.[187] But it is clear that it was alive and well

---

[183] The highest fines recorded were for Gilbert Menzies, the provost's son (and himself provost after 1576), who was fined £10 for fornication on 2 June 1575, and David Menzies, also charged with fornication, who was initially charged a £20 fine, but the amount was reduced to £10 on that same day. The lowest fine was for Elspet Jak, charged with fornication on 15 March 1576, and fined 3 shillings. Fines of 5 shillings, 6s8d, 20s, 2 marks (26s8d), 4 marks (53s4d) and 5 marks (66s8d) were quite common. See *ibid*, 60, 68, 70, 89.

[184] *Ibid*, 106, 109, 111, 112-6.

[185] The "marriage concerns" sin class employed throughout this study includes both cases of breach of promise to marry (resiling), parental objection, and slowness to regularize marriage, where the couple is cohabiting already as man and wife. Whereas most cases in this sin class outside of Aberdeen involve the first two, almost all of the cases from Aberdeen involve the latter.

[186] Georges Duby, *The Knight, the Lady and the Priest*, (New York: Pantheon Books, 1983), *passim*; John Bossy, *Christianity in the West, 1400-1700*, (Oxford: Oxford University Press, 1984), 21-4; John Gillis, *For Better, For Worse: British Marriages, 1600 to the Present*, (Oxford: Oxford University Press, 1985), 11-54.

[187] Rosalind Mitchison and Leah Leneman, *Sexuality and Social Control: Scotland 1660-1780*, (Oxford: Basil Blackwell, 1989), 101-2.

in Aberdeen 'in the 1560s and 1570s.

The Aberdeen session in its two brief early incarnations had expressed the desire to standardize local marriage custom and bring it within the purview of the Kirk. In 1562 it lamented the custom of handfasted couples to cohabit as long as seven years without formal marriage, ordered that all such couples marry within the church, and that future marriage promises be recorded by the session clerk.[188] In 1568 it forbade the minister or reader to be present at handfastings, and declared that couples would not be considered legally married without the public reading of banns and a church ceremony. Those who had sexual relations before the latter would be regarded as fornicators.[189] The suspension of the session's activities shortly thereafter, coupled with the high incidence of recusancy in the area, rendered moot any effort by the Reformed Kirk in this regard until the session was re-created in 1573. But on 22 October 1573, a couple charged with fornication was told to find caution that they would marry by Christmas; their banns had been proclaimed three years before.[190] Two men then appeared in December who were not charged with fathering illegitimate children, but merely with slowness to regularize their marriages.[191] Shortly thereafter a woman had to find caution that she would "fall nev[er] again in blasphemy again[st] ye sacraments off ye kirk or haly band off mat[ri]mony as sho did befoir...."[192]

The following year brought a veritable roundup of couples—in some cases only represented by the male—who were living together without having formalized their marriages. There were 46 couples involved, and 57 individuals actually appeared before the session. Most were given a deadline to marry formally, and threatened with fines for failure. This dragnet cast a wide net, capturing two Menzies as well as many of their humbler neighbors. The fact that irregular marriages were accepted locally is verified by the session clerk's occasional tendency to refer to the woman in these couples as the "wife."[193] Clearly, local opinion regarded them as already married.

But the session (including, apparently, its more conservative elders) wanted to change local marriage custom. It passed an order in June 1574 that all couples who wanted to marry had to give in their banns to be read

---

[188] SRO ms CH2/448/1, 8-9.

[189] SRO ms CH2/448/1, 16.

[190] Matthew Fields and Margaret Ross, *ibid*, 22. Note that this is treated as a sexual case in the database, because it was the child born out of wedlock which brought the matter to the session's attention.

[191] *Ibid*, 26.

[192] *Ibid*, 27.

[193] *Ibid*, 31, 68.

and at the same time find caution that they would remain celibate until formally marrying.[194] Unlike other sessional pronouncements, this one seems to have worked. It became quite common for couples thereafter to appear before the session, request that their banns be read, and find a cautioner (usually the bride or groom's father), that they would not "adheir together" until the formal ceremony.[195] Violators were fined and at least told to perform public repentance as fornicators. As far as marriage questions are concerned, the dwindling caseload after 1574-5 (see table 3.10) is probably reflective of the Aberdeen session's success rather than its flagging interest. Marriage was a legal issue, with implications for property and family alliance. Children who were officially legitimate could inherit whether or not their parents had written wills. This was one area in which the generally conservative Aberdonian elders were happy to use the new apparatus of the Reformed Kirk to clear an old legal thicket.

Otherwise, there was little sign that the behavioral ideology of the Reformed Kirk had had much effect in Aberdeen by 1578, when the session register ends. True, sexual sinners paid fines, but many apparently did nothing more than that. There were scattered cases of Sabbath breach in 1576 and 1578, and elders were delegated in March 1576 to stroll on the links to record the names of those playing golf during Sunday preaching.[196] But offenders were only fined small amounts, or let off with a warning. The burgh council in October 1576 forbade the sale of fish or meat during Sunday preaching, but the rest of the day remained free for commerce, and the order had to be repeated four years later.[197] The only attention the session gave to popular culture was its treatment of five women charged with dancing in men's clothes; one was given a fine and public repentance in 1576, while four others were merely admonished the next year.[198] There were no denunciations of drink, games, music or gambling. The session was very slow to order public admonitions against anyone, and only clearly did so on one occasion.[199] Only once did it resort to excommunication, and that was against an adulterous couple who refused to appear and answer charges in September 1573.[200]

By the time the next extant session register from Aberdeen begins, in October 1602, the elders were willing to fine people for offenses such as

---

[194] *Ibid*, 41.

[195] *Ibid*, 42-3, 44-6, 60 and *passim*.

[196] *Ibid*, 88-9, 101, 129.

[197] *Aber. Recs.*, 2:27-8, 38.

[198] SRO ms CH2/448/1, 87, 108.

[199] *Ibid*, 87, 117.

[200] *Ibid*, 21.

Communion absence, collecting the sums from them before they left the session room.[201] But much had occurred, both nationally and locally, between 1578 and 1602, and new generations had come to maturity, marrying and baptizing children in a burgh church which was at least nominally reformed. Many of the same families (including the Menzies) still predominated in session lists, but those elders had apparently become accustomed to the uses of Reformed discipline. In most respects, the Aberdonian Reformation must have taken place between 1578 and 1602.

In examining the practice of Reformed discipline before 1582 in St. Andrews, the Canongate, Edinburgh and Aberdeen, we have seen how the concept could be adapted to different urban environments, and how it might both reinforce and clash with existing power structures. Many urban Scots opposed the new order, often vocally. Different elderships chose to attack particular problems, with the session of St. Andrews sporadically attempting to pursue the wider Reformed program—including religious orthodoxy, maintenance of the Sabbath and required Communion attendance—more enthusiastically than any of the other sessions scrutinized. The Canongate's elders, on the other hand, used the session to sanctify the burgh council's traditional role as dispute arbiter. Edinburgh, rent by the civil war, found in its overworked session an enforcer of political orthodoxy. In Aberdeen, where nearly all of the elders would have had to perform public repentance for their former political leanings if held to the standards of Edinburgh, the session chose to use Reformed disciplinary procedures to bring marriage more fully under control of the Kirk. Of course in all of these communities, the elders' first concern was to discourage sexual relationships outside of marriage; any particular local campaigns came after that. It was on this issue that the widest consensus existed. Illicit sex was a leading social problem, and the pregnancy which often resulted made it an easy offense to detect. Nevertheless, individual sessions varied in their enthusiasm to track it down and punish it.

But the evidence employed thus far in this chapter has been almost entirely urban. The vast majority of Scotland's population lived in rural areas. Were rural craftsmen, servants, farmers, lairds and feuars feeling the effects of religious revolution to the same extent that their urban countrymen were? Was Reformed social discipline an influential factor in rural Scotland before the creation of the presbyteries?

Reformed Discipline in Rural Scotland Before 1582

The evidence for assessing the impact of Reformed discipline outside of the

---

[201] SRO ms CH2/448/2, 5.

burghs before 1582 is thin indeed. Only two registers from predominantly rural parishes have survived in even fragmentary condition, and their irregularity makes it difficult to use them in any quantitative way, as the urban registers have been employed.[202] Of course, the paucity of surviving material may be evidence that relatively few rural parishes even had sessions. Doubtless some rural registers have been lost, but how many? The St. Andrews Kirk Session sent a letter in 1560 "to all ministeris, eldaris and diacons of the congregatioun of Anstruthir," and its minutes make reference to the existence of elders at Crail in 1565, but these scraps of evidence do not prove the existence of a working session in either parish.[203] The St. Andrews session did feel the need to take up quite a few cases from the villages of eastern Fife, and in many of them there is no reference to local disciplinary proceedings. Firm conclusions are impossible, but any case for widespread rural disciplinary practices before the advent of the presbyteries would have to rely more on faith than reason.

Attempts to establish rural sessions were bound to encounter difficulties not found in cities. First of all, in larger burghs such as Edinburgh, St. Andrews or Aberdeen there were already governing institutions, such as burgh councils and craft guilds, which were accustomed to collective responsibility. These could lend experience, authority and membership to newly-established kirk sessions. Many of these bodies had exercised some control over their urban churches even before the Reformation, so ecclesiastical administration was not foreign to them. In rural areas, barony courts were generally dominated by an individual—the superior or his representative—and their jurisdictional boundaries were not necessarily coterminous with those of the parish. At Monifieth in Angus, for instance, several estates in the parish were part of the Angus Douglas regality of Kerriemuir, while two others (Ardownie and the subdivided Ethiebeaton) were not, being held instead either under the earl of Crawford or directly from the crown.[204] The parish of Anstruther Wester in 1580 contained four tiny burghs in three different baronies, plus at least one additional lordship. The minister took a peripatetic approach to this problem, convening two

---

[202] The registers are Monifieth (Angus), NRH ms OPR 310/1 and Anstruther Wester (Fife), NRH ms OPR 403/1 and StAUM ms CH2/624/1. Anstruther Wester was, technically, a burgh, but it was tiny, and many of the parishioners came from the surrounding countryside or the equally tiny neighboring burghs of Anstruther Easter, Pittenweem, or Kilrenny.

[203] *StAKS*, 1:22-3, 258-9. An (unfinished) order from the Regent Moray in 1567 made reference to a penitent stool in the kirk at Anstruther. See *Historical Manuscripts Commission: Sixth Report*, (London: HMSO, 1877), 643.

[204] J. Malcolm, *The Parish of Monifieth in Ancient and Modern Times*, (Edinburgh: William Green, 1910), 31; Frank Bardgett, *Scotland Reformed: The Reformation in Angus and the Mearns*, (Edinburgh: John Donald, 1989), 99.

sessions (with different memberships) at various locations throughout the parish. One parish laird was given a free hand to choose all the elders and deacons from within his own lordship.[205] But where one laird held the right of ministerial patronage while several others held many of the estates in the parish, the former was bound to chafe at sharing ecclesiastical authority with the latter group, whose members might be at odds with each other over land or jurisdictional disputes.

One possible result of all this was that several local notables would band together and use the kirk session as a forum to attack one or more prominent opponents in the neighborhood. This seems to be what happened at Monifieth, where a clique formed around the Durhams of Grange, using adultery charges to harass another local faction headed by the families of Guthrie and Ramsay in the late 1570s and early 1580s.[206] Being too closely identified with one local patron could present a danger to the kirk though, as in 1565 when William Lovell of Ballumbie took advantage of the absence of William Durham of Grange from the area to sack the parish kirk, eject the minister from his manse, and raze the cottages of kirk tenants.[207]

But, on the whole, lairds such as the Durhams of Grange were able to nurture and protect the infant Reformed kirks in their parishes, as long as the political and economic fortunes of the family were good. Certainly, opponents came under attack in disciplinary cases for political or economic reasons, but many parish functions also had a sound foundation in sincere belief. William Durham of Grange was one of the two representatives from Forfarshire at the original General Assembly in December 1560, and played an active role in several of the assemblies which met in the following decade. He was a nephew of the leading lay reformer of the Mearns, John Erskine of Dun.[208] The kirk session at Monifieth, on which he was the most prominent elder, had established a regular system of alms collection and distribution by the mid-1560s, and there were already at that time scattered examples of individual parishioners being required to do public repentance for adultery or fornication.[209]

Also contributing to the potential strength of a rural kirk session was

---

[205] The burghs were Anstruther Wester and Pittenweem, belonging to the abbey of Pittenweem, Kilrenny, belonging to the family of Beaton of Balfour, and Anstruther Easter, belonging to John Anstruther of that ilk. In addition, the parish contained the lordship of Caiplie and several other rural estates. See NRH ms OPR 403/1, 12r, 22r-24v, 27r, 28r.

[206] NRH ms OPR 310/1, 41r, 42r, 43v, 45v, 47v, 57v; Bardgett, "The Monifieth Kirk Register," *RSCHS* 23 (1988), 175-95, at 186-8; *ibidem, Scotland Reformed*, 117, note 92.

[207] Malcolm, *Parish of Monifieth*, 53; *Register of the Privy Council of Scotland*, 1:685-6.

[208] *BUK*, 1:3; Calderwood, 2:45, 289, 293-4, 378-83; Bardgett, *Scotland Reformed*, 100; Malcolm, *Parish of Monifieth*, 92, 337.

[209] E.g. NRH ms OPR 310/1, 8r, 10v.

continuity of office. Some burgh churches saw the need to replace the entire eldership every year, as seen earlier in the examples of Edinburgh, the Canongate, and, at least on one occasion, Aberdeen. Even where there was, in effect, a rotational system under which nearly all the elders would have had previous experience on the session, the annual turnover would often cripple administrative continuity. This was not a problem on rural sessions where elections were infrequent, and elders generally served for life. Local lairds, feuars and substantial tenants were obvious choices for the eldership, and could rarely be replaced. The Monifieth session recorded only three session elections before the 1590s—in 1573, 1575 and 1579. Of the eight elders of 1573, three were still serving in 1579, while two others had been replaced by sons or other relatives, and a deacon of 1573 had been promoted to the rank of elder. Only one new surname had entered the eldership.[210] Such a session had the advantage of experience and continuous service on its side. Even the diaconate was the preserve of a few families.

An entrenched group, controlling most of the land in a parish, would have faced little opposition from social inferiors, most of them tenants or servants. Whatever disciplinary agenda the elders decided to follow would have had considerable local authority on its side. Opponents would have lacked the forum of rival institutions such as burgh councils or craft guilds in which to attack or impede the session's operations. Even credit could be under the session's control; the Monifieth session loaned out money and threatened with poinding (seizure of goods) a debtor who had not made timely payment in March 1581.[211]

TABLE 3.11—DISCIPLINE AT MONIFIETH, 1579-81

Year	Cases (all sexuality)	Males	Females	No-shows
1579	13	6	7	7
1580	5	3	2	2
1581	6	3	3	1
Totals	24	12	12	10

[210] *Ibid*, 21r, 41v.

[211] *Ibid*, 48r.

Given such power and authority, it is significant that the elders of Monifieth took a very narrow view of what Reformed discipline entailed.The session's register is too fragmentary and heavily damaged to attempt a complete assessment of its disciplinary activities before the late 1570s, but table 3.11 sums them up for the period 1579-81.

The Durhams of Grange had been leading laymen in the regional reform movement since its beginning, and the lairds of Angus and the Mearns have been celebrated for their early zeal in embracing the Reformation.[212] But, as late as 1581, discipline here meant only sexual discipline. There is no trace of concern with religious orthodoxy, Sabbath-breach, Communion attendance, or popular culture. Further, despite a near-monopoly on local authority, the session had considerable difficulty in inducing offenders to appear before it. Ten of the 24 sinners charged during the three-year period never responded to a summons. It is possible that many of these no-shows came from the estate of Laws, whose laird was at odds with the session and who was himself charged with adultery; two of them certainly did.[213] But whatever the reason, the Monifieth Kirk Session was still a remarkably inefficient agent of social discipline.

The session also maintained a low profile in another respect. Combining and dividing the cases in table 3.11 yields an average annual caseload of eight. Yet the parish clerk recorded Communion attendance figures of 700 for 1579 and more than 600 for 1580.[214] Averaging these to 650 yields a ratio of one annual case for every 81 communicants, the lowest level of disciplinary intensity yet encountered in this study.

If, as the Scots reformers maintained, discipline was the third mark of the true church,[215] it was one of which the parishioners of Monifieth had not yet seen a great deal of evidence. Those living in the many rural parishes without sessions would have seen even less. Even major burgh churches such as Aberdeen's were failing in the effort to enforce new behavioral standards. Clearly, the parochial Reformation needed organizational help from above. The superintendencies had withered; the presbyteries would be the next step in the ongoing Scottish experiment in church polity.

---

[212] Knox 1:317; Bardgett, *Scotland Reformed*, 101.

[213] NRH ms OPR 310/1, 41r-v, 43v, 45v-46r, 47v, although Henry Ramsay, laird of Laws did himself appear and perform three public repentances in 1580-1.

[214] *Ibid*, 41v, 45r. No figure is mentioned for the Communion in 1581, if one took place.

[215] G.D. Henderson, ed., *The Scots Confession, 1560 and the Negative Confession, 1581*, (Edinburgh: Church of Scotland, 1937), 75.

CHAPTER FOUR

THE CREATION OF THE PRESBYTERIAN SYSTEM

Becaus thai heve not a pastor and also thair kirk [is] al[to]gether decayit,
thair is na eldaris, deacones nor forme off disciplein in this congregatione
quhairthrow sin and vyce gretlie abundis amangis thame....
- visitor's report from parish of Port of Menteith
(Stirlingshire), 19 August 1586[1]

Quhen we speik of eldaris of particular congregationis we mene not that every
particular paroche kirk cane or may have thair awin particular eldarschip,
especiall to landwart [i.e., in rural areas], bot we think thrie or four, ma or
fewar, particular kirkis may have ane commoun eldarschip to thame all to
judge thair ecclesiasticall causes.
- *The Second Book of Discipline*[2]

Despite the efforts of the Reformed ministry and well-disposed laity in the
first two decades of the Scottish Reformation, Scotland in the early 1580s
included far too many parishes like Port of Menteith, which, aside from
occasional services conducted by a reader, were left by the Kirk to their
own devices. In such communities, most of them rural, the Reformation
could thus far have had little impact.

The first obstacle to thoroughgoing reform in many areas was the
shortage of competent ministers.[3] As a transitional measure, the Kirk had
appointed readers in parishes without ministers, or to assist ministers in
large parishes, such as St. Andrews.[4] But the readers, many of them former
Catholic clergy, lacked the educational qualifications deemed necessary for
the Reformed ministry, and the Kirk was increasingly concerned by the
1580s that readers were dispensing (or selling) baptisms for the offspring
of illicit unions and performing marriages between couples who were not

---

[1] James Kirk, ed., *Visitation of the Diocese of Dunblane and Other Churches, 1586-1589,*
(Edinburgh: Scottish Record Society, 1984), 11.

[2] James Kirk, ed., *The Second Book of Discipline*, (Edinburgh: Saint Andrew Press, 1980),
199.

[3] The proportion of parishes served by ministers varied greatly between regions. In Perthshire, for instance, there were only 21 full ministers for 100 parishes in 1567, while East
Lothian had 13 ministers for its 25 parishes. In both areas there were readers as well, bringing
the total clergy for Perthshire to 78 and for East Lothian to 20. See Gordon Donaldson, *The
Scottish Reformation*, (Cambridge: Cambridge University Press, 1960), 87-8.

[4] *Ibid*, 83-4.

technically free to marry.[5] Such actions undermined the disciplinary authority of the Kirk.

Equally crippling to the Kirk's disciplinary authority was the fact that many parishes, including some of those with ministers, lacked kirk sessions. It was noted in the previous chapter how few rural session registers from the early years of the Scottish Reformation have survived, and this suggests there may have been relatively few to start with. Evidence from the late 1580s suggests that, in Stirlingshire, Perthshire and Clackmannanshire, at least, readers rarely established sessions, and ministers occasionally neglected to do so as well.[6] The lairds resident in a parish might be called "elders" and might convene for visitations, but this does not necessarily mean they met regularly with the minister or reader as a kirk session.

The General Assembly was not blind to these failings in the parochial reformation. This concern, along with discontent over the pro-episcopal policies of the Regent Morton, led the body in 1576 to appoint a committee to draft a new "book of policie," a document which was accepted formally by the assembly in 1581, and eventually came to be called the *Second Book of Discipline*.[7]

The Second Book of Discipline

Much of the discussion of the *Second Book of Discipline* has centered on the role of Andrew Melville (1545-1622). Historians have disagreed both over the extent of his influence in its writing (he was one of 30 on the committee which drafted it), and the degree to which it changed substantially the polity of the Kirk. Melville, the son of an Angus laird, had as his intellectual mentor the Parisian scholar Pierre Ramus, while spiritually he was a protegé of Theodore Beza, Calvin's successor in Geneva. In 1574, after ten years abroad—the first four as a student in Paris and the last six as a professor in Geneva—he returned to Scotland to take a principal's post in the University of Glasgow.[8]

---

[5] E.g. *SPR*, 74-5, 90-2, 96-7, 101-2, 130-2, 172-3; *Dunblane Visitation*, 19. It should be noted that ministers were not exempt from such failings, either. See *SPR*, 11-2, 100-1.

[6] *Dunblane Visitation*, *passim*, esp. 11, 15, 29, 33.

[7] *BUK* 1:362, 2:488-512; Calderwood, 3:417, 433-42, 529-54; Kirk, ed., *Second Book of Discipline*, 41-8 *et passim*.

[8] The only full biography of Melville is the hagiographical work of Thomas McRie, *The Life of Andrew Melville*, (Edinburgh: William Blackwood, 1856). He also gets good press in the writings of his nephew James. See Robert Pitcairn, ed., *Autobiography and Diary of Mr. James Melvill, minister of Kilrenny*, (Edinburgh: Wodrow Society, 1842), *passim*, esp. 83-4, 123-6, 143-4, 307-8. For more modern discussions, see James Kirk, *The Development of the Melvillian Movement in Late Sixteenth Century Scotland*, (Edinburgh University Ph.D. Thesis, 1972), 1:164-83; and Michael Lynch, "Calvinism in Scotland, 1559-1638," in Menna

The archbishop John Spottiswoode (1565-1639), recalling events which occurred when he was only ten (but with which his father, one of the original superindendents, would have been familiar), said Melville was "a man learned...but hot and eager upon any thing he went about, labouring with a burning desire to bring into this Church the presbyterial discipline of Geneva."[9] James Kirk, who rejects the notion of Melville as a radical, dismisses Spottiswoode as "an obviously hostile commentator." To Kirk, it was Morton, with his attempts to revivify the episcopate in the 1570s, who was the real innovator.[10] But even the Presbyterian David Calderwood, an ardent admirer of Melville, suggested that Morton was wary of Melville's "new opinions, and over-sea dreames tuiching discipline and policie of the Kirk."[11] Significantly, the controversy created by Melville's ideas caused Lord Glamis, Morton's chancellor, to write to Theodore Beza in Geneva, seeking clarification.[12] In hostile eyes, the Scottish Kirk was certainly now associated with "the Babilon Geneve," as a 1581 ballad-style lampoon of Melville and his fellow ministers characterized it, urging them "to Geneve haist with speid."[13] In this particular debate, Gordon Donaldson's position—even if somewhat exaggerated with its characterization of Melville as a "presbyterian missionary" from Geneva—makes more sense than Kirk's.[14] Melville (although not working alone) sought further reform in the Scottish Kirk, and the *Second Book of Discipline*, however limited his contribution to it, was a blueprint for significant change.

The *Second Book of Discipline* was firmly anti-episcopal, and contained proposals for educational reform and the financial strengthening of the Kirk. The disciplinary role of the elders remained essentially unchanged from the *First Book*. Elders were "to watche diligentlie upon the flok committit unto

---

Prestwich, ed., *International Calvinism, 1541-1715*, (Oxford: Clarendon Press, 1985), 225-55, at 234-6.

[9] Spottiswoode, 2:200.

[10] James Kirk, "The Polities of the Best Reformed Kirks: Scottish Achievements and English Aspirations in Church Government After the Reformation," *Scottish Historical Review* (1980), 22-53, at 39-41; *ibidem, Development of Melvillian Movement*, 1:223.

[11] Calderwood, 3:369.

[12] Gordon Donaldson, ed., "Lord Chancellor Glamis and Theodore Beza," *Scottish History Society Miscellany* 8, (Edinburgh: Scottish History Society, 1951), 89-116.

[13] Nicol Burne, *Ane Admonition to the Antichristian Ministers in the Deformit Kirk of Scotland*, (n.p., 1581), reproduced in D.M. Rogers, ed., *English Recusant Literature, 1558-1640* 135, (Menston, Yorkshire: Scolar Press, 1973) (no pagination).

[14] Donaldson, *Scottish Reformation*, 190-3. Donaldson also claims that that with Melville and his following, the leadership of the reform party within the Kirk passed from men who were primarily pastors to those who were academics, although this is debatable. While Andrew Melville was a professor, other Kirk leaders of the 1580s and 1590s, such as Robert Bruce, Nicol Dalgleish, David Lindsay and James Melville, were parochial ministers.

thair charge, bayth publicklie and privatlie, that no corruptioun of religioun or maneris enter thairin."[15] But there was one important difference: rather than being elected annually, these new elders were to serve indefinite terms, possibly for life.

While some have sought to downplay its significance,[16] the creation of what could be in essence a life eldership was a significant break with past practice in some areas. Many of the elders of the St. Andrews kirk session were already serving for life, as we have seen, but other communities, such as Edinburgh, the Canongate and (on occasion) Aberdeen, replaced some or all of their elders on a regular basis. Granted, this did not preclude a yearly rotational system, as seems often to have been practiced, but there was an important philosophical distinction between elders who served for life (like the minister with whom they sat on the session), and those who faced annual election. One aristocratic critic welcomed this change, specifically noting that it was "playne contrarie [to] the ordor that hes bene observit quhair eldaris hes bene zeirlie electit through the haill realm."[17]

The initial creation of the Reformed consistory can be seen as part of the effort by laymen across all of Europe to wrest some control over the Church from the clergy. But the *Second Book*, written by parochial ministers and academic theologians, sought to co-opt this movement by making lay elders and deacons clergy of a sort themselves. As Walter Makey has written, "the *Second Book of Discipline* rested on the assumption that the godly society had failed and the assertion that its failure had sprung from the futility of the lay church of the reformers."[18] So, it specified that ministers, elders and deacons should all be considered "ministeris of the Kirk," with a special vocation.[19] Under its terms, elders would only be replaced for gross moral failings, or if they had served for several years and found the task too burdensome.[20] In addition to sitting on the local session, one or two lay elders would represent the parish in a district eldership.

While never mentioned in it by name, the presbytery was certainly an outgrowth of the program laid out in the *Second Book*. The idea seems to have originated in the "exercise," a group of ministers from adjacent parishes who would gather to discuss scripture and doctrine.[21] In July 1579,

---

[15] Kirk, ed., *Second Book of Discipline*, 193.

[16] Such as James Kirk. See his introduction to *Second Book of Discipline*, 89-92.

[17] NLS ms Adv. 29.2.8, 128v.

[18] Walter Makey, *The Church of the Covenant, 1637-1651: Revolution and Social Change in Scotland*, (Edinburgh: John Donald, 1979), 10.

[19] Kirk, ed., *Second Book of Discipline*, 174, 178.

[20] *Ibid*, 192. A draft of the *Second Book* was already in circulation by June 1578, when the General Assembly held at Stirling endorsed the life eldership. See Calderwood, 3:413.

[21] Ian Cowan, *The Scottish Reformation*, (New York: St. Martin's Press, 1982), 131-2.

with the *Second Book* already under consideration, the General Assembly ruled that, until presbyteries were formally established, "the exercise may be judged a presbyterie."[22] This new body was the equivalent of the colloquy, present in the structure of the French Huguenot churches since at least 1572.[23] The term actually used in the final draft of the *Second Book* was "commoun eldarschip." As proposed, this would be composed of ministers and elders of "thrie or four, ma or fewar, particular kirkis," and was held to be particularly necessary in rural areas, where the parochial structure was weak.[24] In a later passage, the authors of the *Second Book* suggested that every parish need not have an eldership, "bot onlie in the townis and famous places quhair resort of men of jugement and habilitie to that office may be had."[25] The General Assembly apparently took "commoun eldarschip" to mean "presbytery," and in October 1580 appointed a committee "to lay and devyse a platt of the Presbytries."[26]

Political Crisis and Ecclesiastical Uncertainty, 1581-86

The resolution passed in April 1581, under which the General Assembly assigned parishes to 13 pilot presbyteries, reflected the limited regional strength of the Reformed Kirk at that point.[27] These presbyteries were to be set up as "examplatour to the rest that may be established heirafter." They were: Edinburgh, Dundee, St. Andrews, Perth, Stirling, Glasgow, Ayr, Irvine, Haddington, Dunbar, Chirnside, Linlithgow and Dunfermline. Their sizes ranged from 13 parishes (Dunbar) to 28 parishes (Perth), with a total of 266 parishes placed in some presbytery. Even the smallest of these was more than three times the size suggested for the common eldership in the *Second Book*. And, since Scotland at this time included over 900 parishes,[28]

---

[22] Calderwood, 3:450.

[23] Although the colloquies met only infrequently. See Glenn Sunshine, "French Protestantism on the Eve of St. Bartholomew: The Ecclesiastical Discipline of the French Reformed Churches, 1571-72," *French History* 4 (1990), 340-77, at 341, with text from 1571 *Discipline* of La Rochelle at 365; François Méjan, ed., *Discipline de l'Eglise réformée de France*, (Paris: S.C.E.L, 1947), 254-5; Michel Reulos, "L'Histoire de la Discipline des Eglises Réformées Françaises, élément de l'histoire de la Réforme en France et de l'histoire du Droit Ecclésiastique Réformé," in Leo Olschki, ed., *La Storia del Diritto nel Quadro delle Scienze Storiche*, (Firenze: Societa Italiana di Storia, 1966), 533-44, at 542, (although Reulos exaggerates the uniqueness of the Huguenot polity); James Kirk, "The Influence of Calvinism on the Scottish Reformation," *RSCHS* 18 (1972-4), 157-79, at 171.

[24] Kirk, ed., *Second Book of Discipline*, 199.

[25] *Ibid*, 231.

[26] *BUK*, 2:469-70.

[27] *BUK*, 2:482-7.

[28] Donaldson, *Scottish Reformation*, 94.

The Thirteen
Proposed Presbyteries
of 1581

North

Sea

Moray Firth

Highland Line

Dundee
Perth
St.
Andrews
Firth of Tay

Dunfermline
Firth of Forth
Stirling
Linlithgow
Edinburgh
Haddington
Dunbar

Glasgow
Irvine
Ayr
Chirnside

Irish

Sea

• Indicates the thirteen proposed
presbyteries of 1581

England

50 Miles

considerably less than a third of the country was thus organized.

Clearly, presbyterian discipline at first could only have been a regional phenomenon. There is also little firm proof that many of these presbyteries actually began to meet. The only presbytery records prior to 1586 which have survived are from Stirling and Dalkeith; the fact that Dalkeith was not even mentioned in 1581 should serve as a warning against assumptions based purely on General Assembly records.[29] Other evidence suggests that the presbyteries of Glasgow and Edinburgh were active in 1582, and the General Assembly was told of "elderships" (which, in the context, may have meant presbyteries) meeting in Montrose, Brechin, Dundee, Perth, Strathearn, Dunkeld, Linlithgow, Ayr and Irvine that same year.[30] While several of these were not among the 13 presbyteries of 1581, it is in most cases impossible to say whether lay elders were participating in meetings, or what sorts of disciplinary matters (if any) were being handled. As late as 1595, the presbytery of Peebles, just 22 miles south of Edinburgh, professed uncertainty as to whether it had the authority to try disciplinary cases.[31]

Commissioners who had been ordered to oversee the foundation of presbyteries would be questioned by the General Assembly, and some may have simply told the assembly what its increasingly presbyterian leadership wanted to hear: that the presbyteries were in operation. But some of the more obvious weaknesses in the system could not be covered up. A commissioner reported in April 1582 that he had made no progress toward establishing a presbytery in Aberdeen, and that northern presbytery remained unfounded a year later.[32] This problem was not unusual, particularly in the north. "None were present to declare what was done in Caithnes, Ross, Sutherland or Murrey" at the April 1582 General Assembly.[33] George Hay, who had been given responsibility for those areas, did appear in October 1582, but could report no progress.[34] All he could offer the assembly the following April was a plan to locate presbyteries in Moray.[35]

Nor was the north the only problem area. The assembly of April 1582

---

[29] *SPR*; SRO ms CH2/424/1. The records for Stirling begin in 1581, and for Dalkeith a year later.

[30] *BUK*, 2:549-50, 598-600; Calderwood, 3:596-8, 621-2.

[31] James Kirk, ed., *The Records of the Synod of Lothian and Tweeddale, 1589-1596, 1640-1649*, (Edinburgh: Stair Society, 1977), 94.

[32] *BUK*, 2:549, 613. The records for the Aberdeen Presbytery do not commence until 1598. See SRO ms CH2/1/1.

[33] *BUK*, 2:550.

[34] *Ibid*, 2:586-7; Calderwood, 3:680.

[35] *BUK*, 2:613.

was told that there were only three ministers in the vicinity of Falkland, "quhairof ane was found slanderous." This shortage of competent manpower torpedoed plans for the creation of a presbytery there, in the heartland of protestant Fife.[36] Teviotdale, in the border region, was declared poor ground for presbyteries later that same year, also due to a lack of ministers.[37] The presbytery of Haddington, one of the original 13, was dissolved in October 1583 "be reason of the many enormities occurreand ther," which were tolerated by lackadaisical elders and contemptuous residents.[38] Dunbar Presbytery was threatened with similar action in 1593, due to the "greit negligence amangis the brether [ministers of the presbytery]."[39] Haddington and Dunbar were both in the immediate neighborhood of Edinburgh, where the General Assembly usually met. Negligence was probably even greater, if less detectable, farther away.

Hampered by the chronic manpower problems of the parish ministry, the presbyteries were also beset by political controversy. The period 1578-86 was one of great uncertainty as to the future government of Church and state. The earl of Morton had lost the regency in 1578, but continued as the dominant influence in government until his removal and execution in 1580-1. Upon Morton's demise, the teenage king began ruling in his own name in fact, as he had been doing in theory since 1578. The creation of the presbyteries had been a political challenge to the monarch, since they took over many of the functions which Reformed bishops might have performed. The Leith Convention of 1572 had envisioned an episcopate which would continue as long as the king was a minor, but all bets were off once he took the reins of government into his own hands. The Godly Monarch would have little role to play in the presbyterian system as formulated in the *Second Book of Discipline.*

The king soon fell under the influence of his francophone cousin, Esmé Stewart, seigneur d'Aubigny, who had returned to Scotland in 1579, was made earl of Lennox in March 1580, and duke in August of the next year.[40] His meteoric rise was accompanied by his efforts to reassert traditional

---

[36] *BUK*, 2:549.

[37] *Ibid*, 2:586-7; Calderwood, 3:681.

[38] *BUK*, 2:635; Calderwood, 3:747.

[39] Kirk, ed., *Records of the Synod of Lothian*, 62.

[40] Gordon Donaldson, *All the Queen's Men: Power and Politics in Mary Stewart's Scotland*, (London: Batsford, 1983), 132-5. Esmé was the nephew of Matthew Stewart, earl of Lennox, the king's paternal grandfather, who had briefly served as regent in 1570-1, before his death in the civil war. Since Matthew's eldest son, (James' father) was dead, the earldom passed to his younger son Charles, who died in 1576. From there it went to Matthew's brother Robert, an elderly bishop, who resigned it in Esmé's favor, receiving the earldom of March in exchange.

Lennox Stewart claims to land and influence, mainly at the expense of the Douglases (Morton's family) and Hamiltons. Captain James Stewart, a younger son of Lord Ochiltree, was soon rewarded with the earldom of Arran, held to be vacant due to the insanity of the Hamilton earl. While the king was nominally ruling on his own, Lennox and Arran were dominant influences by the middle of 1581.

Lennox's nomination that year of Robert Montgomery, minister of Stirling, to the vacant archbishopric of Glasgow, further politicized the presbyteries, and encouraged Lennox's political foes to seize upon the issue of church polity in their struggle against him.[41] In October 1581, the General Assembly ordered Montgomery to remain minister at Stirling and not take up the archbishopric under pain of excommunication. He was charged with having been negligent in assisting the elders of Stirling in their enforcement of discipline, and with having taught that "the discipline of the Kirk is a thing indifferent."[42] Montgomery's case was then referred to the Stirling Presbytery.[43] After battling the Stirling Presbytery for several months, he was excommunicated, apparently by the Edinburgh Presbytery, in June 1582.[44] That same month the Stewart laird of Minto, provost of Glasgow, led a band of his retainers into a meeting of the Glasgow Presbytery, demanding that the Kirk stop all proceedings against Montgomery. Unsatisfied by the presbytery's reply, Minto's group beat up the moderator, knocking out one of his teeth, and locked him in Glasgow's tollbooth for three days.[45] Subsequent efforts by the General Assembly to take action against Minto and his followers were blocked by the king. The populace of Edinburgh, however, displayed its sympathies by pelting Montgomery with stones and eggs as he was led out of the burgh after the Edinburgh Council expelled him in July.[46]

Lennox himself was exiled from the realm when his foes, headed by the earl of Gowrie, staged a palace revolution—the "Ruthven Raid"—in August 1582, seizing the king.[47] The Edinburgh Presbytery and the Synod of Lothian were quick to back the raid, ordering ministers John Durie and John Davidson to canvass the barons of Lothian and Teviotdale and seek signatures for the political band drawn up by the Gowrie faction.[48] Later,

---

[41] Donaldson, *All the Queen's Men*, 139-40.

[42] *BUK*, 2:533-4, 542; Calderwood, 3:579-80, 582-3; *SPR*, 6-10.

[43] *BUK*, 2:546-7; *SPR*, 12-15.

[44] *SPR*, 17-22, 31, 35-40; Calderwood, 3:621.

[45] *JMD*, 131; Calderwood, 3:621. The Glasgow Presbytery had previously been summoned before the Privy Council for its refusal to accept Montgomery as bishop. See *ibid*, 3:596-8.

[46] *BUK*, 2:579-80; Calderwood, 3:626, 633.

[47] Donaldson, *All the Queen's Men*, 140-1.

[48] Calderwood, 3:675.

the General Assembly formally endorsed the raid on the grounds that the perpetrators had been acting to protect the Kirk, and the laird of Minto and some of his followers confessed their offenses before the assembly.[49]

This did not quell anti-presbyterian activities in outlying areas, however. David Russell, bailie of St. Andrews and elder on the session there, reportedly read a letter before the local congregation in March 1583 denouncing the presbyterian system as lacking scriptural warrant.[50] And the Kirk did not long enjoy the luxury of a sympathetic governing faction; in June 1583, King James escaped from the Gowrie faction. Arran was soon free from the confinement to which the Ruthven Raid had condemned him, and by the end of the year he was the leading influence in James' government.[51]

One of Arran's first targets in the Kirk was Andrew Melville, who was charged in February 1584 with seditious preaching. After he claimed that complaints regarding his sermons in St. Andrews could only be tried before the presbytery of St. Andrews, he was ordered imprisoned in Blackness Castle. Melville fled to England instead, the first drop of what would become a flood of Presbyterian refugees later that year.[52] An attempt by Gowrie and some followers to mount a counter-coup in April 1584 led to Gowrie's execution and an attack by Arran's government on the presbyterian system, now tainted by association with the defeated faction. The General Assembly which convened at St. Andrews that same month was sparsely attended and soon broke up, reportedly due to royal intimidation.[53] More importantly, the Parliament of May 1584 passed the so-called "Black Acts." These noted that a number of courts not approved by Parliament had been created since 1560, "contrare ye custome observit in ony vther christiane kingdome" and tending to the weakening of the king's authority. Such courts (i.e., the presbyteries) were therefore banned. Further, all ministers were to subscribe to an oath recognizing the king's ultimate authority over the Kirk.[54]

The crisis occasioned by the "Black Acts" left wounds among the

---

[49] *BUK*, 2:594-9; Calderwood, 3:676-9, 688.

[50] *BUK*, 2:616-7; Calderwood, 3:710-11.

[51] Donaldson, *All the Queen's Men*, 144-5.

[52] *JMD*, 142-4; Spottiswoode, 2:308-9. For the exiles generally, see Gordon Donaldson, "Scottish Presbyterian Exiles in England, 1584-8," *RSCHS* 14 (1960), 67-80.

[53] Calderwood, 4:37.

[54] *APS*, 2:293. Patrick Adamson, archbishop of St. Andrews, appeared before the St. Andrews Kirk Session on 17 June to clarify the legislation, specifying that the session was to continue meeting and handling disciplinary cases. The acts of Parliament had only aimed "to inhibeit the new erectit Prisbittreis," he said. The Edinburgh session received a similar license to meet. See *StAKS*, 2:529; Calderwood, 4:72-3.

Reformed ministry which would take more than a decade to heal. Many ministers, particularly in Edinburgh, St. Andrews and the Lothians, chose exile over subscription, while another group, headed by John Craig and John Duncanson, ministers to the royal household, and John Brand, minister of the Canongate, signed the acts after adding the clause "according to the Word of God." The elders and deacons of Edinburgh were summoned to Falkland Palace to face the king's wrath for refusing to condemn their ministers' flight as desertion. Nicol Dalgleish, an Edinburgh minister who remained but refused to subscribe, was convicted by an assize of treason (on the grounds of his correspondence with the exiles) though spared execution.[55]

The political crisis, unlike the ecclesiastical one, passed more quickly. The earls of Angus and Mar, leading nobles of the Gowrie faction who had fled with their ministers into exile, returned to Scotland near the end of 1585, and Arran, increasingly unpopular as an upstart, was soon out of power. The result was a government by coalition, including on the one hand former supporters of the queen as well as members of Arran's faction, and on the other members of the Gowrie group.[56] A February 1586 agreement between the king and many of the exiled ministers, now returned, cleared the way for the re-creation of the presbyteries and for the General Assembly to meet again.[57]

The Growth and Consolidation of the Presbyterian Disciplinary System, 1586-96

While the presbyterian system did not receive formal approval from Parliament until 1592,[58] it was by then already on fairly solid footing in parts of lowland Scotland. The crown and the Kirk still disagreed over polity and procedures (especially when the latter sought to discipline noblemen friendly with the king[59]), but the period from 1586 to 1596 was one of increased cooperation between the two. This was based on a mutual interest in the suppression of disorder and in defending the crown against both foreign Catholic intrigue and domestic diabolical *maleficia*. The

---

[55] Calderwood, 4:123-4, 210-11, 236-7, 246-7; *JMD*, 218-9; *Pit. Crim.*, 1(pt. 2):136-8.

[56] Donaldson, *All the Queen's Men*, 147-9.

[57] Calderwood, 4:491-4. This recognized the existence of bishops as well, but gave the General Assembly and its subsidiary courts - the synods, presbyteries and sessions - control over discipline and excommunication.

[58] *APS*, 3:541-2. This, the so-called "Golden Act," approved by name the kirk session, presbytery and synod, although it gave to the monarch the power to dictate the time and location of general assemblies.

[59] This issue will be discussed in chapter seven, below.

ministers and the king were particularly united on the dangers posed by the latter; royal intervention followed the revelation in 1590 of a plot against James' life by a coven of witches in North Berwick in cooperation with Francis Stewart, earl of Bothwell, leading to the first widespread witch hunt in Scottish history.[60] A year earlier, when the king departed for his marriage in Denmark, the Edinburgh minister Robert Bruce, an ardent Presbyterian, was placed on the privy council.[61] James, attending the General Assembly of August 1590, gave thanks to God "that he was born in such a time, as in the time of the light of the Gospell, to such a place to be King, in such a Kirk, the sincerest Kirk in the world."[62]

In September 1594, Andrew and James Melville accompanied the king northward as he sought to quell the rebellion of the earl of Huntly and his allies.[63] It seemed that James was willing to treat the Kirk as a buttress to his monarchy on terms largely proposed by the ministers themselves, in an effort to promote the rule of law, and attack the problems of endemic feud and rebellion. Never again would the Reformed Kirk wield such influence with the Stewart monarchy.

This growth in influence began with the February 1586 agreement between the king and representatives of the Kirk noted above. The General Assembly of May 1586 held one of its sessions in the Chapel Royal at Holyrood Palace, and approved an ambitious plan for the creation (or, in some cases, re-creation) of 51 presbyteries. The vast majority were still in the southern lowlands, though, and only two were proposed north of the Dornoch Firth.[64] An inquiry by the General Assembly in April 1593 found only 47 presbyteries in operation, and it is impossible to say how diligent these were; some may not have been disciplinary bodies, or may have met only infrequently.[65] Only 19 presbyteries were active (or informed) enough

---

[60] *Pit. Crim.* 1(pt. 2):185-6, 191-204, 206-13, 230-57; Spottiswoode, 2:411-12; Christina Larner, *Enemies of God: The Witch-hunt in Scotland*, (London: Chatto and Windus, 1981), 60-1; Arthur Williamson, *Scottish National Consciousness in the Age of James VI: The Apocalypse, the Union and the Shaping of Scotland's Public Culture*, (Edinburgh: John Donald, 1979), 48-9, 53, 55, 59-61.

[61] *JMD*, 277.

[62] *BUK*, 2:771.

[63] *JMD*, 318-22.

[64] Nor was a commissioner named to create the two, to be located at Thurso and Dornoch. See *BUK*, 2:648-9; Calderwood, 4:555-6. The convening of one session of this assembly at Holyrood was to prove significant in light of later claims by the king to dictate the time and place of general assemblies.

[65] *BUK*, 3:799-800; Calderwood, 5:245-6. Peebles Presbytery, while listed among the 47, apparently did not handle disciplinary cases and tolerated pilgrimages to the "preistis hauch" at Peebles. The burgh kirk's minister told the Synod of Lothian and Tweeddale in April 1592 that he did not preach regularly out of fear of his life. See Kirk, ed., *Records of the Synod of*

to send representatives to the assembly held at Perth in February/March 1597, and it was reported in March 1600 that the presbyteries at Ayr and Irvine, two of the original 13, still did not meet regularly.[66] Fifty-three presbyteries were listed as active in December 1606, however, with the lowland regions south and east of the Grampian Mountains generally covered.[67]

The presbyteries were an important addition to the disciplinary apparatus of the Kirk. Those which met regularly and were diligent in pursuit of their mission gave previously isolated ministers the moral (and sometimes physical) support of their peers, and a forum for the discussion and dissemination of General Assembly directives. They also provided an intermediate district court to which recalcitrant or serious disciplinary offenders could be summoned in lieu of referral to the semi-annual synods and general assemblies. This had the potential of making discipline much more effective, because the infrequency of synods and general assemblies, coupled with the distance of travel involved, had made it difficult to force sinners to attend.

One way the presbyteries did not develop as initially planned, however, was in the early exit of lay elders from their ranks. The minister/historian John Row, son of the co-author of the *First Book of Discipline*, claimed that, in the early days at least, each minister attending a presbytery meeting brought a lay elder with him.[68] The presence of prominent laymen could have greatly enhanced the disciplinary authority of the presbyteries, but it appears that lay elders virtually ceased to participate after the restoration of the presbyteries in 1586. The Edinburgh Presbytery was moved the following year to lament the absence of the "baronis and gentilmen" who had helped found the presbytery, but had little luck getting them to return to meetings.[69] No lay elders were listed in the sederunts of the Stirling Presbytery between 6 September 1586 and 31 October 1592, and the presence of two on that latter date was not soon repeated, even at half

---

Lothian, 41, 81, 88, 94. The 47 listed presbyteries did not include Stirling, which was certainly in full operation at this time, but Dunblane was listed among the 47, and the Dunblane ministers were then part of the Stirling Presbytery, so the listing of Dunblane must be taken for Stirling instead. See, for example, WRH ms CH2/722/2, 21 August 1593, 4 September 1593, 18 September 1593 (no folio markings).

[66] *BUK*, 3:910-11, 950; Calderwood, 5:607, 6:23.

[67] *BUK*, 3:1035-8. For a brief sketch of the development of presbyteries after 1600, see Walter Roland Foster, *The Church Before the Covenants: The Church of Scotland, 1596-1638*, (Edinburgh: Scottish Academic Press, 1975), 85-8.

[68] Row, 1:13-4.

[69] SRO ms CH2/121/1, 29v. The Edinburgh Presbytery did sometimes include laymen in the delegation it sent to the General Assembly, though. See *ibid*, 46r, and 10 June 1589, 25 February 1590. (foliation stops in late 1588).

strength.[70] The records of the St. Andrews Presbytery do not include sederunts, but the presence of John Beaton, laird of Balfour, on 27 October 1586 was rare enough to be considered worthy of mention.[71] Lay elders may have lost interest as the presbyteries became less concerned with discipline and more involved in supervision of the ministry, a professional responsibility which occupied most of their time by the late 1580s. Such oversight was likely quite tedious to the typical lay elder, who would have had to defer to the ministry in such technical matters anyway. Whatever the ultimate reason, the decline in lay influence had been presaged back in April 1582, when the General Assembly ruled that presbyteries had to have fewer lay elders than ministers and doctors (professors of theology).[72] By monopolizing the presbyteries, the ministry could overcome lay control of local kirk sessions, where elders vastly outnumbered ministers. Laymen did not return in significant numbers to presbyteries until the revolutionary year of 1638.[73]

What were the behavioral concerns of this increasingly ministerially-dominated Church? Discipline at the parish and presbyterial level after 1581 will be discussed in subsequent chapters, but it would be worthwhile here to examine the rhetoric of the national Kirk during the same period. As noted in chapter two, sexuality was the leading concern of the General Assembly during the 1560s and early 1570s, with this obsession waning somewhat in the late 1570s. By 1580, a clear change in emphasis was underway. The politicization of the Kirk in the late 1570s and early 1580s, coupled with a perception by the Melvillians that the nobility was turning away from its earlier commitment to reform, made Catholicism and "apostacie" the primary concerns of the national Kirk in the last two decades of the century.[74] The leading ministers saw themselves surrounded by backsliders within the nation, and threatened by the machinations of Spain and the revived papacy from without. In August 1588, expecting an imminent attack by the Spanish Armada, the General Assembly proclaimed

---

[70] *SPR*, 228; WRH ms CH2/722/2, (unfoliated) 31 October 1592. Laymen previously named as elders were also present to aid the presbytery on 12 March and 27 August 1588, although they were not listed in the sederunts. See WRH ms CH2/722/1, 12 March 1588, 27 August 1588. The attendance of lay elders in the period 1581-4 was not uncommon in either Stirling or Dalkeith, the two presbyteries for which pre-1586 records have survived. See *SPR* and SRO ms CH2/424/1, *passim*.

[71] *StAP*, 4. There are no further instances of laymen mentioned as present except those who were summoned or sought the presbytery's aid in some matter.

[72] *BUK*, 2:567; Calderwood, 3:616.

[73] Foster, *Church Before the Covenant*, 89-90; Makey, *Church of the Covenant*, 37.

[74] For a discussion of the Kirk's growing disappointment with the nobility, see K.M. Brown, "In Search of the Godly Magistrate in Reformation Scotland," *Journal of Ecclesiastical History* 40 (1989), 553-81, especially at 556-66.

an emergency fast and ordered the Edinburgh Presbytery to take action against Catholics and "apostates" frequently at court, particularly the earl of Huntly, Lord Seton and Sir John Chisholm.[75] Earlier in the year, the assembly had appointed a special commission to keep track of Jesuits and seminary priests, and report their names and locations to the crown.[76]

It is reflective of the changing priorities of the Kirk that the General Assembly's July 1591 petition to the king to enforce laws stressed the need to punish Jesuits, idolaters, participants in pilgrimages, excommunicants and sabbath-breakers, but made no mention of sexual sinners.[77] A convention of ministers held in Edinburgh late in 1592 concluded that the Kirk faced four major threats, headed by domestic and foreign conspiracies to "execut that blodie decrie of the Counsall of Trent against all that trewlie profes the Relligioun of Chryst." Other dangers were the lack of ministers or money to pay them in "the graittest part" of the realm, "a feirfull defection" to Catholicism, particularly among the nobility, and a general disorder in society.[78] The General Assembly of April 1593 threatened to excommunicate Scots who travelled to Spain for any reason, until the king could get a guarantee from the Spanish monarchy that his subjects would not be troubled for their religious beliefs.[79] Traffic with Spain was particularly suspect in the Kirk's eyes, not only because of the failed Armada, but also because of the Spanish intrigues of the earls of Huntly and Errol, leading Catholic noblemen.

The language of purity previously invoked to condemn sexual sins was now employed in the service of religious orthodoxy. The very Melvillian Synod of Fife in September 1593 lamented that, along with suffering from the actions of rebellious Catholic noblemen, "the land [was] defiled in diverse places with the devilish and blasphemous masse."[80] Where an earlier generation of ministers would have feared divine punishment on a society which abounded with lechery and blasphemy, it was now sensed that a return to the old religion was most likely to earn His wrath. The Edinburgh minister Robert Bruce preached in February 1589 against "that idolatrous doctrine of that dumb messe":

---

[75] SRO ms CH2/121/1, 47r; *BUK*, 2:730, 738; Calderwood, 4:682-3, 691. Another fast was later proclaimed for three Sundays in October and November, to give thanks for the failure of the Armada. See Calderwood, 4:696.

[76] *BUK*, 2:704-5; Calderwood, 4:651.

[77] *BUK*, 2:784; Calderwood, 5:134-5.

[78] *JMD*, 299-300. Adultery was mentioned as one of the elements of societal disorder, but only alongside contempt, blasphemy, treason, bloodshed and witchcraft.

[79] *BUK*, 3:799-800.

[80] Calderwood, 5:263-8.

I cast this unto you, because I see that our haill youth (for the maist part) are given to it; and the Lord is beginnand to abstract his mercie and grace from this countrey for the contempt of this quickning word, quhilk has sa clearlie sounded here, and quhilk our noblemen, for the greatest part running headlong to the devile, in a dumb guise, traveils utterlie to bannish.... The Lord of his mercie give you eyes in time![81]

A month later, with the king himself in his audience, Bruce chose his text from Isaiah 38, in which the prophet told King Hezekiah to put his house in order, for he soon would die (a prediction which did not come true):

Then I say, praised be the living God, our king is not diseased, but surely his country is heavily diseased; for so long as Papists and Papistrie remain in it, so long as thir pestilent men remain in it, and so long as thir floods of iniquitie quhilk flows from the great men remains, there is a heavy judgement hanging over this country....[82]

At times, Bruce's pessimism was overwhelming. After the defeat of the Spanish Armada, he could still speak of the "work of reformation" as "not...only unended but unbegun," and predicted such calamity would strike the land that it would "spew forth the inhabitants."[83]

But the Kirk did not fear Catholicism to the exclusion of all else. The General Assembly of February 1588, after presenting the king with a shire-by-shire list of Jesuits and known Catholics, passed a general lament for the disorders plaguing Scottish society:

For what part of this land is there that is not with a spaitt overwhelmed, with abusing the blessed name of God, swearing, perjurie and lies...profaning of the Sabbath day with merkats, gluttonie, drunkness, fighting, playing, dancing etc., with rebelling against magistrats and laws of the countrey, with blood touching blood, with incest, fornication, adulteries and sacriledge, theft and oppression, with false witness, and finalie, with all kind of impiety and wrong; and how can the wrath of God already kindled [plague was present in some parts of the realm] be any wayes quenched so long as it hath such matter to turn upon; and albeit there be some good laws for repressing hereof, yet none of them are put in execution, or take any effect.[84]

Even allowing for ministerial exaggeration, the Kirk's efforts at social

---

[81] William Cunningham, ed., *Sermons of Robert Bruce*, (Edinburgh: Wodrow Society, 1843), 113.

[82] *Ibid*, 171.

[83] *Ibid*, 210.

[84] *BUK*, 2:724; Calderwood, 4:666.

discipline seem still to have accomplished little, 30 years into the Reformation.

There was also growing fear that, in addition to ignoring the laws of God, some were actively in league with the Devil. The increase in witch-hunting which began in 1590-1 has already been mentioned, and the Kirk sought to foster cooperation between its own courts and also with civil authorities in the prosecution of witches.[85] And, in May 1594, the General Assembly asked Parliament to pass a law regarding "the horrible superstitioun used in Garioch [Aberdeenshire] and diverse parts of the countrey, in not labouring ane parcell of ground dedicate to the Devill, under the name of the Goodmans Croft." The assembly suggested legislation that such land be either farmed or forfeit to the crown.[86]

Poverty was another joint concern of Church and state, and the Kirk was increasingly trying to make charity contingent on responsible behavior. Collection and distribution of alms was often a major part of the business of kirk sessions, easily tied in with their disciplinary function.[87] The General Assembly in August 1588 ruled that henceforth couples requesting alms had to present evidence of their marriage and the baptism of their children before they would be given any aid. Continued charity would depend on their participation in Communion.[88] Such a carrot-and-stick approach was designed to bring the poorest and most troublesome elements of Scottish society into the disciplinary net and force them to behave according to social norms.

This last concern highlights the philosophy which was at the foundation of the disciplinary efforts of the Kirk. Ministerial advocates of the system felt that a regimen of chastisement and public humiliation would, over time, develop the conscience and turn it into an agent of remorse as the sinner internalized the reformed ethos. Of course the most committed of the ministers felt that this moral education was necessary for all elements of society, not just the lower orders. Many influential laymen whose assistance was required to impose the system agreed that the general population needed to be brought under control, but were not eager to have their own behavior subject to the same scrutiny. This discord, coupled with the controversy

---

[85] E.g. *BUK*, 2:725, 3:937-8; Calderwood, 5:685-7; James Kirk, ed., *Records of the Synod of Lothian*, 4-7, 12, 22, 35, 74, 76, 90, 98; *StAP*, 41, 221-2, 273, 290.

[86] *BUK*, 3:834; Calderwood, 5:326. I have been unable to find any record of the passage of such a law. In September 1586, a commissioner conducting a visitation of the parish of Logie, near Stirling, was directed to inquire about "peces off grond dedicat to Satan onder the name off Kynd Knycht." See Kirk, ed., *Dunblane Visitation*, 13.

[87] The kirk sessions of Edinburgh and Monifieth were particularly careful to record weekly totals of alms collections. See SRO ms CH2/450/1 and NRH ms OPR 310/1, *passim*.

[88] *BUK*, 2:731; Calderwood, 4:689.

created by the dispute between episcopacy and Presbyterianism, spawned a full-scale debate over discipline in the last three decades of the sixteenth century.

The Debate Over Discipline

The General Assembly's embrace of the books of discipline, coupled with the ready passage of legislation against vice and certain traditional practices by burgh authorities and the estates in Parliament, demonstrates that there was at least a philosophic consensus among the leading elements in Scottish society that steps had to be taken to curb social disorder. But the actual implementation of the disciplinary system, involving attacks on traditional practices and kin loyalties as well as a challenge to the role of the crown in governing the Kirk, severely tested this consensus, and exposed its limits.

David Fergusson (d. 1598), a former skinner who became minister of Dunfermline after 1560, is representative of many ministers of rather humble origins who served in the early Reformed Church in Scotland. In his view, discipline was necessary not because it would help bring salvation, but because the habits of sin were all too easily learned. Preaching in January 1572 on Israel's repeated apostasy, he declared:

> Of this we leirne, that lang custume to sinne, is a thing maist pernitious, for it makis that thing, quhilk of the self, is the maist abhomiable to appear nathing to thame that ar hantit thairwith, specially if God defer punischment for ony quhyle, for then beginnis man to flatter him self, to abuse the patience of God, and to wrap him self in that cairles and maist perrillous perswasioun, that God regaires not his doingis, nor is thairwith sa heichly offendid...and so precedis to heap sinne upon sinne until ye day of wraith....[89]

Fergusson argued that sinners had to be made to display repentance, thus conditioning them to realize the unacceptability of their behavior. But while this repentance might be initially the result of outward pressure, it had to involve a true recognition of sin, for "it is but loste labour and a vane purpois to perswade men to repent that acknawledgis na fault."[90]

But such correction would not necessarily be welcomed by the sinner, and we have already seen evidence of resistance to the imposition of the new order. In 1563 Fergusson had written that "the greatest nomber of carnall Gospellers in Scotland this day hateth the ministers of the Evangle, for no vther cause then for their seveir reboking of vice, for the which I for

---

[89] John Lee, ed., *Tracts By David Fergusson, Minister of Dunfermline: 1563-1572*, (Edinburgh: Bannatyne Club, 1860), 63-4.

[90] *Ibid*, 64.

one...am hated to the death...."[91]

This resentment was doubtless particularly common among prominent sinners unaccustomed to public criticism from men of low social origin.[92] But the minister Robert Bruce (c. 1554-1631), a laird himself, agreed with Fergusson on the necessity to bring discipline to all social strata. In 1589 Bruce preached that many of the social and political ills facing Scotland were the result of a lack of conscience and discipline among the nobility: "Thir oppressions of the poor, thir deadlie feids with their awin companions, would not burst out in sick ane high measure, gif they had advised weill with their consciences."[93]

For Bruce, the conscience was natural to man, but had to "be reformit according to the Word of God."[94] It was "a certain feeling in the heart, resembling the judgement of the living God, following upon ane deed done be us, flowing from ane knowledge in the mind, accompanied with ane certain motion of the heart, to wit, feare or joy, trembling or rejoicing."[95] Most notable is Bruce's explicit rejection of a conscience which might help determine human actions in advance.

David Sabean has highlighted the differences between modern and sixteenth-century notions of conscience. The modern conscience is a Freudian superego, a regulator of behavior which operates while we consider various courses of action. In contrast, the early modern conscience (*gewissen* in Sabean's German sources) even at its most functional merely supplied remorse after the fact.[96] Bruce's writings support Sabean's conclusions. The conscience described by Bruce was a court, a kirk session within the self. Its purposes were to observe and record one's deeds, "to be ane accuser of thee," "to beare ane true and steadfast witnes against thee," and, finally, "to do the part of ane judge against thee, to give out sentence against thee, to condemn thee."[97] For Bruce, the only real advance solution to the problem of sin was to avoid temptation. This being often impossible, "thou sall amend thy life by repentance, and be repentance thou sall get peace."[98] Social discipline administered by the Kirk was necessary as an external conscience, to prod the sinner to repentance while developing the

---

[91] *Ibid*, 10.

[92] For further discussion of this issue, see chapter seven.

[93] Bruce, 143.

[94] *Ibid*, 105.

[95] *Ibid*, 103.

[96] David Sabean, *Power In the Blood: Popular Culture and Village Discourse in Early Modern Germany*, (Cambridge: Cambridge University Press, 1984), 51, 91-2.

[97] Bruce, 105-6.

[98] *Ibid*, 111-3.

conscience within.[99]

The only alternative Bruce could envision was a slide into anarchy, a possiblity which seemed all too real to him and his contemporaries. Without external and internal regulation of behavior,

> how would it be possible that a society could be kept; how would it be possible that a kirk could be gathered; how would it be possible that any man could have company or conversation among men?...The restraint that cometh by discipline and execution of laws, it taketh not away the tyranny of sin; it taketh not away the absolute command and sovereignty quhilk sin hath, it holdeth wicked men in awe; it maketh them to keep ane external society, and holdeth them in some honesty and civil conversation; but it taketh not away the sovereignty and empire of the affections.[100]

Thus even a fully-developed system of ecclesiastical discipline assisted by an enthusiastic magistracy would never usher in a Calvinist utopia. The latter was unimaginable on this side of eternity; external discipline would always be necessary for most of the population.

Also significant is Bruce's emphasis on the role of God, or the Kirk as His surrogate, as a necessary participant in the healing of all strife. Scottish social and legal custom had long encouraged the settling of disputes, assaults and even murders through negotiation and compensation between the parties.[101] The courts were a last resort, if all private efforts had failed. But Bruce insisted that even sins which victimized individuals, such as slander or assault, be brought before the Kirk for adjudication. There was to be no private justice; only the Kirk could recognize penitence:

> So this is the true repentance, where men and women, suppose they have offended the creatures, yet they run to God only and seek remission. And indeed, this is the right way; for why? It is only God [i.e., the Kirk] that may forgive them their sins, suppose they have offended men and women.[102]

The formal Scottish legal system was in many ways still in its infancy. But

---

[99] For a seventeenth-century English example of someone who had internalized discipline to the extent that he would fine himself for various offenses, see Paul Seaver, *Wallington's World: A Puritan Artisan in Seventeenth-Century London*, (Stanford: Stanford University Press, 1985), 31-2.

[100] Bruce, 351.

[101] Keith M. Brown, *Bloodfeud in Scotland, 1573-1635: Violence Justice and Politics in an Early Modern Society*, (Edinburgh: John Donald, 1986), 50-2; Bruce Lenman and Geoffrey Parker, "Crime In Early Modern Scotland: A Preliminary Report on Sources and Problems," (End of Grant Report, Social Science Research Council, London, 1977), 2.

[102] Bruce, 358.

the development of courts and the expansion of their jurisdictions was a necessary aspect of early modern state building. In Scotland it was the Kirk and its courts which were taking the lead.[103] Ultimately, by making discipline a necessary mark of the true church, the reformers would play a major role in making the rule of law a necessary mark of the well-governed state.

But the disciplinary system the reformers were trying to build was not without critics, both within and without Scotland. Perhaps the best-known (or, in Presbyterian eyes, most notorious) Scottish critic was Patrick Adamson (c. 1537-1592). Originally a client of the moderately-protestant James Hamilton, duke of Châtelherault, Adamson was made minister at Ceres in 1562. A Latin poet of some merit, Adamson was certainly a firm protestant, but had little interest in the parochial ministry, abandoning it in 1564 to study abroad.[104] By the early 1570s, he had returned to Scotland, and became chaplain to Regent Morton. In 1576, Morton appointed him archbishop of St. Andrews, placing the ambitious Adamson on a collision course with Andrew Melville and his followers over the acceptability of episcopacy. For it was in 1576 that Melville returned from Geneva to take an academic post at Glasgow and then, four years later, at the reorganized university in St. Andrews. Melville and his party attacked the very idea of episcopacy and argued that churchmen like Adamson, who held high office but did not preach on any regular basis, had no legitimate function within the Kirk. Related to the episcopacy debate were questions regarding the lay eldership, particularly whether lay elders should serve on presbyteries, and over who should hold the ultimate power of excommunication.

During the crisis of 1583-4, Adamson had gone to England, where he sought to convince Queen Elizabeth's government, particularly Archbishop John Whitgift, that the Melvillians were trying to cut the Scottish king out of the government of the Kirk.[105] Whitgift declined to offer Adamson any public support, coolly informing the latter in January 1584 that he (Whitgift) would need the queen's permission to write about any of the topics in question. Meanwhile, the English archbishop forwarded Adamson's "articles" to Francis Walsingham, the puritanically-inclined secretary of

---

[103] For a discussion of this theme in a later period, see Stephen Davies, "The Courts and the Legal System 1600-1747: The Case of Stirlingshire," in V.A.C. Gatrell, Bruce Lenman and Geoffrey Parker, eds., *Crime and the Law: The Social History of Crime in Western Europe Since 1500*, (London: Europa, 1980), 120-154.

[104] Michael Lynch, ed., *Mary Stewart, Queen in Three Kingdoms*, (Oxford: Basil Blackwell, 1988), editor's introduction, 2, 23; Mullan, *Episcopacy in Scotland*, 54-5, 71-2.

[105] Collinson, *Elizabethan Puritan Movement*, 276.

state, who was not likely to read them with sympathy.[106] Clearly, Adamson had made a poor impression on his English counterpart. Whitgift's aversion must have been more personal than philosophical, because the two were in substantial agreement on matters of church polity and the royal supremacy. Thus rebuffed, Adamson sent his own theories of church polity to Geneva for review. In these, he denied the scriptural warrant for the eldership, and opined that "presbytereis to be appointed of gentlemen, lords of the ground, and others associat with the ministers, is no other thing but to induce a great confusion in the kirk, and an occasioun of continuall seditioun."[107]

But Adamson was not the only controversial Scottish churchman in England in 1584. As noted earlier, the "Black Acts" spurred a southward exodus of several of the leading Melvillians, following Andrew Melville himself. While these exiles received no official welcome from the government of Queen Elizabeth, William Davison, her ambassador to Edinburgh and a committed puritan, happened to be in Berwick to greet several of them as they entered England, and he seems to have offered some assistance. Later, Melville and several others met with Walsingham in London.[108] One of the Scots exiles, James Lawson, died while in England, and his London funeral served as a rally for the Calvinist international, drawing 500 mourners, including the English presbyterians John Field and Walter Travers, and the three ministers of London's Huguenot congregation.[109] At least two of the Scots exiles, Walter Balcanquhal and John Davidson, did some freelance preaching from London parish pulpits, but the bishop of London put a halt to this in January 1585.[110] The young Welsh puritan John Penry "had heard of a remarkable Puritan movement [in Oxford] stimulated by the visit of ministers from

---

[106] *Historical Manuscripts Commission, Seventh Report*, (London: HMSO, 1879), 429. Adamson complained to Whitgift in a later letter that someone (Walsingham?) had sent the articles on to his Scots opponents "to inflame the faction," forcing Adamson to defend himself against charges of popery. See *ibid*, 430.

[107] Calderwood, 4:50-5, with quotation at 54. For further details on Adamson's trip to England, see Gordon Donaldson, *Scottish Church History*, (Edinburgh: Scottish Academic Press, 1985), 166-9.

[108] Donaldson, *Scottish Church History*, 182.

[109] *The Miscellany of the Wodrow Society* 1, (Edinburgh: Wodrow Society, 1844), 449-51; Donaldson, *Scottish Church History*, 184-5.

[110] Donaldson, *Scottish Church History*, 186. Richard Bancroft later alleged that the preaching of the exiled Scots had been suppressed at the request of the Scots ambassador in London, offended by statements the preachers had made from the pulpits about king James' government. See [Richard Bancroft], *Daungerous Positions and Proceedings Published and Practised Within This Iiland of Brytaine...*, (London: John Wolfe, 1593), 26.

Scotland."[111] Given the divisions within the English Church, the Scots faced the danger of being viewed as sowers of sedition. Indeed, one of the charges against Field when he was suspended from preaching in 1585 was that he had associated with the exiled Scots during their stay in London.[112] It is no coincidence that the English Parliament of 1584-5 briefly considered a bill which would have created parish consistories and district presbyteries in England, and replaced the *Book of Common Prayer* with the *Form of Prayers and Administration of the Sacraments*, used by John Knox's congregation in Geneva in the 1550s, and later adapted into the Scottish Reformed Kirk.[113] A crisis in Scotland had spilled over the border, and the presence of the refugees had awakened conflicts within the English Church.

By 1586 Patrick Adamson was back in Scotland, as were the Melvillian ministers. The Arran government had been toppled by a *coup d'etat* at Stirling in November 1585. Eager for conciliation, the king had agreed to the revival of the presbyteries. But Adamson was now claiming for the monarch, rather than the Kirk, ultimate control over the use of excommunication, a view which was widespread in the English Church.[114] The issue affected him in particular, because the same Synod of Fife before which he made the claim proceeded to excommunicate him for contempt of the Kirk and suspicion of heresy. The king sided in part with his controversial archbishop, temporarily exiling Andrew Melville to his birthplace,[115] but nevertheless confirmed in general the power of presbyteries over excommunication.[116] Adamson's problems with the Kirk continued. Finally, in June 1589 a joint commission of the presbyteries of St. Andrews and Edinburgh concluded he was still holding to numerous erroneous positions, and that "ye said bischop hes bene ane plane hinderer of the p[ro]moting & propagating [of] the evangell in yis c[on]trei," both in terms of discipline and preaching. The commission debarred him from ever holding any office in the Kirk.[117] In 1591, abandoned even by the king, he submitted a

---

[111] Albert Peel, ed., *The Notebook of John Penry, 1593*, (London: Camden Society, 1944), x.

[112] Collinson, *Elizabethan Puritan Movement*, 276-7.

[113] Collinson, *Elizabethan Puritan Movement*, 286-7. The bill, proposed by the London physician and MP Peter Turner, received little support.

[114] Calderwood, 4:542; Kirk, *Patterns of Reform*, 259.

[115] Calderwood, 4:498, 552-3; *BUK* 2:662; *JMD*, 247-9; Mullan, *Episcopacy in Scotland*, 66.

[116] *BUK*, 2:665-6.

[117] SRO ms CH2/121/1, 10 June 1589. The Edinburgh Presbytery had also chastised him in August 1588 for having "inorderlie pr[ocee]dit" in performing the marriage ceremony of the earl of Huntly when the presbytery and General Assembly had ordered a stay of the proceedings. See *ibid*, 46v.

recantation of his beliefs before the Synod of Fife, and was dead within the year.[118] At that time the Scots presbyterian John Davidson wrote of him: "...it is much better that the legend of his leud life bee buried in eternall oblivion, then that Christian eares should bee polluted with the unsavorie mention thereof."[119]

After Adamson, the anti-Presbyterian cause was taken up by Richard Bancroft (1544-1610), an English divine who later became bishop of London (1597) and archbishop of Canterbury (1604). While Bancroft, responding to the anti-episcopal charges of the anonymous pamphleteer "Martin Marprelate," aimed his attacks at the English presbyterian movement, he often cited examples from the Scottish Kirk to demonstrate the evils he viewed as inherent in the Presbyterian system. His opening salvo came in a sermon he preached at Paul's Cross in London in February 1589, based on 1 John 4:1: "many false prophets are gone out into the world." Drawing on the writings of Adamson and (curiously) the English separatist Robert Browne, he excoriated the ministerial tyranny which he claimed reigned in Scotland, where "the nobles & people [are] at great discord and much distracted, & yet all men made slaves to the preachers & their fellowe elders."[120] Referring to the creation of the presbyteries in Scotland in 1581, he charged that the leaders of the Kirk had usurped the spiritual authority of the king of Scots, and, "under the pretence of their presbyteries...trod upon his scepter."[121]

Bancroft drew a quick response north of the Tweed. In April, the Edinburgh Presbytery ordered the ministers Robert Bruce, Robert Pont and John Davidson to write a reply to "ye sclanderous s[er]m[on] p[rea]chit at Pauls croce be D. Bancroif," and in December the presbytery decided to write to Queen Elizabeth herself, asking her to "tak ordor" with Bancroft for "traducing in [the sermon] ye haill Discipline of ye Kirk of Scotland."[122] While there is no evidence of a response from the Queen, her secretary Lord Burghley did require that Bancroft send an explanation of his remarks to King James, who had been in Denmark when the news of the sermon

---

[118] Recantation given in Row, 1:25-34; see also Mullan, *Episcopacy in Scotland*, 71. Adamson was one of the few victims of James' *rapprochement* with the Kirk in the late 1580s and early 1590s.

[119] John Davidson, *D. Bancroft's Rashness in Rayling Against the Church of Scotland*, (Edinburgh: Robert Waldegrave, 1590), (no regular foliation).

[120] Richard Bancroft, *A Sermon Preached at Paul's Cross the 9 of February...1588*, (London: Gregorie Seton, 1588), *passim*; Mullan, *Episcopacy in Scotland*, 67-8; Donaldson, *Scottish Church History*, 170-1; Leo Solt, *Church and State in Early Modern England*, (Oxford: Oxford University Press, 1990), 117.

[121] Bancroft, *Sermon Preached at Paules Crosse*, 72-4.

[122] SRO ms CH2/121/1, 29 April 1589, 10 June 1589, 9 December 1589.

arrived in his kingdom.[123] Davidson wrote and published a response to Bancroft, as did John Penry, living in exile in Scotland at the time. Both were particularly critical of Bancroft's use of Browne "and other known and confessed infamous persons" as sources.[124] But Bancroft and Davidson were in agreement on one thing: the international nature of the British presbyterian movement. Davidson granted that the causes of presbyterianism in England and Scotland "are most neer linked togeather," and Bancroft later charged that the Scots "doo iustifie the proceedings of our disturbers here, & animating them to go forward as they have begun, doo tell them, that both their causes...are most nerely linked together.... They seek under hand to steale away the harts of her Maiesties subiects...."[125]

Bancroft was undeterred by the controversy he had engendered, and in 1593 published *Daungerous Positions* and *Pretended Holy Discipline*, two full-length critiques of Presbyterian pretensions.[126] The latter work began with his history of the Genevan Consistory, for him an evil example of ministerial usurpation of magisterial authority. Despite such perversion of the proper relationship of church and state, he wrote:

> certaine persons of the consistoriall humour, doe daily vpon euery occasion, still dash vs in the teeth, with the orders of Geneua: the discipline at Geneua: and the Consistorie in Geneua: as though that forme of discipline, had come lately from heauen; with an embassage from God....[127]

Bancroft held that the "Black Acts" of 1584 had been the ultimate fruit of John Knox's infatuation with Genevan polity, and accused Calvin's successor Theodore Beza of directing the leaders of the Scottish Kirk in "a pope-like manner."[128] He took delight in sneering at the humble folk who (he claimed) dominated the elderships in Scotland—"Husbandmen, Taylors, Butchers, Carpenters, Shomakers, thatchers, dawbers," or "such artizans,

---

[123] In the sermon, Bancroft had accused the king of inconsistency in his attitude toward the Scottish Church, basing part of his argument on a 1585 royal declaration actually written by Adamson. See Donaldson, *Scottish Church History*, 175; Stuart Barton Babbage, *Puritanism and Richard Bancroft*, (London: Church Historical Society, 1962), 31-2.

[124] Davidson, *D. Bancroft's Rashness*; [John Penry], *A Briefe Discovery of the Untruthes and Slanders (against the true Governement of the Church of Christ) Contained in a Sermon, Preached the 8 of February 1588, by D. Bancroft*, (London: n.p., 1589). Penry was to join Browne in the separatist camp within a few years, however. He was executed in 1593 on charges arising out of the Marprelate Tracts controversy. See Peel, ed., *Notebook of John Penry*, editor's introduction.

[125] Bancroft, *Daungerous Positions*, 5-6, 31.

[126] *Ibid*; Richard Bancroft, *Pretended Holy Discipline*, (London: John Wolfe, 1593).

[127] Bancroft, *Pretended Holy Discipline*, 38.

[128] *Ibid*, 49, 51.

& mean persons"—suggesting they acted as "seven or eight Archbishops in every parish."[129]

This is not to say that Bancroft thought the behavior of the general population was not in need of reform. Rather, he scoffed at the disciplinary apparatus the Scots reformers had created on the grounds that it lacked scriptural warrant, was inimical to the traditional ordering of society, and was ineffective. The Presbyterians required the appointment of elders, he claimed, "not that they find them in the word of God, but because they fit their turnes, and doe account them necessary to set vp their own kingdom."[130] Bancroft was not averse to invoking the jeremiads of the Scots Presbyterians themselves to prove that their "pretended holy discipline" had failed to reform societal mores.[131] To him, Presbyterianism was a new papacy, a new attempt by the Church to bully the secular magistrate, with the regicide proposed by "the Scottishe consistorian" George Buchanan a natural result.[132] Bancroft was so committed to a condemnation of the Scottish Reformed Kirk that, when giving an account of its history in *Daungerous Positions*, he neglected to mention the (considerable) aid given by queen Elizabeth's government to the Lords of the Congregation in 1559-60.[133] Such embarrassing evidence could only pollute the patriotic tone of his rhetoric.

Matthew Sutcliffe (1550-1629), another English critic of Presbyterian discipline, found public censure of sin particularly unedifying, lamenting that "admonitions that are private, are lewdly made part of the church censures that are publike, and with publike authoritie executed."[134] He claimed that the eldership usurped royal power by claiming legal jurisdiction over so many cases, taking the profits of justice and refusing to recognize the monarch's control over excommunication.[135] The first two complaints might have had some resonance in England, where the legal system was more fully developed, but the courts of the Scottish Kirk were not stealing any business from the crown. Rather, they were among the most conscientious of the new, public, courts which were taking justice out of

---

[129] *Ibid*, 154, 160-1.

[130] *Ibid*, 180.

[131] E.g. *ibid*, 458-60, where the language echoes Robert Bruce.

[132] *Ibid*, 254, 258-9. Bancroft's reference was to the tyrannicide justified by Buchanan in his *De Jure Regni Apud Scotos*.

[133] Bancroft, *Daungerous Positions*, 10-13.

[134] Sutcliffe, *Ecclesiasticall Discipline*, 2 (although the page is marked "8"). Sutcliffe was dean of Exeter, and opposed the Arminians in the 1620s. See *DNB*, 19:175-7; Nicholas Tyacke, *Anti-Calvinists: The Rise of English Arminianism, c. 1590-1640*, (Oxford: Clarendon Press, 1987), 215.

[135] Sutcliffe, *Ecclesiasticall Discipline*, 177-81.

private hands and placing it in the public domain, an effort which, in the long run, could only enhance the powers of the central government. Jurisdictional conflicts were relatively rare; most cases handled by kirk sessions and presbyteries would never have been heard in any other court.

Far more controversial north of the Tweed was the question of who should hold the ultimate control over excommunication. When Andrew Melville in 1596 told James VI that, in God's Kingdom, the king of Scots was but a "sillie vassal,"[136] he meant that there were certain matters in his realm over which he could have no control, and excommunication—the power to bind and loose—was one of them. Of course, since no one was to have any dealings with an excommunicated person, the Kirk was claiming through control of excommunication the right to bar certain individuals (such as the earl of Huntly) from the royal presence. After 1596, James sought to gain ultimate control over all jurisdictions in his kingdom and, by implication, the right to choose his companions. Once again, the argument was mainly over episcopacy, but the disciplinary structure of the Kirk was bound to be affected.

The Post-1596 Reaction

The period 1586-96 had been one of continued growth in the power and prestige of the Presbyterian Kirk. Although the king was becoming increasingly annoyed at the tone of politically-tinged sermons,[137] it would only become clear in retrospect that 1596 represented a pinnacle in the powers of the Church imagined in the *Second Book of Discipline*. Calderwood opined that "the Kirk of Scotland was now come to her perfectioun, and the greatest puritie that ever she atteaned unto, both in doctrine and discipline."[138] It was in 1596 that the General Assembly ordered all synods, presbyteries and kirk sessions to supervise the renewal of a national Covenant, based on the "Negative Confession," an anti-papal diatribe which had been aimed at Esmé Stewart in 1581.[139] Ministry, crown, nobility, gentry and commons would thus be united in a sacred national effort, firmly rooted in the traditional Scottish practice of the band, a contractual agreement.[140] James Melville, writing of the period 1596-1610, placed it under the heading "the Declyneing Aige of the Kirk of Scotland,"

---

[136] Calderwood, 5:439-40.

[137] *JMD*, 323-6; Calderwood, 5:466-8, 522, 526; Spottiswoode, 3:19-22; Mullan, *Episcopacy in Scotland*, 76.

[138] Calderwood, 5:387.

[139] *JMD*, 353-67; *BUK*, 3:873-4; Row, 1:38-9; *StAP*, 203-5.

[140] Williamson, *Scottish National Consciousness*, 74-5. The covenant had also been renewed in 1590.

and held that 1596 had been, in retrospect a "fatall yeir."[141]

But even in 1596, 36 years after the "Reformation Parliament" and the *First Book of Discipline*, some ministers still had to be reminded by the General Assembly that they were expected to establish kirk sessions.[142] And the assembly's motion to renew the Covenant was prefaced by a litany of lamentation for "the commoun corruptiouns of all Estates within this realme," headed by "superstitioun and idolatrie maintainit, quhilk utters itself in keiping of festuall dayis, and boonefyres, pilgrimages, singing of carrels at Yoole." The Sabbath was still openly violated with dancing, drinking and markets, bloodshed and feuds were rampant, sexual sins abounded, food hoarders drove prices up and the nation was plagued by "ane great number of idle persons without lawfull calling, as pypers, fidlers, sangsters...[and] strang beggers, living in harlotrie, and having thair children unbaptizit, without all kynd of repairing to the Word."[143] As late as October 1595, the Synod of Lothian had been unable to banish "monumentis of idolatry" from the kirk at Peebles, and to prevent pilgrimages there.[144] Covenant or no, much of Scottish society was still beyond the pale of godliness.

Perhaps the pivotal event of 1596 in terms of the polity of the Kirk was the anti-episcopal riot which broke out in Edinburgh on December 17.[145] In the aftermath, the ministers of Edinburgh fled the town and were put to the horn, although reinstated the following May. The king prohibited the convening of general assemblies, synods or even presbytery meetings in the capital.[146] In preparation for the General Assembly which he was calling in the less seditious and more northerly burgh of Perth in February 1597, he gave the Synod of Fife a series of leading questions drawn up by John Lindsay, Lord Menmuir, a senator of the College of Justice, concerning the disciplinary powers of the Kirk. These were aimed at exposing the level of ministerial control to which the Melvillians aspired.[147]

The synod told the king that a minister could exercise disciplinary

---

[141] *JMD*, 330-1.

[142] *BUK*, 3:865.

[143] *Ibid*, 3:873-4.

[144] Kirk, ed., *Records of the Synod of Lothian*, 100.

[145] Calderwood, 5:511; Spottiswoode, 3:28-9, 37-8; Foster, *Church Before the Covenants*, 13.

[146] *JMD*, 374, 384-5, 415; Calderwood, 5:536-7, 626.

[147] Questions and answers given in Calderwood, 5:585-97, and Spottiswoode, 3:41-5. For related queries, possibly a draft version of the same set, see NLS ms Adv. 29.2.8, 103r-106v. Some of these, regarding presbyteries, were clearly aimed at the practices of the Presbytery of St. Andrews, of which Andrew and James Melville were members, as shown by the tag "questiounis of ye presbiterie of Sanctan" written vertically at the bottom of 106v.

jurisdiction even in matters on which most of his kirk session disagreed with him, provided the "best part" of the eldership backed him. While the king had proposed the annual election of a session moderator, the synod insisted that only the parish minister was qualified to moderate at session meetings. In a clear rejection of the principles of 1560, the synod endorsed ministerial appointment of elders, rather than election by the congregation. Although James cast doubt on the propriety of issuing public admonitions without first privately warning offenders (and thus opened the door for eminent people who simply refused to appear to avoid public embarrassment), the synod replied that "where the slander is become publict, the place of privat admonitioun is past," and affirmed that refusal to answer a summons could by itself merit excommunication. The synod pointedly refused to grant that the monarch had any power to overturn a sentence of excommunication, any more than a church court could annul a horning or forfeiture.

David Calderwood denigrated the composition of the General Assembly that met in Perth in February 1597, claiming "the ministers of the North conveened in suche numbers as were not wont to be seene at anie tyme before, and everie one of them great courteours."[148] In his radical view, northern conservatism was *prima facie* evidence of courtier sympathies, even though relatively few of the northern ministers had ever had the time or opportunity to spend much time at court. Granted, religious conservatism was a regional phenomenon, but so was Melvillianism, with the latter strongest in Fife and the Lothians, previously almost always a short horseback ride to General Assembly meetings. Calderwood argued that the Perth meeting was not a true General Assembly, "because it was not to edifie, but to demolishe the discipline established," and because David Lindsay, minister of Leith and "one suborned by the court" was chosen moderator.[149] Never mind that Lindsay had impressive Presbyterian credentials, having been imprisoned in Blackness Castle in 1584, when the Melvilles fled into exile.[150] Calderwood could see only toadyism in his actions, confirmed by his later acceptance of the bishopric of Ross.

King James presented 13 articles to the assembly, many of them concerning discipline.[151] He proposed that ministers refrain from public admonitions, except in the cases of fugitives and excommunicates, and that excommunications only take place after three citations, each separated by at least eight days. As the Kirk's actions against the courtier earl of Huntly had piqued much of the king's discontent with the disciplinary system, he

---

[148] Calderwood, 5:606.

[149] *Ibid*, 5:622-3.

[150] *Ibid*, 4:76, 167-9.

[151] *BUK*, 3:890-2; Calderwood, 5:609; Spottiswoode, 3:49-50.

argued that the earl's case should be handled by the ministers of his home district of Aberdeen and Moray, rather than by the Melvillians who dominated the presbytery of Edinburgh and the Synod of Fife, who had previously taken action against him.[152] While the assembly was willing to negotiate on the matter of summary excommunication, it refused to forbear public admonition of those who ignored the summonses of the Kirk. It remitted the Huntly case to the presbyteries of Aberdeen and Moray, but named five reliable ministers to assist and encourage them.[153]

A General Assembly called later that spring in Dundee absolved Huntly and his followers, and granted that the king could stay excommunication proceedings against someone in a case "of any thing prejudiciall to the civill jurisdictioun."[154] In 1605, James was to insist that no nobleman be excommunicated without the approval of the Privy Council.[155] He had been disturbed by the political uses of excommunication, as demonstrated in the case of Huntly and his allies, and was not unaware that the sanction had been in episcopal hands in the pre-Reformation Church. Clearly, after 1597 the king was resolved to restore the bishops to their pre-Reformation constitutional position, but their role, as royal appointees, in the polity of the Kirk and its disciplinary structure was unclear. In 1598, the place of bishops in Parliament was the issue,[156] but within ten years royal pressure had made many of them permanent moderators in presbyteries.[157]

James' choice of Bancroft as archbishop of Canterbury in 1604 (after he had succeeded to the English throne) is clear evidence of his complete disdain for Presbyterian sentiment by then. But this was no sudden royal conversion. Representing the king at the General Assembly at Glasgow in 1610, the earl of Dunbar said James had turned to episcopacy because "after he had suffered anarchie to bring furth suche evill effects, as that it could not be longer tolerated...he has spaired no expences or travell to vindicat the jurisdictioun spirituall out of the hands of civill men."[158] Of course, Presbyterianism had hardly put spiritual jurisdiction in the hands of "civill men." The presbyteries had been dominated by the ministry since 1586. At the parish level, the king was perfectly happy with the powers of lay elders, as shown by the questions to proposed to the Synod of Fife in 1597. It was a seditious ministry which could not be held accountable for political

---

[152] SRO ms CH2/121/1, 43v; *JMD*, 309-10; Calderwood, 5:263-8, 309; *BUK*, 3:821.

[153] *BUK*, 3:895-6; Calderwood, 5:614-6; Spottiswoode, 3:53-4.

[154] *BUK*, 3:918-22, 926; Calderwood, 5:643-4.

[155] Foster, *Church Before the Covenants*, 105.

[156] Calderwood, 5:697-9; Spottiswoode, 3:68-9.

[157] Calderwood, 6:648; Foster, *Church Before the Covenants*, 20.

[158] Calderwood, 7:95.

sermons that troubled him. Now, he looked for reliable landlords and burgh councils to bridle the ministers in their home parishes, and loyal bishops to police them in the episcopally-moderated presbyteries. The General Assembly was fading into irrelevance, and met only sporadically after 1603.

With the rejuvenation of episcopacy came a restoration of the bishops' disciplinary functions. The resulting changes should not be exaggerated, because kirk sessions carried on as before, and presbyteries (not all of which had bishops as moderators) continued to handle appeals and difficult cases. But in 1610 the king gave powers to his two Scottish archbishops (John Spottiswoode of Glasgow and George Gladstaines of St. Andrews) to hold courts of high commission, and to summon anyone "being offenders either in life or religion, whom they hold any ways to be scandalous...." These courts were given the power to excommunicate, fine and imprison.[159] This carried the potential of creating competing ecclesiastical jurisdictions, and Calderwood attacked it for doing just that, claiming "they have power to advocat causes from the ordinarie judicatoreis, presbyterie, synod, session, yea, Generall Assemblie, upon complaint of anie persoun ather scandelous in life or erroneous in religioun....is it not to weaken or destroy the ordinarie judicatoreis of the kirk?"[160] His complaints were valid insofar as the courts of high commission (combined in 1615) did end up handling many of the same types of cases already common in kirk sessions and presbyteries, particularly those involving prominent people, but they concentrated on religious dissent, both Catholic and protestant.[161] There was still plenty of business for the other church courts.

Theoretically, the most significant change the king imposed on the Kirk's disciplinary system occurred when he pressured the 1610 General Assembly to require that any sentence of excommunication be approved by the bishop in whose diocese the offense took place.[162] This, coupled with the earlier requirement that the Privy Council approve the excommunication of any nobleman, ensured that all excommunications would be in the hands of royal servants. It has been argued that the participation and assistance of the bishops actually strengthened the presbyterian system, both in terms of discipline and ministerial supervision.[163] This may be so, but the restoration to the bishops of their pre-Reformation disciplinary fuctions, and the delegation to them of exclusive control over the ultimate disciplinary

---

[159] *BUK*, 3:1078-82; Row, 1:87; A. Ian Dunlop, "The Polity of the Scottish Church, 1600-1637," *RSCHS* 12 (1958), 161-84, at 162.

[160] Calderwood, 7:63.

[161] George McMahon, "The Scottish Courts of High Commission, 1610-38," *RSCHS* 15 (1965), 193-209.

[162] *BUK*, 3:1096; Calderwood, 7:100; Spottiswoode, 3:206; Row, 1:94.

[163] Foster, *Church Before the Covenants*, 108-9.

sanction of excommunication marked a philosophical rejection of the Reformed disciplinary order. Thus the year 1610 marked not only the golden anniversary of the Scots' break with Rome, but also, at the highest level, the end of the disciplinary regime constructed by the first two generations of reformers. Doubtless this was scarcely noticeable in the parishes, where kirk sessions continued to function as before, but 1610 has been chosen as the terminal date for this study due to the theoretical significance of the change. The full presbyterian system would only be restored with the overthrow of the bishops in 1638, in circumstances far removed from those of 1610.

And while ultimate control over excommunication might have had as little to do with most parochial discipline as the administration of capital punishment today does with shoplifting, the Melvillians discerned more than simple Erastianism in the king's full restoration of the episcopate. Increasingly, they saw in James an overly indulgent monarch, far too willing to wink at, or even encourage, sinful practices. May games, a target of the reformers since the 1560s, were openly endorsed by a royal proclamation at Edinburgh's mercat cross in the spring of 1599.[164] When a group of English comedians scheduled performances under the king's warrant the following November, the four kirk sessions of Edinburgh passed a resolution forbidding attendance by any of their congregations. This led to a row between James and the ministers of the capital, led by Bruce. "To what end, I pray you," the king asked Bruce, "sought I an hous, but onlie that the people might resort to their comedeis?" Bruce replied "we have good reasoun to stay them from thair playes, even by your owne acts of Parliament." To James, this was unwelcome meddling. "Yee are not the interpreters of my lawes," he declared, and the kirk sessions were persuaded by the Privy Council to go against their ministers and rescind the order.[165]

A General Assembly which met in November 1602 at Holyrood Palace, with the royal minister Patrick Galloway in the moderator's chair, passed a resolution that no child be denied baptism whose parents declared their willingness to give it a "Christian" faith.[166] Since it was by then the common practice of many kirk sessions to withhold the baptism of children born out of wedlock until the parents performed public repentance, the Kirk was thus abandoning one of its most effective prods. It is no wonder that Calderwood, James Melville and others felt that Babylon was being rebuilt. The General Assembly at Linlithgow in July 1608 complained that most

---

[164] Calderwood, 5:735-6.

[165] *Ibid*, 5:765-7; Spottiswoode, 3:81.

[166] *BUK*, 3:1002; Calderwood, 6:183; Spottiswoode, 3:106.

actions taken by presbyteries against Catholic recusants were ineffective, because the latter could easily purchase royal warrants, forcing the church courts to drop the proceedings.[167] Compared with the heady days of the early 1590s, it now seemed that the monarch and his government were seeking to undermine the ecclesiastical regime at every turn.

The Synod of Lothian lamented this trend, already apparent, in May 1599. It called for a fast due to the "coldness and loathing of the truthe to be fallin out in all estats..." and a people "not humbling themselves to the obedience and censure of the Word, whereby it appeares that the Lord our God, in his just judgement, is moved to take away both the libertie of preaching, and to loose the yoke of discipline."[168] Of course, ministerial lamentation of widespread sin was nothing new. But what was different here was the sense that the nation was retreating from a standard which it had achieved in the recent past. No only was the yoke of discipline loose, it was becoming looser. Was the trend really regressive? This can only be answered through an examination of the work of the presbyteries and kirk sessions themselves during the period 1582-1610.

---

[167] *BUK*, 3:1053.
[168] Calderwood, 5:737-8.

CHAPTER FIVE

THE OPERATIONS OF THE PRESBYTERIES, 1581-C.1610

Compeirit...Elezabeth Levenox and grantit scho past to Chrystis woll [well] becaus hir foirbearis past thair and becaus scho hade ane sair leg, and confessit that scho belevit the woll sould have helpit it, and confessis scho past ainis about the woll and that scho drank of it. Compeirit...Agnes Blair personallie and confessis scho past to the said woll to gait health to ane scharg bairne [sickly child], quhilk scho hade, and belevit that be the waschein of the bairne with the waltir of the said woll he sould ather dee or leive, and confessis scho past ainis about the woll.

- Register of the Stirling
Presbytery, 16 July 1583[1]

Anent report maid to ye p[res]b[yte]rie of a greit number of people...quha upoun mids[om]er ewin last set up banefyrs to ye festering of sup[er]stitoun & ewill ex[a]m[ple] to uyers. Q[uhai]rof ye p[res]b[yte]rie being surely i[n]formit, it is ordanit that ewery minister try in [his] awin paroche kirkis ye p[er]sones setters up of ye samin & call thame to c[om]peir ye secund of Julij nixtocum before ye p[res]b[yte]rie that order [there]fore may be takin w[i]t[h] thame as effeirs.

- Register of the Edinburgh
Presbytery, 25 June 1588[2]

With the creation of the presbyteries, the Reformed Kirk of Scotland felt it had the means to enforce uniform standards of behavior and worship, at least in those parts of the nation where the new tribunals were established. Historians can speak of Scotland as having a "Presbyterian Church" after 1581, although the term lacks precise meaning, because much definition and evolution remained before the system would become fully developed.

At least some of the original 13 presbyteries resembled the "common elderships" envisioned in the *Second Book of Discipline*, in which ministers and lay elders shared power in discipline and ecclesiastical oversight.[3] But by the late 1580s, the presbyteries had become strictly ministerial bodies,

---

[1] *SPR*, 150.

[2] SRO ms CH2/121/1, 42v. None of those who were summoned appeared on July 2, and the presbytery eventually decided to take up the matter during parochial visitations. See *ibid*, 43v, 44v-45r.

[3] James Kirk, ed., *The Second Book of Discipline*, (Edinburgh: Saint Andrew Press, 1980), 199.

devoting ever-increasing amounts of time to administrative duties such as the examination of prospective ministers, arrangements for stipends, and the visitation of parish churches. By 1610, the presbyteries had become rather regimented, with permanent moderators, many of whom were bishops in the revived Jacobean episcopate. Of course, the lay elders returned with a vengeance in 1638, ushering in a revolution which toppled the bishops and, (soon after) the king himself, but those events are beyond the scope of this study.[4] Here, the concern is the evolution of the presbyteries as disciplinary courts, and it would be best to start at the beginning, using Stirling Presbytery (for which the most complete early records exist), as an example.

Stirling Presbytery, 1581-84

The first incarnation of the Stirling Presbytery lasted from its foundation on August 8, 1581 until May 19, 1584, its last meeting before the abolition of the presbyteries mandated by the "Black Acts."[5] Ironically, the commissioners from the General Assembly who presided over its foundation—Andrew Graham, bishop of Dunblane, and Robert Montgomery, the minister of Stirling who was soon after named archbishop of Glasgow—later became prime targets of its censures, and neither took an active role in its disciplinary or administrative activities.

The boundaries of the presbytery's jurisdiction are unclear. According to the General Assembly's plan of 1581, it was to contain 24 parishes, although the kirk of Stirling itself was curiously omitted from the list.[6] Some were as far away from Stirling as Aberfoyle, 19 miles west (and slightly north), Callander, 14 miles northwest, and Tulliallan, 13 miles southeast. To the north and west the presbytery was bounded by highland regions, and to the south, east and northeast by the presbyteries of Linlithgow, Dunfermline and Perth. But one must keep in mind that the plan of 1581 was more prescriptive than descriptive. The presbytery's first meeting drew ministers from just eight parishes, and elders from only three. Three of the eight ministers came from relatively distant places not listed on the General Assembly's plan: Falkirk (11 miles southeast), Muckhart (15 miles northeast) and Fossoway (16 miles northeast). Andrew Graham (styled

---

[4] Walter Makey, *The Church of the Covenant, 1637-1651: Revolution and Social Change in Scotland*, (Edinburgh: John Donald, 1979), 37. Makey claims the contention of the supplicants of 1638 that lay elders had participated in the original presbyteries was "openly propagandist" and "no longer verifiable." But the records of both the Stirling and Dalkeith Presbyteries record the participation of lay elders. See *SPR* and SRO ms CH2/424/1, *passim*.

[5] *SPR*, 1, 220.

[6] *BUK*, 2:484.

in the register as "minister at Dunblane") and the minister at Kilbryde (just north of Dunblane) immediately protested at being required to attend the Stirling Presbytery, suggesting that they could convene their own presbytery at Dunblane.[7]

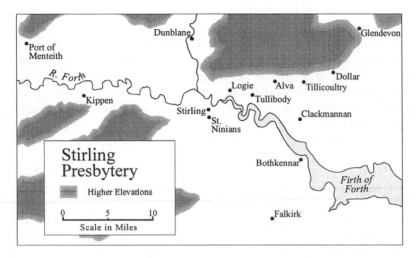

The original elders, of whom there were nine, all came from Stirling or its immediate vicinity, although two others from the distant parishes of Fossoway and Glendevon appeared two weeks later and were sworn in.[8] The presbytery's clerk began to record attendance in October 1581, thereby giving some evidence by which we can judge the enthusiasm, or at least presence, of the various elders (and ministers).[9] Attendance was at times quite low,[10] but 26 lay elders attended at least one meeting between October 1581 and May 1584. Eight of them, such as William Person from Fossoway or William Stalker, a Stirling bailie, made only one appearance, and there were several others whose participation was little better. It was quite

---

[7] *SPR*, 1. On August 22, 1581, Michael Lermonth, minister at Kilbryde, appearing on his own behalf as well as that of Graham at Dunblane and William Stirling, minister at Aberfoyle, argued that they should not be required to attend the Stirling Presbytery "becaus we haif a presbytery of our awin erectit of a lang tyme past in Dunblane be the ordur approvit be the generall kirk...." See *ibid*, 2-3. Lermonth and company seem to have confused the exercise with the presbytery, and were perhaps unaware that the newly-created presbyteries were expected to handle disciplinary cases as well as discussion of doctrine. The General Assembly ruled against the Dunblane group in October, although it continued to resist. See *ibid*, 11-13.

[8] *Ibid*, 4.

[9] *Ibid*, 8.

[10] For example, at the last meeting in October and the first two in November, 1581, when there were five, five, and three ministers, and one, none, and one elder, respectively. Both of these elders came from Stirling. See *ibid*, 10-12.

common for an elder to come once or twice in a year, then disappear, perhaps attending another meeting two years later, if then. Whatever the reason for their apparent apathy, such laymen could have had little influence within the presbytery.

Seven of the 26 elders were clearly lairds, and two others—Adam Erskine, commendator of Cambuskenneth and David Erskine, commendator of Dryburgh—were proprietors of former monastic estates. Both of the Erskines had been tutors to the young James VI, and were close relatives of the earl of Mar, regent of Scotland for a short time in 1571-2.[11] Nine others were Stirling burgesses, and one elder was said to be a notary from Corspatrick. Of the remaining seven, two were commissary judges, leaving five rural elders whose status is unclear. These five were probably substantial tenant farmers, but may have been feuars, portioners or lairds simply not identified as such.

Really, only five or six elders maintained an active interest in the presbytery's business. The two most constant were Umphra Cunningham and James Pont, commissars of Stirling and Dunblane, respectively, who appeared at 71 and 67 meetings. As judges on the commissary courts, they may have attended for official reasons. The commissaries heard divorce and testamentary cases, and the former, at least, often had disciplinary ramifications. Since the powers of the presbyteries and the commissaries alike devolved in part from the pre-Reformation bishops' courts, Cunningham and Pont may have seemed to belong more to the clerical than the lay estate. Of the four other active elders, two were officers of the burgh of Stirling, and two were lairds from the adjacent, expansive parish of St. Ninian's.[12] Another faithful attendee was Alexander Yule, master of the Stirling grammar school, but his identification as a "brethir of exercise" after the resurrection of the presbytery in 1586 suggests that he was considered a cleric rather than a layman.[13]

Just as lay participation came primarily from a small group of elders, only a few ministers played an active role in the presbytery. Here, the clique was somewhat larger (eleven men), but it still represented fewer than half of the parishes assigned to the presbytery (and some not assigned, as

---

[11] William Nimmo, *The History of Stirlingshire*, (London: Hamilton, Adams & Co., 1880), 1:122; Anon, *The History of Stirling*, (Stirling: M. Randall, 1817), 22.

[12] These were Robert Alexander (bailie), William Norwall (burgh treasurer), Alexander Forester of Garden and Duncan Nairn of Torbrex. Alexander appeared at 40 meetings, Norwall 24, Forester (whose estate of Garden was actually in Kippen parish) 30, and Nairn 17.

[13] E.g. *SPR*, 248, 250, 253-4, 257.

noted above).[14] This low level of participation reflected both the shortage
of ministers in the area, and the tenuous status of the presbytery during the
early years of its existence.

This manpower problem and institutional uncertainty are also reflected
in the disciplinary caseload of the presbytery, detailed in table 5.1. Clearly,
a sizeable minority of malefactors had little fear of the presbytery. Just over
a third (66 out of 191) of those summoned simply refused to appear to
answer the charges against them. The St. Andrews Kirk Session had a
similar rate of failure when it acted as the court of the superintendent of

TABLE 5.1—BREAKDOWN OF DISCIPLINARY CASES FOR STIRLING PRESBYTERY, 1581-84

Offense category	Cases	Males	Females	No-shows
Sexuality	89 (47%)	48	41	27 (30%)
Religious practices	43 (23%)	11	32	16 (37%)
Dealings w/outcasts	18 (9%)	16	2	3 (17%)
Disobedient to Kirk	16 (8%)	10	6	9 (56%)
Communion absence	5 (3%)	2	3	1 (20%)
Totals	191	103	88	66 (35%)

(Note: numbers within listed offense categories do not equal totals due to other cases
scattered throughout less numerous categories. "No-show" percentages are calculated for within each category.)

Fife in the 1560s, as did the rural kirk session of Monifieth in the late
1570s.[15] The numbers from Stirling demonstrate that in early 1580s the
mechanisms of social discipline could still be rather ineffective when
operating over a large rural area. Of the 66 alleged sinners who ignored the
presbytery's call between 1581 and 1584, 53 were identified as coming
from a particular community. Dunblane was the most common seat of
contumacity, with 11, or 21 percent of those identified by residence. While

---

[14] The leading ministers were Patrick Gillaspie of St. Ninians, James Anderson of Stirling,
Alexander Chisholm of Muthill, Alexander Fargy of Logie Wallach, Arthur Futhie of Airth,
Patrick Laing of Clackmannan, Michael Lermonth of Kilbryde, Adam Marshall of Fossoway,
Robert Menteith of Alva, William Stirling of Aberfoyle and Andrew Young of Dunblane.

[15] See chapter three, above.

not very far (five miles) from Stirling, Dunblane was the seat of an
uncooperative bishop (Andrew Graham), and a magistracy not very
receptive to the ideology of reform.[16] The minister Andrew Young attended
presbytery meetings regularly, but Dunblane never sent elders, and Young
complained in February 1582 that many of his parishioners had refused to
sign the Negative Confession.[17] Several prominent residents of the town had
been excommunicated, but in early 1583 the presbytery found to its dismay
that they were not being shunned. Not surprisingly, its efforts to discipline
them for not separating themselves from civil society proved unsuccessful.[18]
Moreover, Catholic festival days were openly celebrated in Dunblane as late
as 1589.[19]

Dunblane was not the only trouble spot for the Stirling Presbytery.
Directly west of Dunblane, and shadowed by highland country just to the
north was the sparsely-populated parish of Port of Menteith, which sent no
elders to the presbytery, and lacked a minister as well.[20] Eight of the 66
who refused summonses from the presbytery resided in Port of Menteith,
a number which gains significance when one considers that its population
was much smaller than Dunblane's. And while Dunblane had 12 sinners
who did appear, as against the 11 who did not, no one identified as coming
from Port of Menteith actually appeared before the presbytery during the
period under consideration. The presbytery's writ simply did not run in Port
of Menteith in the early 1580s. In 1586, a visitor's report lamented that the
parish kirk was "altogether decayit," and that there were "na elderis,
deacones nor forme off disciplein in this congregatione...."[21]

Table 5.2 is a crude attempt to compare compliance levels between some
of the parishes mentioned most often in the presbytery record, and thus
suggest where the presbytery's authority was most respected. In this
comparison, the final outcome of cases (sometimes difficult to determine)
is not the issue. Rather, the determining factor is simply whether the sinners
in question appeared when summoned. The numbers for Stirling itself are
probably the least reliable, because, in all likelihood, most of those whose
places of residence were not given (25 in all), came from Stirling. Stirling
and St. Ninians had high appearance rates because offenders from those
parishes did not have to travel far to answer summonses, their ministers

---

[16] James Kirk, ed., *Visitation of the Diocese of Dunblane and Other Churches, 1586-89*,
(Edinburgh: Scottish Record Society, 1984), 37-8.

[17] *SPR*, 32.

[18] *Ibid*, 80.

[19] WRH ms CH2/722/1, 15 April 1589.

[20] The parish was served part time by an "exhortar," or reader. See *SPR*, 22.

[21] *Dunblane Visitation*, 11.

TABLE 5.2—APPEARANCE RATES FOR SOME PARISHES WITHIN
STIRLING PRESBYTERY, 1581-84

Parish	Appeared	Refused	Appearance Rate
Stirling	13	1	93%
St. Ninians	18	6	75%
Kippen	12	6	67%
Dunblane	12	11	52%
Muthill	3	5	37%
Clackmannan	3	6	33%
Port of Menteith	0	8	0%

(James Anderson and Patrick Gillaspie) were two of the most active in the presbytery, and lay elders from the parishes also frequently attended meetings. The high rate for Kippen, a large parish whose center was nine miles west of Stirling, is harder to explain. Kippen did not have its own minister during this period, but its reader, William Stirling, sometimes attended meetings. He also read at Port of Menteith, but the fact that Kippen had a much higher appearance rate might indicate he spent most of his time and effort there.[22] Also, the active lay elder Alexander Forester of Garden, while listed at the presbytery's foundation as a representative of St. Ninians parish, took his lairdly placename (Garden) from an estate in Kippen parish. The elder John Shaw of Broich, less enthusiastic than Forester of Garden, but who nevertheless attended five meetings in 1581 and 1582, was also a resident of Kippen parish.[23]

Muthill, which had an active minister but no elders on the presbytery, was more than 11 miles northeast of Dunblane, so distance may have been the main factor in its low appearance rate, both for offenders and elders. Clackmannan, nine miles southeast of Stirling, had an active minister, but the parish was dominated by Robert Bruce of Clackmannan, a laird hostile to religious reform, and who was himself censured for adultery.[24] Thus an active ministry and cooperation from important laymen, whether elders or not, were more important than distance in getting offenders to appear before the presbytery, but distance could (as in the case of far Muthill) be

---

[22] Stirling himself was investigated by the presbytery for performing unauthorized weddings. See *SPR*, 74-5, 82, 88-9.

[23] Kirk, ed., *Dunblane Visitation*, 9.

[24] The minister, Patrick Laing, was also censured by the presbytery for his timidity in dealings with Bruce. See *SPR*, 127, 134, 164, 171, 198. Bruce was still insisting that the parish bells be rung on Christmas in 1587. See WRH ms CH2/722/1, 16 April 1588.

significant.

The prominence of sexuality in the presbytery's caseload should not be surprising, given what we have already discovered about the practice of Scottish Reformed social discipline before the foundation of the presbyteries. Sexuality generally made up just over half the caseload in urban settings before 1582, except for conservative Aberdeen, where it accounted for 65 percent. But the (scanty) evidence from rural areas suggests that disciplinary concerns outside the burghs during the early period were almost entirely sexual.[25] Much of the population in the jurisdiction of the Stirling Presbytery was rural, so the fact that so many ran afoul of the Kirk for reasons other than sexual misbehavior is evidence that change was afoot. The ministers and elders of the presbytery were now undertaking a major effort to standardize religious practice according to Reformed doctrine, and erase vestiges of Catholic "idolatry."

The widespread practice of making pilgrimages to Christ's Well, a site near Falkirk whose waters were reputed to have healing powers, was a leading target in this effort.[26] The well was first mentioned in the presbytery register in August 1581, when, "undirstanding ane papisticall pilgrimage begun at leat at Chrystis well," the presbytery ordered all ministers to investigate any of their parishioners who might have participated.[27] There was no action taken against any of them until June and July 1583, but in those two months, 38 people (32 of them women) were summoned for having made pilgrimages to Christ's Well. The presbytery had complained in May that James Stewart, Lord Doune, who was steward of the barony of Menteith, was not enforcing laws against idolatry within his bailiwick, particularly by tolerating the pilgrimages. The ministers decided to take enforcement into their own hands, commissioning their Dunblane-area colleagues to hide near the well on a Saturday evening "to espy quhat personis cumis to the said woll and report the naimis of sic personis as thai may gait to the brethrein."[28] The names were given in on May 28, and the dragnet followed.[29]

The statement by Elizabeth Lennox that "hir foirbearis past thair," indicates that making pilgrimages to the well was not a new practice, despite the presbytery's characterization of it as something begun "at leat."[30] Rather, it was a venerable aspect of local piety that the Kirk was only just

---

[25] See chapter three, above.

[26] Nimmo, *History of Stirlingshire*, 1:281-2.

[27] *SPR*, 4-5.

[28] *Ibid*, 115-6.

[29] *Ibid*, 120.

[30] *Ibid*, 150.

beginning to combat. Margaret Downy and Jonet Allane must have been surprised when, just shy of the well, they were met by "ane certane halbert men" (one of the presbytery elders?) who "struik them away," and prevented them from reaching its healing waters. Although the presbytery concluded that they had not succeeded in committing idolatry, they still had to perform public repentance for the attempt.[31]

Those who had made it to the well were asked specific questions about what they did there, and their responses testify eloquently to their fears and uncertainties, as well as their faith in folk remedies. Agnes Graham confessed that she "cust the waltir of it ovir hir schulduris," as did Janet Harvie, who said she had done so "becaus sho was seik in hir hairt and in her hed and lipnit that the woll should have helpit hir seikness." William Kay testified that his baby son was ill, and that he had left an apron string from the boy's clothing at the well, and taken some of the water for him to drink in the hope that it would cure him.[32]

The presbytery's attack on this local tradition certainly aroused opposition; on 9 July 1583, John Adam, a resident of Kippen, was ordered to do public repentance for having proclaimed the medical efficacy of the well's waters to all within earshot at Stirling's mercat cross. He admitted to having said "gif he wist to gait his haill [health] at Chrystis Woll he wald pas thair quha wald quha wald nocht."[33] The battle against pilgrimages was not quickly won, either. In 1586, some parishioners at Port of Menteith reported that there was still "ane universall abuse rinnyng to Chrystis well fra all places in May time," but they would not name guilty individuals.[34] The presbytery summoned several pilgrims in May 1593; James Baird in Muckhart told the ministers he had seen many people there, and that David Morris, who sold aquavitae, had reported "thair was many broght to yat well quha gangs hame on yair feit." Baird was ordered to do public repentance in sackcloth, but many local residents were clearly still willing to risk such a penalty in order to partake of the superior magic of the well.[35] The kirk session of Falkirk was still denouncing the pilgrimages in 1628.[36]

In addition to its actions against pilgrims, the Stirling Presbytery in its early incarnation tried to suppress other aspects of popular culture which it deemed inconsistent with godly practice. These efforts were less concerted

---

[31] *Ibid*, 140.

[32] *Ibid*, 135.

[33] *Ibid*, 147.

[34] Kirk, ed., *Dunblane Visitation*, 12.

[35] WRH ms CH2/722/2, 22 May 1593, 29 May 1593.

[36] Nimmo, *History of Stirlingshire*, 1:281-2.

than the Christ's Well campaign, and therefore involved a relatively small portion of the presbytery's caseload. Often, the presbytery would make a proclamation on a topic, but no cases would result. One colorful example of this is the denunciation of lavish wedding parties issued on 24 December 1583:

> The...brethrein undirstanding ane grit abuse and superstitioun usit be sindrie personis that cumis to parroche kirkis to be mareit in causing pyperis and fidlayeris play befoir thame to the kirk and fra the kirk, to the grit dishonour of God, for avoiding of the quhilk abuse, it is statute and ordeinit be the haill brethrein that na minister within the boundis of the presbytery marie ony personis that ar acompaneit to the kirk with playing on pyppis or ony uthir instrumentis on that day that thai ar swa accumpaneit bot sall suffir thame to depart hame on that day unmareit and swa to do thairefter quhill [until] thay cum to the kirk reverentlie as becumis thame without ony playing.[37]

Marriage, while no longer a sacrament, was nevertheless an ecclesiastical matter, and was not to be made the occasion for revelry. Music and dance were also targeted in August 1581, when the kirk session of Stirling was told to "tak ordur with sic personis as dansis on the Sabboth day speciallie with thai that dansit within the nycht in Robert Wysis hous on sonday last."[38]

In this last instance, the offense was considered particularly serious because it occurred on the Sabbath. While only two of the 191 cases handled by the presbytery in the period 1581-4 involved breach of the Sabbath, the ministers and elders were nevertheless concerned that Sunday be reserved for sermons and quietude, particularly in the burgh in which they met. On 7 May 1583, the minister of Stirling was told to order the town's bailies to punish a group of "servand men and boyis" who had held May festivities and "drum strukin" on the previous Sunday.[39] But it is unlikely that the presbytery had much effect in enforcing Sabbath observance outside Stirling itself until several years later, when cases of Sabbath breach became a significant part of its caseload.

One type of offense—in addition to sexuality and religion—which was already making up a significant part of the presbytery's caseload was contact with outcasts (18 cases, or nine percent). The outcasts were usually excommunicants, and the fact that the presbytery had to summon so many people for their refusal to shun them indicates that, in the area covered by this presbytery, excommunication brought with it little social stigma as yet.

---

[37] *SPR*, 192.
[38] *Ibid*, 4.
[39] *Ibid*, 114.

The ministers and elders found in May 1583 that an adulterous couple in Alva who had been excommunicated ten years earlier were carrying on unconcerned, despite a proclamation in the barony court of Alva that anyone associating with them would be fined. This sentence had been reconfirmed by the bishop of Dunblane in 1577, but remained ineffective.[40]

Avoidance of some people was an unrealistic expectation. Andrew Squire was accused on 17 July 1582 of friendly dealings with the excommunicated Robert Montgomery. Caught between a rock and a hard place, Squire ignored three summonses from the presbytery before he finally appeared and granted that he had led Montgomery's horse down Stirling's High Street. But he protested that this had been an unavoidable obligation; he was Montgomery's tenant. The presbytery was unimpressed by this excuse, and ordered him to perform public repentance, which, under pressure from the Stirling bailies, he finally did.[41] With excommunication the Kirk was claiming the power of the keys, but these still could not unlock the traditional loyalties of Scottish society.

In the records of the Stirling Presbytery for the period 1581-4 there is as yet little evidence of the concern for mending quarrels, particularly among the prominent, which would later become a significant part of the disciplinary business of many of the presbyteries. Three men were charged with violent attacks, and one of them, John Clark, was referred to the provincial synod for homicide, which he said had been accidental, and "for the quhilk he is sorie fra his hairt and hes obtenit remissione fra the kingis majestie and hes satisfeit the partie thairfoir."[42] The process of private justice between him and his victim's family had already taken place, and the Kirk was here seeking to seal it through Clark's public reconciliation to the congregation.

The presbyterian experiment had not gotten far when, in May 1584, it was suspended due to the crown's reaction against the association between the Melvillians and the Gowrie faction. Although restored two years later, the reconstituted presbyteries were significantly different in composition and focus from their ancestors of 1581-4. Nevertheless, the social discipline program under their purview largely picked up where it had left off.

Stirling Presbytery, 1586 and After

The first meeting of the restored presbytery took place on 21 June 1586, when four ministers and the master of Stirling's grammar school met to

---

[40] *Ibid*, 119-20.
[41] *Ibid*, 49-52.
[42] *Ibid*, 174.

consider adultery charges against David Cunningham, bishop of Aberdeen.[43] The fact that no lay elders attended was a harbinger of things to come. Lay elders never really returned to the presbytery after its two-year suspension. John Shaw of Broich made it to one meeting later in 1586, and he appeared again in March 1588, lobbying for provision of a minister to Kippen parish.[44] Another local laird assisted in a disciplinary matter the following August, and two elders (including the commissar Umphra Cunningham) were listed in the sederunt of 31 October 1592.[45] These are the only instances of attendance by lay elders in the first eight years of the restored presbytery, although laymen were occasionally chosen to help represent the presbytery at general assemblies.[46]

While the laymen stayed away, ministers began to attend more frequently. As late as the summer of 1591 there were no ministers or sessions in Glendevon, Tullibole, Tillicoultry and Mure, and no disciplinary practice in Falkirk, but the ministers' ranks were growing.[47] By August 1593, 14 ministers were active in the presbytery. Along with them ministers came increasing numbers of "brothers of exercise," ministerial apprentices who were tested in the scriptural exercise which preceded each meeting, and often later appointed to a parish post.[48] Some of the new appointees brought high status to the ministry, such as Adam Bellenden—whose mother came from the influential local family of Livingston, and whose father was Sir Lewis Bellenden of Auchnoule—appointed to the ministry of Falkirk through his mother's patronage right in 1593.[49]

But all of this scriptural discussion and debate over fine points of doctrine may have contributed to driving the lay elders away, making the presbytery an exclusive club of ministers whose levels of education and wealth were increasing. The absence of lay participation initially threatened the presbytery's ability to act as a disciplinary court; after averaging 79.5 cases per year in 1582 and 1583 (the only complete years during its early

---

[43] *Ibid*, 220-1.

[44] *Ibid*, 228; WRH ms CH2/722/1, 12 March 1588.

[45] WRH ms CH2/722/1, 27 August 1588; CH2/722/2, 31 October 1592. I have not studied the issue of attendance at the Stirling Presbytery beyond February 1594.

[46] Such as William Menteith of Carse and Alexander Bruce of Airth (probably the brother of the Edinburgh minister), chosen on 16 May 1592. The same two, plus John Murray of Touchadam, were chosen the following April. See WRH ms CH2/722/2, 16 May 1592, 17 April 1593.

[47] WRH ms CH2/722/2, 22 June, 3 August and 10 August 1591.

[48] For a general discussion of the process by which one became a minister in the early 17th century, see Walter Foster, *The Church Before the Covenants: The Church of Scotland, 1596-1638*, (Edinburgh: Scottish Academic Press, 1975), 134-8.

[49] WRH ms CH2/722/2, 29 May and 17 July 1593.

incarnation), the restored presbytery took on only six cases in the second half of 1586, and 22 cases in 1587. But the numbers of disciplinary cases soon returned to their former level, with an annual average of 77.7 for the period 1591-3. And, despite this interruption and loss of lay participation, the presbytery's main disciplinary interests remained largely the same.

TABLE 5.3—BREAKDOWN OF DISCIPLINARY CASES
FOR STIRLING PRESBYTERY, 1586-94

Offense category	Cases	Males	Females	No-shows
Sexuality	261 (49%)	140	121	57 (22%)
Religious practices	84 (16%)	75	9	35 (42%)
Sabbath breach	37 (7%)	36	1	28 (76%)
Disobedient to Kirk	36 (7%)	19	17	18 (50%)
Communion absence	27 (5%)	12	15	27 (100%)
Totals	533	351	182	191 (35%)

(Note: numbers within listed offense categories do not equal total due to other cases scattered throughout less numerous categories. "No-show" percentages calculated for within each sin category)

As before, sexuality was the presbytery's main concern. Most (144) of the sexuality cases involved adultery. It appears that by the late 1580s kirk sessions routinely referred adulterers to the presbytery. Typically, they were then ordered to perform public repentance in their parish churches every Sunday until the next semiannual provincial synod. But many offenders refused to make the journey to the synod meeting (often at Perth or Dunkeld), and in early 1591 the presbytery dropped the requirement of a synodal appearance. Instead, it began requiring six months of public repentance, followed by another appearance before the presbytery (this time in sackcloth), and then three weeks of public repentance in sackcloth before offenders were readmitted to Communion.[50] This routine must have become quite familiar to some; John Dryshell, from Tillicoultry parish, was said in September 1593 to be a six-time offender, and had admitted guilt twice

---

[50] E.g. WRH ms CH2/722/1, 24 September 1588; CH2/722/2, 9 February and 30 March 1591.

previously before the presbytery.[51] The definition of adultery was a technical one, applied strictly. For example, the cottar Alexander Dougall was told to separate from the woman with whom he had lived for nine years and by whom he had had several children, because he had been married to another woman 24 years earlier, who had deserted him after a year. Although he claimed he had been granted a divorce by a parish reader, the presbytery refused to recognize it, and held him guilty of adultery because he did not know whether the woman he had previously married was still alive.[52]

In addition to the 144 adultery cases, there were 117 other cases of a sexual nature. Some involved incest, with punishment similar to that for adultery, but with the amount of public repentance in sackcloth doubled.[53] The presbytery considered one charge of bestiality, for which the accused was imprisoned, but eventually freed after finding a cautioner who pledged £100 for his future good behavior.[54] Most of the sexual offenders not charged with adultery were charged with fornication, however. Fornication cases came before the presbytery only if the people involved were habitual offenders, had refused to answer summonses from their local kirk sessions, or came from parishes without kirk sessions. The typical punishment for fornication was a single appearance on the penitent stool, doubled for each repeat offense.[55]

While the presbytery was constantly handling sexual offenses, its other concerns varied greatly from year to year, as indicated by table 5.4. Certain offenses could dominate the caseload one year, even outstripping sexuality on occasion, and be negligible in other years. These sudden shifts are indications of an as yet underdeveloped disciplinary system. The parochial reformation was still in its infancy in many communities within the presbytery's jurisdiction, so the ministers could choose any number of fronts on which to launch a campaign. Thus in 1591, 27 people were charged with absence from Communion, and two more with absence from church. But none of the 27 even bothered to appear before the presbytery, and the fact that Sir James Chisholm of Dundorne, hereditary bailie of Dunblane, was one of them suggests that there was still little pressure to conform from magistrates in some parts of the presbytery's bailiwick.[56] Five

[51] WRH ms CH2/722/1, 24 September 1588, 4 March and 15 April 1589, 13 and 20 January 1590; CH2/722/2, 11 and 18 September, 9 and 23 October and 13 November 1593, 8 January 1594.

[52] WRH ms CH2/722/1, 15 July 1589.

[53] E.g. WRH ms CH2/722/1, 15 April 1589.

[54] WRH ms CH2/722/2, 10, 17 and 18 April 1593.

[55] E.g. *SPR*, 243-4, 277.

[56] WRH ms CH2/722/2, 27 July, 24 and 31 August 1591.

TABLE 5.4—BREAKDOWN OF CASES BY YEAR FOR STIRLING
PRESBYTERY, 1587-93

Column headings:
1 - Sexuality
2 - Religious dissent or unorthodox practice
3 - Sabbath breach
4 - Disobedient to Kirk
5 - Absence from Communion or sermons
6 - Quarrels (violent and/or verbal)
7 - Magic, witchcraft
8 - Marriage questions
9 - Dealings with excommunicants/outcasts

Year	Total	1	2	3	4	5	6	7	8	9
1587	22	15	2	-	1	-	1	-	3	-
1588	67	47	1	-	14	-	2	-	-	2
1589	111	74	30	-	3	-	3	-	1	-
1590	83	33	18	5	5	-	8	5	1	5
1591	98	27	7	21	3	29	3	3	-	-
1592	40	13	4	1	7	3	10	-	2	-
1593	95	40	21	10	3	4	1	1	1	-

(Note: figures in columns do not always add up to annual totals due to additional
scattered cases of different types.)

years earlier, when the minister James Anderson had asked Chisholm to
close the Sunday market in Dunblane, Chisholm said he could not, "becaus
the pepill wald in naways consent to change the same.". Even when it was
clear that Chisholm had no interest in wielding the civil sword in the Kirk's
interest, Anderson nevertheless appointed him and his son as royal
commissioners to punish vice in Dunblane; there were no alternatives.[57]

---

[57] Kirk, ed., *Dunblane Visitation*, 37-8. The Chisholms were related to William Chisholm,
the last Catholic bishop of Dunblane, who returned to the area (and was sought and
excommunicated by the presbytery) in 1587. See *SPR*, 294-5, 303-5, 307-8. For problems of
enforcement and unenthusiastic magistrates, see Michael F. Graham, "The Civil Sword and

For similar reasons, the presbytery had little success in Sabbath enforcement, an area of particular attention in 1591 and 1593. Of 21 men (many of them fishermen or millers) charged with working on the Sabbath in 1591, only three appeared before the presbytery. The trio received only private admonitions; the ministers obviously lacked the support which would have been needed from magistrates and the community on this issue to impose any sterner sanction.[58] The presbytery in 1590-1 resorted to public admonitions against Lord Livingston, his son and his bailies to get them to close the Sunday market within the Livingston barony in Falkirk. After a year and a half of admonitions, the market was at least temporarily halted. But despite similar efforts in Dunblane, the market there was still thriving in 1593, and seven out of ten Sabbath-breakers summoned that year declined to appear before the presbytery.[59]

Religious dissent or "idolatrous" religious practices remained a problem as well, particularly in some areas. Pilgrimages to Christ's Well continued, at least into the 1590s. But whereas most of the religious dissenters sought by the presbytery in its earlier incarnation had been Christ's Well pilgrims, relatively few of those summoned by the restored presbytery were. The switch from targeting pilgrims to taking on other forms of dissent brought with it a significant demographic change in those summoned. The vast majority of the pilgrims had been female, but the new dissenters were mostly male. Some were guilty of traditional practices such as feasting or other social activities marking Easter—"ye tyme callit of auld peace last." Fifteen residents of Dunblane were charged with "papistire" for observing Easter in the traditional fashion in April 1589 but (not surprisingly, given Chisholm control of the town), none of them bothered to appear before the presbytery.[60] Some were happy to remain beyond the pale of Reformed discipline.

If the Reformed Kirk was to acquire a monopoly on popular devotion, one sacramental function over which it needed complete control was baptism. As long as alternative sources of this service were available, Catholicism could survive. It could even gain new converts in the parents of illegitimate children seeking baptism from underground priests in order to avoid the humiliation of public repentance. One way the presbytery could attack this problem was to go after the Catholic priests known to pass

---

the Scottish Kirk, 1560-1610," in W. Fred Graham, ed., *Later Calvinism: An International Perspective*, (Kirksville, Mo.: Sixteenth Century Publishers, 1994), 237-48.

[58] WRH ms CH2/722/2, 22 June, 20 and 27 July 1591.

[59] WRH ms CH2/722/2, 5 May, 7 and 29 July, 1 and 22 September, 8 and 22 December 1590, 6 April, 17 and 24 August, 7, 21 and 28 September, 19 and 26 October 1591, 3 and 10 July, 21 August, 4 and 18 September 1593.

[60] WRH ms CH2/722/1, 15 and 29 April 1589.

through or inhabit the area. The friar George Livingston was charged with performing unauthorized baptisms in May 1588. But, like the Dunblane Catholics, he simply ignored the summons.[61] The presbytery soon abandoned this approach, since itinerant Catholic priests were unlikely to fear even excommunication, and concentrated instead on those who presented their children to unlicensed baptizers, or witnessed such baptisms. Witnessing a baptism was a social as well as a religious function, and many protestants may have been willing to witness the baptisms of Catholic neighbors as a mark of friendship or family alliance. While the Kirk still had little control over Catholics, it did have some power over their protestant friends, and could isolate the Catholics by disciplining those who participated in their rituals.

The first step in this direction came in May 1589 when Isobell Fargy confessed incest, adultery and fornication, with three different men, to the presbytery. Pressed on the details of the baptisms of her children, she admitted that the youngest had been baptized a year and a half earlier by a Catholic priest in Tillicoultry. Under further questioning, she gave the names of the witnesses to the baptism, as well as those to another baptism the priest had performed at the same time.[62] The presbytery was unable to get any of these witnesses to appear, but continued to investigate similar incidents. In early 1590 it succeeded at least in getting several witnesses to another unauthorized baptism to appear, and ordered them to perform public repentance, two of them in sackcloth.[63] Such sentences became standard practice thereafter, and parents of children baptized this way were told to have the children rebaptized by a Reformed minister.[64]

Another aspect of traditional religious practice that the presbytery sought to eliminate was burial within kirks. The leading families in every parish had customarily buried their dead beneath the kirk floor, but, by the late 1580s, the Scots reformers were seeking to preserve the kirk for the edification of the living, rather than the commemoration of the dead. That these could be viewed as competing interests is plain from the case of John Christie and John Henderson, parishioners of Logie, who admitted in 1593 to having snuck into the kirk on a Saturday night, removed the pew of David Balfour, a local laird, and broken it up. Henderson claimed they had done so because the pew "stude on yair foirbears beans [bones]."[65]

---

[61] *Ibid*, 14 May 1588.

[62] *Ibid*, 6 May 1589.

[63] *Ibid*, 3 and 17 February 1590. It is not clear whether the required public repentances were actually performed.

[64] E.g. WRH ms CH2/722/2, 5 May and 14 July 1590, 1 June and 7 September 1591.

[65] *Ibid*, 21 and 28 August and 11 September 1593.

The Stirling Presbytery charged 13 men with burying relatives in kirks between 1589 and 1593, requiring most of them to perform public repentance. Not surprisingly, some were slow to accept that it was now sinful to inter parish notables alongside their ancestors. The entire kirk session of Logie parish faced censure in February 1593 for having allowed Margaret Alexander's family to bury her within Logie kirk. The elders and deacons were made to promise "not to burie any of yair freinds in ye kirk frathymefurt and [not to] give consent to burie any p[er]son yair in tymis cu[m]ing undir ye paine of ten punds money to be payit be everie one of yame that dois in ye contrar." One elder from the Alexander family who refused to grant that the practice was sinful was deposed from the eldership.[66] Two years earlier, the messenger James Lennox had been ordered to do public repentance for accusing the minister of St. Ninians of embezzlement and for claiming there "was na warrand in ye word of god for removing bureall furt[h] of ye kirk."[67]

Many offenders, particularly prominent ones, when called before the presbytery, would claim that they were ignorant of the new policy. John Bruce, laird of Auchenbowie, charged with burying his son within St. Ninians kirk, said "he knew not that bureall in yat kirk was stayit." He also argued that the burial was "na wrang" because Alexander Callendar, another local laird, brought a book from the minister of St. Ninians "in taiken" [as a token] to the interment. This book, a psalter, turned out upon further investigation to have been stolen from the minister's house, and the two men seem to have believed that it sanctified the ceremony, regardless of its provenance. But the psalter had no such apotropaic properties in the ministers' eyes. They demanded that Callender return it and do public repentance, and that Bruce swear an oath that he did not know the book had been stolen. Callender proved stubborn, and Bruce refused to return to the presbytery, although he did purge himself before a delegation of ministers sent to his home.[68]

The campaign against burial in kirks was not unique to the Stirling Presbytery. The bailies of the Canongate were summoned to appear before the Edinburgh Presbytery twice in the late 1580s for allowing the practice in their parish, and at least one laird from the rural area around Edinburgh was charged with supervising a burial within a kirk.[69] The presbytery of St.

---

[66] WRH ms CH2/722/2, 27 February, 6, 13 and 20 March and 29 May 1593.

[67] Lennox refused to submit to discipline for several months. See *ibid*, 25 May, 1 June, 13, 20 and 27 July, 24 and 31 August 1591.

[68] *Ibid*, 23 and 30 March, 13 and 27 April and 4 May 1591.

[69] SRO ms CH2/121/1, 7r-8r, 61r-v, 8 and 29 April 1589. On the other hand, there was apparently no protest over the 1588 burial of the Countess of Argyll next to the remains of her husband, the popular earl of Moray, in St. Giles Kirk. Moray, in death even more than in life,

Andrews also dealt with the offense a number of times, and in October 1595 the Synod of Lothian vowed that in the future those who buried relatives in kirks would be forced to dig up the corpses and do public repentance.[70]

Another effort visible in the records of more than one presbytery during this period is the attack on the practice of setting bonfires to mark certain occasions. On June 25, 1588 the Stirling Presbytery lamented "ye greit multitude of bonfyris" lit two nights previously, "callit of auld midsomer evin, to ye greit dishonor of god & contemp[t] of ye kings auc[thori]tie & lawis made in ye contrar." Two ministers were delegated to speak to the earl of Mar, sheriff of Stirlingshire, and ask him to punish those who had set the fires.[71] That same month, the Edinburgh Presbytery sought unsuccessfully to round up people guilty of the same offense within its jurisdiction.[72] In October 1589, Stirling-area ministers were warned to beware of "ane sup[er]stitius forme usit be div[er]ss p[er]sonis in setting out of bon fyrs on ye evin callit alhall[ow]evin," and to warn their parishioners against doing so.[73] It is likely that such warnings availed little; no one was summoned for having lit fires, and in May 1593, the Stirling Presbytery vowed again to take action against midsummer celebrants, noting that there had been a "great nu[m]bir" of fires set the previous year.[74]

In addition their pagan undertones, these seasonal celebrations provided a forum for other activities the ministers considered dangerous, such as drinking, dancing, unsupervised courtship and riotous behavior. The same concern led the Stirling Presbytery in August 1593 again to try to restrict marriage celebrations, this time by inhibiting the reading of banns until couples found caution not to spend more than five shillings on their festivities. Of particular concern were "penny brydells," said to be scenes of "drunkines and gluttony com[m]ited be many p[er]sonis...."[75] Presumably, the wedding parties of the sons and daughters of lairds and burgesses were viewed with more indulgence. But, like the orders against bonfires and the previous proclamation against fiddlers and pipers at weddings, there is little evidence that the presbytery tried to enforce these guidelines by punishing offenders. Some aspects of popular culture were

---

was much beloved by the leadership of the Kirk. See *Edin. Recs.*, 4:525.

[70] *StAP*, 189-91, 205, 232, 251-2, 254, 260, 263, 265, 267, particularly 1598 case of Robert Bruce of Pitlethie; James Kirk, ed., *The Records of the Synod of Lothian and Tweeddale, 1589-1596, 1640-1649*, (Edinburgh: Stair Society, 1977), 99.

[71] WRH ms CH2/722/1, 25 June 1588.

[72] SRO ms CH2/121/1, 42v. The order is given in full at the beginning of this chapter.

[73] WRH ms CH2/722/1, 21 October 1589.

[74] WRH ms CH2/722/2, 22 May 1593.

[75] *Ibid*, 14 August 1593.

just too deeply rooted to be effectively outlawed by the new order of social discipline.

TABLE 5.5—APPEARANCE RATES FOR SOME PARISHES WITHIN STIRLING PRESBYTERY, 1586-94 (minimum of nine cases)

Parish	Appeared	Refused	Rate	(1581-84)
Tillicoultry	12	0	100%	-
Alva	20	3	87%	-
Stirling	19	3	86%	93%
Clackmannan	17	3	85%	33%
Kippen	19	4	83%	67%
St. Ninians	70	15	82%	75%
Glendevon	7	2	78%	-
Logie	25	8	76%	-
Tullibody	9	3	75%	-
Muckhart	7	3	70%	-
Falkirk	29	15	66%	-
Dunblane	7	18	28%	52%
Port of Menteith	2	14	12%	0%

Despite all the frustrations the presbytery was facing in its efforts to reform behavior, it was successful in extending its authority into areas which had previously been largely immune, as demonstrated in table 5.5. Discounting Stirling itself, (for which these figures are suspect due to the large number of offenders whose domicile was not mentioned, most of whom probably came from Stirling), the appearance rate improved in every major parish except Dunblane. In Dunblane, the disaffection of the Chisholms apparently weakened the presbytery's authority. Also, sinners from Muthill, 11 miles northeast of Dunblane, disappeared entirely from the records. But there were large improvements elsewhere. In Clackmannan, for instance, the appearance rate more than doubled. This may in part have been due to the declining fortunes of Robert Bruce, laird of Clackmannan, who had previously proved so uncooperative. In June 1590, the presbytery was able to force a reconciliation between him and the minister Alexander Wallace, whom he had attacked, and in August 1592 Bruce was captured by a band of Perth craftsmen after he had kidnapped two of their deacons. The townsmen of Perth kept him locked up until the following year.[76]

Another parish showing significant improvement was Kippen. Here, the placement of a regular minister was probably the critical factor; Andrew Murdo was installed as minister to replace the reader William Stirling in March 1588.[77] But in addition to strengthening its authority in parishes where it had already had some success in the period 1581-4, the presbytery was extending its powers into parishes which had been previously almost untouched by the new disciplinary order. The presbytery had charged only four sinners from Alva in its earlier incarnation, and a visitor's report in September 1586 suggested that the kirk session there did not meet regularly.[78] In 1589, the presbytery deposed Alva's minister for incompetence and appointed a new one early the next year; thereafter its residents became much more familiar with the disciplinary system.[79] The same was becoming true for residents of more distant parishes such as Muckhart and Glendevon, although the latter (along with Tillicoultry, a less-distant community with a very high appearance rate) still had no minister or kirk session as late as August 1591.[80] Even Falkirk, where it was reported in 1591 that Communion had not been celebrated for three years due to the "misordur of the pepill," was being introduced to the yoke of discipline.[81]

Of course, there remained difficult areas. Port of Menteith, on the western fringe of the presbytery's jurisdiction, was still largely beyond the pale, as was the area north of Dunblane. Dunblane itself was now even less receptive to the presbytery's intervention than it had been before the "Black Acts." But along the banks of the River Forth, from Kippen in the west to Airth and Kincardine in the east, and even up into the northeastern hills around Tillicoultry, Dollar, Muckhart and Glendevon, the presbytery was making its presence felt. When Madie Menteith, a parishioner of Clackmannan, protested in October 1589 that "ye Kirk was als gredie as evir it was," and "it wald mak ane ill end for ye gredines [there]of," she was speaking from the perspective of one who was unaccustomed to ecclesiastical intervention in her life. She apparently remembered, or at least had heard about, the financial exactions of the Catholic Church, and was

---

[76] *Ibid*, 2 and 16 June, 14 July and 18 August 1590; *The Chronicle of Perth: A Register of Remarkable Occurrences From the Year 1210 to 1668*, (Edinburgh: Maitland Club, 1831), 5.

[77] *SPR*, 292-3; WRH ms CH2/722/1, 12 March 1588.

[78] Kirk, ed., *Dunblane Visitation*, 15.

[79] WRH ms CH2/722/1, 21 October 1589, 3 and 17 February 1590. No cases originated from Alva in 1586, and only one did in 1587. The rest of the cases in table 5.5 date from after the deposition of Robert Menteith.

[80] WRH ms CH2/722/2, 3 August 1591.

[81] *Ibid*, 22 June 1591.

dismayed to find the clergy, in a different form, making a comeback. But these new clergy intruded in non-fiscal ways as well. They admonished her and made her apologize before the presbytery for her statement, and her husband was told to do public repentance for calling them "knavis & lownis."[82]

The Edinburgh Presbytery, 1586-90

The Edinburgh Presbytery differed considerably from its counterpart in Stirling. While the understaffed Kirk in Stirling and its environs sought to extend order into unruly rural parishes, many of them hitherto untouched by the new disciplinary order, the ministers of the Edinburgh Presbytery saw themselves as defenders of the cause of Christ against the worldly political interests of the nation's capital. As a result, they acted less as a disciplinary court and more as a standing committee of the General Assembly, devoting much more attention to Edinburgh and the court at Holyrood than to the surrounding rural parishes.

Several ministers who served on the Edinburgh Presbytery were among the most prominent in the national Kirk.[83] These included David Lindsay, minister of Leith, Robert Pont, Nicol Dalgleish and William Aird, ministers of St. Cuthberts, Walter Balcanquhall and Robert Bruce, ministers of Edinburgh, John Craig, Patrick Galloway and John Duncanson, ministers to the king's household, John Brand, minister of the Canongate and Patrick Simpson, minister of Cramond who later became minister of Stirling and moderator of the presbytery there. Most of these men had taken leading roles in the church polity battles of 1578-86. Balcanquhall and Aird had been exiles in 1584-5, and Dalgleish had been tried for treason for his correspondence with them.[84] Lindsay was imprisoned for his opposition to the "Black Acts," while Craig, Duncanson and Brand gained presbyterian infamy by signing them.[85] Pont, provost of Trinity College and a senator of the College of Justice, had been moderator of the General Assembly of October 1583, and therefore made the opening exhortation at the first meeting of the restored General Assembly in 1586.[86] Bruce was moderator of the assembly in February 1588, Galloway in August 1590, Dalgleish in

---

[82] WRH ms CH2/722/1, 28 October 1589.

[83] List of ministers belonging to the presbytery given in SRO ms CH2/121/1, 1r. Patrick Simpson was, ironically, the nephew of Patrick Adamson. For a short sketch of his life, see Row, 1:223-4.

[84] Calderwood, 4:236-7; *Pit. Crim.*, 1(pt. 2):136-8.

[85] Calderwood, 4:76, 167-9, 246-7.

[86] *BUK*, 2:626; Calderwood, 4:548.

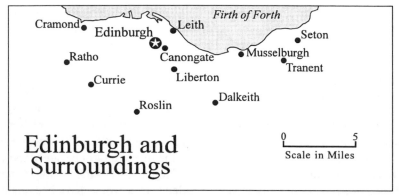

July 1591, Bruce again in May 1592 and Lindsay in April 1593.[87]

Thus the presbytery was in closest contact with the leadership of the national Kirk, and one might expect that its disciplinary activities would best reflect the latter's aspirations for moral reform. Table 5.6 gives a portrait of its caseload from its earliest meeting for which records survive (19 April 1586), until a break in the register after the meeting of 24 March 1590.

TABLE 5.6—BREAKDOWN OF DISCIPLINARY CASES
FOR EDINBURGH PRESBYTERY, 1586-90

Offense category	Cases	Males	Females	No-shows
Sexuality	58 (42%)	33	25	21 (36%)
Religious practices	32 (23%)	30	2	16 (50%)
Sabbath breach	14 (10%)	14	0	14 (100%)
Marriage questions	10 (7%)	8	2	5 (50%)
Absence from kirk	10 (7%)	7	3	8 (80%)
Non-domestic disp.	4 (3%)	4	0	3 (75%)
Totals	138	105	33	70 (51%)

(Note: numbers within listed offense categories do not equal the total due to other cases scattered throughout less numerous categories. "No-show" percentages are calculated for within each category.)

[87] *BUK*, 2:703, 767, 779, 786, 3:795; Calderwood, 4:649, 5:156, 240.

Perhaps the two most remarkable findings here are the high proportion of male offenders (76 percent) and the fact that just over half of those charged by the presbytery never answered the summons.

In terms of gender, even sexual offenders were significantly more likely to be male than female, and only eight women were charged with non-sexual sins, compared with 72 men. This was primarily due to two factors. First, as will be discussed later, the Edinburgh Presbytery was concerned to a remarkably high degree with the sins of the political élite, which was male. Secondly, this was a region where parochial discipline was not as much a novelty as in the Stirling area, so the presbytery only rarely had to fill the role of the nonexistent or non-functioning local kirk session. Given the social structure of early modern Scotland, men would have been much more able than women to resist the authority of an effective kirk session. Since the cases which reached the presbytery were generally those of the recalcitrant or prominent (or both), they mostly involved males.

The high rate of refusal to appear is deceptive, as it counts quite a few common offenders named in late 1586 who the presbytery seems to have lost interest in pursuing once it received commissions from the General Assembly to go after several eminent men, including John, eighth Lord Maxwell, Patrick Adamson and Robert Montgomery, whose loyalty to the Kirk was in doubt.[88] Fifty of the 70 who refused to appear before the presbytery were named in 1586, and 43 of them were referred to royal commissioners, ostensibly for action by civil magistrates.[89] After 1586, the "no-show" rate was a much more modest 25 percent, although a high proportion of the prominent individuals who did appear were able to drag out their cases interminably, with no clear conclusion.

While the presbytery was more successful in getting offenders to appear after 1586, this reflected more a redirection of effort than an increase in authority. As the "no-show" rate plummeted, so did the total caseload, from 59 in the last nine months of 1586 to 12 in all of 1587. After that it rebounded somewhat to 33 (1588) and 28 (1589). In contrast, the Stirling Presbytery averaged 67 cases during the three years 1587-89. The Edinburgh Presbytery did not even charge anyone with Sabbath breach during the period 1587-90, perhaps due to its inability to do anything about the 14 Sabbath-breakers named in 1586.

The magistrates of Edinburgh may have been fairly reliable in instilling

---

[88] SRO ms CH2/121/1, 14v-15r, 19r-v, 22r-v, 26r-v.

[89] *Ibid*, 11r-12v. Many of these were offenders the Kirk had been pursuing for several years, and one case (Margaret Patrick) dated to 1576.

godliness by this time,[90] but there were still 'dark corners' close by, such as Newtown (five miles southeast of Holyrood), whose residents had been directed to attend church in Musselburgh but refused, and "levis lyk infidells."[91] There was a thriving Sunday market at Tranent (10 miles east of Edinburgh) in September 1589, under the protection of the crypto-Catholic Lord Seton.[92] The presbytery did conduct parochial visitations, but relatively few sinners from outlying parishes were summoned to presbytery meetings, which were largely devoted to administrative matters related to the local and national kirks, and to disciplinary cases involving the élite and urban-dwellers.

One type of disciplinary matter in which the Edinburgh-area ministers took a greater interest than their Stirling counterparts however, was the dispute between parents and children over betrothal. For instance, in August 1586 Sir Archibald Napier complained to the presbytery that his son Francis was trying to marry Margaret Mowbray "w[i]t[h]out his knawledge or consent." The presbytery ordered the Edinburgh ministers to stay the banns of the couple while it investigated, and sent a similar directive to the ministers of Dunfermline, presumably Mowbray's domicile. Young Francis, an Edinburgh burgess, ignored a summons the following week, but his father appeared, craving a delay in the matter.[93] The fact that the presbytery kept no further record of the case suggests that father and son settled their dispute privately. The ministers had to arbitrate a similar dispute between Thomas Williamson, another Edinburgh burgess, and his son William the following February, though. Asked his objection to his son's choice, Jonet Nicholson, Williamson said she was "defamit," a charge he was challenged to prove by witnesses. Williamson brought witnesses with him two weeks later, but they testified only that Nicholson was a "virgin undefamit w[i]t[h] ony man." As a result, the presbytery concluded that William Williamson's parents had "no ressonable caus to hinder & stay ye proclama[tio]n of bands & solempniza[tio]n of mariadge," and ordered that the marriage proceed.[94]

---

[90] For example, in the Sabbath ordinance, which also ordered merchants' booths to be shut during afternoon preaching on Wednesdays and Fridays. See *Edin. Recs.*, 4:449-50, 462-3, 488-9, 492. The town's magistrates also banished one Bartholomew Bell in November 1587 for being "ane vicious and sclanderous persoun and for singing oppinly of filthie and badrie sangs." See *ibid*, 4:508. One female resident of the burgh was sentenced by the magistrates to two hours in the jougs for verbally abusing the minister William Aird after he "gently admonist hir and hir spous for blasphemyng of God...." See *ibid*, 4:510.

[91] SRO ms CH2/121/1, 12v.

[92] *Ibid*, 30 September 1589 (manuscript foliation ceases in January 1589).

[93] *Ibid*, 9r-v; Charles Watson, ed., *Roll of Edinburgh Burgesses and Guild Brethren, 1406-1700*, (Edinburgh: Scottish Record Society, 1929), 375.

[94] SRO ms CH2/121/1, 19v-20v.

In both of these cases, the ministers were following the directions of the *First Book of Discipline*, to encourage parental consultation in marriage, but if parents "have na other caus [to object] then the commoun sorte of men have; to wit, lack of guidis, or because thei ar nott so hyght-borne as thai requyre," to marry the couple anyway, provided the prospective bride and groom were adults.[95]

Both the Williamsons and Napiers were burgess families, but such prominence was not unusual in those called before the Edinburgh Presbytery. Indeed, 32 percent of those summoned can be identified with certainty as having had some sort of élite status, either as a laird, burgess or courtier. This proportion of cases involving notables is far higher than that of any other presbytery or kirk session examined in this study.[96] The Edinburgh-area ministers were particularly concerned with Catholics at court, and expended a lot of effort, with little success, trying to ensure the orthodoxy of the king's companions. Some of the latter did sign the confession of faith (probably the "Negative Confession" of 1581) proffered by the ministers,[97] but most seem to have had little fear of or respect for the Kirk's disciplinary system.

James Bellenden, the justice clerk's brother, was summoned in September 1586 for his alleged apostasy while in France. He declined to appear before the presbytery, disingenuously protesting that he could not enter Edinburgh "for feir of warding," a statement presumably based on the burgh's anti-Catholic civic ordinances. This forced the ministers to refer the matter to the Canongate Kirk Session, whose elders would not proceed against Bellenden. Later, the presbytery complained about the session's inactivity and the fact that Bellenden was in Edinburgh "daylie," but it was unable to force him to answer the apostasy charge or to do anything else about him.[98] When commissioned by the General Assembly in October 1586 to take steps against the Catholic Lord Maxwell, the presbytery deputized two of its members to phrase a summons, "and in cais of his non co[m]peirance to proceid agaínes him & give him ye first admoni[tio]n." This was obviously a delicate matter, and Maxwell declined the summons. There were no further proceedings against him by the body, though he was imprisoned at the king's command for treasonous dealings with Spain two

---

[95] James Cameron, ed., *The First Book of Discipline*, (Edinburgh: Saint Andrew Press, 1972), 192-3.

[96] For further discussion of the disciplinary courts and the élite, see chapter seven.

[97] Such as William Stewart, commendator of Pittenweem. Robert, Lord Seton declined to sign on the grounds that he had already done so in 1581. See SRO ms CH2/121/1, 47v-48v, 49v, 50v-51r, 52v, 53v.

[98] *Ibid*, 11r-v, 14v, 17r.

years later.[99]

The most prominent offenders the presbytery sought to discipline during this period were the earls of Bothwell and Huntly. Bothwell performed public repentance for his numerous misdeeds, with Bruce preaching a special sermon for the occasion, but he was seeking the mantle of champion of the Kirk which became available after the death in 1588 of the earl of Angus.[100] Huntly, on the other hand, placed little value in the Kirk's support. He was summoned for his Catholicism before his proposed marriage to a daughter of Esmé Stewart, late earl of Lennox, and did appear before the presbytery on 3 July 1588. Pressed by the ministers on his religious convictions, he agreed that good works were only produced by faith, and seemed to deny the Real Presence at Communion. Perhaps cheered by this, the presbytery allowed John Craig to proclaim the couple's banns in the Chapel Royal, in hopes of Huntly's "full reformatioun afore ye day of ye solempnizatioun." But Huntly had no interest in further reformation, and simply had the marriage performed by Patrick Adamson instead, resulting in a *fait accompli* which the presbytery was powerless to alter.[101] Huntly was the most powerful nobleman in the realm and a close friend of the king; the censures of the Kirk could bother him little.[102]

The presbytery repeatedly issued warnings to the king like that of November 1586, which lamented "ye greit number of papistes and Iesuits that daylie flockis hame & resortis in his ma[jest]ies c[om]panie to ye greit sclander of ye gospell preichit w[i]t[h]in yis c[on]traie and to ye danger of his ma[jest]ies p[er]sone," but James was little concerned.[103] Of course, the power to excommunicate carried with it by implication the power to keep someone out of the king's company. James recognized this and had no qualms about interceding to delay processes against courtiers before the Kirk invoked the ultimate sanction. By doing so he could stave off excommunication indefinitely.[104] James was happy to have his companions

---

[99] *Ibid*, 14v-15r; *Edin. Recs.*, 4:528; Keith M. Brown, *Bloodfeud in Scotland, 1573-1625: Violence, Justice and Politics in an Early Modern Society*, (Edinburgh: John Donald, 1986), 148-9.

[100] SRO ms CH2/121/1, 4 November 1589; Bruce, 349-66.

[101] SRO ms CH2/121/1, 43v, 46v.

[102] For further discussion of the Kirk's efforts to discipline Huntly, particularly in the early 1590s, see chapter seven.

[103] SRO ms CH2/121/1, 16r-v, 32r, 47r.

[104] E.g., the case of William Schaw, master of works. See *ibid*, 48r-v, 50v, 52v, 54r, 56v, 65r, 1 and 8 July, 12 August and 21 October 1589. Schaw is regarded by David Stevenson as the father of Scottish freemasonry, which may have also made him suspect in the Kirk's eyes. See David Stevenson, *The Origins of Freemasonry: Scotland's Century, 1590-1710*, (Cambridge: Cambridge University Press, 1988), 26-32.

embrace the Reformed religion, but refused to make conversion a precondition for membership in his circle.

Thus the Edinburgh Presbytery's campaign to make the court subject to
Reformed discipline met primarily with frustration, and the energy it
expended in the effort may have shortchanged other aspects of its mission.
The big fish were not biting, and many of the little ones who had slipped
through the parochial nets, particularly in the rural areas around Edinburgh,
got free while the ministers' attention was drawn to the glare of Holyrood.
The balanced effort present at Stirling was lacking here. It was lacking in
the St. Andrews Presbytery as well, although the primary distraction there
was infighting between the Melvillians and their opponents.

The St. Andrews Presbytery, 1586-1605

While several ministers on the Edinburgh Presbytery played leading roles
in the Melvillian battles of the 1570s through the 1590s, the St. Andrews
Presbytery had as members Andrew Melville (principal of the university)
and James Melville (minister of Kilrenny) themselves. Whatever their
contribution to the polity and ideology of the Reformed Kirk, the Melvilles
and their followers did little toward fostering harmony among the ministers
of St. Andrews and eastern Fife. The intensity of the disputes which
resulted crippled the presbytery at times, rendering it ineffective as an agent
of discipline, and calling into question the Melvillians' commitment to
practical moral reform if the latter required compromise on any issue they
had cast in ideological terms.

Granted, early modern Scotland was a contentious society, and the
nation's religious reformers rarely fled controversy. But the discord which
afflicted the St. Andrews Presbytery, both within its ranks and in its
relations with other local powers, surpassed even contemporary norms.
Perhaps this was inevitable, once fate and patronage had conspired to place
Andrew Melville on the faculty of the university in Patrick Adamson's
archiepiscopal seat, but it did not end with Adamson's death in 1591. The
two original protagonists set the terms of the debate in the 1580s—the
powers of the ministry and the degree to which the Kirk was subject to lay
(including royal) interference[105]—and the contest lasted into the seventeenth
century. As it continued, the two sides clashed over numerous issues barely
(if at all) related to the main questions, as if they were seeking confrontation above all else.

The first evidence of this quarrel in the presbytery register dates from

---

[105] For a discussion of these questions as they related to the Kirk's disciplinary powers,
see chapter four, above.

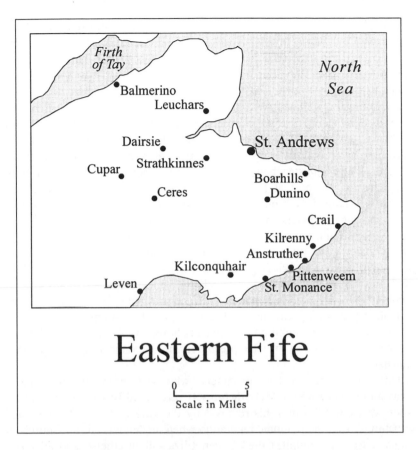

Firth
of Tay

North
Sea

Balmerino
Leuchars

Dairsie
Strathkinnes
Cupar
Ceres

St. Andrews

Boarhills
Dunino

Crail
Kilrenny
Anstruther
Kilconquhair
Leven
Pittenweem
St. Monance

Eastern Fife

0 ____ 5
Scale in Miles

late December 1586, when Adamson was charged by the presbytery with
having "altered his ordiner text of preaching" on December 25. On January
5, he granted that he had done so, explaining that he "meaned no super-
stitione," but that he "speciallie teachit that day of the nativitie to schew
himselve to be disagreand and dissasenting fra the neoteriks that hes
wretting of the birthe of Christ quhome Mr Androw Melvine [Melville]
followis." Adamson also refused to recognize that the presbytery had any
power over him as archbishop of St. Andrews.[106] Adamson himself seems
to have largely ignored the presbytery as irrelevant to his office, but some
of its members were apparently sympathetic to his views. In August 1591,
the very Melvillian Nicol Dalgleish, minister of Pittenweem and (for that
term) moderator of the presbytery, reminded several unnamed ministers that
they had not yet signed the "buik of polecie" (*Second Book of Discipline*)

---

[106] *StAP*, 11-2.

as required by the General Assembly. The dissident ministers had been given twenty days to consider the matter, but still refused to sign because they "as zitt findis thameselfis not resolut in all poyntis." Thus there was opposition to the Melvillian manifesto (however broad-based the group which had drawn it up) in the Melvilles' own backyard. As of June 1593, several ministers still had not signed the book.[107]

A disagreement in 1591 over choosing a minister for the parish of Leuchars, northwest of St. Andrews, so divided the presbytery that it split into two rival bodies, with one meeting at Cupar. A delegation of Edinburgh-area ministers had to be called in to mediate, and it chose a third candidate for the post at Leuchars. Spottiswoode, who was one of the mediators, claimed the group headed by Melville had been outvoted twenty to seven, but had defended secession from the presbytery on the grounds that "voices ought not to be numbered, but to be weighed and pondered." The division into two presbyteries proved permanent, perhaps giving Melville a more sympathetic group; he was elected moderator for the first (and only) time in 1593.[108] In 1597 King James ordered that doctors of theology (Melville was one) not sit with the presbytery when it considered disciplinary matters, leaving the latter to parochial ministers only. The implications of this inhibition are unclear, however; Andrew Melville was among those censured by the presbytery in November 1603 for poor attendance.[109]

One Melvillian on the presbytery who was probably even more contentious than Andrew Melville himself was David Black, minister at St. Andrews from 1590 until his removal by the king in 1597. Black gained something of an international reputation when he denounced the Church of England from the pulpit, called Queen Elizabeth an atheist, and all kings "the devil's bairns."[110] In January 1592, the provost and burgh council of St. Andrews complained to the presbytery that Black, who had been their minister just over a year, would no longer serve their parish, due to a "gruge of his conscience." Black defended himself from the charge of

---

[107] *Ibid*, 82, 139. Dalgleish had become minister of Pittenweem in 1589. See *ibid*, 28; *Fasti*, 5:226. For a discussion of the group which authored the *Second Book*, see the editor's introduction to James Kirk, ed., *The Second Book of Discipline*, (Edinburgh: Saint Andrew Press, 1980), 46-8.

[108] *StAP*, 83, 110-1, 147-8; Spottiswoode, 2:416-7. Moderators' terms usually lasted half a year.

[109] *StAP*, 226, 379. It is possible that, under the 1597 royal order, doctors of theology were still expected to attend the exercise which preceded each presbytery meeting.

[110] Spottiswoode, 3:21; Anne Cameron, ed., *The Warrender Papers*, (Edinburgh: Scottish History Society, 1931-2), 2:418-9; David George Mullan, *Episcopacy in Scotland: The History of an Idea, 1560-1638*, (Edinburgh: John Donald, 1986), 76.

desertion, protesting:

> he never acceptit absolutlie of the said charge and ministerie utherwys than for tryall saik to try quhether thai menit to settell ane profitable ministerie amangis thameselfis, quhilk mycht bere rewl over thaim in the richt information of thair consciences and censuring of thair maneris in everie respect....

He claimed he had found the parishioners wanting on this score, and therefore owed them no further obligation. In addition, they had refused to appoint a fellow minister to help him in the large parish, and elders were "withdrawing...ther personis from the sessioun." So, "hawing sustenit the grieff of thame as he culd...and finding no amendment by repentance," Black said he would not "disgrace his ministerie any mair amangst thaime."[111] In essence, he was arguing that a congregation which did not display 'godly' behavior did not deserve a minister, a standard which doubtless would have left most of the nation without cure of souls, or hope of reform. This was more than the presbytery was willing to swallow, and in the following weeks it ordered Black to return to the ministry of St. Andrews, while agreeing to seek a helper for him, an effort which was ultimately successful.[112]

Black's extremism alienated him from his fellow ministers as well as from his congregation. In 1595, Robert Wilkie, principal of St. Leonard's College and a former minister of St. Andrews himself, complained that Black had preached "that na man dar or can cum to god bot first he man cum to the minister," a view which would have found favor with Pope Innocent III, that thirteenth-century champion of pontifical power. Andrew Moncrieff, minister of Crail, accused Black and his fellow minister Robert Wallace of seeking unjustly to have several residents of St. Andrews imprisoned, and John Rutherford, minister of Kilconquhair, claimed Black had preached "that it was not gud and expedient that ministeris suld be at concord and unitie amangis themselfis."[113] Black flatly denied the second charge, and, as to the first, granted that he had preached that the only path to salvation came through the ministry of the Word. He admitting placing no high value on harmony among ministers, declaring "concord in wickednes was not to be inter[t]enit amangis comone Cristianis mikill les among ministers." He also admitted to an additional charge from the Synod

---

[111] *StAP*, 93-4.

[112] *Ibid*, 95-7.

[113] *Ibid*, 169. For Moncrieff, whom James Kirk has labelled a Melvillian, see *JMD*, 289, and James Kirk, *The Development of the Melvillian Movement in Late Sixteenth Century Scotland*, (Edinburgh University Ph.D. Thesis, 1972), 2:645.

of Fife that he had railed against his fellow ministers, "calling sum of them pynt aill ministeris, bellie fallowis, cycophantis, gentillmenis ministeris, leiders of the pepill to hell, and that a gritt pert of them war worthie to be hangit."[114] Rutherford (doubtless one of those he had in mind) eventually sent on to the king "a book" in which he detailed some of Black's sermonic pronouncements; this began the process which ended in Black's removal from the ministry.[115]

The view, held by Black and some of his colleagues, that the people were hopelessly corrupt, and that only a small intellectual élite within the ministry held the key to their amendment, did not endear them to their flocks. What little time the presbytery had free from ideological infighting to consider disciplinary cases was often devoted to censuring laymen who dissented from their exalted view of the ministry. In November 1595, William Simpson, bailie of Pittenweem, was brought in on the charge that he had slandered his minister, Nicol Dalgleish, before the king. Simpson allegedly told James that Dalgleish was stirring his flock to rebellion by preaching that the king was a Catholic in league with Spain, and that "the tym wald come quhen ministeris micht tak ane mendis at thair awin handis of sic as injurit or shorit them." Simpson denied that he had made any such report to the monarch, or that he had ever heard Dalgleish make these claims.[116] Whether or not he was telling the truth, the case itself is reflective of the distrust which had arisen between the clerical and lay estates, at least in eastern Fife.

If the presbytery, as a disciplinary court of the Reformed Kirk, was to help make Communion a celebration of Christian harmony, it would have to mend feuds where possible. But this peacemaking role was made more complicated when the ministers themselves engaged in violent conflict. Patrick Arthur, minister at Monimail, became embroiled in a dispute with the laird of Carslogie in 1586. The laird was summoned by the presbytery on the charge that he had hidden by a roadside, waiting to kill Arthur. He denied that he had sought to kill the minister, and avowed that any action he had taken, "he did the same in his owen defens." Witnesses testified later

---

[114] *StAP*, 170. Rutherford was subsequently deposed from the ministry, although reinstated by the king in 1597, when Black and Wallace themselves were deposed during a royal visitation of St. Andrews. See *JMD*, 417.

[115] Cameron, ed., *Warrender Papers*, 2:418.

[116] *StAP*, 178. For further disputes between Dalgleish and his parishioners, including Sir William Stewart, commendator of Pittenweem, see *ibid*, 226-8, 236-45, 260-1, 342, 375-400, 412. Dalgleish may also have been resented due to his stipend of 1822 marks per year, which would have been one of the highest in Scotland, and much of which was probably gathered from local sources. For a comparison of some ministerial stipends, see Foster, *Church Before the Covenants*, 157-8.

that the two had scuffled, and that it was unclear who had started the fight, although Carslogie "set on" Arthur again after they had been separated.[117] A gap in the register makes it impossible to tell how the case was finally resolved.

A similar dispute arose in 1586 between John Forrett, brother to the laird of that Ilk, and Thomas Douglas, minister of Balmerino. The presbytery tried to treat the matter as a "sklander" against the Kirk, and demanded that Forrett repent for it as such. But to Forrett, it was simply a feud between men; Douglas offended him first, he protested, and he (Forrett) "hes donne nane in speciall to the Kirk." Nevertheless, the presbytery found Forrett guilty because he was the first of the pair to resort to violence, and had him summoned before the Privy Council, though he never appeared and was denounced as an outlaw.[118] Four years later, he still had not performed public repentance as ordered, but came before the presbytery on a separate charge of fornication. When reminded of his previous offense, Forrett railed against the ministers,

> saying we mycht writt upon in our buikis quhat we pleasit, saying he wes not of purpose to persew the said Mr Thomas and gif it hed bene his purpose to have persewit him it suld not have bene his bluid bot his lyfe. Quhairunto Mr Thomas answerit that he praisit god that his lyfe was never in his hand bot contrare, the said Jhonis lyfe wes in his hand and god gave victorie our him at that tyme.

Douglas then took Forrett's sword and broke it, which only angered him further. "Thou nor nane that appertenis to the[e] dar stand up and wow that in my face," he fumed. "And thairupon he cutt his gluif and kiust the halt thairof to the said Mr Thomas provoking him sayand, gif thou or any in the kin dar, tak it up and meit me in ony place."

As far as Forrett was concerned, this was a simple feud, between his kin network and the Douglases. When Nicol Dalgleish stepped in and upbraided him, he replied "I ken zow [you] weill aneuch, we sall meit in ane uther place," to which Dalgleish replied:

> Supposs ze slay ane minister this day, an uther in the morn, the thrid the thrid morn, thair wilbe ay sum that will call blak blak, condem zour wikitnis and discharge thair conscience nochtwithstanding all zour bosting. As for me this is the first day that ever I saw zow or knew zow. I have not to say to zow bot

---

[117] *StAP*, 9-10, 16, 22.

[118] *Ibid*, 3, 5-6, 7-8; *Register of the Privy Council of Scotland*, (Edinburgh: Register House, 1877-98), 4:117-8.

I heit thir zour maneris.[119]

Dalgleish was here invoking the language of kin, too, but with a new twist. To him, the ministry was a family. He refused to accept that Forrett would simply take revenge on Douglases; all ministers were endangered in this grudge. The Gospel substituted the new bond of the Christian community for the carnal bonds of blood. The minister Robert Bruce had made a similar claim in 1589 when he preached, "let no community of name, ally, proximity of blood, or whatever it be, move you to pervert justice...." Christian love and justice were to prevail over tradition.[120]

Discipline could be a major weapon in this struggle, but ministers belonged to families as well, and this was something people like Forrett could not forget. When his brother the laird had a child to baptize, he refused to take it to Douglas, and had it baptized by Patrick Adamson, at that time suspended from the ministry, instead. The presbytery did succeed in getting the laird to admit this was a sin, however, and extracted a promise from him that he would "renunce...the dewtie of ane brother to Jhone Forret gif he satisfiit not the Kirk." John Forrett never did satisfy the Kirk, but was dead by January 1591, bringing the case to an end.[121]

Attacks on tradition from ministers like the Melvilles, Black and Dalgleish earned the St. Andrews Presbytery a national reputation for controversy, as well as the local enmity already discussed. John Lindsay, lord Menmuir, a lord of session and one of the "Octavians" who dominated the government in the late 1590s, drew up a list of questions regarding presbyteries which referred to several acts of the St. Andrews body he clearly considered unlawful. He questioned the secession by the Melvillian group in 1591, the involvement of the presbytery in factional squabbles within the burgh government of St. Andrews, and its slowness to excommunicate Andrew Hunter, one of its own ministers, who had joined Bothwell in rebellion.[122] Actions like these gave the king ammunition in his campaign to take control of the Kirk after 1596.[123]

In such an ideological crucible, the practice of discipline suffered. Table 5.7 offers a picture of the presbytery's disciplinary activities during the

---

[119] StAUM ms Deposit 13, 32v-33r.

[120] Bruce, 355. For further discussion of this point, see Arthur H. Williamson, *Scottish National Consciousness in the Age of James VI*, (Edinburgh: John Donald, 1979), 69-70.

[121] *StAP*, 52-3, 63, 74. Forrett is referred to as "umquhill" in the last entry, but there is no mention of how he died.

[122] NLS ms Adv. 29.2.8, 103r-v. The political feud within St. Andrews will be discussed in the next chapter. For Hunter, who the presbytery finally suspended from the ministry in 1594, see *StAP*, 159.

[123] See chapter four, above.

TABLE 5.7—BREAKDOWN OF DISCIPLINARY CASES FOR ST. ANDREWS PRESBYTERY, 1586-1605

Offense category	Cases	Males	Females	No-shows
Sexuality	164 (50%)	93	71	36 (22%)
Violent attacks	39 (12%)	38	1	20 (51%)
Magic, witchcraft	26 (8%)	6	20	13 (50%)
Slander, quarrels	20 (6%)	19	1	13 (65%)
Religious practices	16 (5%)	16	0	8 (50%)
Disobedient to Kirk	9 (3%)	9	0	4 (44%)
Totals	329	218	111	126 (38%)

(Note: numbers within listed offense categories do not equal the total due to other cases scattered throughout less numerous categories. "No-show" percentages are calculated for within each category.)

period 1586-1605. The fact that 38 percent of offenders refused to appear seems at first glance unexceptional, given the similar rate of 35 percent for the Stirling Presbytery during the period 1581-94, and it compares favorably to the 51 percent rate for the Edinburgh Presbytery between 1586 and 1590. But, as discussed earlier, the Edinburgh figure is inflated due to a large number of long-time recalcitrants sought in 1586. If the period under consideration is narrowed to 1587-90, the Edinburgh figure is a more modest 25 percent. And, much of Stirlingshire, Perthshire and Clackmannanshire was uncharted territory as far as the Kirk was concerned, whereas Fife had been one of the first regions to embrace the Reformation.[124] Fife also lacked the natural barriers with which the Stirling Presbytery had to contend. Thus the "no-show" rate of the St. Andrews Presbytery requires explanation.

The most important reason for this ineffectiveness was probably the fact that ministers like Black and theologians like Melville represented an extreme faction which secular authorities were reluctant to support. Magistrates and the general population in east Fife were committed to protestantism (indeed, there were hardly any disciplinary cases involving

---

[124] Knox, 1:224-5; Ian Cowan, *Regional Aspects of the Scottish Reformation*, (London: Historical Association, 1978), 28, 31.

Catholicism *per se*), but were wary of radicalism. The potentially seditious sermons of Black and Dalgleish placed local authorities in a difficult situation. On the one hand they appreciated the Kirk and its disciplinary system because it buttressed their own power, but Fife was not far from Holyrood, and they could not afford to be seen as tolerating attacks on the king. Significantly, the non-appearance rate dropped to 20 percent after 1600, as the controversies died down.

    Also contributing to the "no-show" problem may have been the disciplinary interests of the presbytery. Most cases involved sex, and the 22 percent non-appearance rate for sexuality cases was identical to that of the Stirling Presbytery for the period 1586-94. But the ministers of east Fife devoted a lot of disciplinary attention to other matters largely absent elsewhere, such as violence, witchcraft and verbal disputes. These (with the exception of the concern for peacemaking shown by the Canongate Kirk Session in the 1560s[125]) were mostly new to the Kirk's disciplinary system, thus yielding high rates of non-appearance. Obviously many people did not yet accept that these offenses fell within the Kirk's bailiwick. The St. Andrews Presbytery was more than a forum for radical ideology; it attempted innovations in the realm of discipline as well. Table 5.8 identifies the timing of some of those innovations.

TABLE 5.8—BREAKDOWN OF CASES BY YEAR
FOR ST. ANDREWS PRESBYTERY, 1586-1605

Column headings: 1 - Sexuality
                        2 - Violent attacks
                        3 - Magic, witchcraft
                        4 - Slander, verbal quarrels
                        5 - Religious dissent or unorthodox practices
                        6 - Disobedient to Kirk
                        7 - Marriage questions
                        8 - Dealings with excommunicants/outcasts

Year	Total	1	2	3	4	5	6	7	8
1586*	7	4	3	-	-	-	-	-	-
1587*	10	6	-	-	-	-	-	-	-
1589*	14	7	-	-	-	-	-	3	-

---

[125] See chapter three, above.

Year	Total	1	2	3	4	5	6	7	8
1590	42	26	-	2	4	1	1	-	4
1591	23	18	1	-	-	3	-	-	-
1592	22	14	1	-	-	2	2	-	-
1593	23	5	10	1	4	-	-	-	-
1594*	17	8	-	-	1	-	1	-	-
1595*	5	-	-	-	1	1	1	-	-
1596	18	5	6	-	2	2	-	-	1
1597	32	6	8	16	1	-	-	-	-
1598	27	8	1	3	5	6	-	-	-
1599	15	13	-	-	-	-	-	-	-
1600	18	10	-	1	-	-	2	2	-
1601	9	8	1	-	-	-	-	-	-
1602*	14	9	1	-	-	1	2	-	-
1603*	17	11	3	3	-	-	-	-	-
1604	11	6	1	-	2	-	-	-	-
1605	5	-	3	-	-	-	-	-	-

*indicates incomplete year, due to gaps in the register. There are no records at all
for the period from 20 April 1587 to 9 October 1589. Note that figures in columns
do not always add up to annual totals due to additional scattered cases of different
types.

One point this table makes clear is that the number of disciplinary cases
handled annually by the presbytery was still quite variable as late as the
early 1600s. The busiest period in terms of the total number of cases was
the 1590s, when the Melvillian party was at its strongest. As well as taking
on greater numbers of cases in the 1590s, the presbytery sought to enlarge
the disciplinary net. Feuds and other disputes received attention, as did
witches and those who consulted them. In particular, there were crusades
against violence in 1593 and 1596-7, and a campaign against sorcery in
1597-8.

The latter coincided with a national outbreak of witch hunting, although an earlier widespread hunt, in 1590-1, had been reflected by only two charges from this presbytery.[126] By 1597, the presbytery was ready to play a significant role in the local roundup of sorcerers. It ordered a fast for two Sundays in August 1597 as a response to disease, poor harvests, and "the discoverie of the gryt empyre of the deivill in this countrey be witchecraft."[127] It had charged four women and one man with practicing sorcery in May and June, and would charge two others (one of each sex) the following year. In addition, numerous area residents were accused of consulting the witches. Several of these clients came before the presbytery and were suspended from Communion pending public repentance, but none of the accused witches actually appeared. Rather, their depositions, already given before secular officials, were read to the presbytery and the ministers made a ruling, finding five out of the seven guilty.[128]

It is difficult to determine whether the initial pressure to pursue witches came from the ministers or magistrates, but the latter were at least enthusiastic accomplices, if not primary agents. If anything, one gets the sense local notables feared the ministers were too soft on Satan's accomplices. One of the charges brought against Dalgleish by some of his parishioners in 1597 was that he was slow to move against sorcerers and their customers.[129] The minister Andrew Duncan apprehended Geilis Gray upon the presbytery's orders in early 1599, but then the laird of Lathocker, an occasional elder of the St. Andrews Kirk Session, took her from him "and careit hir to his place of Lathocker and their torturit hir, whairby now scho is become impotent and may not labour for hir living as scho wes wont."[130] The clerk's language suggests that the ministers felt that this particular witch hunt had gone too far. Nobody else was charged by the

---

[126] *StAP*, 41, 51. The St. Andrews Kirk Session did not make any accusations related to witchcraft in 1590-1, so the church courts of eastern Fife seem to have been largely uninvolved in that hunt. As for presbyteries elsewhere, the Edinburgh Presbytery did not charge anyone with witchcraft or consulting between 1586 and 1590, although a gap in the register between March 1590 and April 1591 may conceal some cases. That presbytery was not uninterested in the subject. See SRO ms CH2/121/1, 4 May 1591. There were several cases at Stirling in 1590-1. See WRH ms CH2/722/2, 21 April, 1 and 12 May, 2, 10 and 23 June, 21 and 28 July, 18 and 25 August, 8, 17 and 29 September 1590, 3 August, 19 October and 2 November 1591. For the dates of national outbreaks, see Christina Larner, *Enemies of God: The Witch-hunt in Scotland*, (London: Chatto and Windus, 1981), 60-1. For a general discussion of the role of the Kirk's disciplinary courts in attacking witchcraft, see chapter eight, below.

[127] *StAP*, 231.

[128] *Ibid*, 221-4, 271-3, 283, 290. Those who consulted witches were given the same ritual of multiple public repentance ordered for adulterers.

[129] *Ibid*, 226, 228, 236-8.

[130] *Ibid*, 290. The laird of Lathocker had earlier been ordered to do public repentance for the murder of Alexander Brown. See *ibid*, 213-4.

presbytery with actually practicing witchcraft until late in 1603, when three accused witches appeared before the ministers, with no clear outcome.[131]

In general, the crusading spirit displayed by the presbytery in the 1590s seems to have declined after 1600. The ministers still sought to punish sexual offenders, and violent attacks continued to form a significant, if reduced, portion of their disciplinary caseload. This effort to pacify feuds and other disputes was a lasting legacy of the Melvillian years,[132] but by 1604-5, Black and Robert Wallace had been removed, Andrew Melville no longer attended meetings regularly, and Dalgleish, although elected moderator in September 1605, was often ill.[133] The extraordinarily low case total for all offenses in 1605 was certainly due in part to the plague outbreak in St. Andrews, which led the presbytery to hold meetings in other parishes,[134] but a trend toward fewer cases per year was already apparent. Black and Wallace had been replaced at St. Andrews by George Gladstaines, who was made bishop of Caithness in 1600 and archbishop of St. Andrews in 1604, and David Lindsay, who was censured by the presbytery in 1604 for poor attendance.[135] Neither those two nor most of their colleagues of the early 1600s seem to have devoted as much energy to the presbytery as their predecessors had. The "no-show" rate for offenders decreased, as noted above, but this may have been partly due to the fact that not as many were summoned, and 61 percent of the charges after 1600 involved sexual improprieties. The presbytery was retreating to safe ground after the storms of the 1590s.

This exploration of the activities of three presbyteries has demonstrated the different forms the presbyterian experiment could take in the first few decades after its genesis. As we have seen, there was often tension between the parochial needs of the Kirk, concern with which had forged the broad coalition that produced the *Second Book of Discipline*, and the ideological aspects of Presbyterianism, which aroused considerable controversy and created a backlash of resentment against the ministry. The Stirling Presbytery, while not unconcerned with ideology, concentrated primarily on strengthening the parocial system both in preaching and—more importantly for our purposes—discipline. Stirling was not a center of political power, like Edinburgh, and had no theology faculty with which to contend. These

---

[131] *Ibid*, 375, 382-3.

[132] For a general discussion of the role of presbyteries and kirk sessions in making peace between neighbors, see chapter eight, below.

[133] *StAP*, 379, 426, 435. Dalgleish died in July 1608. See *Fasti*, 5:226.

[134] *StAP*, 427-31.

[135] *Ibid*, 388; *StAKS*, 2:827, 830.

factors, and the clear weaknesses of the reform effort in the rural areas the presbytery served, made it easier for the ministers to concentrate on the parochial mission.

In Edinburgh and St. Andrews, on the other hand, politics and ideology often got in the way. This may have been a luxury the Kirk could afford in those areas, already better served by qualified ministers than most other parts of the country. The goal of making the royal court subject to discipline and thus forcing the king to choose 'godly' companions was an ambitious (and potentially revolutionary) one which the Kirk ultimately failed to achieve. Connected with this effort was the battle between the Melvillians and the crown, which resulted in the former being marginalized, within both the Kirk and the political realm. The 'Golden Act' of 1592, which gave official recognition to the presbyteries, cleared the way for parochial reform in most of the Lowlands, but it was no *carte blanche* for ministerial domination, as some of the ministers of the St. Andrews Presbytery had interpreted it. The latter were on the cutting edge of a knife which was soon broken, although their disciplinary innovations, particularly in trying to mend disputes among laypeople, outlasted their brief ascendancy.

There were also similarities between the disciplinary activities of all three presbyteries studied here. The presbyteries were less concerned with sexuality than the kirk sessions, although it was still the leading element in their caseloads, comprising 48 percent.[136] By contrast, 55 percent of all kirk session cases involved sexuality. The presbyteries as a group were also much more likely to summon prominent offenders, (19 percent of presbytery cases as opposed to seven percent of kirk session cases) and made greater efforts to enforce religious orthodoxy (15 percent as opposed to four percent). This concentration on more difficult cases, as well as the distance of travel involved, gave the presbyteries a non-appearance problem from which the kirk sessions did not suffer much. Thirty-eight percent of those charged by the presbyteries never appeared to answer the accusations, while for kirk sessions this rate was a much more modest 18 percent. On the other hand, the presbyteries were starting to get institutional recognition from unexpected corners; the "Second Schaw Statutes" of 1599, a document associated with the early history of Scottish freemasonry, specified that the wardens of masons' lodges were to be answerable to presbyteries for offenses committed by lodge members.[137]

Walter Foster has suggested that "at the beginning of the seventeenth

---

[136] The figure of 48 percent is for the total caseload of all three presbyteries. Individually, their concern with sexuality ranged from 42 to 50 percent.

[137] Stevenson, *Origins of Freemasonry*, 45.

century, the presbytery was the newest and probably the weakest unit of church government," but that it was much strengthened by 1640.[138] This chapter has confirmed the presbyteries' weakness around 1600, while shedding light on their development prior to that date. It was at the level of the presbytery that the Kirk's political role merged with its disciplinary function, often an uneasy combination. The kirk sessions were usually better able to concentrate on discipline, and it is to them that we now return.

---

[138] Foster, *Church Before the Covenants*, 86.

CHAPTER SIX

THE DISCIPLINARY NET WIDENS, 1582-1610

Wirk na euill wark on Haly day, Fle from all sinfull lust and sleuth,
Walk and be sober, fast and pray, Heir him that prieche the word of treuth.
Commit na kinde of licherie, Bot leif ane chaist and sober lyfe,
Want thow the gift of Chaistitie, Burne not in lust, bot wed ane wyfe.
- The Good and Godly Ballads[1]

The quhilk day [21 November 1599], in consideration that divers personis...in
making repentance befoir the pulpeit for thair evill lyiff and conversation,
uteris proud and querelling speiches, testifying thairby the pryid of thair hartis
and the litill regaird of God and disciplene; it is thairfoir ordinit that
quhatsumevir person or personis, in making of repentance befoir the pulpeit,
uteris proud and querellous speiches, and behaves nocht thame selffis humblie,
sal be repellit for that tyme, and put and keipit in pressoun, till thai find
cautioun to satisfie on the penitent stule of repentance the nixt Saboth
following.
- Register of the kirk session of St. Andrews[2]

In the three decades after the foundation of the presbyteries, most rural
lowland Scots got what was probably their first real taste of the new
disciplinary order. Their urban counterparts experienced this earlier, but in
rural areas the ministers and elders had much more to overcome—distance,
isolation, uncooperative lairds, absentee landowners and the fragmentation
of authority—before their powers could be made effective. It was also only
during this period that the practical disciplinary agenda moved beyond
sexuality and marriage and into new areas of concern to the Kirk, such as
the preservation of the Sabbath, attendance at sermons, Communion and
catechism, repression of "idolatry" and magical practices, and the fostering
of neighborly and familial harmony. Although some urban kirk sessions had
taken up one or more of these issues earlier, in most places they did not
become important until 1585 or after. The presbyteries played a major role
in directing, encouraging and policing local sessions and ministers, as we
have seen, and they deserve a large part of the credit (or blame), for both
bringing the disciplinary system into parishes hitherto untouched and

---

[1] *A Compendious Book of Psalms and Spiritual Songs, Commonly Known as the Gude and
Godlie Ballates,* (Edinburgh: W. Paterson, 1868; follows Edinburgh: John Ross, 1578 edition),
7-8.

[2] *StAKS,* 2:910.

drawing a wider range of offenses under its umbrella.

As before, local practices varied widely, and there were also significant differences in the roles played by urban and rural kirk sessions. To assess properly the evolution of the system, we should continue to explore widely, incorporating the experiences of several scattered communities. Once again, the St. Andrews Kirk Session supplies the most complete record, and we will begin in that urban setting, where some form of discipline had been practiced since 1560, before branching out into rural areas with less experience of the new order.

St. Andrews

The previous chapter included a discussion of the activities of the St. Andrews Presbytery after 1586, and the controversies which raged, both within and around it. The burgh of St. Andrews itself was the storm center of these disturbances. There, the perennially uneasy relationship between town and gown, combined with the strong personalities of Andrew Melville and his local followers, continued resistance to kirk session discipline in some quarters, and conflicts within the burgh oligarchy, created a highly volatile mixture. Certainly, the first two decades of the Reformation in St. Andrews had not been entirely free of conflict,[3] but the burgh had been relatively receptive to the new order. The local consensus broke down in the 1580s and 1590s, however, as religious radicals like Melville, David Black and Robert Wallace sought to use the pulpit and the kirk session in the service of an ardent presbyterianism distasteful to both a large part of the town's leadership and the crown.

Andrew Melville came to St. Andrews from Glasgow in 1580 to serve as principal of St. Mary's College. In 1590, he was elected rector of the university.[4] One should not conclude that, just because of his academic importance and influence in the Kirk nationally, he was necessarily a powerful figure in burgh affairs.[5] Indeed, his other obligations probably left him little time for civic matters, and the burgh authorities were ever wary of the colleges, anyway. But he and his nephew James, as well as Robert

---

[3] See chapter three, above.

[4] Thomas McRie, *Life of Andrew Melville*, (Edinburgh: William Blackwood, 1856), 76, 153.

[5] As has Geoffrey Parker. See his "The 'Kirk By Law Established' and the Origins of the 'Taming of Scotland': St. Andrews 1559-1600," in Leah Leneman, ed., *Perspectives in Scottish Social History: Essays In Honour of Rosalind Mitchison*, (Aberdeen: Aberdeen University Press, 1988), 1-32, esp. at 15. This essay was subsequently republished, with minor changes, in Raymond Mentzer, ed., *Sin and the Calvinists: Morals Control and the Consistory in the Reformed Tradition*, (Kirksville, Mo.: Sixteenth Century Publishers, 1994), 159-97.

Pont, minister of St. Cuthbert's, Edinburgh, did fill in as part-time preachers after the death in 1581 of Robert Hamilton, the burgh's minister, until a full-time replacement could be found.[6]

Andrew Melville was blunter in calling attention to the sins of the local notables than the more politic Hamilton had been, and the full-time ministers who followed continued in Melville's style. James Melville reported: "sa Mr Andro, coming in the pulpit, spak the treuthe of all thingis with grait ardentness and zeall," chastizing the town's leadership. "This was takine sa hiche, that a grait space ther was na thong bot affixing of plackarts upon the Collage yett [gate], bosting with batoning, burning and chassing out of the town." James Lermonth of Dairsie, the burgh's provost, was so offended that he stormed out of the kirk during a sermon. His son James posted a placard in Italian and French denouncing Andrew Melville after the latter publicly denounced him as a "Frencheist, Italianist, jolie gentleman, who has defyled the bed of sa manie maried," and warned that young Lermonth would never have legitimate offspring—a prediction which, James Melville avowed, came true.[7]

An archery accident in 1592, in which a student wounded one of the burgh's elderly maltmen, led to a riot by craftsmen against the university, with Andrew Melville's residence chosen as a particular target.[8] Clearly, he remained unpopular with much of the burgh establishment; this division was underscored by Melville's support of a civic coup in the fall of 1593 which ousted Lermonth of Dairsie as provost, inaugurating a two-year regime under William Murray of Pitcarleis. Melville and his followers could not have been pleased by the restoration of the Lermonths in 1595.[9]

Such factionalism no doubt contributed to the burgh's chronic difficulties in finding and paying suitable ministers, a shortcoming particularly evident in the 1580s and early 1590s. Instability in the ministry was bound to have an adverse effect on the kirk session's disciplinary powers, and this factor must be considered when examining the session's caseload. After Robert Hamilton's death in 1581, the session and burgh council sought, unsuccessfully, to lure Robert Pont to St. Andrews on a permanent basis.[10] Why he declined is unclear, but he may have found the stipend too small; Pont was a senator in the College of Justice in Edinburgh, and an important figure in the Kirk nationally. Alexander Arbuthnet, principal of King's College, Aberdeen, likewise refused to accept the post in August 1583 (he

---

[6] McRie, 86-7.

[7] *JMD*, 125-6.

[8] *Ibid*, 307-8.

[9] For a fuller discussion of these events, see chapter seven, below.

[10] *StAKS*, 1:460-1, 463, 2:488.

died soon afterward), and the pulpit was still vacant in February 1584, when the presbytery of St. Andrews named Henry Leiche and Thomas Wood as temporary co-ministers.[11]

But these appointments apparently did not long survive the dissolution of the presbyteries in May, because on 22 July 1584, John Rutherford, provost of St. Salvator's College and a former kirk session elder, was installed as minister. His tenure also proved short; he fell victim to the plague outbreak which ravaged St. Andrews and several other Scottish burghs in 1585-6.[12] There are no records of kirk session meetings between August 1585 and June 1586; the dislocation caused by pestilence may have prevented any from taking place. Robert Wilkie, a member of the St. Andrews theology faculty, was named burgh minister when a new session convened on 29 June 1586.[13] Significantly, the session ruled at its next meeting that all business conducted at meetings be kept secret, and that all disputes between members of the session be tried fully by the session before being passed on to "ony uther juge," a move probably aimed at the newly-revived St. Andrews Presbytery, of which Wilkie was a charter member, and of which the lay elders remained suspicious.[14]

Wilkie stabilized the ministry for a time, serving just over four years. His mildness probably appealed to the burgh authorities; later, he was one of those who opposed the firebrand Melvillian David Black within the presbytery.[15] When Henry Hamilton, a burgess of the town and client of Archbishop Patrick Adamson, publicly criticized Wilkie's doctrine in October 1588, the session rushed to its minister's defense, and ordered Hamilton to confess publicly that he had offended Wilkie and the Kirk.[16] Wilkie was assisted in his responsibilities by a reader, but there were also efforts to find a second minister to serve the large parish. An offer was made to Robert Bruce, minister of Edinburgh, in May 1589, but he declined, possibly because he was placed on the Privy Council later that

---

[11] *Ibid*, 2:506, 514, 520.

[12] *Ibid*, 2:532, 559; *JMD*, 222, 245.

[13] *StAKS*, 2:560-1; Calderwood, 4:513, 517.

[14] *StAKS*, 2:563. For evidence of earlier opposition to the presbytery, see Calderwood, 3:710-11; *BUK*, 2:616-7. For a later jurisdictional battle involving the reading of a couple's banns, in which the session appealed to the burgh council against the presbytery, see *StAKS*, 2:593-6, 599, 601, 604.

[15] *StAP*, 169. For more on opposition to Black within the presbytery, see chapter five, above.

[16] *StAKS*, 2:626-7, 629-30. Hamilton was also involved in a fatal scuffle in 1589 which led to a bloodfeud pitting the Smiths and Welwoods (supported by the Melvilles) against the Arthurs and Lindsays. See *JMD*, 272-5, as well as chapter eight, below.

year.[17] Always more suited for the academic than the civic life, Wilkie was in late 1590 transferred by the General Assembly to the post of principal of St. Leonards College, where he could resume his professorial duties while ministering to the small university parish of St. Leonards. Replacing him in the burgh pulpit was David Black, who was to prove an entirely different sort of minister.[18]

We have already discussed the battles between Black and his parishioners which were carried to the presbytery of St. Andrews, including his "strike" in the winter of 1591-2 owing to the unruliness of the congregation and the burgh's unwillingness to hire a second minister to assist him.[19] In September 1592, Black was still complaining to the kirk session that the Sabbath was ignored, the poor not supported and "the maneris of the pepill" uncorrected. He wanted to divide the parish in two, with another minister taking half.[20] This plea got some response, as the number of cases handled by the session increased dramatically for a time. Twenty-two of the 39 cases handled by the kirk session in 1592 date from September and after, and the annual total went up to 82 the following year, and 118 in 1594, before declining. In May 1593, the presbytery formally installed Robert Wallace, another firm Melvillian, as co-minister, despite the objections of the provost, bailies and 33 burgesses, who said they would not pay his stipend.[21]

The removal of Lermonth of Dairsie as provost in October 1593 brought in a more sympathetic civic regime, and in November Black and Wallace were finally able to divide the parish.[22] A huge kirk session was then elected, with six elders from the university, 22 from the burgh, and 11 from the surrounding rural area, plus 12 urban and eight rural deacons. The new provost, William Murray of Pitcarleis, took a seat on the session, something his predecessor had never done. Most of the elders and deacons were assigned to one or the other parish, although the session continued to meet *en masse*.[23] The two-parish system survived the Lermonth restoration in 1595, but not the removal of Black and Wallace in 1597.

The two ministers enjoyed a stormy tenure. The new civic regime used

---

[17] *StAKS*, 2:641-2; *JMD*, 277. Geoffrey Parker has written that Bruce became minister in St. Andrews, and given him partial credit for the tightening of discipline there in the 1590s. He is in error on this point, however; Bruce was the most prominent preaching minister in Scotland at the time, and his career at court and in Edinburgh's pulpit is quite well-known. See Parker, "Kirk By Law Established," 16.

[18] *StAKS*, 2:687-8; *StAP*, 68.

[19] See chapter five, above; *StAP*, 93-7, 107-8.

[20] *StAKS*, 2:725.

[21] *Ibid*, 2:751; *StAP*, 126-30, 131, 133.

[22] For their earlier efforts in this regard, see *StAKS*, 2:754-5; *StAP*, 138-9, 140-6.

[23] *StAKS*, 2:760-3.

the session to buttress its tenuous hold on power, threatening burgesses who challenged the elected council with censure by the Kirk.[24] But, one by one, supporters of Lermonth crept back onto the council and session. Steven Philip, elder and dean of guild, was deposed from the session and fined £10 in September 1595 for speaking "without license" in a meeting, using the occasion to attack Andrew Melville and another elder, and to denounce the "form of the discipline of the kirk ressavit and observit in this kirk." The session voted that all elders or deacons making such comments in the future would also be deposed.[25] But Lermonth emerged victorious from the civic elections the following month and, significantly, had himself elected to the kirk session as well.[26] Within a couple of years, Philip had returned to the eldership.[27] In December 1596, just after "gravlie and sinceirly reproving the enormeteis and sinnes" of the congregation from the pulpit, Wallace was assaulted by one of the provost's kinsmen "with bosting and thret[en]ing behaviour in the face of all the peipill." Neither the session nor the presbytery were able to do anything about it.[28]

Always controversial at home, the burgh's two ministers were by late 1596 incurring the wrath of higher powers as well. The anti-episcopal riot in Edinburgh in December proved a turning point nationally, convincing James VI that the crown had to take control of the Kirk, but Black already had a bad reputation with the king. In August 1595, James had summoned him to Falkland because he had denounced the king's late mother in a sermon.[29] In November 1596 Black was again called, this time to face the Privy Council in Edinburgh, for a sermon in which he had criticized the king and council, branded all kings as offspring of the Devil, and England's Queen Elizabeth as an atheist. Although Black protested that only his own presbytery could censure him for what he said in sermons, King James banished him north of the Tay, thus preventing his return to his parish.[30]

Black seems to have had some supporters within the burgh establishment, particularly on the kirk session, but in most quarters he had worn out

---

[24] See chapter seven, below.

[25] *StAKS*, 2:799.

[26] *Ibid*, 2:802.

[27] *Ibid*, 2:870-1.

[28] The presbytery did request that the burgh's bailies "renew" the attacker's caution, but it is not clear that they did. In any case, this would not have been much of a punishment. See *StAP*, 211.

[29] *JMD*, 323-6.

[30] Annie Cameron, ed., *The Warrender Papers*, (Edinburgh: Scottish History Society, 1931-2), 2:419; Spottiswoode, 3:13-26; Calderwood, 5:453-98. Note that Edinburgh's ministers were themselves banished after the disturbance in December, although allowed to return several months later. See Calderwood, 5:536-7, 624-6, 651.

whatever welcome he originally received. On 9 January 1597, the kirk session deputized Wallace and two elders to urge the burgh council to petition the king "for releif of Mr. Daud Blak our pastour," but when a delegation from the council and session complained to the presbytery that they lacked "the comfort of the word" due to Black's removal, they were coldly told "it wes they themselffis that wer the cause of it."[31] No petition from the council for his restoration has survived, although the session continued to intercede on his behalf through the spring.[32] By February, Wallace was under fire as well, for his public charge that John Lindsay, lord Menmuir, one of the "octavians" who were the king's principal advisers in the late 1590s, had practiced bribery, and been unfair in his dealings with Black.[33] Both Wallace and Black were formally removed from the ministry at St. Andrews during a royal visitation in July, the same visitation during which Andrew Melville was replaced by Wilkie (the former burgh minister) as university rector.[34]

Black and Wallace were replaced by George Gladstaines and David Lindsay, men more palatable both to the burgh establishment and the crown. Gladstaines was a future bishop (Caithness) and archbishop (St. Andrews), although less is known about Lindsay, who apparently lacked enthusiasm, at least in the presbytery's eyes.[35] Significantly, Gladstaines later reviewed the session register and crossed out at least one entry which detailed punishment for members of the Lermonth party for their legal challenge to the 1593 burgh elections.[36] He was an Erastian who opposed the Melvillians, both locally and nationally. After the confrontational relationship between ministers and magistrates favored by Black and Wallace, the burgh now had a moderate-conservative ministry which shared the outlook of its provost and council.

Since the minister likely was a major influence on the actions of any kirk session, one must keep this ministerial history in mind when examining the session's disciplinary record.[37] The examination commences with table 6.1.

---

[31] *StAKS*, 2:823; *StAP*, 213.

[32] *StAKS*, 2:825-6.

[33] *StAP*, 215-7, 219.

[34] Spottiswoode, 3:62-5; *JMD*, 417-9.

[35] He is not to be confused with the David Lindsay who was minister of Leith and later Bishop of Ross, although like that David Lindsay he might have been related to Menmuir, which perhaps helped him get the ministerial post. He was censured by the presbytery in 1604 for poor attendance. See *StAP*, 394.

[36] *StAKS*, 772.

[37] For a discussion of session membership, see chapter three, above.

TABLE 6.1—BREAKDOWN OF DISCIPLINARY CASES FOR
ST. ANDREWS KIRK SESSION, 1582-1600

Offense category	Cases	Males	Females	No-shows
Sexuality	894 (64%)	447	447	146 (16%)
Sabbath breach	173 (12%)	151	22	15 (9%)
Violent attacks	44 (3%)	35	9	6 (14%)
Slander/bickering	41 (3%)	18	23	8 (20%)
Church absence	41 (3%)	30	11	2 (5%)
Domestic disputes	32 (2%)	21	11	5 (16%)
Political dissent	22 (1.5%)	22	0	9 (41%)
Relig. diss/practice	22 (1.5%)	22	0	1 (5%)
Dealing w/outcasts	21 (1.5%)	11	10	7 (33%)
Drunkenness	18 (1%)	17	1	1 (6%)
Dancing, gaming	14 (1%)	11	3	0
Totals	1405	843	562	214 (15%)

(Note: numbers within listed offense categories do not equal the total due to other cases scattered throughout less numerous categories. "No-show" percentages are calculated for within each category.)

Just as it had been during the period 1559-81, (discussed in chapter three), sexuality remained the kirk session's main disciplinary concern. Indeed, the session seems to have been even more obsessed with sex after 1581, when sexual offenses comprised 64 percent of cases, as against 58 percent during the early period. With this increased concern came an increased effectiveness; the "no-show" rate for sexual offenders declined from 21 percent in 1559-81 to 16 percent during 1582-1600.[38] Punishments also

---

[38] There are several cases in the register during the later period of men seeking to shield themselves from sexual charges by preventing the women involved from appearing to testify. The fact that they were finding this expedient necessary suggests that it was increasingly difficult to avoid disciplinary action once a woman had testified under oath against her paramour. See *StAKS*, 2:716-7, 724.

became stiffer. Fines were only mentioned in 11 of the 437 sexual cases (2.5 percent) during the early period, but 195 of the 894 post-1581 sexual offenders (22 percent) are recorded as having been fined, in addition to performing public repentance. The amounts of fines levied steadily increased as well. In 1582, they ranged from 10 to 30 shillings, (with fines mentioned in 19 percent of sexual cases), while in 1590 the minimum amount mentioned was one mark (13s4d) and the maximum £6, with 18 percent of sexual offenders fined. In 1594 this range had risen to a minimum of 20 shillings and a maximum of £24, with a sexual "fine rate" of 40 percent.[39] Corporal punishments had been introduced for those who could not pay. One notorious female fornicator had been ordered to spend time in the "jougs" (an iron bridle with a gag set up in the marketplace) as early as 1564, but by 1593 this was standard procedure for women who had offended more than once.[40]

This new strictness was due in part to better support from local magistrates. In December 1593, the new burgh council (Lermonth of Dairsie having been ousted as provost two months before) resolved to enforce fully a 1567 act of Parliament mandating that first-time fornicators of both sexes pay a fine of £40 or else be imprisoned for a week on bread and water, followed by a spell in the jougs. This civil punishment was to be imposed in addition to the ecclesiastical punishment of public repentance, and was to be doubled for repeat offenses.[41] In fact, the full £40 does not seem to have ever been imposed, but fines of 20 shillings, and usually more, became quite common for first-time fornicators, with those unable to pay given imprisonment and the jougs. In April 1599, "finding the syn of fornicatioun and huredum grytlie to incres in this citie and congregatioun," the session requested that local magistrates force offenders to pay at least £4 to avoid prison.[42] Unlike many previous pleas for magisterial strictness, this one seems to have gotten some results; roughly half of the fornication fines in 1599 for which the amount was mentioned were £4 or more, and in 1600 the percentage increased to 89 percent.[43]

---

[39] Urban Scots laborers' wages during this period ranged from three to six pence Sterling per day, or 30-60d Scots. See L.M. Cullen, T.C. Smout and A. Gibson, "Wages and Comparative Development in Ireland and Scotland, 1565-1780," in Rosalind Mitchison and Peter Roebuck, eds., *Economy and Society in Scotland and Ireland, 1500-1939*, (Edinburgh: John Donald, 1988), 105-16, at 107.

[40] *StAKS*, 1:191, 2:766.

[41] *Ibid*, 2:767; *APS*, 3:25-6.

[42] *StAKS*, 2:887, 891.

[43] Of course, the fact that a fine was listed does not always mean it was collected. Several elders who had been delegated to collect fines in 1597 apparently had not done so, and sought extensions of deadlines to collect them in November. See *ibid*, 2:840-1.

Of course, those guilty of more serious sexual offenses were not spared. Sometimes they received exemplary punishments, as on December 8, 1594 when the adulterer James Kingzow was, on kirk session orders,

> jokit, cartit and that throw the haill streitis of the town, and cariit to the North Hauche of this citee, the haill scolaris and utheris, ane grea[t] multitude of pepill, upon Mononday ane merkat day, being his convoy, casting rottin eggis filth and glar at him, [he] wes at last dowkit ower the heid diveris tymes.

He was also banished from the town "in the will and optioun of the magistratis," but this may have only been an empty formality designed to coax a fine out of him, as he was also told to do public repentance in sackcloth several times, until the kirk session was satisfied with him.[44] While the punishment was relatively severe, it was still far milder than the death penalty which Parliament had mandated for adulterers in 1563, and reconfirmed in 1581.[45]

As can be seen in table 6.2, sexual cases dropped precipitously in 1595-6. This has led one historian who has examined social discipline at St. Andrews to opine that the stiff punishments had spurred a true "reformation of manners."[46] It is rash to conclude that sexual behavior could have been changed so quickly, though, particularly in light of the fact that sexuality cases returned in large numbers after 1596. It seems more plausible that the vow of the council to enforce the act of Parliament in December 1593 led to a gradual shift of sexual cases out of the session and into the burgh bailies' court, for which the records have not survived. After the restoration of the Lermonth regime in late 1595, burgh officials eventually decided that sexual cases were an ecclesiastical matter after all, a conclusion similar to that reached by a criminal assize in Aberdeen in 1599.[47] But while illicit sexuality was ultimately to remain a matter for the session to punish, by the 1590s, under the ministry of Black and Wallace, it was sharing space on the disciplinary ledger with quite a few other kinds of offenses.

In the early period 1559-1581, religious dissent, mainly lingering Catholicism, had been the kirk session's second leading concern, after sexual misbehavior.[48] But, as the above table indicates, it was no longer much of an issue locally by the last two decades of the sixteenth century. There was a crackdown in 1599-1600 on the celebration of Trinity Sunday in the nearby villages of Raderny and Kincaple, but the activities to which

---

[44] *StAKS*, 2:793.

[45] *APS*, 2:539, 3:213.

[46] Parker, "Kirk by Law Established," 17-8.

[47] *Aber. Recs.*, 2:203.

[48] See chapter three, above.

the celebrants admitted—playing football, piping, dancing and "ryiotus usage"—were devoid of religious content.[49] This was more an attack on popular culture and Sabbath breach than on Catholicism. Indeed, the session was now much more concerned with proper Sabbath observance than with "papistry" or "idolatry."

TABLE 6.2—BREAKDOWN OF CASES BY YEAR FOR
ST. ANDREWS KIRK SESSION, 1582-1600

Column Headings:
    1 - Sexuality
    2 - Sabbath breach
    3 - Violent attacks
    4 - Slander, quarrels
    5 - Absence from kirk
    6 - Domestic disputes
    7 - Political dissent
    8 - Religious dissent or unorthodox practices
    9 - Dealings with excommunicants/outcasts

Year	Total	1	2	3	4	5	6	7	8	9
1582	80	43	22	1	5	-	-	-	1	4
1583	57	41	7	-	2	-	2	-	-	-
1584	109	101	-	-	-	-	3	-	-	1
1585*	39	34	-	-	-	-	3	-	-	-
1586*	53	49	-	-	1	-	-	-	1	1
1587	77	74	-	-	-	-	1	-	2	-
1588	49	44	-	-	-	-	1	-	1	-
1589	77	67	-	-	-	-	3	-	-	1
1590	99	85	5	-	4	-	1	-	-	3
1591	76	63	4	2	1	1	-	-	-	-

---

[49] *StAKS*, 2:892-3, 897, 925-7.

Year	Total	1	2	3	4	5	6	7	8	9
1592	39	37	-	-	-	1	1	-	-	-
1593	82	70	3	3	-	-	-	-	3	-
1594	118	35	40	-	2	2	2	20	1	-
1595	45	6	3	3	3	9	6	-	-	-
1596	37	4	15	1	2	6	4	-	-	-
1597	49	13	11	4	3	9	2	-	-	3
1598	99	42	15	3	8	7	2	2	-	4
1599	143	50	33	21	8	5	1	-	4	4
1600+	77	36	15	6	2	1	-	-	9	-

*plague years
+partial year—register ends in October
Note: numbers within years may not add up to the listed annual totals due to
leftover cases which do not fit the listed categories.

There had been sporadic attempts to enforce the Sabbath prior to 1582, but
virtually all of those who bothered to appear before the kirk session when
charged with its violation were released with private admonitions.[50] The
wide fluctuations in numbers of cases handled suggest that the session's
periodic efforts lacked the support needed from the local magistrates and
population to inflict punishments which might have deterred others. The
community was willing to grant that the Sabbath ought to be respected, but
was not prepared to make examples of those who dishonored it. The
roundup of Sabbath-breakers in 1582 (22 cases) probably reflects the
influence of Pont and the Melvilles, who were filling in the burgh's pulpit
for the time, but all 22 offenders were released with a mere warning. Most
of those summoned for the offense in 1583 did not bother to show up.

The session then abandoned further efforts in this area, concentrating
almost exclusively on illicit sexuality—a type of sin that all local powers
agreed deserved punishment—for the rest of the 1580s. It was not until
Black replaced the mild-mannered Wilkie in 1590 that the Sabbath again
became an issue. Five people were charged with violating it that year, and
they all received private admonitions. There were a few cases the following

[50] Of 66 cases of Sabbath breach before 1582, only one person was told to do public
repentance (a case from 1577), and no fines for the offense are recorded in the register.

year (one offender being ordered to do public repentance), but it was only
with the installation of a sympathetic burgh regime in late 1593 that Black,
Wallace and the kirk session were really able to enforce the Sabbath. Forty
Sabbath-breakers were charged in 1594, resulting in five sentences of public
repentance, 28 private admonitions and two fines.[51] Indeed, 1594 was the
second busiest year overall for the session between its foundation and 1600,
with a total of 118 cases from all disciplinary categories. Numbers tailed off
in the following years, and cases of Sabbath-breach were particularly rare
in 1595, but all three of those charged received fines and sentences of
public repentance. Thereafter, Sabbath-breakers made regular appearances
before the session, and the imposition of public repentance, often with a
fine, became the rule. The practice of allowing some first-time offenders to
go free after a private rebuke resumed after the removal of Black and
Wallace in 1597, but most of the guilty were still made to sit on the penitent
stool, and some were even imprisoned for brief periods.[52] Most importantly,
Sabbath enforcement had become an integral part of the disciplinary regime
at St. Andrews.

There were several other types of malfeasance which also received
regular attention from the kirk session in the 1590s. In particular, the
ministers and elders became quite concerned with fostering harmony within
the community. This was not an effort of the kirk session alone; in burghs
like St. Andrews, burgh councils were often active in settling business
disputes.[53] In addition, the short run of burgh court records (1589-92) for
late sixteenth-century St. Andrews reveal a burgh coucil which regularly
appointed assizes to try cases of slander or assault if the parties involved
were important in burgh affairs.[54]

The kirk session had attempted to heal domestic squabbles prior to 1582,
and continued to do so after, as when David Lees, who had "dung" [struck]
his father, was ordered to do public repentance barefoot in sackcloth,
holding a hammer and a stone (the two weapons he had used against his
father), wearing a paper crown bearing the words "behald the onnaturall
sone punisit for putting hand in [sic] his father and dishonoring of God in

---

[51] On 13 February 1594, the session had passed a decree calling on the burgh's bailies to
collect fines mandated by an act of Parliament against Sabbath breach. See *StAKS*, 2:779.

[52] E.g. *StAKS*, 2:887.

[53] For examples of the St. Andrews burgh council doing this, see StAUM ms B65/8/1, 9v,
11v, 12r, 14r-v, 16r, 20r, 28r, 59v, 80r, 82v, 88r-v.

[54] E.g. StAUM ms B65/8/1, 39v-40r, 45r-v, 50r, 53r, 92v. Those convicted were ordered
to acknowledge their offenses publicly, and ask forgiveness from the plaintiff. But, unlike the
practice in cases handled by the kirk session, these rituals of reconciliation would only take
place in church if the offense in question had been committed there. For an instance of the
latter, see *ibid*, 88v-89r.

him." Then he was to ask his father's forgiveness in front of the congregation, stand two hours in the jougs, and be carted through the town.[55] But after 1590 the session brought its peacemaking efforts to the wider Christian family as well, particularly by attempting to punish slanderers and those guilty of assault. While violence, like Sabbath breach, was an offense to which men were much more prone than women, slanders and verbal quarrels involved more women than men. ·

Quite typical was the case of Mirrabel Moody, told to sit on the "goik stuill of this citee" for two hours on a Monday morning in the spring of 1591 for having called Isobel Kay a "commoun huir;" or Magdalene Motto, forced to confess publicly in 1597 that she had falsely accused Margaret Taylor of witchcraft.[56] But it was recognized that women could be violent as well. In August 1589, Margaret Lyell admitted to the burgh council that she had struck Andrew Turner, an officer of the town. She was fined and told to ask his forgiveness.[57] In November 1599, the servant Margaret Parky appeared at a kirk session meeting and accused her mistress Marion Adie, daughter-in-law of the bailie and elder William Lermonth, of "cutting hir heir by the plattis out of hir heid with ane knyiff, and in striking of hir, and burning of hir fleshe with ane hot irn tayngis, and speciallie betuix hir leggis." The nature of the act suggests sexual jealousy; several men of the Lermonth family (including Adie's husband) had been disciplined for fornication and/or adultery. The elders seemed eager to avoid another scandal involving the prominent family in this case. Concluding that Parky had proven nothing except the hair-cutting, they "sharplie rebuikit" Adie "for hir pryid and misbehaviour," and ordered the two to reconcile themselves. The minister was then told to announce from the pulpit that no offense warranting public repentance had been proven.[58] Parky may have taken the case to the kirk session because, given her lowly status, she had little hope of obtaining justice from the Lermonth-dominated burgh council.

Public reconciliation was considered critical in such cases. Efforts by both the session and presbytery to patch up the longstanding Arthur/Smith feud, which involved at least two murders, proved less successful, but by 1599 arbitration of disputes was considered an essential preparation for the celebration of Communion.[59] The previous year, the elders had ordered an investigation of all those not participating in Communion; refusal to take

---

[55] *StAKS*, 2:785-6. The burgh council also sought to arbitrate disputes between family members when property settlements were involved, as it did in the case the widow Ellen Melville lodged against her son, James Dick, in 1589. See StAUM ms B65/8/1, 29r, 35r.

[56] *StAKS*, 2:702, 838, 840.

[57] StAUM ms B65/8/1, 92v.

[58] *StAKS*, 2:910, 915.

[59] *Ibid*, 2:884. For the Arthur/Smith feud, see chapter eight, below.

part could reflect religious dissidence, but in the late 1590s in St. Andrews it was more likely to be an indication of enmity against others in the congregation.[60]

The session ordered in October 1595 that "all flytaris flatteraris bykbytaris of thair nichbouris drunkardis nicht walkaris and wikked sklanderaris" pay fines of ten shillings for the first offense, sixteen for the second, and be banished from the town for the third, all in addition to public confession or repentance.[61] While this resolution may not have been enforced (relatively few fines were recorded for such offenses), it does indicate that the elders were by then prepared to combat discord and drunkenness as well as illicit sexuality and breach of the Sabbath.

Drunkenness and poverty could be related, and the session gave considerable attention to pauperism by the 1590s.[62] Of course, like all early modern (and many modern) social reformers, the Kirk was more likely to see heavy drinking as a cause of destitution than as an effect. This had been the concern in February 1594, when two laborers were admonished "for extraordinar drinking and mispending of thair geir, and commandit to spend thair geir at hame with thair wyffe and barnis ressonabile."[63] In the censurious eyes of the elders, drinking at best begat idleness, at worst poverty, violence and debauchery. All were to be avoided. It was in the same spirit that the session in June 1598 warned the matron Elspet Brydie to stop hosting local youths "in hir hous, to pley at the kairdis at extraordinar tymes."[64] It was not enough to avoid serious sin; by the 1590s misuse of one's time as well as one's money could be a matter for discipline.

This new social puritanism attacked more public aspects of popular culture as well. In the spring of 1591, three pipers were admonished for "filthy playing" of music on the streets after dark, on the Sabbath as well as other evenings, and two women were ordered to do public repentance "for singing of bawdy songis, play at durris, dansing and ryning throw the town eftir supper, and under silence of nycht on the Sabbath day." In 1598, an Englishman was turned down when he sought a license to have a play performed. The times and types of public entertainment available to the population in St. Andrews were becoming strictly regulated.[65]

But there are signs that these reforms met continued resistance. Granted,

---

[60] *StAKS*, 2:863.

[61] *StAKS*, 2:808.

[62] E.g. *ibid*, 2:883-4.

[63] *Ibid*, 2:776.

[64] *Ibid*, 2:856-7.

[65] *Ibid*, 2:701, 705, 870.

we must be wary of imposing modern standards of behavior on sixteenth-century people, but the baxter Alexander Scharpe's act of "making watter unreverendlie in the kirk," in April 1595 was probably not random, particularly in light of the fact that he was also accused of denouncing the ministers and session. He had a kindred spirit in Marion Ogilvy, who later that same year told elders who inquired after her regular absences from kirk "lett thame gang to the kirk that wynnis thair mait in the kirk!" Both she and Scharpe were forced to do public repentance for their sins.[66]

But the mere performance of public repentance came to be insufficient in the eyes of the ministers and elders, as the quotation at the beginning of this chapter indicates. Sinners had to convince the session that their repentance was sincere, which must have been difficult (or even impossible) in cases like Scharpe and Ogilvy, who clearly found the disciplinary apparatus intrusive. The session found it necessary in 1595 to forbid those summoned for offenses to carry swords or guns to its meetings, and also decreed that those forced to sit on the kirk's penitents' stool do so unarmed.[67] It is not hard to imagine the menacing sight of an unreconstructed offender, fully armed upon the penitent stool, glowering at Black or Wallace as they preached and condemned the sins of the congregation.

The widening net of disciplinary practice was accompanied by an increase in overall numbers of cases. While the session had averaged 36 cases per year in the 1570s, this increased to 66.4 cases in the 1580s and 76.5 cases by the 1590s. Meanwhile, the non-appearance rate declined, from 20 percent in the 1570s to 19 percent in the 1580s and 13 percent in the 1590s, indicating that the session was not only becoming busier, but more effective as well.[68] An order for the preparation of 2,000 communion tokens in July 1590 gives us an estimate of the number of active parishioners at that time,[69] meaning that in an average year in the 1590s, one in 26 adults was called by the kirk session to answer for some offense.[70] The increase in business forced the session to meet more frequently. Before the 1590s, the session met weekly, if that. By 1599 this had increased to two or three times per week. Small wonder then, that

---

[66] *Ibid*, 2:796, 811.

[67] *Ibid*, 2:806.

[68] Parker claims that by 1600, "there were scarcely any cases outstanding in which those delated would not appear." This seems an exaggeration. Out of 220 cases for 1599-1600, there were 20 "no-shows," for a non-appearance rate of nine percent - certainly low, but not negligible. See Parker, "Kirk by Law Established," 14.

[69] *StAKS*, 2:677.

[70] While this indicates an intensification of disciplinary practice, St. Andrews in the 1590s still had not attained the annual ratio of one case for every ten adults shown in the Canongate in the mid-1560s. See chapter three, above.

elders had to be reminded (with fines) to attend meetings instead of playing golf![71]

By 1600 then, the practice of Reformed social discipline at St. Andrews had been transformed. Two decades earlier, once the danger of local Catholic reaction had subsided, the ministers and elders had chosen mainly to restrict their disciplinary efforts to the control of bastardy, with occasional attempts to remind people of the Sabbath. This was no longer the case in the mid and late 1590s, however. The restriction of illicit sexuality was still usually the leading concern, but alongside it now came vigorous efforts at Sabbath enforcement, conflict mediation, and some attempts to stifle some of the favored amusements of popular culture. The expansion of the disciplinary agenda brought with it both a sizeable increase in the numbers of cases handled, and in the severity of punishments. Much of this transformation occurred during the controversial ministry of Black and Wallace, and they seem to have been leading agents in the effort. But the group of burgesses and lairds which ousted Lermonth of Dairsie as provost in 1593 and governed the town for two years also played an important role. A clear alliance existed between the ministry and this group. Even after the Lermonth restoration, the changes in disciplinary practice survived; the traditional "misrewlars" of the town (to use James Melville's label for them) had come to see the benefits of Reformed social discipline, particularly after the installation of more moderate ministers in 1597 lessened the likelihood that they would be its targets.

The changes which took place in St. Andrews also occurred elsewhere, as kirk sessions evolved from unfamiliar intruders into recognized local institutions older than most residents. This is not to say that the 1580s and 1590s were the critical decades everywhere. In many communities this institutional maturation came later; the kirk session at St. Andrews was, after all, one of the oldest in the nation, and discipline was much slower to take hold in rural areas. But one semi-rural parish in which similar changes did occur at roughly the same time as in St. Andrews (possibly in part due to its proximity to the latter) was Anstruther Wester, only about ten miles to the south. Its experience merits examination at this point.

Anstruther Wester

Due to the shortage both of ministers and endowment for their support, Anstruther Wester in the early 1580s was not one parish, but several, served by one minister, along the southeast coast of Fife. This group of congregations centered on the parish kirk for the western half of the village

---

[71] *StAKS*, 2:913.

of Anstruther. Anstruther 'bewest the burn' became a burgh of barony, belonging to Pittenweem Abbey, in 1549, and a royal burgh in 1587.[72] It was tiny; as late as the 1790s, it had a population of only 370, with an additional 46 in the nearby rural area.[73] But in the early 1580s its minister also had to serve the communities of Anstruther Easter, Pittenweem, Kilrenny, and Abercrombie. Anstruther Easter, smaller than Anstruther Wester, was a burgh of barony belonging to the Anstruthers of that Ilk.[74] Abercrombie was a relatively insignificant inland village, but both Pittenweem and Kilrenny were larger than either of the Anstruther burghs. Indeed, Pittenweem was ranked fourth among Fife burghs (behind St. Andrews, Dysart and Kirkcaldy) in a 1575 tax roll. Its valuation of £137 10s was the same as that for the Canongate and North Leith, two Edinburgh suburbs.[75] Its population in 1750 was 939, but had probably been higher in the late sixteenth century.[76] Kilrenny, which included the seaside fishing enclave of Cellardyke, was a burgh of regality for the Beatons of Balfour, becoming a royal burgh sometime in the late sixteenth century. Its population in 1750 was 1348.[77] A list of active adult communicants from the several parishes around 1578 contains 833 names, but this may well be incomplete.[78]

Fishing and sea transport formed the main livelihood of most residents of all these communities in the late sixteenth century, although there were also significant numbers of craftsmen and farmers. The waters around the Isle of May, five miles southeast of Anstruther, teemed with fish, and the fishermen and mariners of Anstruther Easter developed a new harbor sometime between 1541 and 1587.[79] Local merchants and shipmasters sailed to Bordeaux, Spain, Norway, Denmark, and through the Danish Sound to

---

[72] Stephanie Stevenson, *Anstruther: A History*, (Edinburgh: John Donald, 1989), 35-6; Walter Wood, *The East Neuk of Fife: Its History and Antiquities*, (Edinburgh: David Douglas, 1887), 343. The Dreel Burn was the stream which ran through the center of the settlement.

[73] Sir John Sinclair, ed., *The Statistical Account of Scotland, 1791-1799*, (Wakefield: EP Publishing, 1978-83), 10:34. There is no evidence that the population in the 1790s would have been any lower than that of the late sixteenth century. See Michael Flinn, ed., *Scottish Population History From the 17th Century to the 1930s*, (Cambridge: Cambridge University Press, 1977), *passim*.

[74] Stevenson, 128-9.

[75] In contrast, Anstruther Wester was valued at only £74 5s. See Wood, *East Neuk of Fife*, 299-300.

[76] Sinclair, ed., *Statistical Account*, 10:695-6.

[77] *Ibid*, 10:477; Harry D. Watson, *Kilrenny and Cellardyke: 800 Years of History*, (Edinburgh: John Donald, 1986), 22-3, 33.

[78] StAUM ms CH2/624/1, 1-17 (manuscript paginated rather than foliated).

[79] Watson, 9, 23.

Danzig, Königsberg and Lübeck.[80]

The leading lairdly families in the area were the Beatons of Balfour (closely related to several bishops, including the cardinal David Beaton), the Anstruthers of that Ilk, the Scotts of Abbotshall, the Borthwicks of Grangemuir and the Inglises of Tarvit. Also significant locally were the Strangs, portioners of Kilrenny. The courtier William Stewart, commendator of Pittenweem after 1583, was an important absentee landlord. The Beatons, Anstruthers, Scotts and Strangs were all connected by marriage, while the Barclay family, of some stature in Pittenweem, had married into the Strangs and Inglises. The Simpsons and Dairsies, Anstruther Wester burgess families, had married into the Strangs and Beatons, respectively.[81] The Alexanders, burgesses in Anstruther Easter, had married into the Anstruthers.[82]

At the beginning of the 1580s, one William Clerk was minister to all these communities. In addition, Kilrenny had its own reader, John Anstruther, possibly a son of the laird.[83] Clerk was relatively obscure, but James Melville praised him for his "godlines, wesdome, and love of his flok."[84] He died in February 1584.[85] His replacement, Robert Wood, was appointed by Archbishop Adamson and (predictably) denounced by Melville as "ane of whome they [the parishioners] lyked nathing," and who caused "very grait dissentioun in thair bowelles."[86] One ought to consider the source of these criticisms, though; Melville himself was appointed minister by the presbytery of St. Andrews in November 1586, whereupon Wood refused to step down.[87] The Laird of Anstruther, with whom Melville was on good terms, had complained to the presbytery in October that Wood was preaching in Kilrenny "without any lauchfull [lawfull] calling or liciens had

---

[80] NRH ms OPR 403/1, 64r, 74v; Stevenson, *Anstruther*, 21, 130-1. The importance of sailing to the local culture was underscored by a kirk session order of 1575 which stipulated that the children of fornictors could not be baptised until the parents performed public repentance unless the child seemed close to death "or ye father absent at his guid voyadge." StAUM ms CH2/624/2, 3 (manuscript paginated rather than foliated).

[81] Stevenson, *Anstruther*, 197; Watson, 25; Wood, *East Neuk of Fife*, 356, 376-7, 380.

[82] Stevenson, *Anstruther*, 167.

[83] *Fasti*, 5:182; 211-2; Wood, *East Neuk of Fife*, 355.

[84] *JMD*, 3, 140-1.

[85] Both Melville and Scott (in *Fasti*) report that he died in February 1583, but that must be by old style reckoning, because the kirk session register records him as still living in June 1583, and the handwriting in the register changes abruptly in February 1584. See NRH ms OPR 403/1, 34v, 37v.

[86] *JMD*, 3-4; *Fasti*, 5:182. As will be seen below, 1584 brought a marked increase in the disciplinary activities of the kirk session, which may account in part for Wood's unpopularity.

[87] *Fasti*, 5:182; *JMD*, 4-6; *StAP*, 7. Melville is recorded as performing baptisms beginning on 6 November 1586. See NRH ms OPR 403/1, 44v.

tharto be the elders of the said kirk."[88] Challenged to produce a testimonial of his appointment, Wood did so, but local notables such as Anstruther of that Ilk and Beaton of Balfour (a lay elder on the St. Andrews Presbytery) clearly preferred Melville, and seem to have driven Wood from the parish. By 1590, he had moved to within the boundaries of the presbytery of Kirkcaldy.[89]

Meanwhile, Melville and the presbytery of St. Andrews sought to improve the provision of ministers to the area. Robert Durie, son of the Edinburgh minister John Durie, began assisting Melville in December 1586.[90] Soon, Durie was ministering to the western half of the parish (Anstruther Wester and Pittenweem), and Melville to the eastern half (Anstruther Easter and Kilrenny). In November 1588, Pittenweem was formally created as a new parish by royal charter, and a church was constructed there on land donated by William Scott of Abbotshall.[91] Nicol Dalgleish, formerly minister of St. Cuthbert's in Edinburgh, was installed as minister of this new parish in late 1589.[92] In 1590, the presbytery ruled that Durie was minister in Anstruther Wester, now a parish unto itself, and Melville in Kilrenny and Anstruther Easter, where the latter took up residence that Whitsunday in a new manse constructed by the Laird of Anstruther.[93]

William Clerk had sought to handle the problem of authority over multiple congregations by creating two kirk sessions, one for the western part of his charge (Anstruther Wester, Pittenweem and Abercrombie), and another for the eastern part (Anstruther Easter and Kilrenny). The eldership for the western half was headed by Peter Borthwick of Grangemuir, and included two Barclays as well, doubtless because of the latter family's importance in Pittenweem. A listing of elders in 1581 made no distinction between those resident in Pittenweem and Anstruther Wester, but the next listing, in December 1583, divided the eldership between the two communities, with the Anstruther Wester eldership headed by Borthwick of Grangemuir and Alexander Simpson, a burgess.[94] This latter group included

---

[88] *StAP*, 2.

[89] *Ibid*, 2-4, 60-1. The St. Andrews Presbytery informed the Kirkcaldy Presbytery in September 1590 that Wood had fathered a child out of wedlock, and had been involved in a dispute with Beaton of Balfour.

[90] NRH ms OPR 403/1, 44v. Robert Durie is among those listed by James Kirk as "Melvillians." See Kirk, *The Development of the Melvillian Movement in Late Sixteenth Century Scotland*, (Edinburgh University Ph.D. Thesis, 1972), 2:610.

[91] *Fasti*, 5:226, 8:463.

[92] *StAP*, 28.

[93] *Ibid*, 46, 55; *JMD*, 5-6.

[94] NRH ms OPR 403/1, 12r, 37r.

three rural elders (Borthwick was one), and twelve others who were probably from the burgh itself. Little can be said for certain about them; the few who left behind wills which have survived were merchant burgesses.[95]

The eastern session (Anstruther Easter and Kilrenny) elected in 1581 was already clearly divided between the various jurisdictions in the area. The Kilrenny group was, naturally, headed by John Beaton of Balfour, and also included representatives of the Strang and Anstruther families. Anstruther Easter had no fewer than eighteen names listed (with no distinction made between elders and deacons), including the shipmasters Alexander and William Black and William Low and the merchants John Alexander, senior and younger.[96] Several elders from other villages, such as Innergellie, Pitkierie and West Barns, were also mentioned, and John Inglis of Tarvit was given free rein to choose elders and deacons from his lordship of Caiplie, a privilege he got again when the next session was named in December 1583.[97]

Clerk kept one register for both kirk sessions, and his notation that meetings sometimes took place in Anstruther,[98] sometimes in Kilrenny[99] and sometimes in Pittenweem[100] suggests that he was really dealing with three or four sessions, with only the local elders and deacons attending particular meetings. The problems inherent in working with so many groups may have made it difficult to sustain any more than minimal disciplinary efforts, and the enthusiasm and diligence of the elderships could have varied considerably.

The nearly simultaneous arrival of James Melville and Robert Durie as ministers in late 1586 may have eased these difficulties. The register gives session lists for Pittenweem and "Anstruthir" (Wester?) in December 1587, but none for Kilrenny.[101] Presumably Melville was by then concentrating on Kilrenny and Anstruther Easter, and keeping a separate register, which has not survived. Then, on 1 July 1589, the clerk (probably Durie himself) noted that the residents of Pittenweem now had their own kirk "and therfor they refused to be under anie ordour of this kirk of Anstruther."[102] Thereafter, all listings of session members were for Anstruther Wester

---

[95] E.g. John Thomson, (d. 1620 - see *StART*, 346); James Strang, (d. 1591 - see *ERT*, 1:266); John Cuik, (d. 1598 - see *StART*, 80).

[96] NRH ms OPR 403/1, 28r. For more on the Blacks and Alexanders, who were also involved in brewing, see Stevenson, *Anstruther*, 130-1, 167.

[97] NRH ms OPR 403/1, 28r, 37r.

[98] E.g. *ibid*, 22r, 34v, 35v.

[99] E.g. *ibid*, 22v-24v, 35r.

[100] E.g. *ibid*, 27r.

[101] *Ibid*, 57v.

[102] *Ibid*, 64r.

alone.[103] Nevertheless, the session continued occasionally to order baptisms or approve marriages for residents of Pittenweem[104] and Kilrenny.[105] This may have been necessary because of the involvement of Nicol Dalgleish and James Melville in the national affairs of the Kirk, which often drew them

TABLE 6.3—BREAKDOWN OF CASES FOR ANSTRUTHER
WESTER KIRK SESSION, 1583-85, 1588-98.[106]

Offense category	Cases	Males	Females	No-shows
Sexuality	198 (36%)	104	94	32 (16%)
Sabbath breach	90 (16%)	61	29	49 (54%)
Church absence	86 (16%)	38	48	46 (53%)
Slander/bickering	45 (8%)	12	33	8 (18%)
Dealing w/outcasts	16 (3%)	8	8	9 (56%)
Magic, witchcraft	15 (3%)	0	15	2 (13%)
Commun. absence	10 (2%)	6	4	6 (60%)
Domestic disputes	9 (1.5%)	3	6	1 (11%)
Violent quarrels	9 (1.5%)	7	2	3 (33%)
Dancing, gaming	8 (1.5%)	8	0	4 (50%)
Disobeyed Kirk	8 (1.5%)	4	3	2 (25%)
Totals	546	284	261	183 (34%)

(Note: numbers within listed offense categories do not equal the total due to other cases scattered throughout less numerous categories. "No-show" percentages are calculated for within each category.)

---

[103] *Ibid*, 70v, 74r, 88r, 94r.

[104] *Ibid*, 67r, 73r.

[105] *Ibid*, 67v, 75r.

[106] Data for 1586-7 are not included because of inconsistencies caused by the apparent keeping of separate registers by the ministers Wood, Melville and Durie. By 1588 the register appears trustworthy again, with one minister concentrating on the parish of Anstruther Wester itself.

away to St. Andrews, Edinburgh, and beyond. Recalling his parish ministry, Melville admitted "I was often absent...occupied ever in comoun causses, to my great peanes and spending of all I haid...."[107] Still, in Durie, Melville and Dalgleish, the area was served by three enthusiastic Melvillians, and the wide range of cases handled by the Anstruther Wester Kirk Session after 1586 certainly reflects their committment to expanding the authority of the Kirk. Table 6.3 gives a profile of the session's disciplinary activities.

What is most remarkable, given the experience of other communities previously examined, is the relatively low percentage of sexual cases at Anstruther Wester during this period. Granted, sexuality still led all categories, but it made up considerably less than half of the total caseload. Cases were much more widely distributed between different offense categories here, with a particular emphasis on religious observance and the fostering of peace between neighbors. But, as table 6.4 will demonstrate, this distribution was not present during the early 1580s, and seems tied to the arrival of Melville and Durie on the scene.

The distribution (or lack thereof) of offenses during the years 1583-5, when Clerk and then Wood served as minister, demonstrates that the ministers and elders of that period regarded their disciplinary task as restricted largely to keeping sexual relations confined to lawful marriage and to the linked problem of curbing illegitimacy. For some, the issue may have been one of spiritual pollution, while for others the concern for the growing burden of poor relief may have been more important. Whatever, the primary motivation, of 93 cases during the period, only two did not involve sexual misbehavior. Not only was the kirk session very conservative in this respect, it was also quite passive. The non-appearance rate for this three-year period was a mere six percent, but that is because the session almost never summoned anyone. Rather, it waited until the parents of illegitimate children came in seeking baptism for their offspring, and then made the baptisms contingent on the parents paying fines and performing public repentance. Those who did not seek baptism, or found an alternative source for it, could avoid the disciplinary system entirely. The regular use of the term "concubine" in the register during this period suggests recognition, even by the minister and session, of cohabitation unsanctioned by official marriage.[108]

---

[107] *JMD*, 434.

[108] E.g. NRH ms OPR 403/1, 33r, 34v, 35v; StAUM ms CH2/624/2, 3 (manuscript paginated rather than foliated).

TABLE 6.4—BREAKDOWN OF CASES BY YEAR
FOR ANSTRUTHER WESTER KIRK SESSION, 1583-85, 1588-98

Column Headings: 1 - Sexuality
                        2 - Sabbath breach
                        3 - Absence from kirk
                        4 - Slander, quarrels
                        5 - Dealings with excommunicants/outcasts
                        6 - Magic, witchcraft
                        7 - Communion absence
                        8 - Domestic disputes
                        9 - Violent attacks

Year	Total	1	2	3	4	5	6	7	8	9
1583	13	12	-	-	-	-	-	-	-	-
1584	44	44	-	-	-	-	-	-	-	-
1585	36	35	-	-	-	-	-	-	-	-
1588	65	45	11	-	1	1	-	-	-	-
1589	59	7	14	21	3	8	1	-	-	2
1590	15	6	2	-	2	-	1	-	-	-
1591	17	10	-	-	-	-	1	-	-	-
1592	32	7	13	7	1	-	1	-	-	-
1593	33	5	10	-	3	4	1	7	-	-
1594	50	14	8	1	7	1	2	-	5	1
1595	25	4	3	7	2	1	-	-	3	2
1596	68	-	9	36	12	-	1	1	-	-
1597	33	7	2	8	6	-	5	-	-	2
1598	56	2	18	6	8	1	2	2	1	2

Note: numbers within years may not add up to the listed annual totals due to left-over cases which do not fit the listed categories.

There were some efforts to change future behavior, rather than merely to impose punishment after the fact, but these were restricted to the area of sex and marriage as well. For example, the session passed a resolution in July 1583 against wedding customs which included lavish dress and a train of virgins accompanying the bride. In such cases, participants were to be punished, and "the brydis to gang hame again unmarrit...." This was necessary, the resolution stated, "becaus the honorabill band of mariege is dyverslie abusit bie vaine and licentius and uncumlie behavior."[109] The session was also prepared to act as a social welfare agency in protection of the children of wetnurses. Noting that nurses had often borne children out of wedlock, and concerned that they took other women's babies to nurse for money, "not regarding quhat sal bec[o]m[e] of ther awin," the session ruled that no woman in the parish was to put her own child out to nurse without the elders' approval. Further, it resolved "that na manis wyfe in thir tua parochis resaife ony nurische [nurse] but be the advyse of the assemblie [session] that it may be knawin quha the nurische be and quhow she hes done w[i]t[h] hir awin bairn."[110] This demonstrates that the minister and elders did not attack illicit sexuality merely out of some levitical concern for purity; they felt an obligation to guard the well-being of children as well.

Clerk's death and the entrance of Wood into the pulpit brought an increase in numbers of cases (see table 6.4), but they remained virtually all sexual in nature. Wood's increased vigilance may have accounted for some of his alleged upopularity, but if the local notables who pushed Melville as a replacement in 1586 expected the latter to revive Clerk's *laissez-faire* regime, they were disappointed. By 1588 the total caseload was about five times that of 1583, while the splitting of the parish meant that the population of potential offenders was much smaller than at the earlier date. In other words, each adult resident was perhaps ten times more likely to be charged by the kirk session in 1588 than he/she had been in 1583. Sexual ethics were no longer the only issue, either; the kirk session charged 11 residents with Sabbath-breach in 1588 and 14 the following year. The disciplinary net was also widening to take in various types of quarrels, and even those who had declined to attend services. In addition, the session was taking reports of misbehavior and summoning offenders by 1588, rather than simply waiting for them to come in.[111]

Not surprisingly, the community did not flock to seek chastisement from the minister and elders. If one were simply to chart numbers, based on table

---

[109] NRH ms OPR 403/1, 35r. No examples of the enforcement of this resolution have survived.

[110] *Ibid*, 35v.

[111] E.g. *ibid*, 57v-58r.

6.4, one might conclude that 1588-9 was a period of quite intensive activity from which the session retreated in the following years. But in fact, a large proportion of those summoned during that two-year span refused to accept the session's intervention in their lives. The 65 and 59 cases of 1588-9 were accompanied by 29 and 43 "no-shows," a problem which decreased noticably in the following years when the session charged fewer people. Table 6.5 demonstrates this trend by comparing total case numbers with the numbers of those who refused to appear before the session.

TABLE 6.5—COMPARISON OF TOTAL CASES VS. NO-SHOWS
FOR ANSTRUTHER WESTER, 1583-85, 1588-98

Year	Total	No-shows	Total who appeared
1583	13	4	9
1584	44	1	43 (Wood replaced Clerk, Feb.)
1585	36	1	35
(Melville and Durie assigned to parish, late 1586)			
1588	65	29	36
1589	59	43	16
1590	15	5	10 (Durie alone as minister)
1591	17	6	11
1592	32	18	14
1593	33	17	16
1594	50	21	29
1595	25	6	19
1596	68	20	48
1597	33	5	28
1598	56	7	49

While wide fluctuations remain in the third column of this table, they are not nearly as wide as those in the first column. The table demonstrates that sudden increases in cases were not necessarily accompanied by increases in compliance. By restricting themselves to sexuality cases in 1584, Wood and the session got 98 percent of those summoned to appear. Under Durie, the session never enjoyed such a high percentage, and did not get as many sinners (43) to appear until the Covenant year of 1596, albeit drawing from a smaller parish. It was those charged with non-sexual offenses who were most stubborn; the non-appearance rates for those charged with Sabbath-breach, absence from kirk or Communion, and dealings with outcasts or excommunicants were all over 50 percent (see table 6.4). It took some time for the residents of Anstruther Wester to accept that such offenses merited ecclesiastical punishment, although by the end of the period under consideration most of them had. By 1596-8, for example, only four of 29 charged with Sabbath-breach refused to appear before the session. It took nearly a decade of behavioral indoctrination to reach that level of obedience.

When the minister and elders discovered on 28 January 1589 that Alexander Young and his wife, charged with violating the Sabbath, were "ignorant of all christian Doectrin," the time seemed ripe to launch an educational effort. Soon after, the session resolved that one of its members would walk around the parish each Sunday during sermon time and record the names of those absent from the kirk. Further, in preparation for the next Communion celebration, all adult parishioners would be examined on points of basic doctrine and belief.[112] These steps resulted in 21 people being charged with absence from the kirk in 1589 (three times the number charged with sexual offenses), but 18 of them ignored the summons. Efforts to enforce attendance were then effectively abandoned for two years. It was not until 1595-6 that the session was able to get more than half of those charged with this offense to appear. And while the few who answered the summons in 1589 were ordered to perform public repentance, the session later moderated such punishments in the interest of encouraging some form of obedience. Kirk absentees who appeared in the late 1590s were given the chance to explain their absence, and, even if unable to provide an excuse, were usually let go with a warning.

But, in general, the session did not win obedience by backing down. Rather, it became better able to enforce its expanding disciplinary code in the 1590s as it became a familiar local institution, accustomed to a close relationship with the burgh council. Together, the session and the council became the twin pillars of the edifice of order. This symbiotic relationship was developing in March 1591, when the session voted to bring insubordination to local magistrates clearly within its own bailiwick:

> Because of the great co[n]tempt of magistrates & disobedience to them be ignorant & orderles persones herefore it is statut & ordeined be the session that whosoever sall be convict in this offence sall be debarrit fra all benefit of the kirk till thay have satisfied according to the ordinance of the consell of the town and session of the kirk.[113]

That October the elders, headed by George Trail, bailie of the burgh, signed a band with the minister Durie that they would stand together in upholding the laws of God and His commonwealth, and that they would

---

[112] NRH ms OPR 403/1, 62v. Couples seeking marriage were also examined, such as Sandy Trail and Isobel Deal in April 1589, who were found to lack basic knowledge, perhaps the Lord's Prayer and Ten Commandments. They were told to learn them and return in a week. See *ibid*, 63r.

[113] *Ibid*, 68r.

make the law applicable to all estates, high and humble.[114] The band was the classic form of contract in early modern Scotland, and the National Covenant of 1638 would be written in such a form.[115] This agreement can be seen as a kind of local covenant, presaging the national, and far more binding in the eyes of the elders than any directives from the General Assembly or the presbytery of St. Andrews.

By late 1593, Durie had begun occasionally recording which elders missed meetings, and in the session election that September, elders were assigned to police particular quarters of the parish.[116] Within two years, attendance was noted regularly. This makes it possible to examine participation in the session. Twenty-one men were named to the session in September 1595 (with no distinction made between the eldership and diaconate), all from the burgh of Anstruther Wester itself. Neither Peter Borthwick of Grangemuir nor his son Walter were listed, but they apparently served as elders *ex officio*, because of their dominant position in the countryside around the burgh. Although they were infrequent attendees, their status as elders was important in legitimating the session's powers, and one or the other was usually among the one to three elders chosen to represent the parish at the General Assembly or the Synod of Fife.[117]

A survey of session attendance at three-month intervals beginning in late 1595 demonstrates what a small clique the active eldership was. For the 13 meetings surveyed, the average attendance was 6.75, or just under one-third of the session's official strength. The 21 men named to the session in 1595 attended an average of 3.8 meetings each, less than a third of the meetings in the survey. Elders were rarely removed or added. A glance at the attendance pattern reveals that, while three of the 21 did not attend any of the meetings in the survey (one of these was said to be poor and sickly[118]), all but one of the rest continued to participate, at least minimally, up to the end of the survey in 1598. The disappearance of the merchant burgess John Cook, who had been an active elder, is explained by his death in late 1597 or early 1598.[119] In fact, the truly active eldership was a group of seven, all

---

[114] *Ibid*, 70r-v.

[115] Keith Brown, *Bloodfeud in Scotland, 1573-1625: Violence, Justice and Politics in an Early Modern Society*, (Edinburgh: John Donald, 1986), 18; Arthur H. Williamson, *Scottish National Consciousness in the Age of James VI*, (Edinburgh: John Donald, 1979), 68-9; for the band of the Lords of the Congregation, which contributed to the religious revolution of 1559-60, see Knox, 1:273-4.

[116] NRH ms OPR 403/1, 80r. This division was repeated in September 1595. See *ibid*, 94r.

[117] E.g. *ibid*, 83v, 94v, 104r, 114v.

[118] This was John Carse. See *ibid*, 98v.

[119] His will was proved in 1598. See *StART*, 80 ("John Cuik").

of whom attended at least six of the 13 meetings.[120]

Attendance was lean at times, particularly in summer. The meeting of 14 June 1597 attracted only one elder, and that of 26 July drew two.[121] Autumn seems to have been the peak participation period; it was then that burgh elections took place, new elders (if any) were named, and parish accounts audited. The importance of the last should not be underestimated, because one major function never mentioned in either of the books of discipline—which the Anstruther Wester session had adopted by the 1590s was that of municipal credit bank, with revenues from fines and fees for burials providing its capital base. In September 1594, it collected 110 merks (including 10 merks of interest) which the burgh council had borrowed, and in turn loaned £100 to the merchant Thomas Thomson, with ten percent interest due on 1 January.[122] These were not isolated events; within a couple years the margins of the register were filled with financial accounts, both of lending and charity.[123] The session was becoming a central community institution in more ways than one.

The financial activities of the session aroused resentment in some quarters. In April 1597, David Philip, questioned on his habitual absence from sermons, catechism and Communion, lashed out at the elder Andrew Melville (not to be confused with the St. Andrews academic), who was parish treasurer for the year,

---

[120] The seven were, in descending order of activity, and with the number of meetings attended listed after their names: David Wead (10), John Thomson, Sr. (9), George Trail (8), Andrew Melville (8), Cook (7), James Dischington (7), and William Dairsie (6). Wead is difficult to identify, but had been an elder since 1583, and was a leading contributor in a collection taken up to support the kirk in February 1593—see NRH ms OPR 403/1, 37r, 76v. Thomson's son was a burgess (his will was proved in 1620), so the father probably was as well—see StART, 346. Trail had served as bailie in the past, and was thus undoubtedly a burgess also—see NRH ms OPR 403/1, 70v. Melville should not be confused with the theologian, and was probably related to the Melville lairds of Carnbee, whose estate was about three miles northwest of Pittenweem. He was a burgess—see StAP, 3. I have been unable to identify Dischington from any other source, but he may have had to attend the session frequently in order to defend himself. He was charged with offenses three times in the period 1596-8, once for hiring a juggler, once for attending a joust on the Sabbath, and once for slandering Andrew Melville, his fellow elder. He was fined for the first, made a private confession of the second, and denied the third—see NRH ms OPR 403/1, 105v, 117v, 121r. His standing had been good enough in September 1594 to represent the parish at the Synod of Fife, however—see ibid, 89r. Dairsie was a merchant shipmaster and burgess, who represented the town at the convention of royal burghs in 1606 and 1610—see StART, 23; Stevenson, Anstruther, 21.

[121] NRH ms OPR 403/1, 110r, 111r.

[122] Ibid, 89r.

[123] E.g. ibid, 102v-103r. For additional accounts, see StAUM ms CH2/624/1, 23-4.

and affirmed yt he wald prov him to be a steirer up & interteiner of sedition & discord and yt he wald prove that the said Andro payed him self better of uther menes purses, as of penalties & unlawes [fines] yt he tuik up, nor [than] the said david wes payed of his waiges awin him.

The session ruled that, unless he could prove his accusation by witnesses, Philip had slandered Melville. Philip's protest several weeks later that his witnesses were out of the country did not win him a delay, and he stormed out of the next meeting rather than accept punishment. The matter was eventually referred to the St. Andrews Presbytery.[124] In the meantime another parishioner had attacked Melville, calling him a "mainteiner of witchcraft [one of Melville's kinswomen had a reputation as a healer] and a taker of reward." When the accuser offered no acceptable evidence, he was told to perform public repentance three times—once each in Anstruther Wester, Kilrenny and Pittenweem.[125] The elders, whose power was grounded partly on their godly reputations, could not allow such attacks to go unpunished. But although the session's multiple roles—morals police (including collector of fines), ecclesiastical treasury board and local bank—left it open to charges of impropriety, its growing financial clout in most instances enhanced its disciplinary powers.

Those involved in commerce may have obeyed the kirk because they were wary of offending the local bank, but the poorest of the community needed its charity. "Strange" beggars (i.e. those not native to the parish), were regularly ordered to move on, and the local poor were from 1588 expected to go to the kirk at a particular time for alms and religious instruction.[126] By 1595 the parish had a school, and parents who did not ensure that their children attended were told to expect no charity. This carrot-and-stick approach even offered the well-behaved poor three hours daily of licensed begging at preordained times, in addition to parish alms, "and the peiple ar to be desyred to be helpful to sic as will give them self

---

[124] NRH ms OPR 403/1, 108v, 110r-v, 111v; *StAP*, 225-6. Philip appeared before the presbytery and promised to do public repentance. He then returned to the session and gave in a bill of submission, but ignored subsequent summonses. At other times, he was sought by the session for excessive drinking and swearing. See NRH ms OPR 403/1, 104r, 105v, 111v.

[125] NRH ms OPR 403/1, 109r. Melville had earlier squabbled with his fellow elder, George Trail. See *ibid*, 108v. A year and a half later, he was at odds with the elders Andrew Richardson and James Dischington as well. The latter may have been a friend of David Philip's. They attended a joust together (on the Sabbath) in July 1598. See *ibid*, 117v, 119r, 120v-121r.

[126] *Ibid*, 59r, 95v. In November 1597 the session voted a regular salary of two shillings per week to Sandy Myln, whose job was to drive "vagabond strangers" out of town. See *ibid*, 113r. Parish residents were occasionally summoned by the kirk session for receiving "ydle beggars" in their homes. See, e.g., *ibid*, 64r.

to ony vertue, and as for utheris to deall hardly w[i]t[h] them, to dryve
them to seik eftir vertue."[127] But some had fallen irrevocably, and those who
had been banished from their native parishes, such as Isobel Clerk, expelled
for theft, could prepare for a lifetime of wandering. Such people had
nowhere to go; the session gave Clerk two shillings "to mak hir expenses"
and sent her on her way.[128] James Melville himself lamented the increasing
numbers of poor, wandering the land "in swarms [like] Turks or Infidelles,
godles and lawles, without mariage, baptesm, or knawlage of dewtie to God
or man."[129]

Thus the session was more than a disciplinary court, although many of
its other responsibilities, such as the supervision of poor relief, reinforced
its disciplinary function. But the elders recognized that sin was not peculiar
to the poor, and their censures could reach the highest echelons of local
society, as when Peter Borthwick of Grangemuir was ordered to make a
public confession of sin from his pew for striking a miller's servant.[130] The
town's merchant seamen, who made up the backbone of the local economy,
were not immune either. Several of them were summoned on reports that
they had committed "idolatry" by conforming to local religious practices
while in Spain or Portugal. Two admitted in July 1589 that for such an
offense "god might haiff left thayme in bodie and saul," and promised "in
tymes comming never to put thame selvis in ye lyke Danger, craving god
and ye congregatioun forgiffnes."[131] Even the occasional elder John
Thomson the younger faced such a charge in 1598. He and several others
granted that they knelt (out of fear, they said) as a procession came by in
Lisbon, and they were admonished never to do so again.[132] The fact that no
one was forced to repent publicly for these offenses may reflect an
understanding on the session's part of the hazards of foreign trade, in which
many of the elders were involved. The community had seen the other side
of the coin in 1588, when a ship from the Spanish Armada had been forced
ashore at Anstruther by heavy weather. James Melville reported that the
crew was treated cordially, and eventually made its way back to Spain,
where the ship's captain arranged the release of an Anstruther crew which
had been confined in his home port.[133]

---

[127] *Ibid*, 95r, 96r.

[128] *Ibid*, 85v.

[129] *JMD*, 191.

[130] NRH ms OPR 403/1, 108r, 109r.

[131] *Ibid*, 64r. See also 74v for three sailors who admitted only that "thay had left ther bible
behind them" when they went ashore.

[132] *Ibid*, 116r.

[133] *JMD*, 261-4. These events were commemorated at Anstruther, with a visiting delegation
of Spanish sailors, in 1988.

But, on the whole, the case of Borthwick of Grangemuir, involving conflict within the community, was more reflective of the session's disciplinary concerns in the 1590s than were debriefings of sailors concerning their behavior in Catholic ports. Many residents were quick with insults, and it became common practice to carry disputes to the session. In December 1592, the session ruled that

> Because of the gret abuse in flyting & sclandering ane ane uthe[r]s, it is ordained yt whasoever co[m]plaines of ony sclander & cane not prove it sall be debared fra the benifits of the kirk till thay have satisfied the act of the magistrates in paying fourtie S[hillings].[134]

This penalty for false accusation was less than that for slander itself, however. By 1595 "sclanderous speikers" and those guilty of "flyting & reprochfull speiking" were to be placed in the branks at the kirk door while the congregation filed in for services, and then made to sit in front of the pulpit for a half hour as well as paying a fine of 40 shillings.[135]

Slander cases could consume a great deal of the session's time, because of the interrogation of witnesses necessary to determine who suffered the first wrong.[136] Often, such a determination proved impossible. Slander accusations could also raise other disciplinary issues, as the interrelated cases of Nannis Melville, Isobel Smith, Jonet Mill, Jonet Wardlaw, Marjorie Ferny, William Ferny and Jonet Durham demonstrate.

On 4 June 1594, the session was investigating a quarrel between Durham and Marjorie Ferny, her daughter. Jonet Cook testified that, during a conversation between Durham, Nannis Melville and others, the subject of where Ferny customarily slept came up,

> & the said Jonet Durham said yt sumtym M[ar]iorie wald creip in at hir fathyrs bak & that thir dyvers zeirs she [Jonet Durham] lay not w[i]t[h] hir housband W[illia]m Ferny & yat when thay [her husband and daughter] past to ther supper thay wald clos hir up in the place yt is behind the door.

Ferny, a sea captain, was prominent enough in the community that his house was used as a landmark in dividing the parish into quarters. Mother and daughter appeared together before the session on 16 June, but the matter was tabled "till it plecis god to recu[nc]eill farther."[137] The elders could see that this was no ordinary domestic quarrel, but they only had

---

[134] NRH ms OPR 403/1, 75v.

[135] NRH ms OPR 403/1, 93v.

[136] E.g., case of Jonet Mill v. James Milton, July-August 1596 in *ibid*, 102r-v.

[137] *Ibid*, 85v-86r, 94r.

hearsay evidence. There were no witnesses to any suspicious relationship between Ferny and his daughter.

This changed on 15 December, when Nannis Melville told the elders that one Sunday late the previous spring Marjorie and William Ferny had entered Melville's house when the latter was not home:

> m[ar]iorie w[i]t[h] hir father taried in the hous the stair dor being closed & did what thay pleased and afterward, the said m[ar]iorie cursed hir fa[the]r maist terriblie & when Isobell Smyt reproved hir, schoe ansred in thir wordes—O ze know not what he hes done to me.

A servant girl of Smith's had been watching the house while Melville visited Smith for dinner, and she told the session on 17 December that Marjorie Ferny had ordered her to leave, and that William Ferny had then closed the door. Smith also testified, saying that the servant had returned from Melville's house while the women were eating dinner and said, "Nanse, it is an evill haddin hous that ye keip," reporting that the pair were inside, whereupon the three of them went to Melville's house. She added that William Ferny told Melville "he had his will of hir [his daughter]." The latter then cursed him. In response, he moved as if to strike her, but did not. Marjorie refused to leave Melville's house that night, so Smith had her servant girl stay with the two women. At this point, the elders felt they had to summon William Ferny, who happened to be "in the kirk" at the time. He admitted making the statement to Melville, but said "he ment nathing saving only, that he had hir in his [sic] house & had comandment of hir."[138]

At this point it should be noted that Melville herself had a reputation. Her activities as a healer had brought her under suspicion of witchcraft several times, and she had broken promises to the session to cease her activities.[139] Most notably for our purposes, her name, as well as that of

---

[138] *Ibid*, 90r. Melville may have been seeking revenge on Marjorie Ferny for an accusation of thievery the latter had made against a man who was probably Melville's husband. See the next footnote.

[139] *Ibid*, 64v, 65r-v, 66r, 69r-v, 73v, 75r-v, 80v, 81r, 83r, 87v. She may have been put to death in August or September 1595, if she is the same person as "Agnes" Melville, also a witch from Anstruther, reported to have been executed before 10 September 1595, and whose healing techniques as reported in 1588 sound similar to those of "Nannis." A "Nannis" Melville in Anstruther was charged with several offenses after 1595, but none of them involved magic or witchcraft. She, too, was known in St. Andrews as "Agnes," (or else the clerk of the presbytery there simply made an error in recording her name in 1597). See *ibid*, 110r-v, 115r, 116r, 122r; *StAKS*, 2:620-3, 799-800; *StAP*, 223-4. A couple pieces of circumstantial evidence suggest that Nannis the healer and Agnes the witch were the same person. In her 1588 deposition before the St. Andrews session, "Agnes," a native of Anstruther, said she had been married to David Beanes, son of a St. Andrews burgess, although they had subsequently parted. It is possible that she later returned to Anstruther and they were reconciled there,

Isobel Smith, had come up in 1590 when Jonet Mill and Jonet Wardlaw had quarreled. Wardlaw claimed Mill had slandered her by saying that she [Wardlaw] had "laid an seikness upon Isobel Smith." Since Smith had returned to good health, her recovery required an explanation, and this was provided by her friendship with Melville. Both Smith and Melville testified, denying that Wardlaw had made Smith sick, or that Melville had removed any curse, although Smith said Melville had given her "sum parsell rutes and bade hir teik southe running water." Questioned again the following week, Smith changed her story, claiming that Melville had told her Wardlaw "wes ane witche and haid layed...w[it]chcraft and saikness upon [Smith]." Melville denied this, and both she and Smith (as well as Mill and Wardlaw) were suspended from Communion, at least temporarily.[140]

So, four years later, when faced with charges of incestuous rape, William Ferny decided to use the reputation of his leading accuser against her. If Melville could be suspected of removing curses, she could be suspected of laying them as well. Ferny said Melville had previously threatened him "when he sailled w[i]t[h] Alex Thomson and said to him if he sailled at that tym he suld never cum hoam again," and that while ashore on that trip he and Thomson met a mysterious man from Dysart and "wandered all yt nyt, thay knew not how & wer in perrell of ther lyf & wer caried over ye river w[i]t[h]out ane boit & on the morn wer 8 or 9 myles fra the ship." He had apparently taken a trunk belonging to Melville to St. Andrews, on this or some other occasion, and added (perhaps thinking that this would be his best defense from the charges) that since then "he never had power to haif to do w[i]t[h] ane woman." Melville denied all of this, and added that she knew he had "strugled w[i]t[h]" a woman from Pittenweem named Isobel Halladay since then. Smith and her servant also swore that they had never heard of Melville threatening Ferny. All the session could determine for certain at the moment was that Marjorie Ferny

---

because when Marjorie Ferny called David Beanes in Anstruther a thief in 1594, "Nannis" Melville responded with her charges against Ferny and her father. When a child of "Nannis" Melville's was presented for baptism in Anstruther in May 1595 by the elder Andrew Melville, "becaus the parentes were lying under a sclander," "Nannis" was identified as Beanes' wife. Then, a David Beanes was charged with fornication while engaged in 1597, a sin of which he would have been incapable if his wife were still alive. But if his wife had been executed for witchcraft in the summer of 1595, he could have committed fornication in 1597, when the other Nannis/Agnes Melville was also in trouble, for adultery with William Brown. On 23 November 1595, Beanes had applied to have his banns read. His prospective bride was, of all people, Marjorie Ferny. For Beanes, see *StAKS*, 2:621; NRH ms OPR 403/1, 90r, 92r, 96r, 107v.

[140] NRH ms OPR 403/1, 65v. For the allegedly magical properties of south running water, see Christina Larner, *Enemies of God: The Witch-hunt in Scotland*, (London: Chatto & Windus, 1981), 141.

(who had yet to testify) had cursed her father.[141] Nearly a year later, (after Melville herself may have been executed for witchcraft), the elders required Marjorie to confess privately her remorse for the curse before they would allow her banns to be read; she wished to marry a man who may have previously been Melville's husband.[142]

But the eldership determined that something yet had to be done about Ferny. He was again summoned,

> and being accused of words spoken be him yt wer sclanderous…he authored that he remembret not yet he wald refer h[i]m self to sic witnesses as wald testifie in it and And[rew] Melvill testified of his misbehaviur q[uhe]rupon W[illia]m Ferny confessed his offense upon his knies & craved god & the session forgivness.[143]

Since Nannis Melville may have been dead by then (and, if so, Ferny's accusations had a hand in sending her to the stake), Ferny might have known the lead witness against him was no longer available. In such circumstances, Smith would have feared testifying again because of what had happened to Nannis Melville. The only other witness was the servant girl. Andrew Melville, perhaps seeking some revenge for his kinswoman's death, probably just read the three witnesses' previous testimony from the session register. Ferny backed down, but his punishment proved minimal: a private confession, just as had been required of his daughter. She, the other victim in this plot, had meanwhile fallen into poverty received alms regularly in 1596.[144]

These related cases draw on several threads of the session's activities in the 1590s—conflict mediation, suppression of sexual sins, witchcraft and poor relief—and demonstrate the connections between them. They also show the relative inability or unwillingness by the session to reach within the family in a sensitive case where the accusers were female and the accused male. It was relatively easy to order a son to support his aging father, or a wife to stop nagging her husband. But when William Ferny stood accused of incestuous rape, the elders recast the accusation in other terms—his daughter had cursed him, and he had uttered words tending to impugn her reputation. And as long as society was terrified of diabolism, women (and sometimes men) on the margins of society could be discredited by accusations of witchcraft.[145]

---

[141] NRH ms OPR 403/1, 90r-v.

[142] *Ibid*, 96r. See also note 139 above.

[143] *Ibid*, 96v.

[144] *Ibid*, 103r-v, 104v, 106r.

[145] For more on church discipline and witchcraft, see chapter eight, below.

In other situations (particularly when women were the accused) the session was not afraid of confronting the dark side of family life. Nannis Melville herself had been very careful to shield herself from accusations that she had provided women with abortifacients, recalling that one man who had sought one for his paramour or wife had threatened to kill her "becaus she had not put away yt lump."[146] The elders took great interest in the suspicious death of Molly Thomson's infant child in the summer of 1593. The baby had been in bed with Thomson's sister Jonet, but the latter reported that since it had still been alive after she got up, and was later found dead by servants, "how [it died] scho can not tell." One William Pausta hinted at an earlier death when he said "he hard na din of the bairne yt nyt bot u[the]r nyts he hard it greit." Cristin Pausta said she heard nothing, but when she was called into the room where the baby lay, she "sa the bairne wes bot new dead, for it wes hot & ane bew of foame at [t]he bairnes mouth & [she] sa na taiking of ony hurt on the bodie of the bairne or ony p[ar]t of." Mystified, the session referred the case to the presbytery, although no trace of it appears in the presbytery's records.[147]

These cases, which moved into sensitive areas beyond the session's original concern merely to discourage illegitimacy, were not unique to Anstruther Wester. But the influence of Melvillian ministers like Durie and James Melville should not be underestimated. The widening of the disciplinary net certainly came earlier here (and in St. Andrews) than in many other communities. Monifieth in Angus, despite important local protestant connections dating from to the 1540s, held much longer to a traditionalist pattern of social discipline.

Monifieth

The kirk session of Monifieth, which had held its first recorded meeting in 1562, was still handling only sexual cases when it came under the jurisdiction of the presbytery of Dundee in 1581.[148] In this respect, it was not unlike its counterpart in Anstruther Wester. But although the Monifieth session later developed other disciplinary interests, sexuality remained its leading concern (by far) as late as the early 1600s. Frank Bardgett, using the parish of Monifieth as a prime example, has written that "Angus and the Mearns were among the first areas of Scotland where the parochial reformation was to be generally implemented within a few years of

---

[146] NRH ms OPR 403/1, 81r. For a 1589 case of a male from Leuchars allegedly providing a potion to induce abortion (he denied it) in St. Andrews, see *StAKS*, 2:649-50.

[147] NRH ms OPR 403/1, 79r.

[148] *BUK*, 2:483. See also chapter three, above.

1560."[149] Historians may differ over what is meant by "parochial reformation," but, in terms of disciplinary practice, Monifieth had already lagged far behind parishes such as St. Andrews and Anstruther Wester by the late 1580s.

The Durham lairds of Grange continued to lead the Monifieth Kirk Session at the end of the century, as they had since the early 1560s.[150] William Durham of Grange was the first of the six elders named in 1595, and his kinsman Andrew Durham, a substantial tenant on the divided estate of Ethiebeaton, was one of the others.[151] The timing of the next session election, two weeks after the burial in 1606 of William Durham of Grange, was surely not coincidental. This new session was headed by his son William Durham of Grange, and also included as an elder one James Durham, presumably from the Ethiebeaton branch of the family.[152] As had been the case before 1582, the Durhams of Grange did not shrink from using the censures of the Kirk against their local rivals, such as the Guthrie and Ramsay families.[153] By the early 1600s, the Durhams were involved in disputes over land with both the Ramsays of Ardownie and the Lauders of Omachie, with the latter disappearing from the eldership between 1595 and 1606.[154]

The Durhams showed their disdain for at least one of the national Kirk's concerns (preventing burial within churches) by building a family monument around 1600 which covered one wall of the choir of the parish kirk.[155] The session they dominated also showed its traditionalist tendencies in 1600 (and again on the anniversary of the event a year later) by ordering a proclamation of thanksgiving for the king's deliverance from the Gowrie conspiracy. The earl of Gowrie and his brother the master of Ruthven, so

---

[149] Frank Bardgett, *Scotland Reformed: The Reformation in Angus and the Mearns*, (Edinburgh: John Donald, 1989), 101. Elsewhere, Bardgett labels Monifieth a "model reformed rural parish." See *ibid*, 160. As part of his evidence, he points to the "radical terminology" employed in the kirk session register, in which couples were "proclaimed in marriage," later appearing to "ratify" their contracts. Baptisms had "witnesses" rather then godparents. See *ibid*, 103. But it should be noted that such language was quite common in kirk session registers by the end of the century, when the evidence becomes plentiful enough to make a useful comparison.

[150] See chapter three, above.

[151] NRH ms OPR 310/1, 87v.

[152] *Ibid*, 117v-118r.

[153] *Ibid*, 57v, 101v.

[154] J. Malcolm, *The Parish of Monifieth in Ancient and Modern Times*, (Edinburgh: William Green, 1910), 59-60, 321, citing *Register of the Privy Council of Scotland*, 8:162, 10:349; Alexander Warden, *Angus or Forfarshire: The Land and People*, (Dundee: Charles Alexander, 1880-5), 4:411.

[155] Malcolm, 82-3.

beloved by some of the more radical elements in the Kirk, had been killed in their attempt to capture the king, but many influential presbyterian ministers considered them heroes rather than traitors.[156]

Despite the conservatism of the Durhams, there was one important figure at Monifieth by the century's end who might have tried to push the session in a more innovatory direction. This was the minister Andrew Clayhills, a son of a burgess in nearby Dundee. Clayhills had attended the university at St. Andrews in the 1560s. Identified as a Melvillian because of his subscription to a 1586 letter denouncing episcopacy, Clayhills actually had two stints as minister of Monifieth.[157] He was listed as minister there in 1569, but by 1574 had been transferred to the border parish of Jedburgh. Monifieth was then served by a reader, James Lovell, under the oversight of Andrew Auchinleck, minister of Barry, a parish three miles to the east. But in April 1598, Clayhills returned to Monifieth.[158] This may have had some impact, as an examination of the session's caseload demonstrates. This kirk session was never particularly busy, considering that there were just over 1,000 communicants in the mid-1590s (up from 7-800 ten years earlier).[159] Even during the busiest period indicated above (1600-1), the session only sought to discipline about one in 77 adults per year. But even at that low level of activity, it still had difficulty persuading offenders to honor its summonses. The non-appearance rate for all kirk sessions in this study was 18 percent, and the Monifieth elders, despite (or perhaps because of) their mild approach were generally well above that.

The increase in cases for 1600-1 was probably a reflection of Clayhills' return as minister. Although transferred to the parish in 1598, his arrival may have been delayed until September 1599; it is at that point that the handwriting in the session register changes markedly. Alexander Guthrie, appearing on 24 August 1600 to answer a charge of fornication, protested that his offense "was auld" before Clayhills' return, suggesting that one parishioner, at least, sensed that a new disciplinary regime had begun when Clayhills came back to the parish.[160]

---

[156] NRH ms OPR 310/1, 102r, 105v.

[157] Calderwood, 4:604. James Kirk includes him in his roster of melvillian clergy. See Kirk, *Development of the Melvillian Movement*, 2:592.

[158] *Fasti*, 5:361; Charles Haws, *Scottish Parish Clergy at the Reformation 1540-1574*, (Edinburgh: Scottish Record Society, 1972), 181; Frank Bardgett, "The Monifieth Kirk Register," *RSCHS* 23 (part 2) (1988), 175-95, at 192. Clayhills had a daughter, Margaret, baptised at Monifieth in April 1600. See NRH ms OPR 310/1, 100r.

[159] *Ibid*, 51v, 54v, 57v, 83r.

[160] *Ibid*, 102r. Guthrie's protest availed him little, however; he performed public repentance on 4 January 1601. See *ibid*, 103r.

TABLE 6.6—BREAKDOWN OF CASES FOR MONIFIETH KIRK
SESSION, 1579-81, 1593-94, 1600-1, 1603-6.*

Offense category	Cases	Males	Females	No-shows
Sexuality	78 (74%)	40	38	21 (27%)
Sabbath breach	11 (10%)	10	1	5 (45%)
Communion absence	3 (3%)	3	0	0
Violent attacks	2 (2%)	2	0	0
Dealing w/outcasts	2 (2%)	1	1	0
Disobedient to Kirk	2 (2%)	1	1	0
Totals	105	63	42	30 (29%)

*Sample years chosen due to poor condition of register
(Note: numbers within listed sin categories do not equal the total due to other cases
scattered throughout less numerous categories. "No-show" percentages are
calculated for within each category.)

TABLE 6.7—ANNUAL VARIATIONS IN DISCIPLINARY
CASELOAD AT MONIFIETH

Years	Cases (ann. avg.)	Sex	Sabbath	Other	No-shows
1579-81	24 (8)	24	-	-	10 (42%)
1593-94	19 (9.5)	17	-	2	2 (11%)
1600-1	26 (13)	12	7	7	9 (35%)
1603-6	36 (9)	25	4	7	9 (25%)

The session had passed a series of ordinances the previous March, vowing
stern action against Sabbath violators, keepers of "superstitious" holidays,
blasphemers, disobedient children, adulterers, fornicators and slanderers.
The promised punishments included two weeks of incarceration in the
church steeple for first-time adulterers, and 24 hours of the same for first-
time fornicators. Those who "willfullie" declined to attend sermons were to
perform public repentance dressed in linen.[161] Some of the more vulnerable
residents of the parish felt the sting of these resolutions: Jonet Clark, who
had been disciplined for fornication before, was on 20 April 1600 "found

---

[161] *Ibid*, 99r-v.

to be gyltie of ye final fall." As a result, she was "ordaynit to be banished and intimatioun thairof to be maid publictlie ye nixt Sonday." Her partner, who came in seeking baptism for the child, was forced to do two Sundays of public repentance.[162] The elders were happy to rid the parish of women like Clark, who had no husband and possibly no male relatives with any influence to defend her. The same was true for Jonet Guild, "suspected of oppressing [suffocating] hir bairn," who was forced in 1606 to perform public repentance in sackcloth three times and then depart the parish.[163] Such women were thereby condemned to nomadic, marginal lives; it was becoming increasingly difficult for anyone to settle in a new locale without a testimonial from the minister of their former parish.

But other local residents, more established in the community, were not troubled much by these new efforts to enforce order, partly because not all parish authorities were as enthusiastic as Clayhills and the more zealous elders. The ordinances of March 1600 had commissioned several area notables to round up Sabbath violators, but some were unwilling to do so. Two of these reluctant enforcers were admonished from the pulpit for foot-dragging in July 1600, and the fact that one, William Guthrie of Kingennie, was a leading elder on the session does not speak well for the group's unity of purpose.[164] Numerous Sabbath-breakers were charged in the months after March 1600, but none was actually induced to appear before the session until January 1601, when Adam Wylie, accused of carrying cloth on a Sunday, promised "to abstane thairfra provyding that ye lyk ordor be tane with ye rest."[165] He could tell that the session was incapable of vigorous enforcement of the Sabbath.

Even the Durhams were losing enthusiasm. The younger William Durham of Grange was summoned to a visitation by the presbytery of Dundee in August 1603 for failure to attend Communion. The fact that Alexander Guthrie, another area laird, was summoned for the same offense suggests that the laird of Grange was letting a feud get the better of his family's reputation for piety. The lairds were probably using abstention from the most important ceremony of the local kirk to display their mutual enmity.[166] A problem like this could cripple the disciplinary apparatus; there were only three cases brought up in all of 1603, and two of them were those of Durham and Guthrie. Once Durham was persuaded to return to Communion, case numbers returned to normal.

---

[162] Ibid, 98v, 100v.

[163] Ibid, 118v-119r.

[164] Ibid, 101v.

[165] Ibid, 103v.

[166] Ibid, 111r-v.

One area connected to discipline in which the local kirk was growing stronger was its response to poverty. After Clayhills' return to the parish, the clerk (probably Clayhills himself) took regular note of who received alms, and how much was distributed. Alms collections had been faithfully recorded since the 1560s. Table 6.8 traces the growth in alms collection, using as sample periods in the years surveyed the five Sundays from mid-February through mid-March.

TABLE 6.8—AVERAGE WEEKLY ALMS COLLECTIONS IN LATE WINTER AT MONIFIETH FOR VARIOUS YEARS, 1583-1606

Year	Weekly average (in pence)
1583	37.2
1593	43.2
1601	66
1603	62.6
1605	51
1606	80.8

This table shows fairly steady growth in alms collection, even if one takes inflation into account. It also demonstrates that the heightened disciplinary efforts which followed Clayhills' return may have been accompanied by a temporary surge in receipts. By 1603, collections (and numbers of disciplinary cases) had tailed off, however, partly because of the Communion boycott of the young laird of Grange. The even lower average for 1605 is probably due to an outbreak of plague, said to be present in the area in 1604 and 1605.[167] By 1606, collections were quite high, showing the strength of local charity efforts.

But these efforts were intended to benefit native paupers only, particularly those who did not add to the poverty problem by giving birth to illegitimate children. The banishments of marginal women already discussed reveal the elders' eagerness to lower the number of potential alms recipients, however drastic the method. In August 1600, the session urged "that order be tackin w[i]t[h] the resettaris of vagabound boyis and young hussies."[168] The minister and elders wanted to ensure that the wandering poor would find no safe haven in Monifieth. Some stangers were associated with diabolism. John Henderson was summoned in October 1601 "for dealing w[i]t[h] the egiyptionis [gypsies]" and allowing them to perform acts

---

[167] *Ibid*, 113r, 116r-v.

[168] *Ibid*, 102r.

of witchcraft in his house. He granted that he had taken them in, but denied that they had engaged in any magical practices, and the case was dropped. Presumably, the "egiyptionis" had already moved on.[169]

While the local kirk thus became established as an institution of charity for some, its disciplinary practices remained one-dimensional, aimed at curbing illegitimacy. The session of this rural parish was far too dependent on the authority of one lairdly family—the Durhams of Grange—and the disputes in which that family was involved stunted the growth of the disciplinary program. Other local powers were not meaningfully represented on the session, rendering it relatively impotent as an agent of effective social discipline. The expansion of the disciplinary agenda visible at St. Andrews, Anstruther Wester and elsewhere still had not really taken place here. But Monifieth was not unique in this respect. The remote parish of Rothiemay, far to the north, provides a similar example.

Rothiemay

Rothiemay was an expansive, thinly-populated rural parish centered on the 'Milltown' of Rothiemay on the River Deveron, north of the Grampian Mountains and just eight miles downstream from the Gordon stronghold of Strathbogie Castle. The parish stretched seven or eight miles in length (north-south), and five or six miles in breadth. It was a region of small farms, with weaving the leading craft. The parochial population in 1755 was 1190, with just 100 in the milltown itself. The latter contained the church and manse, as well as Rothiemay House, which was in 1600 the home of John Abernethy, eighth Lord Salton.[170] A report that 400 people participated in Communion in April 1605 suggests that the parish population may have been slightly smaller during our period of study. It should be noted, however, that the Salton household communicated separately, so the 400 did not include its members.[171]

The Communion total may also been low because the Reformed Kirk, and perhaps Christianity itself, was still scarcely planted in this isolated area in the early seventeenth century. Many of the neighboring Gordons, so powerful in the region, followed their chief the marquis of Huntly by remaining Catholic. Rothiemay did not have a resident Reformed minister until 1590. In 1606, its session encountered a 16-year-old girl from the

---

[169] *Ibid*, 106r. A gap in the records for the first half of 1602 makes the precise outcome of Henderson's case unclear, but he was an accepted member of the congregation by July 1602, when he had a child baptised. See *ibid*, 107r.

[170] Sinclair, ed., *Statistical Account*, 16:398-402. Sir James Balfour, ed., *The Scots Peerage*, (Edinburgh: David Douglas, 1904-14), 7:413.

[171] NRH ms OPR 165/3, 15r.

nearby settlement of Inchcorsie who had never been baptised by any rite, Reformed or Catholic.[172] The minister in 1605 (the first year for which the session register is complete) was Alexander Smart, who had arrived in the parish in 1599. Smart was an obscure figure, but he was apparently willing to make concessions to powerful interests in the parish. This earned him the censures of the General Assembly, which suspended him in 1617 for improperly marrying Jean Abernethy, lord Salton's sister, to the Catholic George Gordon, laird of Gight.[173]

That Smart would have succumbed to pressure and performed such a marriage is not surprising; the General Assembly met far away and the Abernethys dominated the parish. Lord Salton himself did not serve as an elder (he was often absent from the area), but his kinsmen seem to have controlled the session. Four of eleven elders recorded as attending meetings in the years 1605-6 bore the surname Abernethy, and another, Patrick Livingston, was Salton's brother-in-law. The Abernethy elders were always listed first on sederunts, followed by Livingston, if he was present.[174] The first named was always James Abernethy, bailie of Rothiemay and probably laird of Corgie.[175] The rest of the elders were always identified as "in," rather than "of" some estate, indicating that they were tenants rather than proprietors. Thus other Abernethy landowners in the parish, such as the lairds of Auchencloich and Mayen,[176] left the operation of the session to underlings.

The local kirk seems to have been managed in a traditional and deferential fashion, with little heed paid to the more socially unsettling aspects of Reformed religion. Salton and his household did not take Communion with the rest of the congregation, thereby insulating themselves from parochial life in a way which could only have detracted from the ceremony's symbolic power to unite the Christian community.[177] The session displayed little concern over the practice of burial in the kirk, condemned by the national Kirk. Rather than outlaw the practice, it ruled in June 1606 (long after such interments had been banned elsewhere) that future burials within the kirk would cost relatives of the deceased fines of 40 shillings. The families of those buried since Smart's arrival in 1599 were

---

[172] *Ibid*, 20r. Given the remoteness of the area, it seems unlikely that she was unbaptized because she was illegitimate. Only the sternest of ministers would have prevented another parishioner from presenting her, even if her parents had been excommunicated.

[173] *Fasti*, 6:331; Balfour, ed., *Scots Peerage*, 7:413.

[174] E.g. NRH ms OPR 165/3, 14r, 18v, 23v.

[175] *Ibid*, 3v.

[176] Balfour, ed., *Scots Peerage*, 7:414.

[177] NRH ms OPR 165/3, 15v.

to be charged 20 shillings retroactively.[178] Such fines would not have been prohibitive for parish notables, so the ordinance merely served to reinforce the exclusivity of the practice while raising funds for kirk repairs.

This traditionalism was also reflected in the kirk session's caseload, of which table 6.9 provides a glimpse.

TABLE 6.9—BREAKDOWN OF CASES FOR ROTHIEMAY KIRK SESSION, 1605-6

Offense category	Cases	Males	Females	No-shows
Sexuality	60 (80%)	31	29	14 (23%)
Sabbath breach	7 (9%)	7	0	1 (14%)
Slander, bickering	4 (5%)	2	2	-
Totals	75	40	35	17 (23%)

(Note: numbers within listed sin categories do not equal the total due to other cases scattered throughout less numerous categories. "No-show" percentages are calculated for within each category.)

The session was primarily concerned with preventing illegitimacy through the suppression of illicit sexuality. Such an approach did not require any consensus on finer points of theology, and it did not involve any attack on traditional practices. This was something on which all the elders (and presumably their superiors) could agree. They also seem to have shared the related concern that marriage be clearly defined and upheld. The highest fine recorded in the register during this two-year period was five pounds, levied against Isobel Abernethy for "resiling," or backing out of a promise to marry James Gray. Abernethy's family name may have shielded her from performing any public repentance, however.[179] Couples who did come before the session seeking to marry were required to find caution that they would marry soon or face a hefty fine. Like the equally conservative elders of Aberdeen in the 1570s, the elders of Rothiemay were quite willing to use the disciplinary apparatus to enforce standard, recognized marriage procedures on a population which had previously tolerated irregular relationships.[180]

---

[178] *Ibid*, 21r.

[179] *Ibid*, 19v.

[180] See chapter three, above.

As was usually the case in other parishes we have examined, those guilty of sexual sins were fined and ordered to perform public repentance. The fines went toward maintenance of the poor, and those who could not pay were forced to spend time in the stocks instead. Since there is no evidence of any effort to enforce kirk attendance, it may have been quite low except in the spring when Communion was celebrated. Thus time in the stocks was probably more humiliating than public repentance in the kirk. This allowed for a double standard in punishment, because only the poor could not afford to pay fines.

Sabbath breach, generally a male offense and one which usually involved work or commerce, never brought any public form of punishment (or even a fine) during the period under consideration. Offenders were either excused or privately admonished.[181] This was not the case with those who slandered or quarrelled with their neighbors, however. William Runciman complained on 6 July 1606 that Agnes Young had slandered his wife and father-in-law by labelling them a witch and a thief, respectively. She was convicted of the slanders by the testimony of witnesses the following week, and ordained to perform public repentance and spend an hour in the stocks. But, due to the "ongodlie words" that Ruciman used in accusing her (he called her "ane biring bitch"), he was ordered to make a public confession and spend an hour in the stocks himself. It took nearly a month for either to comply, but, after being threatened with excommunication, they both did.[182]

Such efforts to foster neighborly harmony show some similarity to the expanded disciplinary practices we have seen in parishes such as St. Andrews and Anstruther Wester, but they formed a very small portion of this session's caseload. Like its counterpart in Monifieth, the session of Rothiemay was under the nearly exclusive control of one local family, and it did not show any more zeal than the Abernethies were interested in fostering. That it seems to have been slightly more effective (as seen in the "no-show" rate) than the Monifieth session is probably a reflection of Abernethy power in the area; the Durhams faced more rivals in Monifieth. But, lest one should conclude that rural parochial discipline outside the orbit of the St. Andrews Presbytery was almost entirely focused on illicit sexuality in the late sixteenth and early seventeenth centuries, we should consider the example of Dundonald in Ayrshire. There, far from the influence of the Melvillians of St. Andrews, the elders nevertheless were interested in a wide range of offenses by the first decade of the seventeenth century.

---

[181] NRH ms OPR 165/3, 17r-v.

[182] *Ibid*, 21v-22r.

Dundonald

Dundonald in the early seventeenth century was a large, primarily rural parish situated on rich land and seacoast in the Kyle district of Ayrshire. It was seven to eight miles in length, with the River Irvine as its northern boundary. The parish extended as far inland as Caprington, on the western outskirts of Kilmarnock. To the west, it was bound by the sea. Its southern boundary is less clear, but seems to have extended southwest from Caprington to a point on the coast about two miles south of the Troon (a rocky peninsula extending a mile into the sea). These boundaries gave the parish a triangular shape. Dundonald itself was a small village in the middle of the triangle, nearly three miles inland, on higher ground. It contained the church, manse and a castle which, though partly ruined, could still be used for incarceration.[183]

The Claven hills, which rise roughly a mile inland from the Troon, naturally divided the parish between upper and lower parts, but both were quite fertile. The parish population in the mid-eighteenth century was just under a thousand, although the local population growth which marked the late eighteenth century may have already been underway by then, meaning that the figure for 1600 could have been significantly smaller.[184] Local power was divided among several leading families. Although some, such as the Cunninghams of Caprington, the Fullartons of Crosbie, and the Wallaces of Auchans were clearly more important than the rest, land and influence were distributed so that no individual family could dominate the parish.

This last point is worthy of special consideration, because it clearly distinguished the Dundonald Kirk Session from those of Rothiemay and Monifieth, and made it similar to that of Anstruther Wester. The parish of Rothiemay had been largely controlled by the Abernethies, and though Monifieth contained other influential families, only the Durhams of Grange took a longstanding, active interest in the session. At Dundonald, several of the leading local families were regularly represented on the session, meaning that the disciplinary system could not fall under the control of one individual or family.

The register of the Dundonald session is fairly complete for the years 1602-10. A survey of attendance by elders, based on the sederunts of the first meetings in January, April, July and October of each year, includes a

---

[183] For a physical description of the parish, albeit after it had already been somewhat transformed by proto-industrialization, see Sinclair, ed., *Statistical Account*, 6:171-81.

[184] *Ibid*, 174.

total of 33 possible meetings.[185] There were five elders who attended at least ten of the meetings surveyed, led by Robert Wallace, laird of Galrigs (now Newfield), who was present at 29 of the 33. Next came the lairds James Fullarton of Crosbie and John Fullarton of Dreghorn, who both attended 22 meetings. John Wallace younger, laird of Auchans, made it to 18 meetings and his father John Wallace elder, who died midway through the period surveyed, was present at 11.

Although both John Wallaces were present at several meetings, the son in effect replaced the father around 1606. Unlike some of their fellow elders, the Wallaces of Auchans did not hold their lands directly from the crown. Rather, they were tenants of the Boyds, an old Ayrshire family with many protestant connections.[186] John Wallace younger certainly had a firmly Calvinist education; he is listed among the Scots students who attended the Huguenot academy at Orthez.[187] If one counts how many meetings one or the other attended, their participation is second only to Robert Wallace of Galrigs. This may be partly a result of geography. Of all the elders' estates, those of the Wallaces of Auchans were the closest to the parish kirk. Indeed, the John Wallaces were usually styled as "of Dundonald" in the session register. They were also almost always listed first among the elders. The only exceptions to this rule occurred on those very rare occasions when one of the Cunningham lairds of Caprington attended a session meeting. The proximity of the lands of Auchans to the kirk seems the most likely explanation for this, because the Fullartons controlled more land. Proximity may also explain the very active participation on the session of Robert Wallace of Galrigs. His lands lay just east of Dundonald itself.

In contrast, both Fullarton lairds had to travel farther to attend. Dreghorn was nearly three miles north of Dundonald, and Crosbie about four miles southwest. The Fullartons, however, had long been associated with the Reformed Kirk, both politically and religiously. John Fullarton of Dreghorn (d. 1587) had attended the General Assembly of June 1565 in Edinburgh, requesting a minister for Dundonald parish, and promising to help pay his stipend.[188] This same laird had subscribed to the protestant band at Ayr in 1562, along with the earl of Glencairn and lords Boyd and Ochiltree. He

---

[185] For the register, see Henry Paton, ed., *Dundonald Parish Records: The Session Book of Dundonald 1602-1731*, (Edinburgh: Bute Society, 1936). Due to gaps in the register, there are no January or October meetings for 1603, and no July meetings for 1604.

[186] James Gillespie, *Dundonald: A Contribution to Parochial History*, (Glasgow: John Wylie, 1939), 1:157.

[187] John Durkan, "The French Connection in the Sixteenth and Early Seventeenth Centuries," in T.C. Smout, ed., *Scotland and Europe 1200-1850*, (Edinburgh: John Donald, 1986), 19-44, at 38.

[188] *BUK*, 1:61.

was also a participant in the "Chaseabout Raid," an abortive rebellion against Mary Queen of Scots and the Darnley marriage, in 1565.[189] The Fullartons were one of the oldest local families, probably Norman in origin, and Dreghorn was the center of their barony.[190] The Fullartons of Crosbie, while a cadet branch of the family, may have owned more land in the parish than their cousins in Dreghorn. James Fullarton of Crosbie held lands in Fullarton (just south of Irvine), the Troon, Irvine, Harperland, Gailes, Craiksland, Sandyhills, Rowanhill and Brownlee. Even Edward Wallace of Sewalton, a fairly active elder on the session (he attended nine of the meetings surveyed) was a tenant of Fullarton of Crosbie.[191]

This small band of local notables was also linked by marriage. John Fullarton of Dreghorn's wife was a Wallace of Auchans. The elder John Wallace of Auchans had married a woman from the Cathcart family, and her kinsman, Gilbert Cathcart of Collennan, also served as an elder, although he only attended seven of the 33 meetings surveyed. James Fullarton of Crosbie married a daughter of John Fullarton of Dreghorn. Another woman from the latter family married William McKerrell of Hillhouse, an elder whose attendance was infrequent.[192]

While the Wallaces, Fullartons, Cathcarts and McKerrells were parish bigwigs, the Cunninghams of Caprington were notables on a wider, regional scale. The minister and session considered it important that the laird of Caprington and his heir were listed first on the session elected in June 1606 (the only election held during the period under consideration here), but they almost never attended meetings.[193] Their presence on the eldership was probably more honorific than practical. Having the patriarch and heir of the most prestigious family in the parish as elders, even in name only, lent authority to the kirk session. But the cavalier attitude displayed by the Cunninghams may have endangered their prominent position, at least within the kirk itself. In 1613 the Glasgow court of high commission ruled in favor of the Fullartons of Dreghorn in a dispute with the Cunninghams of Caprington over possession of a prime pew.[194] Church seating in a rural

---

[189] James Paterson, *History of the County of Ayr with a Genealogical Account of the Families of Ayrshire*, (Ayr: John Dick, 1847-52), 2:22.

[190] *Ibid*, 2:12; Gillespie, 1:121.

[191] Gillespie, 1:134, 161.

[192] Details on marriages from Paterson, 2:17, 23, 25, 33.

[193] *Dun KS*, 108. William Cunningham, young laird of Caprington, was censured for fornication in 1609, and attended one meeting in connection with that case. Other than that, he did not attend a single meeting between October 1606 and April 1610. See *ibid*, 120, 200, 207, and chapter seven, below.

[194] *Dun KS*, 237. The mother of the young laird of Caprington had apparently tried to claim a pew used by the Fullartons of Dreghorn.

parish was an important reflection of the local hierarchy, and the Cunninghams may have been losing their grip.

One elder who certainly lost his social position during this period was Thomas Wallace of Gulliland. His fall from grace provides an illustration of the way the kirk session and disciplinary system could both reinforce local power relationships and assist in changing them. Wallace of Gulliland had been one of the most active elders during the period 1602-6, and his visage would have been familiar to the many offenders who faced censure from the session during those years. His regular presence may have been more a reflection of geography than social position; Gulliland was a mere stone's throw from the village of Dundonald. In fact, when listed in sederunts his name usually followed those of all the other elders, indicating that he was considered the least important of the group. Whereas the presence of a Wallace of Auchans, a Fullarton of Dreghorn or a Cunningham of Caprington enhanced the session's prestige, Wallace of Gulliland's position on the session probably did more for his own reputation than it did for the eldership's. But he lost this status when a new session was elected on 1 June 1606, and his name was not among those listed.[195]

His disappearance from the eldership certainly did not bring with it his disappearance from the register, however. On 22 June, he was accused of having made his servant, Marion Wallace, pregnant. The following week, both appeared and admitted their fornication, were fined and told to perform public repentance as first-time fornicators. But a month later, the session heard that the couple were still living under the same roof, a situation which it was certain would only compound the scandal. The two ignored several summonses to appear again, and Thomas Wallace had still not performed his public repentance when he finally faced his former colleagues once more on 31 August. Reminded to perform his repentance, he "refuisit to do the samin and opponit him self to the discipline and ordour of the kirk." This earned him a summons to a meeting of the Presbytery of Irvine. It is uncertain whether he obeyed that order, but on 7 September he was again before the session, where he attacked the minister, David Milne, and the elders for having appointed him. Never mind that there was no record of Wallace having opposed Milne while he was an elder, he now felt the minister was only qualified to preach to "ruid plewmen and yeamen men and had neither graces nor doctrine." With this outburst, "the minister and sessioun comportit patientlie for the tyme."[196]

It seems clear that Wallace's transformation from enforcing elder to accused offender had changed his outward opinion of the minister, session

---

[195] *Ibid*, 108.
[196] *Ibid*, 111-4, 117-8.

and disciplinary system. What is not so certain is what caused his ouster from the eldership. Was it the rumor of scandal, or did he lose his position for some other reason? On 1 November 1607, he was styled as "sumtyme of Gullilandis," suggesting that he had lost his estate.[197] By then he had been battling the minister and session for over a year, but that alone would not have caused him to lose his lands. It seems more likely that he was already having trouble meeting his financial obligations in 1606, and his growing impoverishment caused his removal from the session. Once he had been removed, he was more vulnerable to the charge of fornication.

His Wallace kinsmen did make some effort to intercede on his behalf. On 26 October 1606, John Wallace of Auchans/Dundonald asked that action by the presbytery against Wallace of Gulliland for his calumny on the minister be suspended while he met with him privately, and this delay was continued the following January for the same reason. Meanwhile, Marion Wallace satisfied for her part of the offense, and was said in February 1607 to be indigent. But her erstwhile partner remained stubborn. The session ordered public admonitions against him in February, and he was accused of habitual absence from preaching in March. In October 1607 he appeared before the session with further charges against the minister, but was himself convicted of slander instead, "quhilk he confirmit be railling against the minister according to his auld maner." He never seems to have settled matters with the session, and in September 1610, he and Marion Wallace were accused of fornication again.[198]

If Thomas Wallace railed in public against the kirk's disciplinary system, many of his fellow parishioners probably lent a sympathetic ear, although they might have questioned the timing of his conversion. The Dundonald session was an active one, and on those rare occasions when sitting elders or their immediate family members were accused of offenses, they usually got preferential treatment.[199] Not so Wallace (once he was off the session), or more humble members of the community. By 1605-10, the Dundonald session was averaging 77 cases per year, quite an extraordinary figure for a parish with a population under one thousand. These cases were spread over a wide range of offenses, as table 6.10 demonstrates.

There were eight categories of offense which each made up at least four percent of the total caseload for the Dundonald session during this period. By comparison, only two types of offense (sexuality and sabbath breach) did so in St. Andrews during 1582-1600, and only four offense types (the same two plus kirk absence and slander or verbal quarrels) did so at Anstruther

---

[197] *Ibid*, 154.

[198] *Ibid*, 120, 127, 130, 133, 151, 219.

[199] For more on this subject, at Dundonald and elsewhere, see chapter seven, below.

TABLE 6.10—BREAKDOWN OF CASES FOR DUNDONALD
KIRK SESSION, 1602-10

Offense category	Cases	Males	Females	No-shows
Sexuality	230 (36%)	119	111	35 (15%)
Sabbath breach	132 (20%)	109	23	27 (20%)
Violent attacks	44 (7%)	42	2	9 (20%)
Church absence	34 (5%)	20	14	14 (41%)
Slander, bickering	31 (5%)	21	10	5 (16%)
Communion absence	29 (5%)	22	7	3 (10%)
Disobedient to Kirk	26 (4%)	18	8	11 (42%)
Dealings w/outcasts	24 (4%)	10	14	11 (46%)
Magic, witchcraft	19 (3%)	9	10	5 (26%)
Violations of fasts	18 (3%)	11	7	1 (6%)
Domestic disputes	13 (2%)	8	5	3 (23%)
Totals	644	414	229	131 (20%)

Note: numbers within listed sin categories do not equal the total due to other cases
scattered throughout less numerous categories. "No-show" percentages are calculated for within each category.

Wester for 1583-5 and 1588-98. The Dundonald elders during the years
1602-10 devoted more attention to a broader range of cases than any other
kirk session in this study. Table 6.11 sketches out their efforts on an annual
basis. While it reveals what is still an episodic pattern for a few offenses,
such as magic/witchcraft, or dealings with outcasts, annual fluctuations for
most offenses are not nearly as wide here as in other communities in this
study. The Dundonald elders were settling into a broad, consistent
enforcement regimen in which one type of offense could not dominate the
annual caseload. There were only two years (1606 and 1609) when any
category comprised more than half of the total, and none when any totalled
over 60 percent. One does not see here the tendency visible elsewhere (in

TABLE 6.11—BREAKDOWN OF CASES BY YEAR
FOR DUNDONALD KIRK SESSION, 1602-10

Column Headings:
1 - Sexuality
2 - Sabbath breach
3 - Violent attacks
4 - Absence from kirk
5 - Slander, quarrels
6 - Communion absence
7 - Disobedient to kirk
8 - Dealings with excommunicants/outcasts
9 - Magic, witchcraft

Year	Total	1	2	3	4	5	6	7	8	9
1602*	49	11	1	4	9	6	-	-	13	4
1603*	47	15	7	4	6	2	3	-	3	-
1604*	85	13	18	5	2	1	12	5	-	10
1605	94	28	20	2	11	9	2	3	-	-
1606	79	40	23	-	1	3	-	3	-	2
1607	70	26	11	9	1	5	-	6	8	-
1608	94	30	32	6	2	5	2	6	-	3
1609	62	36	14	4	1	-	2	1	-	-
1610	64	31	6	10	1	-	8	2	-	-

*incomplete years in register
Note: numbers within years may not add up to the listed annual totals due to leftover cases which do not fit the listed categories.

earlier periods) to crack down suddenly on a certain offense, only to abandon the effort just as hastily after an adverse community reaction. In Dundonald in the early seventeenth century, the disciplinary system was reaching something like a mature state, and parish residents were willing to accept the session's authority in a number of areas besides sexuality.

One area in which the Dundonald session had enjoyed some success was in bringing reluctant local residents within the pale of Reformed religion through enforced catechism and Communion participation. When Margaret Wallace protested that she could not come to Communion because John McGeachen, a regular participant, had slandered her, she was told that her absence was unacceptable, and admonished "to lay asyd hir rancor and cum to the communioun."[200] Every adult in the parish was also to be examined annually on points of doctrine. Conscientious record-keeping was part of the effort; William Hobkin was fined five shillings for missing a 1596 examination, but had it refunded in 1602 because he had faithfully attended every examination in the interim. Bessie Blair managed to avoid examination and Communion for five years, but the session caught up with her in late 1604 and forced her to perform public repentance in linen. John Findlay was given the same punishment for a similar term of absence the next year. He did not even know the Lord's Prayer.[201] The beggar Margaret Underwood had obviously learned something of the Atonement, but found it difficult to reconcile with contemporary reality. This led her to suggest that "Christ vald not [have] bein sa daft as to haif died for hir." Proceedings against her were tabled, however, when it was suggested she had made the statement "of witlesnes."[202] The session could ensure that all were at least exposed to the rudiments of doctrine, but for some these still surpassed all understanding.

Underwood's marginal status made her difficult to coerce. She, like many other itinerants, had little to lose. She could not afford to pay fines, and imprisoning paupers cost money. The techniques of public humiliation which could be so effective against those with some position in the community were small deterrence to someone with no fixed residence. The elders saw the presence of such wanderers as a threat to the community, but rather than pursuing the vagrants themselves, sought to discipline parishioners who had dealings with them. Thus the herring fishermen who haunted the coastal taverns of the Troon on the Sabbath were effectively out of reach, but the session could, and did, try to punish those who sold them meat and drink. One of the latter, Margaret Bryan, probably did not help her case any when she tartly suggested that the minister "sould haif send his man to gather the teind herring on the Saboth day." Another irony—that she was called in to defend herself on the day which had until the recent past been celebrated as Christmas—passed unmentioned.[203]

Just as the session could do nothing about the Sabbath-breaking fishermen themselves, it was incapable of direct action against "the

---

[200] *Dun KS*, 40.

[201] *Ibid*, 61, 84.

[202] *Ibid*, 49.

[203] *Ibid*, 43.

maisterfull beggar quho callis him self John Burg, Yrland man, with his huris [whores]." But when Burg and company found overnight lodgings in the parish in the spring of 1602, the elders launched an investigation, in order to see who had hosted them. Thirteen people were charged. Hugh Houston admitted that the itinerant group had stayed in his house, but protested that it was not by invitation. Burg had entered, he said, "sat down in his [Houston's] chyr and prowdlie ansuerit he wald not ga out." Houston also claimed that when he had gone down to the village of Barassie seeking aid in ejecting the visitors, no one had been willing to help. Andrew Reid, one of those Houston charged with refusal to help, maintained that Houston had been entertaining the group all day, and had only quarreled with Burg in the evening. Several parishioners were willing to grant that others had volunteered to host Burg and his followers, but all denied that they had done so themselves. In the end, the session dropped the matter, but those involved were given a clear reminder that all vagrants were *personae non gratae* in Dundonald parish.[204] With the disciplinary system in place, the locals could be policed, and vagrant strangers kept away.

In this chapter, we have witnessed a widening of the net of discipline in St. Andrews, Anstruther Wester and, to a lesser extent, Monifieth. From an initial preoccupation with sexual matters, kirk sessions expanded their concerns to include enforcement of the Sabbath, mandatory participation in parochial religious life and the settling of disputes by mediation and arbitration. At Dundonald in the early seventeenth century, the system was in full swing. But the example of Rothiemay at the same time serves as a reminder that the Reformed Kirk still had an uncertain grip on some parishes, and some local authorities were uninterested in further reformation.

Where the disciplinary regime had developed, kirk sessions were no longer merely vice squads; they were becoming primitive social welfare agencies whose concerns included vice, indoctrination and education, poor relief, treatment of children and the aged and relationships between neighbors.[205] This is not entirely a story of what nineteenth-century commentators might have called enlightened "progress," though. The courts of the Reformed Kirk had little toleration of dissent, and made a major contribution to that most unenlightened of early modern phenomena: the witch hunt. Further, while in theory all estates were equally sinful, there

---

[204] *Ibid*, 15-8.

[205] For detailed arrangements made by the Anstruther Wester elders to provide for a foundling infant abandoned by the roadside between Anstruther and Pittenweem in 1588, see StAUM ms CH2/624/1, 32-3. The child was still alive, with the parish still paying many of her expenses, four years later.

were differences (just as in modern court systems) between the treatment of offenders who held power and those who did not. This last issue is the subject of the next chapter.

CHAPTER SEVEN

EQUALITY BEFORE THE KIRK? REFORMED DISCIPLINE
AND THE ELITE

The haill body of the nation, and namlie the graittest members thairof, wha
sould be gydders and guid exemples to uthers, ar defylit with sacrilage,
swearing, blasphemie, blud, adulteries, reaf and oppression, etc., sa that na
mervell it is tho the fleing buik of God's judgments enter in thair housses, and
consume timber with stean.
> \- James Melville, Reformed minister[1]

I can testify by trial of Scotland, which have traveled it over in their best
reformed places, as in Donde, Sct. Andrewes, Edenborowe & sundrie other
Townes. And [I] have knowne the king in great daunger & feare of his lyfe by
their Lordlie Discipline, the nobles & people at great discord and much
distracted, & yet all men made slaves to the preachers & their fellowe elders.
> \- Robert Brown, English separatist[2]

One of the complaints James VI and I had about presbyterian church
government was that its courts took no account of rank. Lecturing John
Reynolds, president of Corpus Christi College, Oxford, at the Hampton
Court Conference in 1604, he warned, "if you aim at a Scottish presbytery,
it agreeth as well with monarchy as God and the Devil! Then Jack and Tom
and Will and Dick shall meet and censure me and my council."[3] The king
saw in what had by then developed into a presbyterian disciplinary system
in Scotland ample opportunity for sedition. To him, elders and presbyters
were unwelcome interlopers in the affairs of their betters.

The king's concern was shared by at least some of the Scots aristocracy.
One such lord in 1585 criticized the *Second Book of Discipline* of 1576-8
because under its provisions, "it appeareth that marchandis and craftisme[n]
or like rabb[le] in ane station may be called ministeris seing throch the haill

---

[1] *JMD*, 188.

[2] Robert Brown, *A New Years Guift*, (ed. Champlin Burrage), (London: Congregational
Historical Society, 1904), 25-6, cited by David George Mullan in *Episcopacy in Scotland: The
History of an Idea, 1560-1638*, (Edinburgh: John Donald, 1986), 68. Brown and his followers
ran afoul of the Edinburgh Presbytery for their baptismal views early in 1584. See
Calderwood, 4:3.

[3] This comes from the tirade which ended with "no bishop, no king." Cited in Caroline
Bingham, *James I of England*, (London: Weidenfield and Nicolson, 1981), 37-8.

realme sic men are electit elders and deacones."[4] This seemed an unhealthy mixture of estates, involving the elevation of the lower to a position above the higher. In 1605, seeking to ensure that the highest estate would judge its own in the face of what the king viewed as clerical pretentions, James tried to insist that no Scots nobleman could be excommunicated without the approval of the Privy Council.[5]

More recent commentators have seconded the king in his estimation of the political and social implications of Reformed discipline, in Scotland and elsewhere. Both Michael Walzer and Henry Heller have seen church discipline as inherently anti-aristocratic, citing the French Huguenot example of Madame de Mornay, wife of a leading ideologue and aristocrat, who was enraged to find that her servants could attend Communion, while the consistory of Montauban forbade her to do so because of her ostentatious hairstyle.[6] In Geneva itself, the *consistoire*'s campaign against the habitual dancing of the captain-general Ami Perrin and his wife, daughter of the prominent citizen François Favre, led to the pair being briefly jailed by order of the town's Council of Sixty. This indignity certainly contributed to Perrin's break with the Reformed party and the formation of the so-called "libertine" opposition.[7]

Discussing the relationship between the nobility and the Kirk in Scotland, Keith Brown has suggested that by the 1590s, discontent at being subject to discipline led the nobility to favor episcopacy over presbyterianism.[8] Examining four kirk sessions in the county of Fife in the mid-seventeenth century, John Di Folco wrote that "apparently free of rigid class distinction, the composition of and method of election to the eldership were, compared to other existing institutions, such as the burgh court, relatively democratic and more widely socially representative."[9] Assessing the same period, Walter Makey argued that local kirk sessions helped complete a revolution set off by inflation and the feuing of lands—a revolution which saw power

---

[4] NLS ms Adv. 29.2.8, 128r.

[5] Walter Roland Foster, *The Church Before the Covenants: The Church of Scotland 1596-1638*, (Edinburgh: Scottish Academic Press, 1975), 105.

[6] Michael Walzer, *The Revolution of the Saints: A Study in the Origins of Radical Politics*, (Cambridge, Mass.: Harvard University Press, 1965), 50; Henry Heller, *Iron and Blood: Civil Wars in Sixteenth-Century France*, (Montreal: McGill-Queen's University Press, 1991), 72-5, 83.

[7] André Biéler, *L'Homme et la Femme dans la Morale Calviniste*, (Genève: Labor et Fides, 1963), 129-30.

[8] Keith M. Brown, "In Search of the Godly Magistrate in Reformation Scotland," *Journal of Ecclesiastical History* 40 (1989), 567.

[9] John Di Folco, "Discipline and Welfare in the Mid-Seventeenth Century Scots Parish," *RCSHS* 19 (1977), 183.

shift from the crown and nobility to the substantial farmers and burgesses who comprised the eldership of the typical session. For Makey, Calvinism in Scotland thus resulted in "the construction of a new apparatus of government [the kirk session] founded on different principles from the old and operated by ministers and elders who would, or at least could, be drawn from a different social strata. In this...guise, Calvinism would, as the price rise wrought its silent havoc, become subversive in more than the obvious sense of the word." Indeed, Makey goes so far as to label the kirk sessions "revolutionary cells."[10] These are strong claims. The question which remains unanswered is how this system, certainly revolutionary in theory, operated in practice. Did the new courts treat the bigwigs (including the elders themselves) like everyone else, thus perhaps justifying the traditionalist king's condemnation of the system, or did rank carry its privileges into the consistory? If kirk sessions were revolutionary cells, when did this revolution begin and how long did it take?

The Limits of Ecclesiastical Power

The General Assembly passed a resolution in December 1563 that "offenders whose offenses war published [announced] sould mak their publict repentance, without exception of persons; and if they refused...after due admonitions, the censures of the Kirk sould strike upon them: and therefore it [is] ordained that Mr. Robert Richardson sould make his publict confession for his whoredome, and satisfie the kirk of Edinburgh."[11] Richardson, a prominent patron of the Protestant cause, was lord high treasurer of Scotland, and prior of St. Mary's Isle.[12] The following October, the kirk session of Canongate/Holyrood, whose location between the capital of Edinburgh and the principal royal palace of Holyrood, gave it some prominent parishioners, passed an ordinance regarding the banishment of women for fornication or adultery. Sentences of banishment in the past had not been sufficiently enforced. So, the elders ruled, any offender banished thereafter who was later found in the burgh was to be put in the branks at the market cross for six hours, and then be warded until she did public repentance, "and this to be observit on all...without exceptioun of person

---

[10] Walter Makey, *The Church of the Covenant 1637-1651: Revolution and Social Change in Scotland*, (Edinburgh: John Donald, 1979), 7, 139.

[11] *BUK*, 1:41.

[12] Michael Lynch, *Edinburgh and the Reformation*, (Edinburgh: John Donald, 1981), 181, 265-6. Richardson was one of the "faithful brethren" who agreed to endow the reformed poor hospital in the burgh in November 1562. John Knox listed him among those who "had renunceit Papistrie, and oppinlie professit Jesus Chryst with us," and attended the 1560 parliament. See Knox, 2:88.

or personis. "[13]

Of course, such pious resolutions did not always result in consistent practice. The records do not specify whether Robert Richardson ever made his public repentance, although the matter was not raised again. In August 1573, the General Assembly passed a resolution reminding its members that noblemen were subject to discipline as were "the poorer sort," and superintendants and commissioners of the Kirk were expressly forbidden to sell dispensations from public repentance in sackcloth to those offenders who could afford to pay.[14] The following March, James Patoun, bishop of Dunkeld, admitted to the General Assembly that he had not executed the sentence of excommunication ordered against the earl and countess of Atholl, Catholics and supporters of the queen's party in the civil war which had just ended.[15] The General Assembly continued to prod the reluctant bishop, but as of March 1575, he still had not excommunicated the earl.[16]

Clearly Patoun, perhaps unenthusiastic himself about the Reformed program, was reluctant to offend a magnate who wielded so much power in and around Dunkeld.[17] The General Assembly was acting as a sort of super kirk session to handle a case far too big for any local session, if indeed any existed in Atholl's home region at that time. Atholl himself had little interest—theological or political—in the new religion. For other magnates, political patrons of the kirk, submitting to discipline could reinforce their standing as "godly magistrates," albeit sinners. Thus on June 26, 1582, the earl of Gowrie, leader of the ultra-protestant Ruthven faction which was to seize power two months later, enhanced his standing by submitting to the Edinburgh Presbytery for violating a fast and receiving the excommunicated Robert Montgomery into his house, although no punishment was mentioned.[18] Gowrie here courted the Kirk by accepting its authority, and distanced himself from Montgomery, who had been made archbishop of Glasgow against the wishes of the General Assembly and

---

[13] *BKC*, 9.

[14] Calderwood, 3:300.

[15] *Ibid*, 3:303. James Stewart, earl of Atholl, was one of only three temporal lords present at the 1560 parliament who voted against the Reformed confession of faith. (Knox, 2:121) After Queen Mary's 1567 deposition, he initially supported the Earl of Moray due to his own territorial feud with Argyll, but switched to the queen's side in 1569. See Gordon Donaldson, *All the Queen's Men: Power and Politics In Mary Stewart's Scotland*, (London: Batsford, 1983), 93-4; and George Hewitt, *Scotland Under Morton*, (Edinburgh: John Donald, 1982), 26.

[16] Calderwood, 3:330-1, 341.

[17] Patoun had also been pressured by the Earl of Argyll into granting the earl several pensions out of his bishopric. Patoun was of obscure origins himself, and seems to have had difficulty taking a stand against nobles. See Mullan, *Episcopacy in Scotland*, 41-3.

[18] Calderwood, 3:622.

through the influence of Esmé Stewart, duke of Lennox and Gowrie's political foe. In October the General Assembly cemented the alliance by officially endorsing the Ruthven raiders on the grounds that they were protecting the liberties of the Kirk.[19]

While Atholl was out of favor with the Kirk and the regency in 1574, and Gowrie was courting the ministers in 1582, the case of George Gordon, 6th earl of Huntly, clearly demonstrates the limits of the Kirk's power when dealing with a magnate who flouted the authority of Kirk and Parliament, but enjoyed the king's favor. The Gordons dominated Aberdeenshire and the northern Grampian region through an extensive network of kin and dependents. The 6th earl, educated as a Catholic in France, returned to Scotland to take his position as head of the family in the early 1580s. By 1589, through a marriage with the Lennox Stewarts and the acquisition of several court offices, he was, after the king, the most powerful figure in the realm.[20]

In 1592 Huntly, along with the earl of Errol and several other lords, was implicated in the affair of the "Spanish Blanks," in which he and his fellows appeared to pledge their support to the designs of Phillip II of Spain. For this, their Catholicism and Huntly's role in the 1592 slaughter of the earl of Moray, they were excommunicated by the Synod of Fife in September 1593.[21] As the earls were national figures, the excommunication was supposed to be broadcast from pulpits throughout the realm, and in some areas it was.[22]

The king and the Kirk closely cooperated on several fronts in the early 1590s, and the ministers of Fife (led by the Melvilles) may have felt confident that they could effectively punish Huntly and thereby quash Catholicism as a political force in Scotland, but they were mistaken. The ministers of the Synod of Lothian and Tweeddale, many of whom (including those who preached in Edinburgh itself) were hardly shrinking violets, favored a cautious approach when dealing with an *éminence* like Huntly. They decided in October "that for a certan tyme sylence salbe keipit of the excommunicatioun...."[23] King James considered Huntly a good friend, and

---

[19] *Ibid*, 3:676-9; *BUK*, 2:594-6. Gowrie may have needed the support of the Kirk to reinforce his social position as well; his was the first earldom created for someone not of royal blood since the reign of James IV, which ended in 1513. See Donaldson, *All the Queen's Men*, 140, 145.

[20] Keith M. Brown, *Bloodfeud in Scotland 1573-1625: Violence, Justice and Politics in an Early Modern Society*, (Edinburgh: John Donald, 1986), 145.

[21] Calderwood, 5:263-8; *JMD*, 309-10.

[22] For example, at Monifieth (Angus) on October 7, 1593. See NRH ms OPR 310/1, 84r.

[23] James Kirk, ed., *The Records of the Synod of Lothian and Tweeddale, 1589-96, 1640-49*, (Edinburgh: Stair Society, 1977), 64-5.

took attacks on the nobleman personally.[24] In November the king pardoned the rebel earls, "provided they satisfy the Kirk." The leading ministers complained that they had not been consulted, but the king coldly replied that he had issued the pardon "by the advice of the three estats [sic]" and was merely informing them of the decision. As for the standing sentence of excommunication, James opined that "the proceedings of some few ministers against them in a corner of the countrie was nothing."[25]

Undaunted, the General Assembly, with Andrew Melville as moderator, endorsed the excommunication of the rebel earls in May 1594.[26] Later that year, the king was even moved for political reasons to march north against Huntly and his followers, although the campaign resulted in little military action and had no lasting effect.[27] Sir James Chisholm, one of Huntly's followers, submitted to the General Assembly at Montrose in June 1595,[28] but Huntly remained recalcitrant. He was persuaded by his brother-in-law the duke of Lennox to go into temporary exile in February 1595, but returned just over a year later, welcomed by the king.[29] A General Assembly called at James' behest in Dundee in May 1597 absolved the Catholic earls, after the ministers of the north succumbed to the royal will "be fear and flatterie," according to the embittered James Melville, who had presided over the original excommunication at the Synod of Fife.[30] The earls did promise to accept the reformed religion, but this pledge proved insincere in Huntly's case; in July 1608 the General Assembly excommunicated him again "because they find no hope [of his accepting the reformed faith] but, be the contrair, greater obstinancie."[31] This apparently troubled the earl little.

Huntly was powerful and the Kirk lacked the means of coercion which could have forced him to comply with its orders. In that respect, it was a simple case; the earl had the preponderance of might and influence on his side. But the conflict was fought using the corporate vocabulary of early

---

[24] Brown, *Bloodfeud*, 148-9.

[25] Calderwood, 5:289.

[26] *Ibid*, 5:309; *BUK*, 3:821.

[27] Brown, *Bloodfeud*, 168-9; Andrew Melville and his nephew James accompanied King James to Aberdeen on this expedition, underlining the temporary alliance between king and Kirk. See *JMD*, 318-22.

[28] *BUK*, 3:851, 853.

[29] Brown, *Bloodfeud*, 169.

[30] *JMD*, 374; *BUK* 3:918-22. Despite the seeming defeat for the Presbyterian party, Gordon Donaldson sees this as "the extinction of Catholicism as a political danger" in Scotland. See Gordon Donaldson, *Scotland: James V-James VII*, (Edinburgh: Mercat Press, 1987) (first pub. 1965), 193-4.

[31] *BUK*, 3:1048; Calderwood, 6:758-9.

modern society. For the Kirk to have sovereign power to judge and punish a great noble seemed, to the king and others, a dangerous mixing of estates. The king of Scots was *primus inter pares*, and, realistically, Huntly was his second. As such, it seemed proper that he be judged by his peers, not by tribunals of ministers, the most highborn of them from mere lairdly families. The traditional authorities of Scotland conceded that the ministers could sit in judgement over the average parishioner (in itself a mixture of clerical and civil functions), but the sacred privileges of higher estates were not to be infringed. For its part, the Kirk was seeking to break down barriers between estates, and that was a revolutionary idea.

The same question arose in 1591 when the lords of Session challenged a summons issued by the General Assembly against their colleague John Graham, lord Halyards. Halyards had allegedly denounced Patrick Simpson, minister of Stirling, as a "suborner" to the other lords of Session. To the General Assembly, this was a case of slander, which, as the highest disciplinary court in the realm, it claimed the power to try. To the lords of Session, such a claim was a breach of their privileges. If Halyards was to be tried for slander, they were to be the judges. In this case, the king staved off a confrontation by persuading Halyards to appear quietly before the Presbytery of Edinburgh and retract his statement against Simpson.[32]

Thus, at the national level the Kirk was unable to coerce noblemen unless, like Gowrie, they needed the Kirk's support for political reasons. King James vigorously defended aristocratic privilege, at least when his friends were involved. Other high officials might claim immunities as well. The Kirk lacked the means to enforce its disciplinary code in the face of more powerful traditional interests. But the synods and the General Assembly only acted as disciplinary courts in the extraordinary cases of obstinate nobleman or other high officials. Cases did not reach that level unless clearly problematic. At the local level, when dealing with local notables, the Kirk might have been more successful.

Kirk Sessions and Presbyteries

Since it involves a large database of disciplinary cases from kirk sessions and presbyteries, this study affords an opportunity to compare the disciplinary experience of the Scots elite with that of the general population. The data for kirk sessions includes 4594 cases, from eight localities, spread

---

[32] *BUK*, 2:781-2; Calderwood, 5:133-4, 138.

over the period 1560-1610.[33] They constitute a fairly representative slice of parish life in lowland Scotland in the first half-century of the Reformed Kirk, although they were at least slightly unusual in that each had a working kirk session, which not all lowland parishes had, particularly in the early part of the period.

Of these 4594 cases, 339 of them (seven percent) involve people who can be identified as having had some sort of local prominence, such as nobles, lairds, burgesses, college degree-holders, or local or central government officials. Some of these individuals were themselves elders or deacons of the kirk, usually in addition to bearing one of these other marks of distinction. One should note that, because of the economy of language used by most of the session clerks, sinners were usually identified only by their names, making status identification difficult. Therefore, figures given here for the percentages of cases involving elite individuals should be considered low estimates. The proportion of cases involving notables ranged from eleven percent in government and merchant-dominated Edinburgh and the Canongate, down to one percent in rural, remote Rothiemay.

One measure of the kirk session's effectiveness was the frequency with which it was able to pursue cases to their conclusions, from original accusation to conviction or acquittal, with the imposition of some sort of reparation for convictions. In the general population, 18 percent of those accused simply ignored the kirk's summons and never appeared. For notable individuals, this "no-show" rate was 23 percent, not a huge difference considering the smallness of the "elite" database. Thus it appears the kirk sessions were at least able to get the bigwigs to appear in the session room at roughly the same rate as the general population, albeit often after more delay. But once they got there, the privileged few were better able to hold up proceedings, pressure witnesses not to testify, or otherwise prevent the kirk session from reaching a clear conclusion. In the general population, three-quarters of all cases reached a clear decision, while for the elite, this figure was just under two-thirds.

But these numbers, while useful for comparing success rates, fail to address two important considerations in any comparison of the treatment of notable sinners with that of the general population: the types of offenses pursued, and the punishments doled out. The Scottish Kirk has been accused

---

[33] The kirk sessions, years tabulated and sources are as follows: 1)Aberdeen, 1562-3, 1568, 1573-8, (460 cases) SRO ms CH2/448/1; 2)Anstruther Wester (Fife) 1583-85, 1588-98 (546 cases) NRH ms OPR 403/1; 3)Canongate 1564-67 (287 cases) *BKC*; 4)Dundonald (Ayrshire) 1602-10 (644 cases) *Dun KS*; 5)Edinburgh General Session 1574-5 (321 cases) SRO ms CH2/450/1; 6)Monifieth (Angus) 1579-81, 1593-4, 1600-1, 1603-6 (105 cases) NRH ms OPR 310/1; 7)Rothiemay (Banff) 1605-6 (75 cases) NRH ms OPR 165/3; 8)St. Andrew's (Fife) 1559-1600 (2156 cases) *StAKS*.

of an obession with sex,[34] and while the quantitative basis for this charge has never been clear, these figures do provide some evidence. Indeed, 55 percent of all accusations involved sexual offenses, far more than the next highest category, violations of the Sabbath (11 percent). The Kirk's third biggest concern regarding its members of all social strata was to prevent slander and other verbal clashes between neighbors (4.5 percent).

TABLE 7.1—TYPES OF CHARGES BROUGHT BY KIRK SESSIONS AGAINST PROMINENT OFFENDERS COMPARED TO THOSE AGAINST THE GENERAL POPULATION, 1560-1610

Prominent offenders		General population	
Sin category	Cases	Sin category	Cases
Sexuality	129 (30%)	Sexuality	2523 (55%)
Religion	43 (13%)	Sabbath breach	485 (11%)
Political acts	34 (10%)	Slander, etc.	207 (4.5%)
Slander, etc.	24 (7%)	Religion	178 (4%)
Sabbath breach	16 (5%)	Church attend.	165 (4%)
Total	339	Total	4594

(Note: Listed categories do not add up to totals due to other cases scattered through less numerous categories.)

The Kirk also peered into the bedrooms of the notables, but not nearly at the same rate. Thirty-eight percent of the elite cases in this sample involved sexual lapses. This was the largest category for elite sinning as well as for the general population, but elite sins were more widely distributed among the various types of offenses. Two categories which did not figure very highly in the numbers for the general population—religious practices/opinions and political offenses—came in second and third, respectively, among the sins of the prominent, at 13 percent and ten percent, although the political cases were concentrated in the urban parishes of Edinburgh and St. Andrews. Thus while the three top categories of malfeasance for the general population were sex, Sabbath-breaking and verbal quarrels, for the notables it was sex, religion and politics, in that order.[35]

---

[34] John Bossy, *Christianity in the West 1400-1700*, (Oxford: Oxford University Press, 1984), 130. Bossy here claims that at least two-thirds of the cases heard before kirk sessions and presbyteries were sexual, but offers no evidence.

[35] It should be noted that a dispute, depending on its nature, could fall into one of three different offense categories according to the classifications employed in this study. The most common type of dispute, both for the general population and the elite, was the verbal dispute, often involving allegations of slander, between two neighbors. The two other categories, both

This highlights the difference in the way kirk sessions valued the obedience of the elite compared with that of the general population. The average parishioner was to restrict sexual activity to lawful marriage, keep the Sabbath and keep the peace. The notables were expected to do the same, but sexual offenses which were not notorious could perhaps be overlooked; at any rate, the illegitimate children of the prominent were less likely to become a burden on the parish poor fund. This may have been what John Inglis of Strathtyrum was thinking in 1589 when he sarcastically told the St. Andrews Kirk session, on which he had once served as elder, that he would perform public repentance for fornication "with the rest of the gentill men of his rank."[36] He certainly was not willing to be the first. But, because eminent individuals were expected to serve as examples for the multitude, their political and religious orthodoxy was closely scrutinized, and deviations were a serious matter, requiring disciplinary action by the Kirk.

The importance of political conformity is vividly demonstrated in the minutes of the Edinburgh General Kirk Session in 1574-5, in the wake of the civil war between supporters of the boy-king James VI and his exiled mother Mary, Queen of Scots. The queen's party took over the burgh in the spring of 1571, driving the king's active supporters to the nearby port of Leith. The following spring the queen's party began demolishing the homes of prominent king's men, but in late summer 1572 the king's party regained control of the burgh.[37] Edinburgh Castle continued to hold out for the queen, but it fell in May 1573, ending the civil war. The surviving kirk session minutes do not begin until April 1, 1574, but on that very day, 28 men appeared before the session and were ordered to perform public repentance in St. Giles' kirk, in black gowns with their heads uncovered, merely for having remained in the town while the queen's party held sway. Two others charged with actively assisting the queen also submitted that day, but their punishments were not specified.[38] In the following 18 months, until the register ends in November 1575, 94 people, almost all male, were charged with political offenses connected with the recent troubles, ranging from merely remaining in town to taking up arms for the queen.[39] These 94

---

less numerous, were conflicts within families, and violent attacks. If one considers all three types together, conflicts make up nine percent of cases for the general population, and 14 percent of cases for the prominent.

[36] *StAKS*, 2:616, 636.

[37] For a survey of these events, see Lynch, *Edinburgh and the Reformation*, 131-143.

[38] SRO ms CH2/450/1, 1r-v.

[39] These cases were probably a response to an act of Parliament passed in early 1573 requiring that all who had fought against the young king in the recent civil war "salbe admonischit be the pastouris and ministeris of the kirk to acknawledge thair offence and return to thair detfull obedience" by June 1, 1573 or face excommunication. This in effect placed

cases made up 29 percent of the total for Edinburgh during the period, second only to sexual offenses (54 percent). But when it looked to the higher echelons of burgh society, the kirk session was more than twice as interested in political offenses as sexual sins. For the Edinburgh notables, 49 percent of the cases were political, only 23 percent sexual. Most of the political offenders still came from the general population, but the elite of the capital were much more likely to be charged on political grounds than on any other.

There were protests against this as well. Perhaps the most recalcitrant of the political sinners was Mr. Thomas MacCalzean, laird of Cliftonhall, former Edinburgh provost and a lord of Session. Originally charged in April 1574, for having remained in town and served as an elder on the kirk session set up by the queen's party, he refused to perform public repentance and appealed to the General Assembly that he was unjustly barred from Communion. In the process, the session complained, he injured the reputation of John Durie, one of the town's ministers, by calling him "ane fantastic man and [saying] yt he [Durie] wes ane evill speker and yt he wes na minister."[40] MacCalzean claimed that he had remained in town out of fear of Archibald Ruthven, with whom he was at feud because MacCalzean had refused to agree to a marriage between Ruthven and his daughter. In March 1575, he still had not performed repentance, and at that point appeared before the session objecting particularly to being made to wear sackcloth, and complaining that no distinction was being made "betuixt me and [the] maist wilfull murder[er]."[41] He later apologized privately for the slander of Durie,[42] but refused to perform public repentance. A kinsman appeared on his behalf on June 9, 1575, this time maintaining that MacCalzean should be allowed to do his public repentance in his own seat before the pulpit, as the General Assembly may have allowed, rather than at the customary pillar of repentance, as the session demanded.

The reasons presented in this *apologia* resonate with an offended sense of corporate equity and social position. MacCalzean, his kinsman argued, believed that his peers on the kirk session (he had served as an elder several times) "wald hav putt na heviar burding nor gret[er] schame to him quha is yr nytbor yan ye generall assemble being straingeris and quha wer men of greit knawlege and discretioun and knew how sic as we salbe handillit alsweill as yai or bett[er]."[43] The session was unmoved by this plea. In

---

political dissidence within the kirk's bailiwick. See *APS*, 3:72-3.

[40] SRO ms CH2/450/1, 26r, 28r.

[41] *Ibid*, 46r-48r.

[42] *Ibid*, 52v, 54v.

[43] *Ibid*, 60r-61r.

October 1575, MacCalzean was again warned that he had to perform his repentance, with no reduction in severity, but the records give no indication of his ever having done so.[44] While the session considered MacCalzean obstinate, he felt that the elders were not giving him his just due as their longtime neighbor and associate. The Kirk was extending its disciplinary agenda to include political correctness, and the liberties of at least two estates were colliding.

The disciplinary system was used in a similar way to reinforce a civic coup resulting from the October 1593 burgh elections in St. Andrews. There, the longtime provost James Lermonth of Dairsie, who had often been at odds with the burgh's Melvillian ministry (Andrew Melville himself was rector of the university there and sometimes took the pulpit), was replaced by William Murray of Pitcarleis. Lermonth's party unsuccessfully appealed the election to a convention of estates at Holyrood palace. Andrew Melville rallied the university behind Murray, and Murray's followers (the new provost had just been elected as an elder) used the kirk session to strike back at Lermonth and forestall further action by his adherents, several of whom were former elders. First, Lermonth's brother Patrick was charged with assault in connection with the burgh elections. He protested that the session was not competent to judge him because the ministers, elders and deacons were "at inammite [enmity] with him, and hes borne armour againis him." Patrick Lermonth appealed to the Presbytery of St. Andrews, which had already failed in its efforts to discipline him and several others for the same offense, and the matter remained unresolved.[45]

Then, in January 1594, nineteen men, most of them prominent, and at least eight of them former elders, were charged by the session with "perjury" for having broken an alleged promise to drop a suit challenging the burgh elections. Only ten of the nineteen appeared, but they were forced to promise that they would abandon the legal action. A month later, David Watson, former elder and dean of guild in the burgh, was censured for having sworn a statement that he had only abandoned the lawsuit "for fer of excommunicatioun." He clearly viewed this as an abuse of the spiritual sword, but the St. Andrews session, just like that of Edinburgh two decades earlier, had no qualms about using discipline to prop up a godly regime; Watson was forced to perform public repentance in St. Andrews and Edinburgh.[46] Significantly, when James Lermonth of Dairsie recaptured the provostship in 1595, he was careful to take a seat on the session as well,

---

[44] *Ibid*, 74v.

[45] *StAKS*, 2:759-60, 764-5; *StAP*, 148-9, 153; *JMD*, 313-4; *APS*, 4:45-6.

[46] *StAKS*, 2:770-6, 778-9.

thus ensuring it could not again be used against him.[47] His kinsman, the laird of Clatto, took the same prudent step when made provost in 1597.[48]

While Thomas MacCalzean had previously held office in the Reformed Kirk,[49] as had several of the Lermonth party in St. Andrews, elders also used their disciplinary powers against local notables who were not at all connected with local reform efforts. In this way, the elders could better their own position by holding rivals up to public scorn. Thus the Monifieth Kirk Session managed to force Henry Ramsay of Laws, a local laird who did not serve on the session, to promise three appearances on the stool of public repentance for adultery in October 1579. He did not actually make the first appearance until the following July, however, nor complete his punishment until February 26, 1581.[50] By April 1584 he was again barred from Communion for adultery, as was Ninian Guthrie, laird of Kingennie.[51] The latter was a former sheriff-depute of Angus.[52] Pursuit of sexual offenders is not by itself so noteworthy, but these cases concerned more than the sins mentioned in the register. The Durhams of Grange, a longtime protestant family whose patriarch was always the first elder mentioned on session lists, were involved in a dispute with the Ramsays of Laws over half the estate of Laws, and Alexander Lauder of Omachie, another elder, had killed Ninian Guthrie's son and heir William in a feud.[53] No Guthrie of Kingennie joined the eldership until 1595,[54] and even that one, William Guthrie, lacked zeal; he was admonished from the pulpit in July 1600 for not enforcing the law against sabbath violations.[55] The Ramsays of Laws never served on the session before 1606 at the earliest, although the Ramsays of Ardownie did.[56]

---

[47] Murray also sat on the session elected in 1595. *StAKS*, 2:802.

[48] *Ibid*, 2:831.

[49] He had served as one of the General Assembly's three advocates from 1564-67. See *BUK* 1:50 and Duncan Shaw, *The General Assemblies of the Church of Scotland 1560-1600*, (Edinburgh: St. Andrew Press, 1964), 150.

[50] NRH ms OPR 310/1, 43v, 45v, 47v. The campaign up to 1580 against Henry Ramsay of Laws and his tenant Henry Guthrie is also discussed in Frank Bardgett, "The Monifieth Kirk Register," *RSCHS* 23, (1988), 186-8.

[51] NRH ms OPR 310/1, 57v.

[52] Alexander Warden, *Angus or Forfarshire: The Land and People*, (Dundee: Charles Alexander, 1880-85), 2:230.

[53] Frank Bardgett, *Scotland Reformed: The Reformation in Angus and the Mearns*, (Edinburgh: John Donald, 1989), 117, n. 92.

[54] NRH ms OPR 310/1, 87v.

[55] *Ibid*, 101v.

[56] Alexander Ramsay of Ardownie was named as an elder in 1575 and 1579 (the session was not elected annually, so he served continuously), but the Ramsays were off the session in 1595. A Henry Ramsay, no estate mentioned, was named to the session in 1606. *Ibid*, 29v,

In Monifieth, the Durhams of Grange felt powerful enough to use the kirk session to pursue their rivals who were not of the reforming party. Elsewhere there were powers the Reformed Kirk and its ministers could not afford or did not wish to offend. The kirk session in the northern, rural parish of Rothiemay was notably uninterested in the sins of the prominent. The leading local family, the Abernathys of Rothiemay, whose patriarch held the title of lord Salton, received Communion in a service separate from the rest of the parish, and had no representative on the kirk session, though several cadet Abernathys were elders. Lord Salton was generally absent on government or family business, and although on at least one occasion, in June 1605, family retainers chose not to communicate, having "pretendit excus of seiknes, bot suspect of relligoun," they were never pursued for this.[57] In 1617 Jean, sister of Lord Salton, married George Gordon, laird of Gight, a Catholic and ally of his kinsman the marquis of Huntly,[58] and the local minister was suspended by the General Assembly for performing the marriage.[59] Most important local residents were Abernathy clients, and the minister and elders were no exception.

Of course, in all these parishes, the elders themselves or their families were sometimes accused of sins, and often made a point of offering public reparation. In Anstruther Wester the elder Peter Borthwick, laird of Grangemuir, admitted on March 8, 1597 to having struck a miller's servant, although the session delayed imposing a punishment on him, because only eight elders were present.[60] Actually, an attendance of eight was above average, and this did not prevent the session from imposing reparations on other, less prominent, sinners. Borthwick skipped the next few meetings, but on April 19 he was given the option of merely standing up in his pew in church and confessing his offense, rather than sitting in the stool of repentance.[61] The matter was not mentioned again, and he probably complied.

The John Wallaces of Dundonald, father and son, were among the most influential elders in Dundonald parish in the decade after 1600. John Wallace younger had reinforced his family's religious credentials when he

---

41v, 87v, 118r.

[57] NRH ms OPR 165/3, 15v.

[58] Sir James Balfour, ed., *The Scots Peerage*, (Edinburgh: David Douglas, 1904-14), 7:413. The Gordons of Gight were known for their recusancy throughout the late sixteenth and early seventeenth centuries. See Margaret H.B. Sanderson, *Mary Stewart's People: Life in Mary Stewart's Scotland*, (Edinburgh: Mercat Press, 1987), 15.

[59] *Fasti*, 6:331.

[60] NRH ms OPR 403/1, 108r.

[61] *Ibid*, 109r.

studied at the Huguenot academy at Orthez.[62] He and his father were only listed second, rather than first, on session sederunts on those rare occasions when the Cunningham laird of Caprington attended. But on May 26, 1605 John Wallace younger's mother Dorothy, from the prominent north Ayrshire family of Sempill, was the only family member present. There, she confessed that she had tried to poison her daughter Mary Wallace, "of the quhilk crevell wickitnes scho earnestlie repentit hir, and the sclander that scho haid thairby geifin to the kirk."[63]

The mention of "sclander" to the kirk indicates that the attempted murder was known in at least part of the expansive rural parish. It seems noteworthy that her husband and son were not in the session that day, because one or the other or both had been present for 18 of the previous 20 meetings. Neither attended the next weekly meeting, either, although they resumed their regular attendance pattern two weeks later. On July 7, the session, with both John Wallaces present, "acceptit" Dorothy Sempill's private confession, and, presumably that was the end of it, with no public ritual of confession or reconciliation.[64] In that same month the session imposed public repentance barefoot and in sackcloth on parishioners guilty of name-calling, unruliness in the kirk, or adultery (with the ritual performed twice for the last), and simple public repentance with a fine for Sabbath-breakers.[65]

William Cunningham, young laird of Caprington, was the only elder considered more important than the John Wallaces, and was always listed first when present, but that was almost never. He seems to have been elder in name only, put on the session due to his family's standing.[66] The Cunninghams of Caprington were direct baronial tenants of the crown, and the elder laird had married Agnes, daughter of Sir Hugh Campbell, sheriff of Ayr. The young laird was eventually to marry a daughter of the Hamilton earl of Abercorn.[67] He attended a session meeting on October 26, 1606, but did not appear again until October 29, 1609, at which point the

---

[62] John Durkan, "The French Connection in the Sixteenth and Early Seventeenth Centuries," in T.C. Smout, ed., *Scotland and Europe 1200-1850*, (Edinburgh: John Donald, 1986), 38.

[63] *Dun KS*, 80-3.

[64] *Ibid*, 84.

[65] *Ibid*, 84-88.

[66] He was elected, along with his equally unenthusiastic father, on June 1, 1606, the only session election recorded between 1602 and 1612. *Ibid*, 108. For more on his and his family's role in the local kirk, see chapter six, above.

[67] James Paterson, *History of the County of Ayr With a Genealogical Account of the Families of Ayrshire*, (Ayr: John Dick, 1847, 1852), 2:410-11, 498. The family was evicted from the estate in the 1640s for supporting Montrose.

session had been considering what to do about his notorious fornication for more than ten months.[68] The woman involved had admitted her sin and promised public repentance, he had submitted a written response to the session's inquiry, and a kinsman had appeared on his behalf, but the session insisted that he appear in person, which he was clearly reluctant to do.

In his appearance in 1609 William Cunningham admitted his fault. But, as might be expected, he protested at having to perform public repentance in "the heich place" at the end of the kirk like everyone else. He offered instead the sum of four pounds Scots, about six times the ten shillings to one mark first-time fornicators were typically fined, and was told he could do his public repentance before the pulpit which was, owing to his high status, where his family's pew was probably located.[69] So, unlike Dorothy Sempill, he did perform a public ritual, but one modified out of deference to his position and generosity.

These prominent individuals were unable to ignore entirely the Kirk's program for reform in life as well as doctrine. It has been claimed that local landlords were never summoned before kirk sessions, but this is simply untrue.[70] What is more, in a statistical comparison like that presented earlier, these noteworthy cases would all be classified as concluded, with personal appearance, verdict and punishment. One might look at them and say the Kirk was able to bring these individuals to heel like anyone else. In doing so, however, it certainly offered them special treatment. All may have been equally subject to God's law in theory, but, in practice, compensation had to be made for earthly distinctions.

In fact, as late as 1588, one of the kirk sessions under the jurisdiction of the Stirling Presbytery seems to have doubted whether church discipline even applied to the elite. On April 9, 1588, under orders from the synod of Stirling and Dunblane, the presbytery summoned the minister and kirk session of St. Ninians for having baptized a child fathered out of wedlock by John Murray, laird of Touchadam, without requiring the father to perform public repentance.[71] A week later Mr. Henry Livingston, the minister, and Duncan Narne, a laird and elder in the parish, appeared to defend their actions. Livingston told the presbytery that the elders ordered him to perform the baptism "allaigein it hes bein ye commone practeis usit in y[air] assembleis befoir his co[m]ing to yame and yat yai knew na act of ye kirk made in ye contrar." Further, Livingston argued that to refuse to

---

[68] *Dun KS*, 120, 179, 189, 192.

[69] *Ibid*, 202.

[70] Christina Larner, *Enemies of God: The Witch-Hunt in Scotland*, (London: Chatto and Windus, 1981), 56.

[71] WRH ms CH2/722/1, 9 April 1588.

baptize the child would have been "to suffir seditione to aryss betuix him [the Laird of Touchadam] & yame [the session], & sua ye haill Disceplein of ye kirk to gang lowss." In other words, it was more important to foster good relations with local notables than to make examples out of them. Narne agreed, and maintained the session did "na wrang" thereby. The presbytery accepted these excuses, but forbade such practices in the future.[72] Such resolution was usually the most that could be mustered in the face of traditional local powers.

One might expect that the presbyteries, including ministers (and sometimes lay elders) from a wider district than the parish kirk session, would have had better luck in bringing the prominent to heel, since the collective status of their membership was generally higher than that of the typical session. Kirk sessions often referred particularly difficult cases to presbyteries, but presbyteries still had many of the same problems in disciplining the elite. In fact, if the experience of three of the original 13 presbyteries established in 1581 is any indication, the presbyteries failed to punish notable sinners as often as they succeeded.

Scrutiny of the extant records of the Edinburgh Presbytery up to 1590, the Stirling Presbytery to 1594 and the St. Andrew's Presbytery to 1605 yields a total of 1191 cases.[73] Of these, only 51 percent reached a clear conclusion, and 38 percent of those charged never appeared. Thus the presbyteries were less successful than the kirk sessions at getting the general population to show up. This trend was even more pronounced for cases involving prominent sinners. Nineteen percent of presbyterial cases involved elite offenders, and while 44 percent of these were brought to conclusion, in another 43 percent the accused never bothered to appear. Table 7.2 compares the charges made against notable offenders with those brought against the general population.

Again, sexuality was the most common sin category for the general population (48 percent), but, for the notables, cases involving religious dissent or unorthodox practices outranked sex, 25 percent to 17 percent. Even more than kirk sessions, presbyteries were careful to ensure that society's leaders demonstrated fidelity to the Reformed faith. Also noteworthy was the fact that 12 percent of elite cases involved violence; the lairds around Stirling and St. Andrews in particular could be masters of intimidation.

---

[72] *Ibid*, 16 April 1588.

[73] For Stirling Presbytery (724 cases) *SPR* goes through December 1587, then WRH mss CH2/722/1-2 (no folio markings—all references below by date); for Edinburgh Presbytery (138 cases), SRO ms CH2/121/1; for St. Andrews Presbytery (329 cases), *StAP* and StAUM ms Deposit 23.

TABLE 7.2—TYPES OF CHARGES BROUGHT BY PRESBYTERIES
AGAINST PROMINENT OFFENDERS COMPARED TO THOSE
AGAINST THE GENERAL POPULATION, 1581-1605

Prominent offenders		General population	
Sin category	Cases	Sin category	Cases
Religion	55 (25%)	Sexuality	572 (48%)
Sexuality	39 (17%)	Religion	175 (15%)
Violence	26 (12%)	Disobedience	64 (5%)
Sabbath breach	17 (8%)	Violence	58 (5%)
Slander, etc.	15 (7%)	Sabbath breach	56 (5%)
Total	224	Total	1191

(Note: Listed categories do not add up to totals due to other cases scattered through less numerous categories.)

The problems the Stirling Presbytery had with Robert Bruce, laird of Clackmannan, provide a good example. On June 4, 1583, Patrick Laing, minister at Clackmannan, admitted to the Stirling Presbytery that he had "sindrie tymis neglectit" to summon Margaret Bruce, accused of adultery with the laird, to appear before the presbytery. She had first been accused ten months earlier, but testimony from her would undoubtedly have led to the implication of her powerful paramour.[74] Two weeks later, Laing "allegit he was manasit and bosted be Robert Bruce of Clakmannan with mony injurius wordis, quhilk he [Bruce] promesit to performe in deid incaice he [Laing] execute the said summondis." Nevertheless, the presbytery ordered him to proceed.[75] Laing was caught between a rock and a hard place; on July 2, 1583 he still had not summoned Margaret Bruce, and on October 29 he admitted that he had baptized her child without obtaining any public repentance from her or the father.[76] The presbytery finally took matters into its own hands and itself summoned Robert Bruce of Clackmannan on January 28, 1584, but he never appeared.[77] He was still reported to be obstinate and unrepentant during a visitation of the parish in October 1586.[78]

Two years later, Clackmannan had a new minister, Mr. Alexander Wallace, but he was no more successful than his predecessor in dealing with

---

[74] *SPR*, 55, 126-7.

[75] *Ibid*, 134.

[76] *Ibid*, 142, 181.

[77] *Ibid*, 198.

[78] James Kirk, ed., *Visitation of the Diocese of Dunblane and Other Churches, 1586-1589*, (Edinburgh: Scottish Record Society, 1984), 55.

the laird. The presbytery called Wallace on the carpet on April 16, 1588 for having allowed the ringing of bells "upone yt day callit of awld Iull day [Christmas]." To the Reformed Kirk, December 25 was a day like any other, and to mark it by bell-ringing smacked of Catholic superstition. Wallace said he allowed the bells to be rung under heavy pressure from the Laird of Clackmannan "quha menasit & co[m]pellit him siclyk agains his will," and that he obeyed the laird "for feir of his lyf." The presbytery, recognizing its inability to bring the traditionalist laird to heel for any of his offenses, accepted Wallace's explanation.[79]

Andrew Graham, bishop of Dunblane and a member of the Stirling Presbytery, might have sympathized with Laing and Wallace, for Graham found himself in a similar bind, but with the additional complication of kinship ties. The presbytery ordered him in March 1584 to admonish John Graham, earl of Montrose and chief of the Graham family, for having entertained several of his tenants who had been excommunicated, including the Catholic David Graham, young laird of Fintry. When asked on March 17 if he had issued the admonition, Andrew Graham, clearly reluctant, excused himself on the grounds that he had been "occupyit utherwayis."[80] It was more than a family connection which made the bishop wary of offending the earl. Montrose's influence had helped him win his bishopric, and he was already in trouble with the presbytery for having let most of the lands pertaining to the bishopric to Montrose on very favorable terms.[81] But, a week after he had offered the excuse noted above, he wrote to the presbytery that he had spoken to the earl on the matter, and that Montrose had replied testily "that quhensoever it plaisit the brethrein of the presbytery to direct unto him the minister of Stirling, accumpaneit with ane barrun, or Johnne Duncansone [minister to the king], with ane barrun, his lordschip sould nocht faill to send ane ressonablle and direct answer...."[82] The requirement that a baron be included in any delegation made the earl's reply sound like a dare. Obviously, the religiously conservative Montrose did not feel he had to answer to what he regarded as clerical meddling in kinship matters. The presbytery considered the reply unsatisfactory, but nothing further came of the matter.

Even the admitted Catholic Walter Buchanan, brother to the laird of Arnprior, avoided excommunication at the Stirling Presbytery's hands for nearly eighteen months. First mentioned as religiously suspect in December 1586, his excommunication was not finally ordered until April 9, 1588. In

---

[79] WRH ms CH2/722/1, 16 April, 1588.

[80] *SPR*, 209-10.

[81] *Ibid*, 71, 73, 77, 111. See also *Dunblane Visitation*, x-xi.

[82] *SPR*, 211.

the interim he ignored more than ten summonses to appear, broke several vows to depart from the realm, and in June 1587 told the presbytery in person that he would neither sign the Negative Confession of 1581 nor have his daughter baptized by the Reformed rite.[83] In the face of such contempt, the presbytery must have realized that excommunication would accomplish little; the standing of Buchanan's family in and around Kippen would minimize the sentence's civil implications, and Buchanan was clearly unconcerned about the spiritual powers of the Reformed Kirk.

The Edinburgh Presbytery confronted another powerful interest—the crown—in the late 1580s when it tried to take action against Catholics at court. One of its targets was William Schaw, master of royal works. First charged in August 1588, Schaw ignored at least six summonses to appear. During the course of the process against him, he did attend several hearings, but only to ask further delays. The king himself also intervened twice to halt excommunication proceedings against Schaw, and the matter remained unresolved in March 1590, when a gap in the register makes it impossible to trace further.[84] At least one courtier suspected of Catholicism did submit,[85] but the king was generally unwilling to allow the presbytery to denounce publicly those of his circle who would not embrace the Reformed faith. James was determined to choose his own companions. He was soon to demonstrate (in the case of Huntly) that he might even wink at intrigue with foreign Catholic powers if he considered the offender a friend.

Robert Bruce, minister of Edinburgh from 1587-1605 and a laird (of Kinnaird) himself, preached a sermon on 2 Timothy 2:22-6, at St. Giles, Edinburgh, on November 9, 1589.[86] The occasion was the public repentance of the Francis Stewart, earl of Bothwell, for numerous sins, including murder and blasphemy. Bothwell was an erratic figure who alternately courted and outraged the Kirk. Taking his cue from Timothy, Bruce began by lamenting the "lusts and affections" to which youth was prone (Bothwell was 26).[87] But soon, he was on a different course, denouncing the

---

[83] *Ibid*, 234-7, 240, 242, 256, 260-1, 266, 299, 310-11.

[84] SRO ms CH2/121/1, 48r-v, 50v, 52v, 54r, 56v, 65r.

[85] This was William Stewart, commendator of Pittenweem Abbey. See *ibid*, 47v, 48v, 50v, 51r.

[86] The text is: "So shun youthful passions and aim at righteousness, faith, love, and peace, along with those who call upon the Lord from a pure heart. Have nothing to do with stupid, senseless controversies; you know that they breed quarrels. And the Lord's servant must not be quarrelsome but kindly to every one, an apt teacher, forbearing, correcting his opponents with gentleness. God may perhaps grant that they will repent and come to know the truth, and they may escape from the snare of the devil, after being captured by him to do his will."

[87] Bruce, 349.

propensity of those who enforced the laws—and he would have included kirk elders as well as the king and his officials—to overlook the offenses of their relatives and allies:

> Let no community of name, ally, proximity of blood, or whatever it be, move you to pervert justice, but let every man be answerable according to the merit of his cause....Let not the thief pass because he is your servant, nor the murderer because he is your kinsman, nor the oppressor because he is your depender.[88]

Bruce was concerned with bringing order to a disorderly society, through the evenhanded enforcement of both civil and ecclesiastical laws by the monarchy and the Kirk. But Scotland was unaccustomed to central power. Most authority was local authority, and local authority had been keeping order, more or less, for centuries. Kirk sessions and presbyteries were newcomers to this scene. Certainly, some of their members had held power in more traditional forms before the advent of Reformed discipline, but the goal then had been merely order itself; there was no egalitarian religious ideology involved. Society had not yet adjusted to accommodate these new corporations, so when they encountered traditional interests, including those dear to the elders themselves, they usually had to yield, taking what they could get in the way of symbolic obedience. The Kirk claimed to encompass all in its membership, but the blanket of order with which it sought to cover society was hardly seamless. The minister James Melville saw the new attempts at order as more resembling "athercape [spider] wobbes that taks the sillie flies, bot the bumbarts [large bluebottle flies] braks throw them."[89] It would be some time yet before the bluebottle flies would accept that they, too, were subject to the new order.

---

[88] *Ibid*, 355.
[89] *JMD*, 188.

CHAPTER EIGHT

REFORMED DISCIPLINE AND SOCIAL ISSUES: SEXUALITY,
CONFLICT AND WITCHCRAFT

*The quhilk day [8 December 1565] it is ordanit that gif thair be ony persone
or personis haif onye gruge of hatrit or malice or onye offence in his hart
aganns his broder, that they and ilke ane of thame come on Tisday in the
mornyng at viii houris to the tolboth quhair four of the kirk salbe present to
juge the offence, and gif that it standis in thame, to reconseill the same....*
— Register of the Canongate Kirk Session[1]

*[Isobel Watson said] the elff quein baid hir refuis god & byd w[i]t[h] yame
becaus scho wald fair bettir.*
— Register of the Stirling Presbytery, 21 April 1590[2]

Much of this study has emphasized local particularism rather than widespread similarities. Significant differences in disciplinary practice from one
community to the next, or from one decade to the next, have been brought
into stark relief by the quantitative methods and organizational scheme used
here. But this must not obscure the fact that there were general trends as
well. Sexuality and marriage are obvious cases in point. The former was a
primary concern almost everywhere, as ministers and elders struggled to
suppress pauperism by discouraging illegitimacy. Conflict resolution, on the
other hand, was something that the early kirk sessions, with the notable
exception of the Canongate, almost never became involved in. But, over
time, ministers and elders began to take part in efforts to restore Christian
love between feuding or bickering neighbors. They also participated in the
periodic witch hunts which were a grim feature of early modern Scottish
life. These three social issues—sexuality, conflict and witchcraft—and the
role the Reformed disciplinary order played in addressing them, warrant
separate examination here.

Sexuality

The problem of too many people exploiting the limited resources of an
underdeveloped economy was endemic in early modern Scotland, and all
authorities, regardless of their particular religious outlook, were willing to

---

[1] *BKC*, 31.

[2] WRH ms CH2/722/2, 21 April 1590.

use the disciplinary apparatus provided by Reformed religion to combat it. The minister James Melville saw a clear connection between vagrancy and irreligion when he complained of the growing army of poor roaming the country "in-swarms...godles and lawles, without mariage, baptesme, or knawlage of dewtie to God or man."[3] Related to this was the question of what constituted legal marriage, and there were extensive efforts, particularly in northerly regions, to change marriage customs and force cohabiting couples to formalize their relationships.

The previous chapters have demonstrated the prevalence of offenses related to sexuality in the caseloads of the disciplinary courts. Of 4,594 kirk session charges, 2,523 (55%) involved sexuality. For presbyteries, the figure was 572 out of 1,191 (48%). Although these numbers cannot really quantify behavior, they do quantify the interests of the elders and ministers who were enforcing discipline, and it makes them seem somewhat obsessed with the issue of illicit sexuality.

If this was indeed an obsession, one way to analyze it is to examine the actions regarding sexuality taken by the General Assembly, the largely ministerial body which governed the Kirk at the national level. This body regularly petitioned the crown, urging stricter enforcement of laws regarding social behavior, and sexuality figured heavily in these petitions. For example, the act of Parliament of 1563 which mandated the death penalty for adulterers was never really enforced, but the General Assembly often reminded the crown of its existence.[4] In addition, the assembly regularly considered questions regarding social discipline at its annual or semiannual meetings, usually passing resolutions in response. An inordinately high number of those resolutions concerned sex and marriage. Indeed, these were the most common subjects of the disciplinary questions considered at meetings during the first couple decades after 1560, when the Reformed Kirk was officially established. These could range from the very basic to the quite complex. For example, the first assembly (1560) concluded that sexual relations between betrothed—but not yet married—couples constituted fornication, requiring public confession by the offenders.[5] Here the real target may have been irregular marriage, a concern shared even by the crypto-Catholic Aberdeen Kirk Session, which vowed in December 1562 that all "handfast" couples (joined by a folk ceremony which rarely involved clergy) would have to marry formally by

---

[3] *JMD*, 191.

[4] Michael F. Graham, "The Civil Sword and the Scottish Kirk, 1560-1610," in W.Fred Graham ed., *Later Calvinism: An International Perspective*, (Kirksville, Mo.,: Sixteenth Century Publishers, 1993), 237-48.

[5] *BUK* 1:5; Calderwood 2:44-6.

the following "Festerans eve" (Shrove Tuesday). Some of them, the session lamented, had been cohabiting for seven years or more.[6] But couples charged with fornication under such guidelines often protested the new interpretation. As late as 1588, a woman stood up in the church of Clackmannan, before the entire congregation, and challenged James Anderson, commissioner from the Stirling Presbytery: "I hade ado w[i]t[h] my awin husband undir promeis of mariage q[uhi]lk is na fornica[tio]n. I will nevir confess fornica[tio]n nor mak repentence for fornica[tio]n." The case was particularly sensitive because her husband was the parish minister, who challenged Anderson from the pulpit: "will ze tak it upon zo[u]r conscience yat it is fornica[tio]n?" The matter was referred to the synod, but the latter concluded that the couple was indeed guilty of fornication, and they performed public repentance.[7]

But the General Assembly's interest in sexuality and marriage extended well beyond this relatively simple concern that cohabitation be legitimized by formal marriage. The assembly of December 1566 considered four disciplinary questions, three of them related to sex and marriage.[8] In June 1567, the figure was three out of three.[9] The assembly of March 1570 took up 17 questions, eight of them related to sex and marriage, including the quandary of whether two men who had slept with two sisters could marry each other's daughters, provided the latter were not the children of either sister (they could).[10] Clearly, sexuality was an issue which puzzled and fascinated the ministers of the Kirk. But this concern at the national level changed over time. By the 1580s and 1590s the public pronouncements of the Kirk at the national level concentrated much more on the threat of Catholic conspiracy, represented by Spain and the Jesuits, and diabolical conspiracy, represented by witchcraft, than on matters of sexuality.[11] Nevertheless, sexuality remained the biggest concern at the local level, despite some forays into other areas of misbehavior.

The reasons for this seeming obsession with sex were both economic and religious. The two-fold nature of the threat was highlighted by the Canongate Kirk Session in 1564 when it referred to fornication as both "hurfull to the commone walth" and "sklander to the kirk of God."[12]

---

[6] SRO ms CH2/448/1, 8-9.

[7] WRH ms CH2/722/1, 16 April, 4 June, 10, 17 and 24 September, 15 and 29 October 1588.

[8] Calderwood, 2:330-1.

[9] Ibid, 2:370-1.

[10] Ibid, 2:541-3.

[11] BUK, 2:704-5, 725, 730, 738, 784, 3:834, 937-8; Calderwood, 4:651, 682-3, 691, 5:134-5, 326, 685-7; JMD, 299-30.

[12] BKC, 10.

Vagrancy was viewed as a growing problem throughout Scotland (and western Europe in general) in the late sixteenth century,[13] and illegitimacy among those who already lived on the margins of poverty—most of the population, really—was certainly a contributing factor. Sex outside marriage was nothing new, but in a context of diminishing resources and growing population it became less socially acceptable. Elders and ministers recognized this and sought to persuade unmarried couples who had conceived children to marry. If they would not (usually because of the male's reluctance), the session often ordered that a sum be set aside by the father for the child's upbringing.[14]

But the numerous examples of kirk sessions pursuing prominent and wealthy offenders demonstrate that the concern with sex was not simply economic. John Dalgleish and Lady Janet Wemyss seemed shocked that the St. Andrews Kirk Session viewed their relationship as "hurdom" in 1566, and accused the elders of being "mer[e] layik and ignorant personis for the maist pairt," but the elders eventually excommunicated them anyway for their refusal to separate and perform public repentance. Wemyss had been unsuccessful in having an earlier marriage annulled, and the session could not but view her relationship with Dalgleish as illegitimate, regardless of the ample provision they could make for their offspring.[15] The St. Andrews session, like most other Scottish kirk sessions, saw no distinction between rich and poor when it came to sin. Sex outside marriage was an attack on marriage itself, and to tolerate it was to hazard the wrath of God, beyond any economic considerations.

Sexual cases usually came to the attention of kirk sessions through unexplained pregnancy, either of an umarried woman, a widow, or a married woman living apart from her husband. Typical was Marion Kirk who on 7 April 1575 admitted to the Edinburgh Kirk Session that she had "sundry tymes...partlie throw ye fregillitie of ye fleche and partlie be ye instigatioun of Sathane...geven ye use of hir body...in ye fylthe syne and vise of fornicatioun."[16] Such language, which cast illicit sexuality in terms of uncleanliness, was common in session registers. The pregnancy provided certain evidence of the woman's guilt, and kirk sessions would follow either rumor or the woman's testimony in identifying her paramour. Most women were relatively cooperative but, in stubborn cases, the session might seek the testimony of a midwife; it was believed that a woman in labor was

---

[13] Jenny Wormald, *Court, Kirk and Community: Scotland 1470-1625*, (Toronto: University of Toronto Press, 1981), 167.

[14] See, for example, *StAKS*, 1:232, 244, 304.

[15] *Ibid*, 1:260-76.

[16] SRO ms CH2/450/1, 51r.

always truthful in naming the father of her child.[17] The men, once summoned, usually appeared before the session, although sometimes after first ignoring one or more summonses. Of 231 males charged with sexual offenses at St. Andrews in the years 1559-81, 172 (74 percent) appeared to answer the charge. Of these 172, 23 expressly denied that they were guilty, although three of these later made confessions. Those who steadfastly maintained innocence could purge themselves by oath, in which case the General Assembly had ruled that they could not be pursued further.[18] But the fact that relatively few did so indicates how seriously the oath was taken; most feared divine punishment for perjury more than ecclesiastical punishment for illicit sex.

The large majority of sexual cases involved fornication. Those determined guilty were almost always required to perform public repentance, which involved sitting through a Sunday church service while seated on a special "stool of repentance" in plain view of the congregation. Repeat offenders might have their penalties doubled or tripled. Adultery and incest were taken more seriously. Disciplinary cases involving charges of incest between blood relatives were extremely rare, but cases of sexual relationships between those related by marriage occurred with some frequency. First cousins Jonat Mont and John Scot admitted to fornication in November 1564, and the St. Andrews kirk session agreed to refer to the General Assembly the question of whether they might lawfully marry, although the General Assembly's reply has not survived.[19] But when Andrew Duncan had a child by his nephew's widow, the session ordered both to perform public repentance six times for "horribill incest."[20] Past marriages (or even illicit relationships) created lines of affinity which could not be crossed. Adulterers, too, were generally required to perform public repentance several times, sometimes in sackcloth.

In addition to these ecclesiastical penalties, kirk sessions sought to have civil penalties, such as fines or imprisonment, imposed on sexual offenders. When the maltman Robert Yule, "citiner" of St. Andrews, was convicted of fornication in March 1566, he was "committit to the magistratis to be punist civile, according to the law, as thar citiner." There is no mention of his partner in sin being likewise punished; she may have lived outside the

---

[17] *StAKS*, 1:382-3. This view was endorsed by the General Assembly in 1574, and was common in the English and colonial American legal system as well. See *ibid*, 1:391; Laurel Thatcher Ulrich, *A Midwife's Tale: The Life of Martha Ballard, Based on Her Diary, 1785-1812*, (New York: Knopf, 1990), 148-50.

[18] The General Assembly made this ruling in July 1570. See Calderwood, 3:5-6.

[19] *StAKS*, 1:228.

[20] *Ibid*, 1:233.

burgh.[21] When David Kyd and Katie Lyall admitted their fornication to the kirk session of Monifieth in the spring of 1593, they were told to pay a fine of twenty shillings in addition to performing public repentance. This same punishment was typical in Dundonald in the early 1600s. In the latter parish, those who could or would not pay the fine were imprisoned for twenty-four hours in a local castle instead.[22] In Anstruther Wester, fines, variable in amount, had become common by the middle of 1583 for those guilty of fornication.[23] Of course, kirk sessions needed the firm support of local officials and notables, be they burgh councilors or lairds, to enforce such non-ecclesiastical punishments, and this was not always forthcoming.[24]

Kirk sessions were sometimes assisted in their detection efforts by informers, such as a "Dame Spence," previously charged with bringing a banished women back into the burgh of the Canongate, who on 24 August 1565 told parish elders that another woman had given birth out of wedlock.[25] Acts passed by the Canongate session in November 1564 instituted fines for landlords who rented rooms to anyone guilty of fornication, masters who concealed the illicit relationships of their servants, and midwives who failed to report all births. The midwife Molly Acheson fell afoul of this last regulation in October 1565 and, when questioned concerning a certain woman, granted that she "was lichter of ane barne in harlattrey."[26]

Employers could be critical to a kirk session's information network. On 4 November 1574 the Edinburgh session ruled that anyone who took into service fornicators who had not yet performed public repentance would themselves be barred from Communion. This inspired the merchant William Scot to appear the following week and produce Jonet Fyft, a servant of his who had "defylit" his house with fornication.[27] Illegitimacy among servants was a concern of the burgh council as well; the council ruled in August 1576 that no servants from outside the burgh could be hired without testimonials from the minister where they had previously dwelt, although such an order must have been difficult to enforce.[28]

This phenomenon—the Kirk's interest in sexuality—is more easily

---

[21] *Ibid*, 1:277.

[22] NRH ms OPR 310/1, 82v-83r; *Dun KS*, 1-2, 8, 29-32, 34, 36-37, 42, 61-2.

[23] NRH ms OPR 403/1, 35v, 38v.

[24] Michael F. Graham, "The Civil Sword and the Scottish Kirk in the Late Sixteenth Century," in W. Fred Graham, ed., *Later Calvinism: An International Perspective*, (Kirksville, Mo.: Sixteenth Century Publishers, 1994), 237-48.

[25] *BKC*, 21, 27.

[26] *Ibid*, 10, 28.

[27] SRO ms CH2/450/1, 26r, 27r.

[28] *Edin. Recs.*, 4:51-2.

described than explained. As suggested above, it was motivated both by material and spiritual concerns. But there is another consideration as well. In seeking to establish its disciplinary system, the Kirk was challenging some of the dearest traditions of Scots society—kinship, social deference and the religious calendar, just to name three. Attacks on Sunday markets, midsummer bonfires and the celebration of Christmas, all three of which eventually became targets of the disciplinary system, were bound to be unpopular and impolitic. But sexuality outside of marriage, like witchcraft, was something upon which everyone—Reformed, half-reformed or unapologetically Catholic—was in theoretical agreement, whatever their personal predelictions (hence the Parliamentary legislation on these matters). In many communities, particularly in rural areas, kirk sessions were established and then handled essentially nothing but sexual discipline for years, even decades. In order for social discipline to work, it was necessary first to coopt local elites into its management. This was done under the cover of an attack on fornication, adultery and incest. Only later would more divisive issues be raised. Seen this way, the concentration on sexual discipline becomes more a sign of the Kirk's weakness and lack of self-confidence than of its strength. As the Kirk gained stature and confidence, and became institutionalized in the localities, it could look to other things.

Gender: Was There a Double Standard?

In recent years historians have noted the "gendered" impact of the Reformation: the differenccs in the ways it might have been experienced by women as opposed to men.[29] One possible outcome of the increased suveillance which resulted from social discipline, particularly in the area of sexuality, might have been the enforcement of a "double standard" which winked at the sexual sins of men while regarding their female partners as guilty temptresses.[30] But a look at the evidence makes this seem unlikely, at least in the first fifty years of the Scottish Reformation.

Of the 4,594 cases from Scottish kirk sessions in the database, 41 percent of those charged with offenses were women. If we restrict ourselves to the 2,523 cases involving sexual behavior, however, the proportion of female offenders increases to 51 percent. To look at the figures another

---

[29] See, among others, Lyndal Roper, *The Holy Household: Women and Morals in Reformation Augsburg*, (Oxford: Oxford University Press, 1989), *passim*; Merry Wiesner, *Women and Gender in Early Modern Europe*, (Cambridge: Cambridge University Press, 1993), 186-203; Jeffrey Watt, "Women and the Consistory in Calvin's Geneva," *Sixteenth Century Journal* 24 (1993), 429-39.

[30] For a discussion of the alleged double standard, see Lawrence Stone, *The Family, Sex and Marriage in England, 1500-1800*, (New York: Harper Torchbooks, 1979), 315-8.

way, dividing them by gender, we find that 45 percent of all men summoned faced sexual accusations, while 68 percent of all women did. Thus women were considerably more likely to be charged with sexual sins than men were. The 1,191 cases from presbyteries followed a similar pattern, although as a general rule, presbyteries were less concerned with sexual misbehavior than were kirk sessions. Further, since presbytery cases often involved those who had managed to avoid punishment at the parish level, the presbytery caseload contains a higher proportion of male cases.

But do such figures have any meaning? The fact that an individual woman hauled before her parish elders stood a two-thirds chance of being charged with sexual misbehavior, while the chances of this happening to a male were less than even, may simply reflect the universe of possible offenses. In fact, there were certain misdeeds, such as political disloyalty, violent assault, or Sabbath breach, which the kirk sessions and presbyteries regarded as much more common in men than women. The kirk session of Edinburgh in 1574-5 charged 92 men with having supported the queen's party during the civil war which had just ended, while only two women faced such charges.[31] Likewise, a factional takeover of the burgh council and kirk session of St. Andrews late in 1593 led to charges of political dissidence against 20 men, but no women.[32] Since women were not active in civic politics, they were incapable of political sins. Accusations against women for Sabbath breach or violent assault were a bit more common, but men nevertheless outnumbered women in these categories by large majorities. Thus the fact that women were much more likely than men to be charged with sexual offenses is largely due to the narrower range of possible sins; males were more versatile miscreants in the eyes of ministers and elders. Their misdeeds ranged widely, while those of women were generally restricted to sexuality, verbal quarrels, religious deviance and the occasional practice of magic.

Though some sins were regarded as common in men and others in women, the nature of most human sexual activity is such that ministers and elders would have had to display wilful bias if they sought to lay the blame on one particular gender. None of the cases in the database involved charges of homosexual behavior or masturbation, and accusations of bestiality were exceedingly rare. Therefore, virtually every sexual offense for which charges were lodged involved at least one male and at least one female. Did the ministers and elders view both parties as guilty and subject to similar sanctions? In general, yes. Kirk sessions charged 1226 men and 1282 women with sexual sins. While women outnumber men slightly in that

---

[31] SRO ms CH2/450/1, *passim.*
[32] *StAKS*, 2:770-6, 778-9.

group, at the presbytery level the situation was reversed, with 314 men and
258 women accused of sexual misdeeds. Some parishes displayed
remarkable evenhandedness; between 1582 and 1600 the kirk session of St.
Andrews lodged sexual charges against 447 men and 447 women.

There were, however, some parishes in which considerably more women
than men were charged in sexual cases—the Canongate in the mid-1560s,
and Edinburgh and Aberdeen in the mid-1570s. Significantly, these are the
most urbanized parishes in my sample. In the tight and crowded confines
of the early modern Scottish town, burgh councilors and session elders
(often the same men) regarded a certain type of single woman as a danger
to public morality.

In the Canongate parish, for example, a notorious red light district in
and around the Cowgate occupied much of the kirk session's attention. In
November 1564, the session drew up a list of sexual sinners "within this
reformit gait," for action by the civil magistrates. Twelve women were
named, as were their partners, but the session was clearly only after the
women, some of whom were rounded up and brought before the session on
2 December 1564.[33] A group trial of sexual sinners held before the kirk
session, burgh bailies and the Justice Clerk of Scotland in December 1565
considered the cases of sixteen women but no men, although one male did
appear before the session the next day because he wished to marry one of
the defendants.[34] And, even when both partners were summoned, they might
be treated differently, as were David Pearson and Isobel Mowtray in
October 1564. The couple admitted to having a child out of wedlock. She
was ordered to leave the burgh within 48 hours "under the pane of
schorging," while he was given four hours in the branks [stocks], which he
avoided by promising to pay a fine of 40 shillings instead.[35] A number of
the women targeted in these roundups seem to have worked as prostitutes,
and the kirk session, at least in its more zealous moments, was eager to
eject them from burgh society. In practice, however, this proved difficult.
Many whippings, head-shavings and banishments were ordered, but few

---

[33] *BKC*, 11-12. It ought to be noted, however, that several of the men were Frenchmen
affiliated with the court of Mary Stewart, and may not have been officially subject to the
session's jurisdiction.

[34] *Ibid*, 34-5.

[35] *Ibid*, 8-9. Different treatment for women far along in pregnancy was specifically mandated by the Dundee Burgh Council in 1562, when it passed a regulation ordaining a two-day
imprisonment for those guilty of fornication, but if a woman were "great with child...and
yfor...there is perrill to presum or handle [her]," she was to be banished from the burgh for
a year. Of course, this would ensure that the child would be born outside the burgh as well,
and thus might not have any claim on Dundee's system of poor relief. See Alexander J.
Warden, ed., *Burgh Laws of Dundee*, (London: Longmans Green & Co., 1872), 25.

seem to have been carried out.[36] As early as 1567, there were signs that the Canongate session was turning the bulk of its attention to resolving conflicts within the parish community, and the sexual double standard was disappearing. A similar trend is evident in Aberdeen, where by 1577, men were beginning to outnumber women among those charged with sexual misbehavior.[37]

Outside of these towns, in smaller burghs such as St. Andrews or rural parishes such as Anstruther Wester (Fife), Monifieth (Angus), Dundonald (Ayrshire) or Rothiemay (Grampians), no such double standard seems to have existed, at least in terms of accusations by elders and attempts at punishment. In every rural or semi-rural parish, men in fact outnumbered women among those accused of sexual impropriety. In the vast majority of cases, both partners were named and summoned. It is true that men found it easier to ignore summonses, delay proceedings, or shift blame on others. Since most of the women accused were pregnant and unmarried, it was difficult for them to flee or deny responsibility. But kirk sessions and presbyteries often went to great lengths to identify the fathers, get them to admit paternity, and force them to perform public repentance along with their paramours. The kirk session of Anstruther Wester in March 1591 tried to prevent any local skipper from hiring the sailor Alan Caddells until he performed public repentance for his relapse into adultery. This effort was unsuccessful; he sailed to the Orkney Islands before he had completed his punishment. But it is a testament to the session's perseverance that he appeared before it when he returned in August 1592, again promising to perform his repentance. The case dragged into the following year, with no clear resolution, but the session displayed no inclination to let the matter drop.[38]

This is not to argue for an egalitarian, gender-neutral Reformation. Certainly, some Scotswomen felt its sting in ways that men could not. The Reformation had shut off many avenues of female spirituality and, in Scotland certainly contributed to the demonification of the witch and the prostitute. But by holding individuals—men as well as women—primarily responsible for their own behavior, it mitigated against the maintenance of any double standard in the area of sexual ethics.

---

[36] See, for example, the cases of Isobell Hill, Katherine Lenton and Molly Young, *BKC*, 58, 60, 66. For the problem of enforcement generally, see Graham, "Civil Sword," *passim*.

[37] In the years 1577-8 (the register breaks off in November 1578), 27 men and 21 women faced sexual charges from the Aberdeen Kirk Session. See SRO ms CH2/448/1, 106-134.

[38] OPR ms 403/1, 62v, 68v, 69v, 71v, 74v-75v, 77r-v.

Peacemaking

There were other general issues besides sexuality which became the common concerns of kirk sessions and presbyteries, particularly once these bodies had established themselves in their communities and become recognized elements in local power structures. Like sexuality, (but unlike Sabbath enforcement or the regulation of holidays or burial practices), these issues drew concern across religious lines. The problems of widespread violence and alleged diabolism provide two leading examples. All local authorities could usually agree that something had to be done about these dangers, and they eventually saw the courts of the Reformed Kirk as an appropriate forum in which to attack them.

By the end of the sixteenth century most kirk sessions and presbyteries had become active as peacemakers. This was an aspect of the disciplinary program that was slow to take hold in most areas. But, as sexuality lost its near monopoly on the disciplinary agenda, elders gave increased attention to mediating disputes so that the Communion celebration (generally held one to four times a year) would not be contaminated by rancor between participants. Even those less concerned about the sacramental aspects of the Reformed rite could see the ill effects of discord within the community. Table 8.1 demonstrates the increasing concern for this issue shown by kirk sessions and presbyteries, drawing on the database of Scottish disciplinary cases compiled for this study.

TABLE 8.1—SCOTTISH REFORMED CHURCH COURTS AND CONFLICT RESOLUTION, 1560-89 AND 1590-1610

Kirk sessions	Total cases*	All conflicts	Violence
1560-89	2592	176 (7%)	18 (1%)
1590-1610	2002	248 (12%)	96 (5%)

Presbyteries	Total cases*	All conflicts	Violence
1581-89+	560	20 (4%)	10 (2%)
1590-1610	631	85 (13%)	48 (8%)

*total for disciplinary cases of all types in the database
+the first presbyteries were founded in 1581

The Scots of the sixteenth century were blunt in speech and quick to fight, particularly when they felt their honor had been threatened. Men often went about armed with a "quhinger" (a short sword), and so were constantly in a state of armed readiness.[39] This bellicosity knew no social boundaries, including those which defined kirk session membership. Thus Simon Wallace, a deacon on the Dundonald session, took offense when John Dickie, with whom he had a longstanding feud, arrived at Communion in April 1602 with a band of armed followers. The result was a brawl, with drawn swords, in the kirkyard. Wallace later told the session elders (several of whom were his kinsmen) that "he tuik [Dickie *et al*'s arrival in church] as done in contempt of him." The session investigated the incident for over a year, trying to determine who had first resorted to violence, before finally finding both parties equally culpable and ordering both to perform public repentance on two consecutive Sundays.[40]

The fact that this *contretemps* took place in the kirkyard might shock modern sensibilities, but it probably did not surprise contemporaries. By encouraging (or requiring) all to attend services on the Sabbath, the Reformed Kirk was forcing parishioners to confront neighbors they might otherwise have sought to avoid. Particularly in rural areas, those at feud could stay away from each other most of the time if they wished, with chance encounters on roads the major danger. But if the whole community was to gather at the kirk on Sunday morning, the kirkyard could easily become a battleground.

It was under such circumstances that three Sinclairs (a laird and his two sons) were slain by a group headed by Archibald Stirling of Keir just after leaving a kirk near Stirling on Whitsunday in June 1593. The Sinclairs and Stirlings were feuding over their competing claims to the lands of Auchinbie in the parish of Dunblane, and the attendance of the Sinclairs at the kirk made them easy to find. Called before the Stirling Presbytery, Stirling of Keir showed little remorse. He claimed he could not be forced to perform public repentance for the deed because the killings themselves had been performed by his servants, not by him. Further, he said, "yai [the Sinclairs] wer men ded of the law [i.e. outlaws], quhairthrow ye fact ca[n] not be accounted sa odius...." Stirling of Keir was here appealing to a legal ruse commonly employed in bloodfeuds; if one group could get its opponents put to the horn the latter were fair game, at least in a legal sense. Stirling maintained that the presbytery could do nothing against him unless he were found guilty in a civil action, which he knew was unlikely. The presbytery countered that he could not present his child for baptism until he atoned for his offense. This had little effect, however, because his wife could still

---

[39] For the role played by violence, see Keith M. Brown, *Bloodfeud in Scotland, 1573-1625: Violence, Justice and Politics in an Early Modern Society*, (Edinburgh: John Donald, 1986), *passim*.

[40] *Dun KS*, 16-17, 20-4, 35.

present the baby on her own.[41]

The Sinclairs had been easy targets as they left their parish kirk. Elsewhere, not even the insides of kirks could be kept free of strife. Edinburgh's town council felt compelled in March 1589 to outlaw "drawing of swords and schoting of pistolets" *inside* the high kirk of the burgh.[42] This may have been a response to an incident the previous month in which Sir William Lauder of Haltoun, with several armed followers, had burst into the nearby kirk of Ratho on a Sunday and attacked James Borthwick of Lochhill "w[i]t[h]out ony feir of god or reverence to his vord." Lauder of Haltoun confessed his offence to the Edinburgh Presbytery, but the latter proved unable to settle the feud, despite nearly a year of mediation.[43] When the kirk itself offered no sanctuary, performance of public repentance could be hazardous. Andrew Clerk's wife complained to the St. Andrews Presbytery in June 1603 that her husband, who had committed a murder and apparently tried to make peace with the victim's family through an assythment (a form of compensation common in Scots law), could not perform public repentance in his home parish for fear of "the inwasioun of the partie." In other words, he feared being attacked by his victim's relatives as he sat helpless on the stool of repentance. The fact that his wife appeared on his behalf suggests that he did not even consider it safe to come to St. Andrews. The presbytery suggested that he perform his repentance in the more remote kirk of Ebdie. He did this several times, but his wife reported back in August that his enemies had tracked him there, and she requested another change of venue, which was apparently granted.[44]

Clerk sought reconciliation, but not everyone did. His enemies seem to have wanted to keep the feud alive. In this highly ritualistic society, most people realized the importance of enmity as a personal attitude. If one gave up enmity, one was closing the door on future avenues for redress. Alan Cook faced this decision in 1598 when summoned before the Anstruther Wester kirk session on the charge of "setting on Patrik Mellvill, wryght, w[i]t[h] a drawin whinger." He was quite willing to admit that he had done so, but said he was not ready to perform public repentance for the act. The

---

[41] WRH ms CH2/722/2, 24 and 31 July 1593. The feud was finally mended by private negotiation, and a bond of reconciliation signed in April 1596 was witnessed by, among others, Mr. Henry Livingston, minister of St. Ninians. Stirling of Keir (who got the lands in question) was said to be settling "be command of his Majestie, and be the earnest trawell of the brether of the ministrie...." See William Fraser, *The Stirlings of Keir and Their Family Papers*, (Edinburgh: Privately Published, 1858), 432-4. For horning as a feud strategy, see Brown, *Bloodfeud in Scotland*, 47-8.

[42] *Edin. Recs.*, 4:539.

[43] SRO ms CH2/121/1, 18 and 25 February 1589, 6 January 1590.

[44] *StAP*, 343, 362, 366-7, 372, 374.

session urged him "to think mair deiplie of the mater & to call to god to giv him a syght of his synne." Later, he was admonished from the pulpit, and referred to the presbytery of St. Andrews, but proved recalcitrant. For the time being, at least, Cook was more interested in maintaining his grudge than in full membership in the Christian community.[45] The same was true of the laird of St. Monance, who told several ministers from the St. Andrews Presbytery who urged him in October 1595 to abandon his dispute with Sir Robert Melville of Murdocairny that "he wes purposett to use no violence bot according to the law of god and be the advyse of his frindis to repair the wrang done to him."[46]

Many lairds found it easy to brush off ministerial intervention, but humbler people could not act with such haughty indifference. James MacKerrill and his wife Marion Kinning were forced by the Dundonald session to perform public repentance in sackcloth in 1602 for having attacked the weaver George Kinning (possibly Marion's brother) and his wife on the Sabbath, "tryand to reif fra thame thair lint eftir that thai had bein at and had cum from the Lordis Tabill that day."[47] Indeed, most people, particularly women, had to bite their tongues as well as to suppress violent urges. In 1598 Kate Brown was accused by the Anstruther Wester session of calling Kristin Scot "drunk harlot" just outside the kirk door in words audible to the worshipers inside. Brown claimed Scot provoked her by telling her to "kis her ers," but the session found Brown the guiltier of the two, and she had to apologize to Scot on her knees as the elders watched, "promis[in]g to walk mair warlie in tym coming."[48] This was actually quite lenient treatment; others found guilty of slander in Anstruther often had to perform public repentance and either pay a fine of forty shillings or spend a couple hours in the "branks."[49] By the early seventeenth century, kirk sessions everywhere were quick to censure the sharp-tongued woman. Janet Thain in Rothiemay denied calling George Mureson a thief, and witnesses testified only to her having used the epithets "murtherer & throtcutter." Considering the mitigating circumstances—Mureson, weapon in hand, had been chasing Thain's husband with apparent deadly intent—the session demanded from Thain only a private apology rather than public

---

[45] NRH ms OPR 403/1, 121r, 122r. Cook never bothered to appear before the presbytery. See *StAP*, 288, 290. For a discussion of the uses of enmity outside the Scottish context, see David Sabean, *Power in the Blood: Popular Culture and Village Discourse in Early Modern Germany*, (Cambridge: Cambridge University Press, 1984), 38-41, 47-54.

[46] *StAP*, 172-4.

[47] *Dun KS*, 2.

[48] NRH ms OPR 403/1, 117r-v.

[49] *Ibid*, 99r, 101v, 104v-105v.

repentance! The elders did not take any action against Mureson.[50]

But the Kirk's disciplinary powers were at times used to protect women from calumny as well. When William Morris, a weaver in Alva, boasted in 1590 of having had sexual relations with Helen Menteith, a married woman, she and her father complained to the Stirling Presbytery. Since Morris' claim seemed groundless, the presbytery ordered him to appear one Sunday in Menteith's parish kirk of Dollar,

> and thair to confes publictlie in p[rese]ns of ye haill congregatione yat he hes innocentlie sclandirit ye said hellein & yat ye words he spak of hir war fals, and [there]for to crave god, ye said hellein & ye kirk forgevenes. And to declair he knawis na thing to hir bot honestie.

Morris apparently complied with this order.[51]

While most disciplinary courts, particularly in rural areas, were not active as peacemakers until near the end of the century, the urban kirk session of the Canongate took on this role quite early. Some mediation had occasionally taken place before the burgh council (several of whose members were session elders) in the past, so the concept was not entirely new.[52] But the need to sanctify the Reformed Communion rite through neighborly harmony, coupled with the significance of the ritual of public repentance in church, gave it a new and expanded meaning, and brought more women into the process. The session hosted a number of mass reconciliations, usually on the eve of Communion celebrations. One such session in January 1567 involved twenty-four parishioners. Usually all parties were found equally guilty, though there were exceptions, such as Bessie Rokart and her daughter Ellen, who were told to apologize to the widow Jonat Cuthbert for having called Cuthbert's late husband a thief while he lay on his deathbed.[53] Other conflicts carried the potential for bloodshed, as in August 1566 when the bailie James Wilkie complained that John Mosman was harboring a man in his house who had killed one of Wilkie's kinsmen. Such a charge threatened to draw Mosman into what was apparently a bloodfeud, and the session admonished him to remove the man

---

[50] NRH ms OPR 165/3, 17v.

[51] WRH ms CH2/722/2, 27 October, 24 November 1590.

[52] E.g. "Extracts From the Records of the Burgh of the Canongate Near Edinburgh," *Maitland Club Miscellany* 2, (Edinburgh: Maitland Club, 1840), 281-359, at 290-301. There is evidence of similar mediation by the St. Andrews Burgh Council in the period 1589-92, the only period in the sixteenth century for which its records survive. See StAUM ms B65/8/1, 35r, 39v-40r, 45r-v, 50r, 53r, 66v. These cases sometimes involved the appointment of an assize to determine which party should be forced to apologize.

[53] *BKC*, 60-3, Rokart-Cuthbert dispute on 62.

from his house.[54]

The disciplinary courts were well structured, both in terms of makeup and theological *raison d'être*, to play the part of peacemaker. By the late sixteenth century, the crown, the Kirk and many leading laymen were united in the belief that the conflicts endemic to Scottish society had to be brought within the purview of the legal system.[55] At the local level, where private justice had hitherto ruled, and where the central courts of the state had made few inroads, the church courts—theoretically impartial and representing an institution which claimed the allegiance of all—seemed the best forum for mediation.[56] They could also lend the weight of their authority to ensure that peace agreements were kept. Thus the Monifieth Kirk Session in May 1593 witnessed a settlement between Henry Howat and Andrew Good in which the pair pledged that if any strife broke out between them in the future, the guilty party would give £10 to the poor.[57] In a similar manner the elders of Dundonald oversaw a band in August 1606 between John Wilson and Thomas Thomson vowing that they and their households would "keip gude nychtbourheid ilkane to vtheris and sall nather fecht nor flyte agains vtheris, and siclyk sall obey the actis of the kirk and sessioun inall tyme cuming vnder the pane of xx li. of penaltie." This contract was notarized by one of the elders.[58]

Of course, one obstacle facing parish sessions when they tried to mend fences between local notables was the fact that the eldership was often identified with one feuding party or the other. Presbyteries could do better, especially after lay elders ceased to play a major role in their memberships. The St. Andrews Presbytery in particular devoted a great deal of attention to patching up differences between the lairds of eastern Fife. Generally, two or three ministers would be assigned to arbitrate between two lairds. It is difficult to ascertain how successful these efforts were, or whether the lairds were interested in this ministerial intervention, but since the presbytery made such arbitration a regular practice after 1590, and the same feuds were not mentioned repeatedly, they may have been resolved in some cases.[59]

---

[54] *Ibid*, 50.

[55] Brown, *Bloodfeud in Scotland*, 267-9.

[56] For the role of church courts within the legal system as a whole in the seventeenth century, see Stephen J. Davies, "The Courts and the Legal System 1600-1747: The Case of Stirlingshire," in V.A.C. Gatrell, Bruce Lenman and Geoffrey Parker, eds., *Crime and the Law: The Social History of Crime in Western Europe Since 1500*, (London: Europa, 1980), 120-154.

[57] NRH ms OPR 310/1, 83v.

[58] *Dun KS*, 115. For a another, similar band, see *ibid*, 195.

[59] *StAP*, 58, 138, 143, 172-4.

Nevertheless, even the presbyteries did not always appear impartial to disputants. This can be seen in the efforts of the St. Andrews Presbytery to reconcile the Smith-Arthur feud, which troubled the burgh and environs of St. Andrews for more than a decade. The feud began in 1589, when Henry Hamilton, a burgess of the town and ally of archbishop Patrick Adamson, allegedly attacked William Welwood, a law professor at the university. This led to a brawl, involving several people, in which James Arthur, "the Bischopes guid brother," was killed. Welwood may have been mortally wounded as well. James Smith, a merchant and former kirk session elder, described by the partisan James Melville as "graitlie beloved of all godlie and guid men for his vertew and guid conditiones," was charged with Arthur's death. After a trial in Edinburgh, he was banished from the realm for six years, as was John Welwood, also involved in the brawl.[60] Melville's praise of Smith and Hamilton's identification with Adamson help to define the political alignments in this dispute. On the one hand were Adamson and the "misrewlars" of the town (the name given by Melville to the group led by Lermonth of Dairsie which controlled the burgh government). On the other were the Melvilles, members of the college faculty, and the more reform-minded among the burgesses, such as Smith.

In June 1594, with the Lermonth party temporarily ousted from power at St. Andrews, Parliament lifted the banishment of Smith and Welwood.[61] But the pair's return to the burgh rekindled animosities. In October 1595, King James ordered the provost and council of St. Andrews to seek a reconciliation between the parties at feud, and the St. Andrews Presbytery appointed several ministers to work with the council in this effort.[62] During that same month, however, the Lermonth party returned to power on the council. The provost appointed six arbiters (all kirk session members), to which the presbytery added six ministers.[63] But the ministers of the presbytery were no more neutral than the burgh government. William Arthur, a close relative of the man killed by Smith, complained in late October that the minister Robert Wallace, while preaching in the burgh church, had called out "murdering knav William Arthour quhair art thow?" Rather than urging moderation on Wallace, considering the ongoing efforts to reconcile the feud, the presbytery "judgit William nocht onlie worthie of that kynd of repruiffe bot of far gryther." Arthur responded by threatening Wallace with bodily harm, whereupon the ministers of the presbytery sent for the bailies to have him warded. When the bailies produced him the next

---

[60] *JMD*, 272-5.

[61] *Ibid*, 317-8.

[62] *StAP*, 168-9.

[63] *Ibid*, 172-3.

week so that the presbytery could order him to perform public repentance for his threats against Wallace, John Johnston, the moderator, rebuked the bailies for not having him punished civilly.[64] It was clear that the burgh government was unwilling to take action against Arthur and his allies, and equally apparent that the ministers on the presbytery were partisans of Smith and the Welwoods.

And so the deadly enmity continued. Smith was the next victim, killed late in 1597 just after leaving James Melville's manse in Anstruther Easter in the custody of one of the bailies of St. Andrews. The latter had been taking him to a meeting which the king had ordered for the following day to try and settle the feud. Naturally, Melville charged the burgh authorities with setting up the murder, and he may have been right.[65] Smith's friends made similar charges; the St. Andrews Kirk Session, now firmly controlled by burgh authorities, convicted four of them of slandering the provost, William Lermonth of Clatto.[66] They appealed the verdict to the presbytery on the grounds that the session was biased against them, but on 20 July 1598 the minister George Gladstaines reported "the mater wes friendly composit and taine away."[67] Such optimism was unwarranted. Three Arthurs—William, Patrick and Henry—and one Patrick Lindsay were excommunicated by the presbytery for the slaughter of James Smith. In May 1599, the presbytery lamented that they had as yet shown

> na repentance...nocht making confessioun of that quhilk is notourlie knowin to all, viz. that that murther wes committit upoun profest feud and lying in wayte with foirthocht, fellonie to that effect. Also...nather magistrate nor partie [Smith's relatives] are satisfeit nor na reasonable satisfaction offerit to the same.[68]

In September the presbytery decided that there was not even any point in the Arthurs and Lindsay attending sermons until they showed some remorse.[69]

The group finally appeared before the kirk session and admitted the crime on 14 December 1599. The elders concluded that two weeks of public repentance would be an appropriate satisfaction, but on 27 December suggested to the presbytery that since the Arthurs and Lindsay already had been banished by royal decree for the slaughter, the sentences of

---

[64] *Ibid*, 174-6.

[65] *JMD*, 421-3.

[66] *StAKS*, 2:851-2, 854-5, 857, 859.

[67] *StAP*, 265, 271-2.

[68] *Ibid*, 294.

[69] *Ibid*, 307-8.

excommunication ought to be relaxed immediately, with the public repentance remaining undone.[70] The presbytery agreed to this on condition that the session would take an obligation from the offenders that they would leave the country when the date of their banishment arrived, and keep off the burgh's streets until then. This the session refused to do, protesting that banishment was a civil, rather than an ecclesiastical, matter "and his Majestie haveand sufficient powar to execute his awin decreit."[71]

The presbytery was treating the session as an arm of the burgh government, knowing that it was controlled by the Lermonth party which also held the reins in the council. The elders responded with the legal fiction that they had no civil powers, probably also sensing that the king lacked the will and resources to enforce the banishment, which they were willing to ignore. In January the presbytery complained that the Arthurs "misbehavit themselffis in resorting on the streitis to the prowocatioun of the partie offendit [Smith's friends]," but the offenders were still ignoring their banishment seven months later, despite repeated protests from the presbytery and Smith's relatives. Not surprisingly, the latter clung to their enmity, and the kirk session sought to bar them from Communion for refusing to shake hands with the Arthurs.[72] Ultimately, neither the session nor presbytery could settle the feud, as each was identified with one or the other party.[73]

But this case, which so amply demonstrates the limits of the disciplinary courts' abilities to settle disputes, must not overshadow their successes. Kirk sessions and presbyteries were seen by many parishioners as legitimate arbiters, and they offered a new, local alternative in conflict resolution—one which, in theory at least, was impartial. They could also draw on the ideology of Christian brotherhood much more convincingly than could the baronial and civil courts to which those at feud had traditionally appealed their grievances.[74] Of course the bloodshed often continued anyway, but the church courts played a major role in the reduction of feuding which marked the latter half of the reign of James VI.[75]

Witchcraft and Magic

Another disciplinary category on which there was a broad societal consensus was witchcraft. An act of Parliament of 1563 mandated the death penalty

---

[70] *StAKS*, 2:912, 915; *StAP*, 315.

[71] *StAP*, 317; *StAKS*, 2:916.

[72] *StAP*, 319, 321-2, 325-6, 330-1.

[73] For other criticisms of presbyteries' handling of feuds, see NLS ms Adv. 29.2.8, 103r.

[74] For an eloquent discussion of this ideology, see Brown, *Bloodfeud in Scotland*, 184-207.

[75] *Ibid*, 270-2.

for practitioners of "witchcraftis sorsarie and necromancie," and those who consulted with them.[76] Keith Thomas, writing about English witchcraft, has suggested that the connection between witchcraft or magical powers and the Devil was a "continental doctrine,"[77] but Scots authorities do seem to have been concerned about the diabolical aspects of the problem. In addition, the use of torture in many of the interrogations carried out by Scots authorities (formal torture not being a part of English legal procedures) probably made it easier for authorities to get the "evidence" of Devil-worship they were seeking.

Witchcraft and related magic made up only a very small part of the caseloads of kirk sessions (43 cases, or one percent) and presbyteries (35 cases, or three percent) in the database compiled for this study, and nearly all of those cases which arose date from 1590 (when the first widespread Scottish witch-hunt began) and after.[78] But despite the slowness of the Kirk's courts to enter the witchcraft battle, once involved they usually treated accusations quite seriously and cooperated actively with secular officials in efforts to seek out and punish offenders. Ministers and elders sought not only those who practiced magic, but their clients as well.[79]

Many women and some men were executed as witches in sixteenth- and seventeenth-century Scotland, but only secular courts could impose the death sentence.[80] Church courts could merely admonish, fine, require public repentance, or excommunicate. As a result, church courts generally played an advisory role in witchcraft cases, reviewing the depositions made by accused witches before secular officials,[81] or handing evidence or suspects uncovered in disciplinary proceedings on to magistrates once it seemed there were grounds for trial. The case of Isobell Watson, a resident of the remote parish of Glendevon (within the boundaries of the Stirling Presbytery) who was accused of witchcraft in 1590, provides a good example of the latter.

---

[76] *APS*, 2:539. The English Parliament passed an anti-witchcraft statute that same year, but it only required the death penalty for those whose practices had resulted in the deaths of others. See Keith Thomas, *Religion and the Decline of Magic*, (New York: Scribner's, 1971), 442.

[77] Thomas, *Religion and the Decline of Magic*, 442-3.

[78] It was in 1590 that a severe North Sea storm threatened the ships bringing the king and his bride, Anne of Denmark, back to Scotland, led to charges of *maleficia* against a coven of witches at North Berwick who allegedly conspired with Francis Stewart, earl of Bothwell, to bring about the king's death. This triggered a nationwide search for Satan's minions. For details, see *Pit. Crim.*, 1(part 2):209-23; and Arthur Williamson, *Scottish National Consciousness in the Age of James VI*, (Edinburgh: John Donald, 1979), 53-63.

[79] Of the 43 kirk session cases in the database involving magical activities, 32 of the suspected offenders were female. At the presbyterial level, 25 of 35 charged were women.

[80] For a sociological study of Scottish witchcraft, see Christina Larner, *Enemies of God: The Witch-hunt in Scotland*, (London: Chatto and Windus, 1981).

[81] E.g. *StAP*, 273.

Watson's story, with all its tragedy and sadness, resembles those of many female paupers throughout early modern Europe. Like the rest, her lowly rank left her vulnerable to witchcraft charges,[82] and the hardships of her life, probably coupled with mental instability, had led her to believe that the charges were true. There is no evidence that torture was employed during her examinations before the presbytery.

On 21 April 1590, James Kinnard from Glendevon admitted to the ministers of the Stirling Presbytery that he had consulted with Watson, suspected of witchcraft, "to haill him of ye worme." Kinnard reported that Watson, "ane pwre [poor] woma[n]," gave him "certane pickills [grains] of quhyt [wheat] q[uhere]of he undirstude yair was ane peice of Rawme tire [mountain ash] and ane peice of ane ded p[er]sonis finger." Probably seeking to appease the presbytery and thus protect himself from being punished for consulting a witch, Kinnard brought Watson with him to the presbytery's meeting.[83] Attention then turned to her. She told the ministers that she was a widow, about 30 years old, who had left her native Perth because of an outbreak of plague there. She got "ye mark on hir hed" (the Devil's mark) when she was 18, having fallen asleep while tending sheep,

> at q[uhil]k tyme scho was takin away be ye fair folk and hauldin w[i]t[h] yame xxiiii ho[u]rs, in ye q[uhi]lk tyme scho said scho past in ane craig undir ye erd [earth] in ane fair hous q[uhai]r yair was folk meikill and litill.

There, a woman offered her an oatcake, but she refused to take it because her maternal aunt, who was present, told the woman to give her meat instead. As she ate the meat, she got the mark with a knife, though her brother later removed the scar. To a poor girl like Watson, oatcakes would have been typical fare, and meat a delicacy. But with her acceptance of the meat had come Satan's mark. To her, advancement was impossible without diabolical assistance: the elf queen told her to "refuis god & byd w[i]t[h] yame becaus scho wald fair bettir."

She also used her relationship with the Devil to explain the death of her child and an illicit sexual encounter. Watson told the ministers that she had given her two-year-old son to

> ye farie furth of ye creddill to lett hir self allane and to succor hir husband quha fell a sleip on ye waltir bray & was lang seik [there]eftir. At ye q[uhi]lk tyme ye fair folk laid in ye creddill ane sloch [a husk] in liknes of hir bairne

---

[82] For European witchcraft generally, see Brian Levack, *The Witch-hunt in Early Modern Europe*, (London: Longman, 1987), *passim*. For the particular attractions of witchcraft to the poor, see Thomas, *Religion and the Decline of Magic*, 520-1.

[83] WRH ms CH2/722/2, 21 April 1590.

to ye q[uhi]lk scho gaif na meat [i.e. food], and yat hir gude mane [husband] caist it in ye fyr q[uhi]lk almaist brunt ye hous. And thaireftir to ye end scho myt recovir hir bairne agane scho made promeis to serve yame, in taikin q[uhai]rof scho retenit yair m[ar]k upoune hir hed be ane Thomas Mcray quha is w[i]t[h] yame [and] quha hade ains carnall deall w[i]t[h] hir.

Since that time, she said, she had ridden out with the fair folk on each new moon, and she named several others who did the same. As to the human finger bone, she first claimed that it had been given to her by John Row, minister of Perth. But, when challenged on this, she said her aunt gave it to her to protect her "fra all straiks [blows] of ye fair folk."[84]

Based on this initial testimony, all given on 21 April, the presbytery asked the bailies of Stirling to imprison Watson in the burgh tollbooth, where she may have been tortured before subsequent interrogations. Clearly, she now saw that her life was in danger. On 1 May, the presbytery met in the tollbooth, and questioned her there. She told the ministers that "ye king of ye court" had given her the mark on her head with an oily substance, telling her that as long as it was on her, no man could harm her. But, she said, "ye same is now all off her," and she blamed this king for taking away all her hair. This suggests that she may have been seriously ill as well as under psychological strain. She also reported that the Devil had visited her in the tollbooth and promised that "gif scho wald serve him out he sould keip hir fra yis danger." But, "scho ansrit yat ye tyme p[ro]mest be hir to serve him was run out. And yat now scho hade gevin her self to God."[85]

Watson remained imprisoned for over a month, and in June the Synod of Stirling, Dunblane, Perth and Dunkeld ruled that she was "ane abusar of ye pepill, consultar w[i]t[h] ye devill & ye ded, and thairfor worthie to die according to gods law." The synod requested that the Stirling magistrates put her to an assize.[86] At this point, her story disappears from the records, but it is unlikely to have had a happy ending.[87]

Watson was willing to admit that she had been involved in diabolical activities. Others denied accusations against them, or argued that the practices involved were not diabolical. Margaret Forgushill told the elders of Dundonald in January 1602 that Katherine MacTeir, a fellow parishioner, had somehow injured a cow which Forgushill had left in her care the

[84] WRH ms CH2/722/2, 21 April 1590.

[85] Ibid, 1 May 1590.

[86] Ibid, 12 May and 10 June 1590.

[87] Watson's case is not listed in the lengthy calendar of Scottish witchcraft cases compiled by Christina Larner, Christopher Hyde Lee and Hugh McLachlan in A Source-book of Scottish Witchcraft, (Glasgow: Social Science Research Council, 1977).

previous midsummer. The cow had begun to give blood instead of milk. She reported that when she had confronted MacTeir, "the said Kaithrein ansuerit hir that hir ky had lyen on ane pismuill hillok, and bad hir rub fresch buttir on the kyis wdderis and papis, quhilk scho did and thay mendit." But the session was evidently already suspicious of MacTeir, and summoned Forgushill back for further questioning the following week. At that meeting, Forgushill admitted

> that scho askit hir kyis milk at the said Kaithrein for Goddis saik. And beand also requyrit quhat wes the ressoun scho sould haif askit it swa or quha teichit her and bad hir ask it swa, for the present could and wald gif no answer, quhairwpoun the session continewit hir to the next session and Kaithrein Makteir to be warnit thairto.[88]

Forgushill was apparently reluctant to accuse MacTeir herself, either out of friendship or fear of her powers.

Forgushill was more forthcoming at the next meeting. She reported that one Marion Blair had told her to make the request to MacTeir, Blair having had a similar problem with one of her own cows. Further, Forgushill said Blair had told her that MacTeir was unlucky "becaus hir mother, Gill Goddie, was ane notit witch." At this point the session decided to call MacTeir into the room, and summon Blair to testify at a later meeting.

MacTeir granted that Forgushill had spoken the words in question to her while kneeling, and that she had replied "God send [you your] kyis milk." To MacTeir, Forgushill and others, this may have seemed an innocent enough exchange. Indeed, Blair later told the session that "it wes the auld fassioun and it wes no falt." But the minister and elders saw it differently, informing MacTeir "it wes the taking of wichrie upoun hir self." To this, MacTeir "ansuerit scho wes but ane pure bodie and could noth cum to complain to the sessioun thairof but scho wald mak sick repentance thairfoir as the kirk wald command hir." MacTeir may have been seeking a quick resolution in order to head off further interrogation, but the session would not agree. One of the elders had heard that she had told others of visions involving her dead mother. Questioned on this the following week, MacTeir told them that she had once been ill, and "eftir the seiknes scho dremit that scho met with hir mother in the Gill and that scho was steyit and that hir mother said to hir, Quhat ailleth ye? Yow sall be weill aneuch."[89] Dreams of departed parents were probably not uncommon, but since MacTeir's mother had been a reputed witch, this added to the elders' suspicions.

At this point, after four weeks of questioning involving Forgushill,

---

[88] *Dun KS*, 1-2.
[89] *Ibid*, 3-4.

MacTeir and Blair, the session decided that a full investigation was warranted. In the next three months it called numerous witnesses who all recalled some odd incident or other involving MacTeir. Some of these dated back more than a decade, and at times the connection between the incidents described and the crime of witchcraft seems tenuous at best. Katherine Geddie recalled that four or five years earlier she had been preparing broth for her husband and some workmen. MacTeir appeared, and Geddie offered her some of the broth, which MacTeir tasted, and then threw back into the pot. Thereafter, the broth was spoiled and full of hair, which Geddie attributed to MacTeir's malevolence.[90] MacTeir was also accused of keeping a magic stone, which the session confiscated and sent to the presbytery of Irvine for examination. An allegation that she had once sold a used pair of shoes while claiming they were new was also aired. John Andrew testified that Geilis Boyd, his late godmother, had been quite healthy when MacTeir told her that she would not live long, a prediction which proved true. Bessie Wilson recalled that MacTeir, then a young servant at the house of Wilson's father-in-law, had been able to make butter on one occasion sixteen years earlier when no one else could. Another woman testified that MacTeir told her five years earlier that she met often with her dead mother

> in the Halie Gill and that hir mother tauld hir that everie seven yeir the teind [tenth] of thame passed to hell, and that scho speirit [asked] at hir mother quhow scho escaipit sway long, and that hir moder sayd that then scho fitched to ane wther maister and sway escaipit....[91]

Despite all the suspicion surrounding MacTeir, the session declined for the time being to make a formal accusation of witchcraft. But, two years later, it began taking evidence against her again. This revival of interest may be related to the fact that several other area sorcerers came to the session's attention at the same time, in the spring of 1604. On 20 May 1604, Agnes Clerk testified that MacTeir had told one of her servants that she (Clerk) would get no more butter or milk. Her cows then escaped from their pen and ran around in the fields, giving thereafter less milk than before. Then MacTeir came into her house "and gripit hir airm and it tuik ane grait dollour [pain] thairof," resulting in a sickness which lasted eight weeks. John Gray corroborated this testimony, swearing that he visited Clerk just after MacTeir left her house, and that Clerk told him "scho docht not steir leg nor airm sen Kathrein Makteir ves at hir."[92]

---

[90] *Ibid*, 5. For a discussion of the implications of food imagery in witchcraft evidence, see Sabean, *Power in the Blood*, 102.

[91] *Dun KS*, 5-7, 9-11, 14.

[92] *Ibid*, 52.

Others implicated MacTeir by associating her with Pat Lowrie, an area vagrant reputed to be a warlock. Margaret Wilson testified that she had seen Lowrie "tary ane quhyll" with MacTeir. Marion Cunningham said she had seen Lowrie scold MacTeir for visiting Janet Hunter, another suspected witch. Lowrie may have been urging MacTeir to tread more warily; MacTeir reportedly snapped at another woman who asked her about her meetings with her dead mother: "will ye gar me leif the cuntre?" Evidently, a number of local residents had used MacTeir's services as a cattle-healer, and their wagging tongues now presented a clear danger to her.[93]

Her fears proved justified. No record of any criminal trial of MacTeir has survived, but she disappeared from the kirk session register. In July 1605, when Lowrie was on trial for witchcraft in Edinburgh, MacTeir (along with Janet Hunter) was listed as one of his deceased accomplices. For his own part, Lowrie was charged with bewitching cows, (including those of several residents of Dundonald parish), digging up and dismembering corpses, and restoring a blind child's sight "be Inchantment and sorcerie." Found guilty by an assize, he was strangled and burnt on Edinburgh's castle hill. Lowrie had never appeared before the Dundonald session himself, but much of the evidence against him was gathered there.[94]

Just as the Stirling Presbytery had done in the case of Isobel Watson, the Dundonald Kirk Session acted as a kind of grand jury in considering the evidence against MacTeir and Lowrie. MacTeir's case originated in the session, but was eventually (after two years) passed on to civil authorities. Lowrie's case evidently began somewhere else, but the Dundonald session played a vital role in gathering evidence against him. Likewise, in January 1597, the Anstruther Wester session heard testimony regarding the activities of Jonet Fogow, an accused witch confined by the commendator of Pittenweem. This evidence was used in her eventual conviction, a verdict to which the St. Andrews Presbytery contributed its own concurring opinion.[95] But evidence of witchcraft evidence aired before a kirk session or presbytery did not necessarily place the accused on a "highroad to the stake."[96] Some were acquitted, as the case of Marion McNab demonstrates.

On 21 July 1590, Jonet Mitchell told the Stirling Presbytery that McNab had given her some cures for her husband, bewitched her husband's malt, and subsequently made the malt good again. McNab denied all the charges, but the presbytery handed her over to the bailies of Stirling to be warded

---

[93] *Ibid*, 53-4.

[94] *Ibid*, 55-9, 85-6; Pit. Crim., 2:477-9; Larner, *Enemies of God*, 149. Larner was apparently unaware of the testimony recorded in the Dundonald Kirk Session register.

[95] NRH ms OPR 403/1, 105r-v, 107r; *StAP*, 223.

[96] The phrase comes from Michael Kunze, *Highroad to the Stake: A Tale of Witchcraft*, (Chicago: University of Chicago Press, 1987).

pending further investigation.[97] Several witnesses testified regarding McNab in the following weeks, although none of their testimony was recorded in the presbytery's register.[98] Finally, on 17 September, after more than a month of confinement (and possibly torture), McNab confessed

> that scho can gar ane cow tak w[i]t[h] ane vy[er] calf, be loying ye skin of ye ded calf befoir ye cow w[i]t[h] ane loik salt on it, and saying thrys in ye name of ye father ye sone & ye holy gost.

Such practices had Catholic and magical overtones, but the presbytery concluded that they did not constitute witchcraft. It ordered the bailies to release McNab, provided that she give a pledge to appear again upon 48 hours notice if any additional evidence were found against her. None was, and this proved to be the end of the matter.[99]

In fact, there are numerous instances of folk healers or suspected witches who admitted to magical practices in testimony before church courts, but were released with a warning not to repeat, or ordered merely to perform public repentance. The career of Nannis Melville, discussed earlier, provides one example. Though eventually executed, she was given repeated warnings by the elders of Anstruther Wester, and may only have met an unhappy end because she levied charges of incestuous rape against a local skipper.[100] Margaret Ferny, who admitted in December 1597 to making healing drinks and baths, based on methods she had learned from Melville, was merely told to make a public confession of her offense before the congregation.[101]

There is also evidence that some ministers and kirk sessions were markedly unenthusiastic in pursuing cases of suspected witchcraft to any conclusion, perhaps out of reluctance to expose suspects to possible criminal proceedings. One of the charges some prominent residents of Pittenweem brought against their minister Nicol Dalgleish in 1597 was that he was slow to prosecute witches.[102] It is unlikely that this reflected a general laxity of discipline on Dalgleish's part; he was, after all, a leading Melvillian.

---

[97] WRH ms CH2/722/2, 21 and 28 July 1590.

[98] *Ibid*, 18 and 25 August and 8 September 1590.

[99] *Ibid*, 17 September 1590.

[100] NRH ms OPR 403/1, 64v, 65r-v, 66r, 69r-v, 73v, 75r-v, 80v, 81r, 83r, 87v. For a more detailed discussion of her case, see chapter six, above. The fact that Melville shared the last name of one of the most active elders on the kirk session may also have helped her avoid serious punishment for so long.

[101] NRH ms OPR 403/1, 113v. Interestingly, Ferny had been the alleged victim in the case of incestuous rape cited above.

[102] *StAP*, 226, 228, 236-8.

Rather, he may have had reservations about the nature of witchcraft accusations and the trials which resulted. Elsewhere, Isobel Trumbull admitted to the elders of Dundonald on 10 July 1608 that she had cured Katherine Walker's sore breast with an elaborate ritual involving Walker's husband's left shoe. The success of this procedure led others to seek Trumbull's assistance, both in curing women's breasts and cows' udders. By August, the session clerk labeled Trumbull as "suspect of witchcraft," but the session then dropped the matter for at least two years, and Trumbull was still alive in 1612.[103] Annie Smith was "sclanderit of witchcraft & charming," but the session of Monifieth released her in June 1601 when she produced a testimonial from the minister of her former parish.[104]

But such cases of leniency or reluctance to prosecute should not blind us to the fact that ministers and elders, like most of their contemporaries, viewed witchcraft and magic as grave dangers. They may have had occasional doubts about their abilities to identify witches,[105] but they were quite convinced that Satan was active in the world, seeking allies in his age-long struggle with God. Particularly vulnerable were those who had experienced misfortune. Whereas an unexplained illness might previously have been treated by participation in a pilgrimage, or some such religious ritual, those practices were now under attack by the courts of the Reformed Kirk.[106] But witches were another source of healing magic, much harder for religious authorities to track down than holy wells. They were often blamed for sudden illnesses, and were just as often in demand as healers by a populace which respected their powers. The Reformed Kirk had attacked Catholic "magic," but had as yet offered no alternative medicine of its own, so it now had to discourage demand for Satanic magic as well.[107]

In May 1591 the Edinburgh Presbytery, responding to a query from the king, reiterated the claim of the 1563 act of Parliament that consulters of witches deserved death just as the witches themselves, but this apparently had little effect.[108] The St. Andrews Presbytery decided in July 1598 to order consulters of witches to do public repentance in the same fashion as

---

[103] *Dun KS*, 169-72, 174, 207, 236. In April 1610, the session finally decided to consult with the presbytery of Irvine on the matter.

[104] NRH ms OPR 310/1, 105r.

[105] Such doubts on the part of magistrates have been cited as the reason for the eventual end of widespread witch hunting elsewhere in Europe. See Thomas, *Religion and the Decline of Magic*, 573-6; Levack, *Witch-hunt*, 215-7; H.C.E. Midelfort, *Witch Hunting in Southwestern Germany, 1562-1684*, (Stanford: Stanford University Press, 1972), 157-8, 161-3.

[106] For examples of this, see chapter five, above.

[107] For this problem in the English context, see Thomas, *Religion and the Decline of Magic*, 494-7.

[108] SRO ms CH2/121/1, 4 May 1591; *APS*, 2:539.

adulterers (another class of offender who deserved death according to statute law).[109] Some form of public repentance became the typical punishment for consumers of magical services. The earliest example from my database of anyone being charged with consulting a witch was the 1590 case of James Kinnard, cited above. Kinnard escaped punishment, probably because he produced the witch in question, Isobell Watson, and she made a lengthy confession of her own crimes. The presbytery was not so lenient two months later with William Culross, who consulted Watson (while she was imprisoned in the Stirling tollbooth) about his cow's sudden inability to give milk. Watson referred Culross to another sorceress, whose help he then sought, and he performed public repentance several times for his offense.[110]

Within a few years, consulters of witches elsewhere were also forced to perform public repentance. Four women received this punishment from the St. Andrews Kirk Session in September 1595 for consulting several condemned witches (including Nannis Melville).[111] Two years later the St. Andrews Presbytery was disturbed to discover "that David Zeman, the warlock, wes sufferit to pas throght the cuntrie to do curis eftir his apprehending, and that peopill wer sufferit to consult with him, he being in the pressoun." The bailies of Pittenweem admitted that they had allowed Walter Gourlay to take Zeman to visit his son, who was ill. Zeman reportedly told Gourlay that his son had been bewitched by one Margaret Smith. Thomas Watson consulted Zeman regarding his cow's inability to give milk, and told the presbytery that Zeman had sent him to see a witch named Beatrix Adie, who proved able to cure the cow. The presbytery ordered that all those who had consulted with Zeman or other witches in the area be suspended from the sacraments "whill they schew teakonis of repentance," as judged by their sessions.[112] John Muckhill in December 1604 admitted to the Dundonald session that he had consulted with the convicted witch Jonet Hunter regarding the illnesses of his son and his cattle. This offense went unpunished for a year and a half, but in the summer of 1606, he and his wife were ordered to do public repentance, barefoot and in linen, for the offense. The session gave Katherine Walker the same punishment in 1612 "for seiking and useing Issobell Trumbillis charmes...."[113]

Thus as far as the elders and ministers were concerned, the witchcraft problem was not merely that of some women and a few men who allied

---

[109] StAUM ms Deposit 23, 93r.

[110] WRH ms CH2/722/2, 2 June, 23 June, 29 September 1590.

[111] *StAKS*, 2:799-800.

[112] StAUM ms Deposit 23, 80r.

[113] *Dun KS*, 66, 111, 113, 236.

themselves with the Devil and practiced evil against their neighbors. It was also that of a population which was all too eager to seek the services of these cunning sorcerers at the risk of offending God. The witches themselves were usually poor, marginal figures, and secular courts were quite willing to execute them. Not so their clients. The latter were often established members of the community. This distinction, so clear in the records examined for this study, is critical to our understanding of witchcraft as a social phenomenon. By forcing those who consulted with witches to acknowledge their offenses and share the stool of repentance with adulterers and other sinners, the Kirk was invoking the sanction of humiliation in a battle against common practice. The widespread belief in witchcraft was not challenged, but the elders and ministers sought to make it socially unacceptable to try and use that belief to one's advantage.[114] Just as the Kirk was using the disciplinary system to try and change the way the Scots defined their intimate relationships, worshipped their God, spent their Sundays and settled their disputes, it was also using it to encourage a revolution in their reactions to illness and misfortune. The ailing and the unlucky were now to seek their solace in prayer and contemplation, not in charms and magic. Even as the witches burned, the ecclesiastical powers partly responsible for the conflagration were undermining the beliefs which made the witch-hunt possible.

---

[114] This is analogous to the modern example of anti-drug or anti-vice campaigns which attempt to reduce demand for illicit goods or services through well-publicized roundups of customers. The underlying assumption is that while drug dealers and prostitutes are not much concerned about their reputations, doctors, lawyers and businessmen are.

CHAPTER NINE

AN ALTERNATIVE DEVELOPMENT—REFORMED SOCIAL
DISCIPLINE AMONG THE HUGUENOTS

*All games prohibited by royal edict, such as cards, dice and other games of
chance, and those which involve avarice, immodesty, notorious time-wasting
or scandal shall be curbed, and the offenders reproved and admonished in the
consistory....*
                    - *Discipline* of the French Reformed Church[1]

*Jean Seguineau the younger appeared...and he was admonished...[for] dan-
cing publicly on the guild festival day and when warned by his mother-in-law
to quit such vanity, nevertheless continued stubbornly; and even more, being
exhorted by the brother Delaye [an elder] to abstain from these things, he
replied haughtily that those who cannot dance do not dance at all. And so it
is found that he will not confess his sin at all, and even debates irreverently
against the remonstrances which are made to him.*
                    - Register of the consistory of Coutras, 20 May 1583[2]

Calvinism was an international movement, and yet its history is still most
often written from the national perspective. Too many historians have
shown too little interest in the impact it might have had outside of their own
territorial bailiwicks.[3] Fortunately, Reformed social discipline is a subject

---

[1] François Méjan, ed., *La discipline de l'église réformée de France*, (Paris: S.C.E.L.,
1947), 297: "Tous jeux défendus par les édits du roi, comme cartes, dés, et autres jeux de
hasard, et ceux ou il y aura avarice, impudicité, perte notoire de temps, ou scandale, seront
réprimés et les personnes reprises et admonestées au Consistoire, et censurées selon les
circonstances."

[2] Ars. ms 6559, 20v: "Jean Seguineau le jeune a compareu en consistoire et luy a esté
remonstré...la faute qu'il avoit commise en dansant publicquement ung jour de confrerie et
de ce qu'estant admonesté par sa belle-mere de se retirer de cette vanité, neanmoins il y avoit
continué opinioniastrement; et encores despuis, estant exhorté par le frere Delaye de s'abstenir
de ces choses, il luy auroit respondu superbement que ceux qui ne savent danser ne dansont
point. Et a-on trouvé par ses propos qu'il ne confessoit point son péché, et mesmes qu'il
debatoit irreverement contre les remonstrances qui luy estoient fetes." Much of this manuscript
has been transcribed and published by Alfred Soman in "Le registre consistorial de Coutras,
1582-1584," *BSHPF* 126 (1980), 193-228.

[3] This problem is remedied somewhat by Menna Prestwich, ed., *International Calvinism,
1541-1715*, (Oxford: Clarendon Press, 1985), but the specialists contributing to that volume
still restrict themselves to national or linguistic boundaries.

which allows the crossing of modern political boundaries.[4] If we take such a journey, we can test the comparative impact of the Calvinist strain of autonomous ecclesiastical discipline. How powerful an element was it in a given society? How might its function differ in alternative political, social or even climatological circumstances? What can its impact tell us about the societies in which it was planted?

The institution and practice of discipline in the Scottish Reformed Kirk and among the Huguenots of France in the late sixteenth century seem ideal for such a comparison. Both were influenced heavily by Geneva, and both were undertaken by a church leadership which was at first uncertain as to how much support it would receive from local and national officials.[5] The language used in the founding documents of both churches was strongly reminiscent of Calvin's own writings.

In addition to these common characteristics, there were direct connections between the reform movements in the two countries. John Knox served as pastor in Dieppe for a short time in early 1559, and may well have taken a copy of the French *Discipline* with him when he returned to Scotland. There is circumstantial evidence that he visited Poitiers in 1557, when the protestants of that town were drawing up their own disciplinary ordinances. The ill-fated earl of Arran, son of the Hamilton duke of Châtelherault, was active in founding protestant churches in the vicinity of Poitiers during that period.[6] Numerous Scots, including the influential

---

[4] Very little has been done on the comparative history of Reformed social discipline. R. Po-chia Hsia's *Social Discipline in the Reformation: Central Europe 1550-1750*, (London: Routledge, 1989), which examines Catholic as well as protestant disciplinary institutions, concentrates primarily on German-speaking lands, and on areas where civil magistrates controlled the power of excommunication. The only studies of early modern discipline which cross linguistic frontiers are: Bernard Vogler and Janine (Garrisson-)Estèbe, "La genèse d'une société protestante: Etude comparée de quelques registres consistoriaux languedociens et palatins vers 1600," *Annales economies, sociétés, civilisations*, 1976, 362-387; Bruce Lenman, "The Limits of Godly Discipline in the Early Modern Period With Special Reference to England and Scotland," in Kaspar von Greyerz, ed., *Religion and Society in Early Modern Europe, 1500-1800*, (London: German Historical Institute, 1984), 124-145; Raymond Mentzer, ed., *Sin and the Calvinists: Morals Control and the Consistory in the Reformed Tradition*, (Kirksville, Mo.: Sixteenth Century Publishers, 1994).

[5] Geneva was viewed as the source of theological wisdom for Scots even after Calvin's death. See, for example, Gordon Donaldson, ed., "Lord Chancellor Glamis and Theodore Beza," *Scottish History Society Miscellany* 8, (Edinburgh: Scottish History Society, 1951), 89-116. For Genevan influence on French protestantism, see, among others, Robert Kingdon, *Geneva and the Coming of the Wars of Religion in France, 1555-1563*, (Genève: Droz, 1956), and *ibidem, Geneva and the French Protestant Movement, 1564-72*, (Madison, Wisc.: University of Wisconsin Press, 1967).

[6] *Hist. Ecc.*, 1:228; W. Stanford Reid, "French Influence on the First Scots Confession and Book of Discipline," *Westminster Theological Journal* 35 (1972), 1-14, at 7-9.

Andrew Melville, spent time in France in the 1560s and 1570s, and one author has suggested that they "became vigorous propagandists for French culture" once they returned to Scotland.[7] The "Auld Alliance" as a political concern may have ended for good in 1560, but intellectual connections continued. Both churches ended up adopting a four-tiered organizational structure of consistory/kirk session, colloquy/presbytery, provincial synod and national synod.[8]

The inchoate reform movements in both countries also crystallized during the same two-year period, 1559-60. This was not entirely coincidental, although the reasons were more political than anything else. In both countries, reformers took advantage of weakened monarchies—in France the accession of a child, François II, and in Scotland the continued absence of the ruling queen Mary Stewart, not much older than François II, who happened to be her husband. Resentment of French political influence was in fact one driving force behind the movement for reform in Scotland. But international politics are not our primary concern here. Rather, it would be useful to trace the development of the disciplinary system among the Huguenot churches, and to offer some comparisons of its operation with that of its Scottish counterpart, examined in earlier chapters.

The First Consistoires *and the* Discipline ecclesiastique

Estimates of the early numerical strength of French Calvinism vary widely. The prince of Condé boasted to Catherine de Medici in 1562 that he was prepared to offer her the support of Huguenot troops raised from 2,150 congregations, if she would offer them liberty of conscience. This figure (and the accompanying assumption that most or all of these congregations had working consistories) has been accepted at face value by partisan historians chronicling the Huguenot movement as an heroic or patriotic struggle. It may have attained verisimilitude simply through repetition; even Menna Prestwich has offered a figure as high as 1,750 churches, with two million members, for 1560.[9] Others have recognized that Condé was

[7] John Durkan, "The French Connection in the Sixteenth and Early Seventeenth Centuries," in T.C. Smout, ed., *Scotland and Europe, 1200-1850*, (Edinburgh: John Donald, 1986), 19-44, at 32, 37-40.

[8] This rather obvious similarity calls into question the assertion of Michel Reulos that the four-tiered system "est proprement français et s'inspire largement du droit public français des Etats provinciaux et généraux." See his "L'Histoire de la discipline des églises réformées en France et de l'histoire du droit ecclésiastique réformé," in Leo Olschki, ed., *La Storia del Diritto nel Quandro delle Scienze Storiche*, (Firenze: Societa Italiana di Storia, 1966), 533-44, at 542.

[9] Prestwich, ed., *International Calvinism*, 73.

probably exaggerating the size of the movement in a bid for power.[10] Mark Greengrass and Janine Garrisson-Estèbe have both suggested the much more realistic figure of around 1,200 congregations as the peak of Huguenot strength in the 1560s.[11]

Whatever the true numbers, it is clear that the movement took off in the period just before 1560.[12] Even those who offer generous estimates have been unable to locate any "erected" congregations (*églises dressées*—that is, with consistories) before 1555. In that year, at least five were formed, including the churches of Paris and Poitiers.[13] The next few years brought the foundation of numerous congregations throughout the realm.[14] But these still lacked any kind of national organization or common agreement on doctrine or procedures. The origins of the latter, at least as far as discipline is concerned, have been traced to the *Articles politiques* drawn up by the Reformed churches in the district around Poitiers in 1557.[15] These established procedures and sanctions, proposing a disciplinary system entirely under the control of lay elders and deacons, without reference to ministers. Ministers were brought into the process by the national synod which met secretly in a house in St. Germain (Paris), in May 1559. This synod approved a *Discipline* and *Confession of Faith*, both of which were intended for acceptance by all Reformed congregations in France.[16] Like their contemporaries among the reformers of Scotland, these ministers and leading laymen held that discipline was the third mark of the true Church,

---

[10] For a discussion of the range of estimates and their pitfalls, see Janine Garrisson-Estèbe, *Les protestants du Midi, 1559-1598*, (Toulouse: Privat, 1980), 62-6.

[11] *Ibid*, 83; Mark Greengrass, *The French Reformation*, (Oxford: Basil Blackwell, 1987), 42-3. A survey undertaken in 1598 to determine the distribution of a royal grant found 760 Reformed congregations in France, but all authorities agree that the protestant population had been in decline for two or three decades by then. See Aymon, 1:226; Quick, 1:198. Philip Benedict has suggested that the Huguenot population in the cities of northern France was already in decline by the 1570s, although numbers remained high in the Midi and center-west regions until the 1620s. See Philip Benedict, *The Huguenot Population of France, 1600-1685: The Demographic Fate and Customs of a Religious Minority*, (Philadelphia: Transactions of the American Philosophical Society, 1991), 29, 50-1.

[12] Prestwich, ed., *International Calvinism*, 87.

[13] *Hist. Ecc.*, 1:117-22; Samuel Mours, *Le Protestantisme en France au XVIe siècle*, (Paris: Librairie Protestante, 1959), 101-2.

[14] *Hist. Ecc.*, 1:124-8, 133-5, 159-67.

[15] Reulos, "L'Histoire de la Discipline...", 535-6. Glenn Sunshine, in his paper "Reforming French Protestantism: The Example of Le Mans, 1561," presented at the Sixteenth Century Studies Conference in Atlanta, Georgia, in October 1992, stressed the variety of ecclesiastical structures within the Huguenot churches before the early 1560s, when a Genevan-style system was imposed through the authority of national and provincial synods.

[16] *Hist. Ecc.*, 1:198-200; Mours, 115.

in addition to preaching and the proper administration of the sacraments.[17]

But it would be rash to conclude that these founding documents were immediately distributed to, and accepted by, all the Reformed congregations in France. The ministers of fewer than a dozen congregations were present at the 1559 synod,[18] and there was as yet no sign that the monarchy was prepared to offer any toleration of protestant worship. Under such conditions, it would have been difficult to maintain regular communications or enforce standards. The second national synod, held at Poitiers in March 1560, passed a motion requiring that every church form a consistory, but this requirement must have been more an optimistic goal than a certification requirement.[19]

The death of François II in December 1560 brought Catherine de Medici, the queen mother, into the regency, and marked a turning away from the ultra-Catholic policies of the Guise faction which had controlled the government of François. The regent's realization of growing Huguenot power led her to offer limited toleration in January 1562, allowing protestants to worship publicly outside of towns, privately within towns, to hold synods, and to form consistories.[20] These concessions were reconfirmed, (but with a complete ban on urban worship), in the edict of pacification which ended the first religious war in March 1563, despite the military defeat of the Huguenot cause, and the fact that the consistories had proved instrumental in recruiting troops from Reformed parishes.[21]

Indeed, while the Huguenots won few decisive military victories in the 1560s, the decade saw considerable growth in the Reformed Church as a national organization, albeit one with its greatest numerical strength in the south. At least five national synods met in the 1560s, and the synod held at La Rochelle in April 1571 had international importance because of the attendance of Theodore Beza (elected moderator), Prince Louis of Nassau,

---

[17] *Hist. Ecc.*, 1:211-2.

[18] Quick, ed., 1:2.

[19] *Ibid*, 1:16. Robert Kingdon has suggested that some French churches may have never formed consistories because of the need for secrecy, and the fact that a church member who had been disciplined might betray the church to Catholic authorities. See his *Geneva and the French Protestant Movement*, 41. But one should keep in mind that there were advantages in the consistorial structure for a "church under the cross." Menna Prestwich has termed the French consistory "the reproductive cell essential to the spreading of the reformed faith." See Prestwich, ed., *International Calvinism*, 73.

[20] J.H.M. Salmon, *Society in Crisis: France in the Sixteenth Century*, (London: Benn, 1975), 141; Prestwich, ed., *International Calvinism*, 88.

[21] *Receuil Gén*, 14:135-40; Salmon, *Society in Crisis*, 141-2.

Jeanne d'Albret, queen of Navarre, and others.[22] These synods were allowed to meet more or less openly after 1562, and attracted increasing numbers of ministers and elders from throughout France. The *Discipline* first passed in 1559 was read and discussed at each meeting, and modifications were made. This ongoing process culminated in the passage in 1571-2 of a new, reorganized *Discipline*, much more comprehensive, and much more widely debated and distributed, than its ancestor of 1559.[23]

One of the leading concerns of the ministers and elders at national synods (and, as it would turn out, a significant disciplinary issue in their home parishes), was the question of relationships with Catholics and the Catholic Church. The Huguenots were a minority nearly everywhere and, although they hoped to bring the whole kingdom (and the monarchy) of France into the Calvinist camp eventually, this was a distant goal, not an imminent prospect. As a result, their strategy during the first decade or so was to walk a tightrope, ensuring that the Huguenot laity did not engage in any dealings with Catholics or the Catholic Church which might enrich the latter, or lead to any reconversions, but at the same time wary of gratuitously offending Catholics or the royal government.

This concern was evident at the outset. The first matter considered at the first (1559) national synod related to Huguenots seeking marriage who had obtained licenses from "des curés & des vicaires de la Papauté." These couples were to demonstrate repentance by tearing up the licenses, either publicly in church or privately before the consistory, at the discretion of the elders. But this did not mean that Huguenots engaged to Catholics were free to break off their betrothals. The synod ruled that such engagements were binding until broken by the Catholic partner, either by marriage to someone else, or infidelity.[24]

On the other hand, the synod ruled that it was permissible for Huguenots to have their children's names entered in Catholic parish registers, since the latter were kept by royal ordinance. The banns of Huguenot couples could also be read in Catholic churches, since this was a matter "purement politique." Moreover, even though the synod held that tithes were used unjustly by the Catholic Church, they were to be paid "as indifferent things,

---

[22] The surviving records of the national synods were collected and published by Quick and Aymon in 1692 and 1710, respectively. Ironically, Quick's English edition predates Aymon's French one, but the two are strikingly similar, suggesting a common source, or even the possibility that Aymon's edition is based on Quick's.

[23] Glenn Sunshine, "French Protestantism on the Eve of St-Bartholomew: The Ecclesiastical Discipline of the French Reformed Churches, 1571-2," *French History* 4 (1990), 340-77, including a transcription of the *Discipline* itself, on 352-77.

[24] Aymon, 1:8; Quick 1:7. The latter requirement was said to be based on the advice of Calvin himself.

due to royal commandments, in order to avoid sedition and scandal."[25]

The national synods considered the danger of backsliding to be the leading hazard in relationships between Huguenots and Catholics. This warning was made explicit in the ordinance regarding the enrollment of Protestant children in Catholic parish registers, and Protestants married to Catholics were cautioned to make every effort to ensure that their children were not baptized by priests. Just as Scots ministers were concerned that Catholic priests gained converts by baptizing the offspring of refugees from parochial discipline, so their French counterparts perceived the baptism of infants as a major avenue of conversion. A mixed marriage could thus lead an entire family down the road to apostasy. The *Discipline* held that no marriage to a Catholic was to be sanctioned unless the Catholic renounced idolatry and the Mass, and agreed to be catechized.[26] Consistent with such an attitude toward marriage with Catholics or use of Catholic rites, any kinds of dealings with Catholics were closely guarded. Printers, painters and other artisans were admonished to take on no business dependent on the Roman Church.[27]

The Huguenots considered themselves a community set apart from its neighbors, a community which must keep to itself and police its own. This view was reflected in the order passed by the national synod of March 1560 that the faithful should only report to the magistrates fellow believers who committed crimes if the offenses were repeated or habitual. Otherwise, the consistory was to be the forum for trial and punishment.[28] In 1579, after nearly two decades of civil war, a national synod made the firm declaration that no evidence gathered in consistories was to be given to civil magistrates, regardless of the circumstances.[29] A synod meeting in Vitré (Brittany) was informed of cases from Lower Languedoc in which offenders had gotten consistorial proceedings against them halted by local judges. This practice was condemned, and the synod told the local consistories to declare publicly that civil judges had no such jurisdiction.[30] In general, institutional separation was reinforced by financial as well as religious considerations; many Huguenots saw the consistory as a cheaper alternative to civil

---

[25] Quick, 1:8-10; Aymon 1:9, 11-12: "eu égard au commandement du Roi, comme des choses indifferentes, & pour éviter sedition et scandale."

[26] Méjan, ed., *La discipline*, 283. But Reformed couples who wished to marry where no Reformed church existed were allowed to partake of Catholic rites. This, too, was defended on the grounds that such a practice was "purement politique."

[27] *Ibid*, 289.

[28] Aymon, 1:20; Quick, 1:18-9.

[29] Aymon, 1:141; Quick, 1:130. This order was discussed and repeated in 1594. See Aymon, 1:181; Quick, 1:162.

[30] Aymon, 1:160; Quick, 1:146.

litigation.[31]

But while the Huguenots may have sought to define themselves as a separate society, they did not claim to seek conflict with their Catholic neighbors, whatever the political reality may have been. The synod of 1560 explicitly condemned violence and calumny against Catholics, including priests and monks.[32] Seven years later a synod granted that Huguenots could attend Catholic weddings or baptisms, provided they were mere onlookers.[33] While religious divisions may have been deep,[34] the Reformed Church at the national level recognized that the residents of many divided communities needed to have social relationships with their Catholic neighbors. Likewise, excommunication had to be handled delicately. The national synod held at Nîmes in May 1572 considered the question of publicly excommunicating apostates, when such action might just make them "plus enragés," and lead to tension with neighbors. The synod reminded consistories that excommunication only applied to those who clearly had belonged to the Church prior to their offenses, and suggested that those for whom there appeared to be no hope ought to be left alone.[35]

Another way in which the Huguenot ministers and elders sought to emphasize the difference between their flocks and the Catholic majority was through the repression of popular culture. Dancing has been termed a "distraction essentielle" for all classes in sixteenth-century France,[36] and gambling, gaming and the celebration of Mardi Gras (to offer a few examples) were also common amusements. Certain holidays had Catholic or pagan overtones, of course, but the Huguenot churches also attacked many pastimes which had no religious significance whatsoever. The passage from the *Discipline* cited at the beginning of this chapter ordered consistories to punish those who participated in games which involved gambling or led to idleness, and this was not an ordinance which was quickly forgotten. As shall be seen, consistories had few qualms about summoning those who participated in such games. A synod which met near Orléans in 1601 condemned all lotteries, even those established by magistrates.[37] As it so happened, games of chance also violated royal ordinances,[38] but the records of consistories suggest that civil magistrates

---

[31] Garrisson-Estèbe, *Protestants du Midi*, 108.

[32] Aymon, 1:17; Quick, 1:17.

[33] Aymon, 1:73; Quick, 1:75.

[34] For violence between neighbors, see Natalie Davis, *Society and Culture in Early Modern France*, (Stanford: Stanford University Press, 1965), 152-87.

[35] Aymon, 1:113; Quick, 1:105.

[36] Garrisson-Estèbe, *Protestants du Midi*, 303.

[37] Quick, 1:213.

[38] Garrisson-Estèbe, *Protestants du Midi*, 300.

did not vigorously enforce them. Just as their Scots counterparts did with statutes concerning sexual offenses and sabbath-breach, the Huguenots here took it upon themselves to enforce laws which were on the books but not used by secular authorities.

But other aspects of popular culture, which violated no civil laws, were also targeted. The national synod of March 1560 added to the *Discipline* a provision which ordered consistories to forbid dancing, mummers' plays and juggling. "Those who make it a profession to dance" were specifically condemned and declared worthy of excommunication.[39] The synod which met at Nîmes in 1572 forbade the faithful to attend "spectacles profanes," such as dances, comedies, tragedies or farces.[40] Similar proscriptions were repeated at later synods, but extant consistory records suggest that many ministers and elders needed no reminding.[41] Enforcement of such behavioral standards was an effective way of dividing the faithful few from the profane multitude, and consistories could be quite strict as long as they did not fear losing membership. Contemporaries sensed this cultural divide; "we shall dance in spite of the Huguenots," declared the peasants in the neighborhood of Montpellier in 1561.[42]

Who were these grim censors, who seemed to expect so much more in the way of behavioral transformation than their Scots counterparts? The *Discipline ecclesiastique* established the office of elder using terminology not unlike that of the Scots' *First Book of Discipline*:

> The office of the elders is to watch over the flock with the pastors, to make sure the people gather and that each is among the sacred congregation; to take notice of scandals and faults, and to know and judge with the pastors; and in general to take care with them [the pastors] of all similar things which relate to the order, upkeep and government of the Church.[43]

The parochial disciplinary ordinance of the Reformed church at Bayeux (1563) gave elders the following charge:

> Make sure that no scandal enters this church and particularly take care that all

---

[39] Quick, 1:15, 17; Aymon, 1:18: "celui qui fait profession de danser."

[40] Aymon, 1:118; Quick, 1:109.

[41] Aymon, 1:151; Quick, 1:139, 194.

[42] Emmanuel Le Roy Ladurie, *The Peasants of Languedoc*, (trans. John Day), (Urbana, Ill.: University of Illinois Press, 1974), 160.

[43] Méjan, ed., *La discipline*, 224: "L'office des anciens est de veiller sur le troupeau, avec les pasteurs, faire que le peuple s'assemble, et que chacun se trouve aux saintes congrégations; faire rapport des scandales et des fautes, en connaître et juger avec les pasteurs; et en général avoir soin avec eux de toutes choses sembables qui concernent l'ordre, l'entretein et gouvernement de l'Eglise."

vices and bad mores are extirpated in the district over which you are given responsibility; procure the peace and union of the church, as much by the example of your lives as by fraternal admonitions....[44]

The national synods held that if a church was being established for the first time, the elders were to be chosen "par voix communes du peuple avec les pasteurs." Once the consistory was operating, it was to choose elders itself by cooptation, but announce the names of the persons chosen to the congregation on three successive Sundays in order to give time for objections.[45] While pastors were chosen for life, the office of elder was not at first held to be perpetual, although the *Discipline* specified no term.[46] The Parisian synod of 1559 ruled that neither elders or deacons could give up their offices without the permission of the Church. Truly incompetent elders could be deposed and replaced, but the language used in the synod's record suggests a real reluctance to see such steps taken.[47] The synod of Nîmes (1572) urged that elders be encouraged to remain in office as long as possible "because frequent changes bring great difficulties to churches."[48]

Thus while there may have been democratic or pseudo-democratic elections of elders and deacons at first, such practices were discouraged thereafter. The synod of La Rochelle in 1571 condemned the method, said to be practiced in Languedoc, of electing elders "recueillant les voix due peuple."[49] A synod held four years earlier complained that parishioners of an unnamed church "because of the grumbling of some of the people against the consistory," had chosen a new group of elders by direct election. The synod expressly condemned this procedure, reaffirming the principle that any new consistory must be chosen by the old.[50]

---

[44] Robert Kingdon, Michel Reulos and Raymond Mentzer, eds., "Disciplines réformées du XVIe siècle: une découverte faite aux Etats-Unis," *BSHPF* 130 (1984), 69-86, at 75: "Vous aurés l'oeil que aucun scandale n'advienne en ceste eglise et singulierement soignerés que tous vices et mauvaises moeurs soient extirpés du milieu de ceux qui vous seront donnez en charge; vous procurerés la paix et union de l'eglise, tant par l'exemple de vie que fraternelles admonitions...."

[45] Méjan, ed., *La discipline*, 222; Quick, 1:5. This method of publicizing the names of prospective elders to allow for objection was also employed in Scotland.

[46] Méjan, ed., *La discipline*, 225-6.

[47] Quick, 1:5, 8; Aymon, 1:10: "S'ils pouvoient satisfaire en quelque sorte à leur charge, ils ne pourront aucunement être deposés sans leur consentement."

[48] Quick, 1:109; Aymon, 1:118: "à cause que les frequens changemens portent beaucoup de prejudice aux Eglises."

[49] Aymon, 1:111; Quick, 1:101.

[50] Quick, 1:76; Aymon, 1:80: "à cause du murmure de quelques-uns d'entre le peuple contre le consistoire..."; Mours, *Protestantisme en France*, 217; Solange Bertheau, "Le Consistoire dans les Eglises Réformées du Moyen-Poitou au XVIIe Siècle," *BSHPF* 116 (1970),

The elders themselves were to be godly and upright men; social or political importance was not prescribed as essential.[51] One wag suggested that the Huguenot church at Le Puy in the Velay in 1561 was led by "bonnet-makers, armor bearers, or other venerable doctors."[52] But once congregations were firmly established, wealth and prominence became more important criteria. Garrisson-Estèbe has argued that through the practice of selecting elders by cooptation "there was...a genuine confiscation of consistorial power by the superior social classes in Calvinist towns and villages."[53] Tracing the origins of 323 elders in the Midi between 1561 and 1609, she found only 37 artisans and 14 rural laborers, while 16 elders were nobles or *sieurs*. Most common were notaries, clerks and procureurs (79 from these three groups), merchants and apothecaries (71), lawyers (33) and consuls (33).[54] But synods debated the suitability of some prominent and wealthy occupations for the eldership. The first national synod declared bankers unfit to be elders, and even threatened them with excommunication if they dealt in dispensations or other "abominations Papales."[55] Nor could anyone who had recently been a Catholic become an elder, according to the 1560 synod of Poitiers.[56]

The inclusion of magistrates on consistories was another significant issue, given the concern, discussed above, to keep evidence gathered in consistories from being used in secular courts. The early national synods concluded that a civil magistrate could serve on the consistory provided that this did not hinder him in the performance of either duty, but there was still enough doubt on the question to warrant writing to the ministry of Geneva.[57] The Genevans replied that, although the mixing of the two jurisdictions made it difficult to keep consistorial proceedings secret, there was little that could be done about this. In some cases, they suggested, sinners could be censured outside the consistory, in order to avoid revealing

---

332-59, 513-49, at 340. For evidence of annual elections by the congregation in one parish in the late sixteenth century, see M. Oudot de Dainville, "Le Consistoire de Ganges à la fin du XVIe siècle," *Revue d'histoire de L'église de France* 18 (1932), 464-85, at 465.

[51] The placement of women on consistories seems hardly to have been considered, in France or Scotland, although four women were appointed by the consistory of Nîmes to seek alms for the poor in the early 1560s. See Davis, *Society and Culture*, 83-4.

[52] Mours, *Protestantisme en France*, 165-6: "de bonnetiers, de couteliers ou autres vénérables docteurs."

[53] Garrisson-Estèbe, *Protestants du Midi*, 99: "il y a...une réelle confiscation de la puissance consistoriale par les couches sociales superieures des villes ou villages Calvinistes."

[54] *Ibid*, 95.

[55] Aymon, 1:10; Quick, 1:8.

[56] Aymon, 1:19; Quick, 1:18. This provision, if strictly interpreted, could have excluded all but a handful in 1560!

[57] Aymon, 1:33, 39; Quick, 1:32, 38; Méjan, ed., *La discipline*, 230.

offenses to magistrate elders.[58] In reality, just as Scots kirk sessions buttressed their authority by including bailies or other local officials as elders,
the consistories of firmly protestant towns such as Nîmes came to be full of
local officials, with little apparent disapproval from synods or other church
authorities.[59] In towns or areas where the Huguenots did not hold sway, but
were a significant minority, the consistory could become a kind of party
cell, the strategic nerve center of the local movement.[60] These "aristocratic"
tendencies, which increasingly placed control of the consistory in the hands
of a chosen few, were not without critics; the most vocal was probably Jean
Morély.

Internal Challenges

While the Huguenot movement faced almost constant political and military
threats from the crown and the Catholic party in the second half of the
sixteenth century, its most dangerous intellectual challenges came from
within its own ranks. Jean Morély, a minor French nobleman living in
Geneva, published in 1562 his *Traicté de la Discipline & Police Chrestienne*, in which he attacked the whole consistorial disciplinary apparatus as
tending toward both oligarchy and sedition.[61] The book was dedicated to
Pierre Viret, the fiery and popular minister of Lyon, who may have agreed
with some of Morély's criticisms of the Huguenot ecclesiastical structure.[62]
    Morély attacked two aspects of Huguenot church polity. First, he
complained that the autonomous system which had developed gave civil
magistrates no effective power within the Church. Morély praised the
historical role played by godly princes such as Constantine in establishing
religions and purifying churches.[63] Under the Reformed system as practiced
by the Huguenots and their spiritual brethren in Geneva, there was no room
for such royal intercession. And yet, according to Morély:

---

[58] Aymon, 1:52-3; Quick, 1:50.

[59] In Nîmes, the consistory picked the town council after the protestant coup of 1561. See
Prestwich, ed., *International Calvinism*, 89; Ann H. Guggenheim, "The Calvinist Notables of
Nîmes During the Era of the Religious Wars," *Sixteenth Century Journal* 3 (1972), 80-96.

[60] As in Rouen. See Philip Benedict, *Rouen During the Wars of Religion*, (Cambridge:
Cambridge University Press, 1981), 98.

[61] Jean de Morely, *Traicté de la discipline & police chrestienne*, (Lyon: De Tournes, 1562)
(repr. Genève: Slatkine, 1968). For Morély and the controversy he generated, see Kingdon,
Geneva and the French Protestant Movement, 43-111; Mours, *Protestantisme en France*, 214;
Janine Garrisson, *Les protestants au XVIe siècle*, (Paris: Fayard, 1988), 222-6.

[62] Kingdon, *Geneva and the French Protestant Movement*, 46-8.

[63] Morély, *Traicté*, 3-6.

...the responsibility of re-establishing this holy discipline belongs to the prince in the first place. Because if, as we have shown, the restitution and conservation of the Word of God is the responsibility of kings and magistrates, [this is] all the more reason that this discipline belongs to their charge, seeing as how without it [pure] doctrine cannot be revived.[64]

What is more, while shutting out kings and their officials from authority at the top, he argued that the Huguenots also paid little heed to the views of the congregations.

This disenfranchisement of the faithful was Morély's second complaint. To him, the consistorial structure led inevitably to a tyranny of the few over the many. He labelled the practice of electing elders by cooptation "aristocratique," and suggested that it was only acceptable for a Church in its infancy, "as if it were still without judgment and not capable of governing itself."[65] Morély was particularly concerned that the powers of excommunication were vested in the ministers and elders alone, without reference to magistrates or the congregation.[66] Thus the debate already heard between Oecolampadius and Zwingli, Bucer and Hedio, and later to echo again between James VI and the Melvilles, was aired in the French Reformed Church, but this time with congregationalist overtones as well.

Morély willingly granted that minister and elders formed "le premier conseil," but he maintained "that which touches all [such as excommunication or the election of ministers and elders] must be heard by all," not considered secretly.[67] In his discussion of Matthew 18, he argued that when Christ told the apostles to take the cases of stubborn sinners to the Church, he meant the whole Church, not merely a council thereof.[68] But this smacked of congregational democracy, which was anathema to the leading Huguenot ministers.

As J.H.M. Salmon has suggested, "Morély's congregationalism was feared by the Huguenot establishment because it contained implications to support Catholic charges of social sedition."[69] Perhaps equally threatening,

---

[64] *Ibid*, 11: "...le soing du restablissement de ceste sainte discipline appartient en premier lieu aux Prince. Car si, comme nous avons demonstré, la restitution & conservation de la parole de Dieu appartient aux Rois & Magistrats, à plus forte raison ceste discipline appartient à leur charge, veu que sans icelle la doctrine ne peut susciter."

[65] *Ibid*, 34-5: "...comme si elle estoit encores sans iugement, & ne pouvoit suffire à son gouvernement."

[66] *Ibid*, 39.

[67] *Ibid*, 112, 41: "Ie pense donc que ce qui touche tous, doit estre entendu de tous."

[68] *Ibid*, 127-8.

[69] Salmon, *Society in Crisis*, 181.

he had supporters within the protestant nobility and ministry.[70] His *Traicté* was condemned by the Synod of Orléans in 1562 as containing "an evil doctrine...tending to the dissipation and confusion of the Church."[71] Morély was excommunicated, and forced to flee Geneva. Many of his followers were hounded as well.[72] Later, Morély served briefly as tutor to the young Henry of Navarre, but pressure from Theodore Beza and leading Huguenot ministers brought his dismissal from that post early in 1567.[73] While his opponents successfully deprived him of influential positions, his ideas were not so easily suppressed. By 1570, his congregationalist ideas had been adopted by Pierre Ramus, the Parisian logician and intellectual iconoclast. The 1572 Synod of Nîmes was forced again to uphold the powers of consistories to excommunicate offenders, and it may have only been the St. Bartholomew's Day Massacres (which claimed Ramus as a victim) which forced unity on the French Reformed Church. Whatever the ultimate reason, church polity was not really an issue thereafter.[74]

Thus the Huguenots after 1572 had an "official" disciplinary prescription, honed and developed in the 1560s, and baptized and sealed by the fires of persecution. Having examined this background, it would now be worthwhile to move from theory to practice, and explore the actual operation of the Huguenot disciplinary apparatus in a few selected parishes.

The System in Action: A Prospectus

The *consistoires* of the Huguenots have drawn considerably more attention from historians over the years than their Scots counterparts. As early as the 1930s, Oudot de Dainville was plumbing consistorial registers for evidence of "une vie intense." He was fascinated by the reports he found, for instance, of a pastor wounded while trying to prevent a *charivari*, or elders making visitations in search of crucifixes or other evidence of continuing

---

[70] Garrisson, *Protestants au XVIe siècle*, 225.

[71] Quick, 1:27; Aymon, 1:29: "...une mauvaise doctrine & tendante à la dissipation & confusion de l'Eglise." Morély was condemned again at the national synod of 1565, which told him he would not be accepted back into Communion with the French Reformed Church until he satisfied the church of Geneva. See Quick, 1:56-7; Aymon, 1:58-9.

[72] Kingdon, *Geneva and the French Protestant Movement*, 63-5.

[73] *Ibid*, 95-6; Salmon, *Society in Crisis*, 180.

[74] Mours, *Protestantisme en France*, 215; Salmon, *Society in Crisis*, 182-3; Kingdon, *Geneva and the French Protestant Movement*, 102-3, 107-9, 122. Kingdon has suggested that these disputes made Beza and the Calvinists of his generation *more* committed to consistorial discipline than Calvin himself had been. See *ibid*, 128.

Catholicism.[75] Dainville's approach was largely anecdotal, and others have continued in this tradition.[76] But some historians in recent years have used the registers quantitatively, classifying and counting disciplinary cases in order to examine social discipline more comprehensively by placing the anecdotal evidence within a measurable context.[77] That will be the approach taken here, just as it was with the Scots material examined earlier. The quantitative research which already exists for French Reformed discipline makes the task here both easier and more difficult—easier because so much work is available from which to draw evidence, but more difficult because, in classifying cases, one can never be sure how closely one's criteria match those of others. Thus, haste to draw comparisons between the activities of consistories in Scotland and France based on other historians' research could lead to a facile contrasting of apples and oranges. Therefore I have determined first to test some of the French evidence myself, using the same criteria employed for the Scottish material, in order to ensure consistency. This will be the basis of comparison here, and it will then be augmented by the work of others.

I have selected three parishes in southern France for which usable registers dating from the late sixteenth century survive—Pont-de-Camarès (today Camarès, in the Rouergue, on the northern fringes of the Lacaune Mountains), Coutras (in Périgord on the Dronne, northeast of Bordeaux), and Labastide St-Amans (today St-Amans-Soult, in the mountains of Haut Languedoc, southeast of Castres).[78] As with some of the Scots registers examined earlier, the condition of the records forces the quantitative historian to be selective and gather cases from particular years, or periods

---

[75] Oudot de Dainville, "Le Consistoire de Ganges à la fin du XVIᵉ siècle," *Revue d'histoire de l'église de France* 18 (1932), 464-85, at 464, 466, 474.

[76] François Martin, "Ganges, action de son consistoire et vie de son église aux 16ᵉ et 17ᵉ siècle," *Revue de théologie et d'action evangéliques* 2 (1942), 17-40, 130-59; Solange Bertheau, "Le Consistoire dans les Eglises Réformées du Moyen-Poitou au XVIIᵉ Siècle," *BSHPF* 116 (1970), 332-59, 513-49; E. Delteil, "Institutions et vie de l'église réformée de Pont-de-Camarès (1574-1576)" in Michel Péronnet, ed., *Les Eglises et leurs institutions au XVIieme siècle: Actes du Vieme colloque du Centre d'Histoire de la Réforme et du Protestantisme,* (Montpellier: Université Paul Valéry, 1978), 95-113.

[77] Most notably Janine Garrisson-Estèbe and Raymond Mentzer. Their work will be discussed more fully below.

[78] The registers are Pont-de-Camarès: Ars. ms 6563; Coutras: Ars. ms 6559 (mostly transcribed and published by Albert Soman as "Le registre consistorial de Coutras, 1582-1584," *BSHPF* 126 (1980), 193-228; Labastide St-Amans: AD Tarn ms I8 (until recently AD Tarn E5383bis).

longer than a year, for which the record seems most complete.[79] Although
all three parishes are in the southern part of the realm and thus geographically unrepresentative, their location is itself a reflection of the numerical
strength of protestantism, largely restricted to the south after 1572.[80]

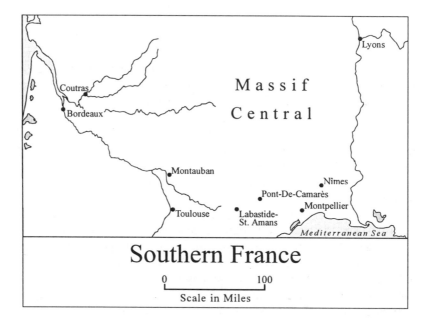

Pont-de-Camarès

Pont-de-Camarès was situated on a small river, the Dourdou, just at the
northern end of a tight valley, at a point where the river meandered north
toward the neighboring town of Montlaur across a wider plain. Mountains
rose immediately to the south and west of Pont-de-Camarès. In the mid-
sixteenth century it was a market town in a region blessed with pasture,
wheat and fruit trees. Although not particularly large, it was a judicial seat,
and home to a royal *procureur*.[81] The date at which its protestant church
was founded is unknown, although there was a Reformed congregation there

---

[79] One should bear in mind, however, that gaps or shortages in registers can indicate more
than simple lapses in record-keeping. Consistories may also have suspended or limited their
activities because of war, disease, or lack of enthusiasm.

[80] Salmon, *Society in Crisis*, 191-3; Benedict, *Huguenot Population of France*, 29.

[81] Delteil, "Institutions et vie...," 95, citing Jacques Bousquet, ed., *L'Enquête sur les
commodités du pays de Rouergue en 1552*, (Toulouse: Privat, 1969).

in 1564, when Catholic troops campaigned in the area.[82] The congregation apparently survived those difficulties, and its records begin in January 1574, with a listing of the minister and consistory at that time.[83] The minister was Bernard Constans, from Montlaur. Eight elders were named, headed by M. de Las Ribes, a local nobleman, and including Raymond Cest, the town's first consul.[84] In addition, the consistory chose a deacon of the poor (a member of the Mazars, a local merchant family which also supplied one elder), a reader (the notary Jean Solier), a clerk and an *advertisseur*, whose duty it was to summon offenders.

While the clerk often claimed the consistory was "complet" for a particular meeting, those occasions on which he did list names of participating elders give the impression that the consistory was dominated by an active clique of four or five, including Las Ribes.[85] In fact, the consistory seems to have primarily represented the town oligarchy.[86] The latter was a contentious group, as the consistory register makes clear. The minister and elders seem to have spent most of their time trying to patch up disputes between prominent residents of the town, some of whom were elders themselves. As table 9.1 shows, more than half of the consistory's disciplinary efforts involved peacemaking, and about half of the disputants were prominent individuals. If one adds the top three offense categories in the table, the resulting total of 54 cases dwarfs the remaining 26 cases from all other categories combined. And although the consistory does not seem to have pried into the domestic squabbles of the town oligarchy, the extrafamilial quarrels of the consuls, elders and notaries of Pont-de-Camarès were its leading concern. Several of these men made regular appearances before the consistory; the most extreme example is that of Guillame de Mazars, who alone accounted for six of the 80 cases in the parish register for 1574-5. Five of his six appearances involved disputes.

The high percentage of élite offenders throughout the disciplinary caseload may be a reflection of both recidivism and the status of protestants in the town and surrounding countryside. Huguenots controlled the town and its major offices, but much of the rest of the population may have been Catholic and therefore not subject to consistorial discipline.[87] The consistory

---

[82] *Hist. Ecc.*, 3:223-4, 233-4.

[83] Ars. ms 6563, 1r.

[84] Cest is identified as "premier consul" on *ibid*, 6v.

[85] E.g. *ibid*, 1v, 2r-v, 3r-v, 4r, 5r, 21r, 27r.

[86] A probability also noted by Delteil. See "Institutions et vie...", 96.

[87] For the failure of protestantism to take hold among the peasantry and lower classes in most regions, see Greengrass, *French Reformation*, 61-2; Garrisson-Estèbe, *Protestants du Midi*, 45-6, 335. J.H.M. Salmon, however, has argued against the stereotype of a uniformly Catholic peasantry, particularly in, among other places, the Rouergue. See his *Society in*

TABLE 9.1—DISCIPLINARY CASELOAD OF THE PONT-DE-CAMARES CONSISTORY, 1574-75

Offense category	Total	Male	Female	Elite	No-shows
Extrafam. disputes	36 (45%)	34	2	20	2
Violent attacks	11 (14%)	11	0	6	2
Domestic disputes	7 (9%)	3	4	-	1
Dances, games	6 (8%)	6	0	2	-
Sexuality	5 (6%)	3	2	-	-
Dealings w/Caths	4 (5%)	3	1	1	-
Totals	80	70	10	34	8

(Note: numbers within listed sin categories do not equal the totals due to other cases scattered throughout less numerous categories.)

did take steps to protect the peasantry, as when it disciplined two men (one of them the elder Simon Mazars) for having stabbed a peasant outside the town gates, but the fact that the peasant was not even named suggests that he was not a member of the congregation.[88] Later, the consistory joined the town's consuls in writing a military governor in the area to complain that his soldiers were extorting too much from the local peasantry.[89] But the peasants themselves rarely appeared before the consistory, and may have had little knowledge of, or concern for, its activities.

The local notables were another matter, however. To them, the consistory was clearly an important institution, and the threat of removal from the office of eldership was, for some, a significant deterrent to misbehavior. The elder Etienne Sabatier, a contentious fellow (judging by his disciplinary record), clashed violently with Simon Bonnet, "quest grand scandalle en leglize de dieu reformee au pont de Camarez" in May 1574. The scandal was so great that the consistory ruled that a public reconciliation was necessary, and threatened to depose Sabatier as elder if he refused. The

---

Crisis, 138.

[88] Ars. ms 6563, 7v.

[89] *Ibid*, 27r-v.

threat apparently worked, as the matter was not mentioned again.[90] There was a sense that, while some quarrels could be settled privately, those which had led to violence could not. In such cases, there had to be public reconciliation or repentance. On 25 December 1574, the consistory considered the question of whether Jehan Paullyan should take Communion, "considering the murder which he has committed." It ruled that he had to abstain, at least for the time being.[91] When B. Marausse and Jehan Alric quarreled in November 1575 because the latter had sent a servant to cut some trees belonging to the former, it was Marausse who had to perform public repentance, because he had struck the servant. The larger issue—a property question—was referred to civil judges for settlement.[92]

This referral suggests that the consistory was wary of intruding upon the jurisdiction of secular courts. In other cases, it explicitly defended the honor and authority of the magistrates. When Gregoire Genes quarreled with Raymond Cest, *premier consul* and consistorial elder, both men were censured, but Genes in particular was warned never again to utter "defamatory words against the magistrate."[93] Of course, the magistrate in question was presumably Cest, so by defending the magistracy, the elders were really defending themselves. The reputation of the consistory was also in part dependent on the reputation of the minister. When the former elder Bernard Raymond publicly berated the pastor Constans in October 1575, "essentially telling him to go to the Devil," the elders ruled that a deacon or the consistory's clerk should make a public pronouncement the following Sunday condemning the use of such language—against the pastor or anyone else.[94]

In addition to these public quarrels among the town's leaders, the consistory delved into some domestic disputes, although the combatants involved do not appear to have been so prominent. Jean Mithau was admonished privately for speaking ill of his mother.[95] In another case, a domestic shouting match came to the consistory's attention. The mother-in-law assured the elders that the issue had been minor, "concerning the affairs of the house [and] of little importance," which had led to the younger

---

[90] *Ibid*, 6r. Garrisson-Estèbe has suggested that such threats carried great weight, due to the prestige associated with the Huguenot eldership. See her *Protestants du Midi*, 114.

[91] Ars. ms 6563, 10r: "...attendu la murtre [que] luy [a] comys."

[92] *Ibid*, 30v.

[93] *Ibid*, 6v: "...parolles Injurieuses [con]tre le Magistraict..."

[94] *Ibid*, 28v: "...semblables parolles alles au diable." For a lengthy dispute between Constans and the Lieutenant Barbut over the former's refusal to allow the latter's 8-year-old niece to serve as godmother during a baptism, see *ibid*, 13r-15r, 17r-v, 18r-19v, 20r, 22v-23r, 25v, 32r-33v. This case is discussed by Delteil in "Institutions et vie...", 102-3.

[95] Ars. ms 6563, 12r.

woman shouting "dirty, wicked words." The two were told to patch things up or face further discipline.[96]

This preoccupation with conflict resolution, which may have been deemed necessary in order to hold together the civic oligarchy and thus preserve its power, left little room for discipline on other fronts. The attack on popular pastimes, particularly dancing and games, so characteristic of other Huguenot consistories, was hardly visible here. The same can be said for Catholic practices or dealings with Catholics, also a subject of much concern elsewhere. In addition, there were relatively few cases involving sexuality, but this is not so unusual among French consistorial caseloads. The consistory's concentration on conflicts among notables meant that women were much less likely to be disciplined at Pont-de-Camarès than elsewhere; seven-eighths of those accused or summoned by the consistory were men, and it was only in the categories of domestic dispute and sexuality that the (small) numbers approached gender equality. The register of Pont-de-Camarès for the period 1574-5 does highlight the significance of peacemaking, a prime concern of Huguenot consistories. The elders of other Huguenot congregations spent a lot of time patching up quarrels, but devoted significant attention to other matters as well. The records of the parish of Coutras, far north and west of Pont-de-Camarès, will demonstrate this.

Coutras

Coutras was smaller than Pont-de-Camarès in the sixteenth century, lacking the latter's legal establishment and local importance. On the other hand, it was close to a major population center (Bordeaux), and it played a greater role on the national political scene. The local castle housed Catherine de Medici during a visit in 1578, and the duke of Alençon in 1580-1. In October 1587, Henry of Navarre's Huguenot army crushed a royal force under the duc de Joyeuse at Coutras, killing Joyeuse in the process.[97] The town was situated on the Dronne river, and its Reformed consistory claimed jurisdiction over the protestants of Lilbourne, just southwest on the Dordogne, as well as those of Coutras and the surrounding countryside.[98]

A recent demographic study of the Huguenot population nationally in the seventeenth century has suggested an annual baptismal rate for Coutras of 14.1 during the period 1600-09, which would yield a population of roughly

---

[96] *Ibid*, 27v: "...touchant les affaires dela maison de petite importance," leading to "parolles salles e[t] meschantes."

[97] Salmon, *Society in Crisis*, 241; Soman, ed., "Registre consistorial de Coutras," 197.

[98] Several elders and deacons from Lilbourne and other neighboring villages were named to the consistory in 1578. See Ars. ms 6559, 1v.

550.[99] A flock that small may have been easier to police than others we have encountered; it is probably the least populous individual parish, Scottish or French, examined in this study. The consistory itself was sometimes smaller than others as well; one list of members given for May 1584 shows only four elders, two deacons, and an *advertisseur*.[100] Election seems generally to have taken the form of cooptation, as it did elsewhere.[101] Because sederunts are not given, it is impossible to discern whether all elders and deacons took an active part in the consistory's activities. The pastor, named du Cygne, had formerly served as minister at Agen.[102]

While the consistory of Coutras devoted significant attention to interpersonal conflicts in the early 1580s, it differed markedly from that of Pont-de-Camarès in the mid-1570s in the amount of time it spent trying to curb parishioners' participation in various aspects of popular culture. Games, dances and other sorts of amusements, which seem to have been particularly popular among the young men of the parish, were not to be

TABLE 9.2—DISCIPLINARY CASELOAD OF THE COUTRAS CONSISTORY, 1581-84

Offense category	Total	Male	Female	Elite	No-shows
Dances, games	16 (24%)	13	3	2	6
Domestic disputes	11 (17%)	9	2	2	1
Dealings w/Caths	9 (14%)	6	3	4	5
Extrafam. disputes	6 (9%)	5	1	-	3
Sexuality	3 (4%)	2	1	1	-
Disobeyed Church	3 (4%)	2	1	-	1
Totals	66	52	14	11	22

(Note: numbers within listed sin categories do not equal the total due to other cases scattered throughout less numerous categories.)

---

[99] Benedict, *Huguenot Population of France*, 135. I have based the estimate of 550 by multiplying 14.1 by the factor of 40 commonly employed for determining population in the rural districts of pre-industrial Europe.

[100] Ars. ms 6559, 9v.

[101] E.g., in June 1582. See *ibid*, 16r.

[102] Soman, ed., "Registre consistorial de Coutras," 196.

tolerated. This concern is demonstrated in table 9.2.

Some of these dancers and gamblers seem to have had little regard for the consistory, or the untraditional morality it tried to impose. We have already heard from Jean Seguineau the younger, who hinted to an elder who censured him for dancing that the censors of the consistory merely opposed dancing because they were no good at it themselves.[103] A third of those summoned for offenses in this category refused to appear before the elders. Daniel Faure and Catherine Arnauld were called twice for dancing on the day they became engaged, but never appeared on that particular charge.[104] Jean Maupille *le vieux* was censured in December 1582 because, "despite all remonstrances, he will not stay away from the dances." Six months later he was back again, this time threatened with excommunication because he had broken his promise to stop dancing, but the consistory decided merely to suspend him from Communion instead.[105] Some of these dancers were also gamblers; Faure and two others faced charges in June 1583 that they had played cards for money "et fet plusieurs blasphemes" on a Sunday during preaching. Others played ninepins on the Sabbath.[106] Like Calvin himself in Geneva, the elders of Coutras faced their own libertine opposition.[107]

As the son of a local *sieur*, Faure may have viewed the elders as social equals or inferiors, and thus fretted little over their scolding. But most of those summoned for dancing, gaming, and other forms of entertainment were not so prominent, and resistance from them was more likely to have been a manifestation of the clash between tradition and innovation. Historians have viewed the early modern period as one during which community leaders began to frown on, and draw away from, popular amusements in which their forbears had happily participated.[108] When Jehan Morin the younger was disciplined for having, with several companions, put on masks and women's clothes and run through the streets of Coutras on Mardi Gras, the consistory called such behavior "an abomination before

---

[103] Ars. ms 6559, 20v, quoted at the beginning of this chapter.

[104] *Ibid*, 18r-v. Faure did eventually appear on other charges, most notably a quarrel with his mother-in-law, which will be discussed below.

[105] *Ibid*, 18v: "...nonobstant toutes remonstrance, il ne s'abstient des dances.", 21v.

[106] *Ibid*, 23r, 28v.

[107] André Biéler, *L'homme et la femme dans la morale calviniste*, (Genève: Labor et Fides, 1963), 129-30.

[108] Peter Burke, *Popular Culture in Early Modern Europe*, (London: Maurice Temple Smith, 1978), 207-22, 270-81.

God."[109] In fact, the elders may have feared the excess and disorder which often resulted from such traditional festivities as much as they feared divine displeasure for allowing them to go on.

Neighborliness and marriage alliances were also traditions which the elders viewed as carrying some danger, since they could bring parishioners into contact with Catholics. In November 1582, Arnauld Biais was made to acknowledge publicly that he had sinned in becoming engaged to Perrine D'Arnauld "before she had renounced idolatry and promised to serve God according to the discipliñe of the Reformed Church."[110] The widow of Jean Berthet de Guîtres refused to make a similar confession; she had allowed her daughter Marie to marry Pierre Coulomb before he had joined the Reformed Church, although he had since done so. Significantly, the elders chose not to press her further on the matter.[111] Likewise, the notary Martial Girault was let off with a private confession before the consistory for having married his daughter to a Catholic, despite the fact that he had even assisted (and danced!) at the wedding. The consistory ruled that such a private confession was acceptable because the offense was not widely known.[112] Clearly, the minister and elders were wary of alienating prominent parishioners and thus driving them back to the Catholic Church.

In other instances, the consistory was quicker to require public rituals. Pierre Chastaignier had sought the aid of a local sorcerer to heal his son of a fever. The sorcerer had given him a small tablet (*brevet*) with words emblazoned on it to cure the boy. Chastaignier claimed he had been unaware that such an act constituted sin, but he was ordered to confess his offense and declare his repentance in front of the congregation. Further, the consistory, "for the common edification of the church," ordered that the tablet be broken up before the same audience "as an instrument of the Devil for abusing those who are weak in faith or rebels against the truth of God."[113] Cases involving such magic were rare among the Huguenots; the magicians themselves were usually beyond the control of the consistories although, like the Scots kirk sessions, consistories could occasionally attack

---

[109] Ars. ms 6559, 26v-27r: "...ce qui est abomination devant Dieu." Morin was required to perform public repentance for the act. His companions were never named, and may have been Catholics not subject to the consistory.

[110] *Ibid*, 18r: "...avant qu'elle eust abjuré l'idolatrie et protesté de servir à Dieu selon la discipline de l'esglise reformée."

[111] *Ibid*, 14v.

[112] *Ibid*, 30r.

[113] *Ibid*, 14v: "Et...le consistoire a esté d'avis, pour la commune edification de l'eglise, que le brevet seroit leu publicquement dimanche prochain en l'assemblée, brisé et cassé comme un instrument du diable pour abuser ceux qui sont informes en foy ou rebelles à la vérité de Dieu."

the problem by discouraging the consumer.

The Coutras consistory certainly heard its fair share of quarrels. Relations within families proved particularly troublesome. Daniel Faure got into a row with his mother-in-law on the day of his wedding in the summer of 1583 over goods which he claimed belonged to his wife. The consistory tried to reconcile the pair, but the woman, Marguerite Langloix, insisted on legal action. Since Faure avowed his willingness to accept reconciliation, he was allowed to take Communion, while she was barred. The matter dragged on for nearly two months before she was induced to forgive him.[114] Pierre Vincent, already in trouble for alleged adultery, was suspended from Communion in September 1582 when he quarreled with his brother, threatening "to slit his throat and throw him in the river."[115] Later, he was accused of beating his daughter, a charge he denied.[116] M. de Serpe, a local notable, was urged in August 1583 to end his estrangement from his wife, despite his claim that her relatives had sent out twenty arquebusiers and fourteen horsemen to ambush and kill him the previous March! Since he was also suspected of adultery and keeping a priest in his house, the consistory suspended him from Communion.[117]

Such suspensions were usually the most severe penalty the Huguenot consistories would impose. Some might carry a specific term, such as one or two Communion celebrations, but many were indefinite, and would last until the offender admitted sinning.[118] Twelve offenders were suspended by the Coutras consistory during the period 1581-4. Excommunication, on the other hand, was reserved for lost causes. This ultimate sanction was only imposed twice by the Coutras consistory during this period; both were cases of apostasy in which the elders saw little hope of bringing the offender back within the fold.[119] Suspension was even more common, and excommunication equally uncommon, in the Reformed church at Labastide-St-Amans in the early 1590s. There, the war on popular culture, of which we have already seen evidence at Coutras, raged on unabated.

---

[114] *Ibid*, 26r-v, 28r.

[115] *Ibid*, 17v.

[116] *Ibid*, 24v.

[117] *Ibid*, 18r, 19r-v, 27v. Serpe gave other reasons for not wanting to be reunited with her as well.

[118] Raymond Mentzer, "Individual, Community, and Church: French Calvinists in the Reformation Era," paper delivered to the American Society for Church History's spring meeting in Richmond, Va., April 1991. I am grateful to Professor Mentzer for providing me with a copy of the paper.

[119] Ars. ms 6559, 29r-v, 32r.

Labastide-St-Amans

Labastide-St-Amans, in a narrow river valley among the mountains of Haut Languedoc southeast of Castres, was a solidly protestant town by the early 1590s. The seigneurs of St-Amans, the Génibrouse family, had avowed the Reformed faith since the early 1560s. The seigneur in 1590 was Guillame Génibrouse, and his younger brother George was a well-known Huguenot officer.[120] Their religion had not prevented them from employing Catholic troops loaned by the governor of Castres to extract seigneural dues from their protestant tenants in 1572, however. The Génibrouses had direct control over the part of the town on the northern side of the river (the *ville-mage*), while an independent town was situated on the southern side.[121] It was there that the Reformed church under consideration here was located.

Although the town had been forced to accept a Catholic garrison in 1570 under the terms of the Treaty of St-Germain, the local Calvinists had risen

TABLE 9.3—DISCIPLINARY CASELOAD
OF THE LABASTIDE-ST-AMANS CONSISTORY, 1591-94

Offense category	Total	Male	Female	Elite	No-shows
Dances, games	35 (32%)	32	3	8	10
Intrafam. disputes	22 (20%)	5	17	5	-
Violent attacks	10 (9%)	9	1	-	-
Dealings w/Caths	10 (9%)	7	3	4	6
Domestic disputes	8 (7%)	7	1	3	4
Absence	8 (7%)	7	1	3	5
Sexuality	7 (6%)	4	3	3	-
Totals	110	79	31	28	28

(Note: numbers within listed sin categories do not equal the total due to other cases scattered throughout less numerous categories.)

---

[120] Jacques Gaches, *Mémoires sur les guerres de religion à Castres et dans le Languedoc (1555-1610) et suite des mémoires (1610-1612)*, (Genève: Slatkine Reprints, 1970), 14; Jean Calvet, *Histoire de la ville de St-Amans*, (Castres: Lucien Granier, 1887), 45-7.

[121] Calvet, *Histoire*, 47, 69-70.

up in October 1572 and ousted the Catholic troops. The last Catholic residents were driven out of town in 1581, and their houses were burned down. After that, Labastide-St-Amans was firmly protestant, although the *ville-mage* continued to be a haven for some Catholics.[122] Its annual baptismal rate at the beginning of the seventeenth century was 20.1, suggesting a population of around 800.[123] The pastor was A. Faure until April 1592, when Faure was replaced by a minister named Beranger.[124]

The makeup of the consistory reflected protestant control of the town. Ten members were listed in April 1592, one of whom was clearly a deacon. Four of the remaining nine were consuls. Four elders were added to the consistory in September 1593, one of them a consul, one an area *sieur*, and one who carried the title of "sire".[125] This was a group of considerable local prestige and importance, which had the weight of secular authority behind it. Table 9.3 gives an overview of its disciplinary activities.

This table gives a good illustration of what the minister and elders could do in a town controlled by Huguenots. Their leading behavioral concerns were dancing and gaming, disputes and assaults, and relations with Catholics. Sexuality, while not ignored, was not a primary concern either. When cases arose involving sex, it was often because some dispute had arisen. The consistory heard evidence in a dispute between Anne Amalrique, a former servant in the house of the consul Pierre Landes, and her ex-mistress. In the course of the case, the *bruit* arose that Landes had committed adultery with Amalrique. His reply (perhaps not entirely honest) was that he had never thought of such an evil deed, and that he had always behaved paternally toward the servant.[126] Josué de Berthomeu had a suspicious relationship with a widow, but he was charged with several other misdeeds as well, including hosting card games, attending masques, and employing servants who sang bawdy songs.[127]

Berthomeu's non-sexual offenses were much more typical of the consistory's disciplinary concerns during this period. When the elders heard that a certain La Balme, who had previously been warned on the subject, continued to host card games, he was summoned to appear and, "raising his

---

[122] *Ibid*, 66-9, 78-9. Many of the activities which the consistory considered unsavory seem to have taken place in the ville-mage. Catholics were not subject to the consistory's disciplinary authority. For a case apparently dismissed when the consistory determined that the offender was a Catholic, see AD Tarn ms I8 (unfoliated), 19 November 1591.

[123] Benedict, *Huguenot Population*, 143.

[124] AD Tarn ms I8, 24 January 1588, 19 April 1592.

[125] *Ibid*, 10 September 1593. I am grateful to Raymond Mentzer for sharing with me his transcriptions of some of the disciplinary cases in this register.

[126] *Ibid*, 9-10 and 12 January 1591.

[127] *Ibid*, 4 and 15 January, 6 February 1591, 18 December 1592, 30 January 1594.

hand to God," promised never to do so again.[128] The consistory considered such games a serious matter, because they induced men to waste their time and money. The Captain Martin became incensed at the consistory, and particularly the elder Antoine Mas, when the latter refused to give him a Communion token. Demanding to know the reason for his exclusion, he was told that he had been suspended for his card-playing and attendance at masques. Since he had ignored all summonses, the consistory had suspended him *in absentia*. Further, the elders decided to treat his rancor toward Mas as a separate offense, requiring public repentance.[129] The consistory apparently had an effective network of informers as well; M. del Toule was charged in September 1594 with having played cards in Castres.[130]

Dancing was likewise regarded as evil. When Balthazar Rey, charged with having danced on the *fête* of Notre-Dame, offered the excuse that someone had grabbed him by the arm and forced him, he was coldly reminded that "it is better to obey God than men," and ordered to perform public repentance, which he did.[131] Mathieu Bouye may have expected speedy forgiveness when he readily admitted to having danced, but the elders replied that since he had danced publicly, he must repent publicly as well.[132]

The consistory of Labastide-St-Amans was also more willing than the other French consistories examined here to to summon women for offenses. Discipline at Pont-de-Camarès was largely a masculine phenomenon, with 88 percent of all cases involving male offenders. This tendency was somewhat less pronounced at Coutras, where the caseload was only 79 percent male. At Labastide-St-Amans male cases still predominated, but 28 percent of those charged were women. This consistory seems to have been more willing than the others to reach into the household and hold women responsible for their own behavior, rather than simply operating through male relatives. A deputation of elders visited the wife of the *sieur* Pierre Landes in the summer of 1594 and scolded her for having worn a fancy hairpiece too soon after her father's death. As a result, she was told to abstain from the next Communion celebration. While the consistory considered her individually responsible, she defended herself with a traditional plea: she had worn the hairpiece on her husband's orders. Landes himself then appealed her suspension to the colloquy of Lauragais, but the

---

[128] *Ibid*, 15 November 1592: "...levant la maien a dieu..." This procedure was common in extracting promises of good behavior.

[129] *Ibid*, 4 September 1594.

[130] *Ibid*, 21 September 1594.

[131] *Ibid*, 10 and 19 September 1593: "Il vaud mieux houbeir à dieu qu'aux hommes."

[132] *Ibid*, 10 September 1593.

outcome is not reported.[133]

Women at Labastide-St-Amans were charged with quarrelling more than anything else. Indeed, 61 percent of cases involving females concerned some kind of dispute, compared with only 27 percent of those involving males. Female wrath could turn as violent as the male equivalent; when Anne Combaire encountered Pierre Averons (who had accused her of suspicious behavior with Josué de Berthomeu) in the *ville-mage* one day she went at him with a knife, crying "scoundrel, give me back my reputation!"[134] Most quarrels between women did not come to blows, however, and private reconciliation was usually all the consistory required.[135]

Public offenses could require public repentance, as we have seen in the cases of dancing already mentioned. Suspension was another option commonly employed; at least 36 of the 110 cases at Labastide-St-Amans led to suspensions for one or more Communion celebrations. While some were thus barred from Communion, the consistory was careful to ensure that all those eligible to participate did indeed partake of the sacrament. Laurence Flottes did not take Communion at Christmas 1590 and was questioned about it. He replied that he had abstained because his son Jacques had been barred (the younger Flottes had mortally wounded another man in a fight the previous summer). Told that he had sinned by thus removing himself from the community, Laurence Flottes apologized, and was told to participate in the future.[136] Janine Garrisson-Estèbe has suggested that consistories were strong in southern France because they were the gatekeepers to Communion, "une nécessité existentielle" in the publicly-oriented meridional culture of the Midi.[137] But the evidence from Labastide-St-Amans suggests that, at least for some individual Huguenots, Communion was not such a necessity, and might be avoided for familial or other reasons.

Despite the disdain of a few, the consistory was a powerful institution in this small Huguenot town. It kept a close watch on the behavior of its flock, trying to ensure that members did not waste time and money in idle

---

[133] AD Tarn ms I8, 15 August, 23 December 1594, 19 February 1595.

[134] *Ibid*, 6 February 1591: "Elle l'avoyt assailli avec ung couteau en sa main, criant: Meschant, tu me rendas icy mon honneur." Averons was apparently unhurt in the attack.

[135] E.g. Marguerite Albert vs. Domingé Fabre, *ibid*, 4 January 1591; wife of Labbuie vs. wife of J. Fabre, *ibid*, 19 November 1591; widow Dammer vs. widow Malz Oncle, *ibid*, 11 December 1594.

[136] *Ibid*, 31 August 1590; 15 January 1591. Similar inquiries were launched regarding the Lieutenant Payrin and the widow Remdomies. See *ibid*, 20 January 1591. The younger Flottes was suspended again in December 1594 for a dispute which led to swordplay. See *ibid*, 21 December 1594.

[137] Garrisson-Estèbe, *Protestants du Midi*, 116, 246.

pursuits, carry grudges, or backslide into Catholicism. Its reach was long, and it rarely excused faults. Of the three Huguenot consistories examined here, it seems to have been the most active and the most firmly entrenched. This may in part be a function of time (the 1590s instead of earlier decades), geography (Languedoc being a protestant stronghold), or unique local circumstances (a few particularly diligent elders, perhaps). But rather than offering generalizations based only on three examples, it might be useful to compare these results with those of some other Huguenot consistories which have been studied in a similar manner by other historians.

Other Case Studies

Both Garrisson-Estèbe and Raymond Mentzer have taken a quantitative approach to the study of French consistory records in the late sixteenth century. While one can never be sure that one is using the same classification system employed by another, a comparison of the data presented above with the findings of Garrisson-Estèbe and Mentzer might strengthen the argument for the importance of some of the tendencies noted here.

In light of the comparison to Scotland, three differences seem particularly important. First, while illicit sexuality made up 55% of the cases handled by Scottish kirk sessions in the period 1560-1610, (and 48% of the cases handled by presbyteries), it did not top six percent in any of the three French parishes examined here. Secondly, disputes and violence, which loom so large in the French examples, ranging between 26 and 68 percent for all three categories of discord,[138] made up less than ten percent of the caseloads of kirk sessions and presbyteries. Thirdly, popular culture, insignificant in the Scots data, accounted for eight to 32 percent of the French caseloads.[139]

Based on her reading of the records of thirteen consistories (but none of the three examined above) during the period 1560-1610, Garrisson-Estèbe has compiled a database of 3485 "cas." But these "cas" are not directly comparable to the cases in my own samples. It appears that she classifies any item of business recorded in a consistorial register as a "cas." About a third of these are not really disciplinary cases, but rather matters of ecclesiastical administration, such as the payment of ministers or communications with colloquies, synods or other churches. This also

---

[138] The three categories are: disputes within families, extrafamilial disputes, and violent attacks. These three categories totalled 68 percent at Pont-de-Camarès, 36 percent at Labastide-St-Amans, and 26 percent at Coutras.

[139] Of 4594 cases in the Scottish kirk session database, only 33 (0.5 percent) involved dancing or gaming. Of 1191 presbytery cases, none did. These types of offenses totalled 32 percent at Labastide-St-Amans, 23 percent at Coutras, and 8 percent at Pont-de-Camarès.

suggests (although she does not make herself clear on this point) that an
individual offense discussed at more than one meeting would be counted as
a "cas" each time it was brought up, whereas I would classify it as one
case. Thus cases which took a long time to resolve would carry more than
their fair share of weight in Garrisson-Estèbe's collection. She also gives
little guidance as to how many "cas" she has gathered from each locality,
although she does make the distinction between urban churches (Nîmes and
Montauban—1349 "cas") and "petites villes et bourgades" (2136 "cas").[140]

TABLE 9.4—SOME ASPECTS OF DISCIPLINE
IN THE MIDI, 1560-1610
(after Janine Garrisson-Estèbe)

Offense category	Number of Cases	Percentage
Extrafamilial disputes	505	22%
Domestic disputes	186	8%
Violence	113	5%
Popular culture	401	17%
Sexuality	188	8%
Total	2343	100%[141]

But keeping in mind the likelihood of double-, triple- and even quadruple-
counting of cases which had to be discussed repeatedly, it is possible to use
Garrisson-Estèbe's listings of items by category to reassemble her data in
a manner comparable to mine, both for France and Scotland, removing
items relating to ecclesiastical administration.[142] I have done this in table
9.4, concentrating on the issues of popular culture, dispute resolution and
sexuality.[143]

These figures suggest that the evidence from Pont-de-Camarès, Coutras
and Labastide-St-Amans examined above was typical. Various forms of
discord account for 35 percent of the total, popular culture received a

---

[140] Garrisson-Estèbe, *Protestants du Midi*, 100-103. Items of ecclesiastical administration
figure more heavily (nearly 50 percent) in the data from urban churches than in that of the
small towns and village churches (25 percent).

[141] Of the 40 percent which is unaccounted for in this listing, seven-eighths of it falls into
Garrisson-Estèbe's broad category of "encadrement religieux," which covers relations with
Catholics, active Catholicism, witchcraft, Sabbath breach, absence from sermons or Com-
munion and a host of other items.

[142] Listings given in *ibid*, 238-9, 244-5.

[143] By "popular culture" I mean dancing, gaming, and charivari.

significant amount of attention,[144] and sexuality made up less than one-tenth of the consistories' disciplinary business. Mentzer's analysis of the consistorial records of Nîmes and two rural consistories in the Cévennes supplies further evidence of these preoccupations.[145] Like my own, his data includes only discipline, so items of ecclesiastical administration do not need to be removed. Table 9.5 is drawn from his data, with the distinction made between urban and rural discipline.

TABLE 9.5—FRENCH URBAN AND RURAL DISCIPLINE, 1560-86
(after Raymond Mentzer)

Offense category	Nîmes (%)	Rural (%)
All disputes	816 (50%)	149 (41%)
"Ecclesiastical" sins*	283 (18%)	108 (30%)
Popular culture	257 (16%)	65 (18%)
Sexuality	121 (7.5%)	6 (2%)
Totals+	1624 (100%)	364 (100%)

*includes relapse into Catholicism, resort to magic, absence from church or Communion, Sabbath-breach, etc.
+listed percentages do not add up to 100 due to other cases scattered throughout additional categories.

Again, the heavy concern to preserve harmony within the community, the eagerness to attack some aspects of popular culture, and the minimal attention given to sexual behavior are all clearly demonstrated. Mentzer also makes gender distinctions in his data which reinforce another trend noted earlier—that French consistories were at first reluctant to discipline women directly, but did so to a greater extent once they became more established. His rural evidence from the 1560s creates a caseload which is 88 percent male, while that from the period 1579-86 is only 70 percent male. Granted, the women summoned were probably not flattered by the attention, but such data may demonstrate an increasing regard for the individuality of women.

---

[144] Popular culture is also probably underrepresented in the percentages because cases involving dancing, gaming or charivari usually did not require repeated discussion.

[145] The rural parishes are Bédarieux (data from 1579-86) and St-Gervais-sur-Mare (1564-8). See Raymond Mentzer, "Disciplina nervus ecclesiae: The Calvinist Reform of Morals at Nîmes," *Sixteenth Century Journal* 18 (1987), 89-115; *ibidem*, "Le consistoire et la pacification du monde rural," *BSHPF* 135 (1989), 373-90.

Comparative Reformed Discipline in Scotland and France

All of the data thus far examined can now be combined, in order to demonstrate clearly the differences in disciplinary practices between Reformed Scotland and Huguenot France in the late sixteenth and early seventeenth centuries which have been identified here. Table 9.6 presents these findings.

The similarities within the French data are clear. Equally apparent are the differences between the Scottish and French caseloads.[146] But the question of how to account for these differences remains. How can two disciplinary systems, remarkably similar both in their theoretical foundations (Calvin and the two national *Disciplines*), and in the nature of their personnel and administration (ministers and lay elders in local consistories

TABLE 9.6—COMPARISON OF DISCIPLINARY DATA FOR
SCOTLAND AND FRANCE, 1560-1610 (all figures are percentages
from the samples discussed earlier)

1 - Scots kirk sessions, 1560-1610
2 - Scots presbyteries, 1581-1610
3 - Pont-de-Camarès, Coutras and Labastide-St-Amans, 1574-94
4 - Various consistories in the Midi, 1560-1610 (Garrisson-Estèbe)
5 - Nîmes, 1561-63, 1578-83 (Mentzer)
6 - St-Gervais-sur-Mare and Bédarieux, 1564-86 (Mentzer)

Offense category	1	2	3	4	5	6
Sexuality	55	48	6	8	7.5	2
All disputes	9	8	44	34	50	41
Popular culture	0.5	-	22	17	16	18
Total cases in sample	4594	1191	256	2343	1624	364

---

[146] This evidence should also call into question the Calvinist/Catholic dichotomy in social discipline asserted by R. Po-Chia Hsia, in which Calvinists were primarily concerned with sexual discipline and Catholics with religious conformity. Clearly, not all Calvinists were obsessed with sex. For the claim, see his *Social Discipline in the Reformation: Central Europe 1550-1750*, (London: Routledge, 1989), 7.

summoning, questioning and disciplining offenders), have taken such divergent paths?

The Huguenot churches were at first gathered, voluntary communities. Even once they became established, their members still had another religious alternative—the Catholic Church—which was entirely legal. It was an option which may have been difficult to choose, depending on time, location and individual circumstances, but it was always there. French protestants who resented the intrusiveness of the elders could return to the faith of their grandfathers, and the consistories had to beware that they did not push them to do so by excessive rigor in the correction of vices. As Pierre Martial told the Ganges elder who would not give him a Communion token in May 1600, "if you do not want to give me Communion, I'll go drink white wine with the papists!"[147]

But it also seems logical that those who joined, or chose to remain a part of, this largely voluntary church were better prepared than the rest of the population to change their own lifestyles in response to religious ideals. Even where the flesh proved unable to maintain the new behavioral standards, the spirit was often willing to continue the struggle. Those Huguenots who were repeatedly warned to stop wasting their time and money on games of cards and dice may have seemed incorrigible to their ministers and elders, but they kept returning to the consistory to be admonished, and to seek renewed acceptance in the community.

The situation in Scotland was markedly different. For the Scots, there was no legal alternative faith after 1560. Of course, Catholicism lingered on in many towns and regions, but its influence steadily declined. Therefore, kirk sessions and presbyteries did not need to worry as much about the danger that excessive rigor would drive away members of their congregations. However, they faced another problem—a population which was in many cases protestant by default, but had little real interest in any Church, new or old.[148] This study has shown that many Scots saw the Church as a source of baptism and little else. They even considered Church-sanctioned marriage unnecessary until they were forced to change their ways by clergy who would not baptize "bastards" until the parents repented. By insisting on a Church which included all, the Scots reformers created a situation in which they had to play to the lowest common denominator, due both to the recalcitrance of much of the population, and the hesitancy of

---

[147] Registre Consistorial de Ganges, 21 May 1600, cited in François Martin, "Ganges, action de son consistoire et vie de son église aux 16ᵉ et 17ᵉ siècle," *Revue de théologie et d'action evangéliques* 2 (1942), 17-40, 130-59, at 20: "Si vous ne voulez pas me donner la Cène, j'irai prendre le vin blanc avec les papistes."

[148] For a discussion of similar problems for Reformed discipline in the Palatinate, see Estèbe and Vogler, "Genèse d'une société protestante," 385.

many traditionally-minded elders to view something like a game, a bonfire, or the celebration of Christmas as sinful. Further, as we have seen, the "official" legal status of the Reformed Kirk did not necessarily translate into vigorous support from secular authorities. In fact, the Scottish Reformed Kirk may have had the worst of both worlds—an unenthusiastic membership *and* little state support.

In many cases, particularly during the early years of reform in a given Scottish community, all that the ministers and elders could agree on was that illicit sexuality was a social problem, and that irregular relationships had to be formalized by marriage or ended.[149] There was also something of a clear and recent mandate on this issue—the parliamentary statutes of the 1560s against adultery, incest and fornication. Next (but not for several decades) came the effort to force Sabbath observance, in many ways an essential precondition for evangelization on a societal scale. Under such circumstances, issues such as the need for communal harmony or the war on popular culture would have to wait, and they did.

But in the religious patchwork which France had become in the late sixteenth century, it was essential for the Huguenots to maintain communal identity and solidarity. A feud between leading members of the Church was a far greater danger than an illicit relationship between them.[150] This does not mean that the latter would be tolerated, but it does mean that the former would be pursued with greater rigor. In this respect it is significant that at Emden in East Friesland, where a Reformed church (and consistory) was created in the mid-sixteenth century, but where other religious alternatives remained, sexual offenses did not even reach ten percent of the consistory's caseload until the 1640s, while various forms of quarrels were two to three times as common in the sixteenth century.[151]

In such circumstances certain codes of behavior came to define membership in the community. Even the Huguenot soldiers had something

---

[149] Sexuality was also the leading concern of English church courts in the late sixteenth century, although their structure and operation differed vastly from the Reformed Church courts of Scotland or France. See Martin Ingram, *Church Courts, Sex and Marriage in England, 1570-1640*, (Cambridge: Cambridge University Press, 1987), 68; Ralph Houlbrooke, *Church Courts and the People During the English Reformation 1520-1570*, (Oxford: Oxford University Press, 1979), 75-6; Robert Friedeburg, "Sozialdisziplinierung in England? Soziale Beziehungen auf dem Lande zwischen Reformation und 'Great Rebellion,' 1550-1642," *Zeitschrift für Historische Forschung* 17 (1990), 385-418.

[150] Studies have found that illegitimacy was widely spread throughout all social classes in sixteenth-century France, although no scholar has yet tried to compare illegitimacy rates for Catholics and Huguenots. See Michael Anderson, *Approaches to the History of the Western Family, 1500-1914*, (London: Macmillan, 1980), 21.

[151] Heinz Schilling, *Civic Calvinism in Northwestern Germany and the Netherlands*, (Kirksville, Mo.: Sixteenth Century Publishers, 1991), 44-8.

of a reputation for godliness. The commander François de la Noue bragged of the protestant troops in the first religious war: "among such a large gathering we heard no-one blaspheme the word of God...you could not find a box of dice or a pack of cards in the camp."[152] There is doubtless some exaggeration in this, but nobody would have made a similar statement about a sixteenth-century Scots army.

King Henri III of France issued an edict in May 1583 prohibiting the sale and transport of cards, tarot cards and dice without payment of a license fee. The French crown was always in need of cash, but the author of this particular edict seems to have had mixed feelings about the state making a profit from items which led to so much evil behavior. After explaining the provisions of the law, he added:

> Nevertheless it is seen by experience that games of cards, tarots and dice, instead of serving for pleasure and recreation as they were intended by those who invented them, only serve at present for notorious harm and public scandal, being games of chance subject to all sorts of cheating, fraud, and deceptions [which] bring great despair, quarrels, and blasphemies, murders, debauchery, ruin and perdition to families, and to those who make them their regular profession.

The edict went on to relate how the king preferred that his subjects would reform themselves and no longer partake of such vices, but that "this is very difficult, or even impossible to do." So, regulation of the trade in cards and dice was the best alternative.[153]

The king's ministers were aware of the dangers of gambling, but knew the limits of coercion. Most importantly, the crown needed revenue. Games of chance were an integral part of French popular culture, and an effort to restrict them, doomed as it was to failure, would only lead to resentment. Like the ministers and elders of the Scottish Kirk, the king of France had to concern himself with the whole population, and he knew better than most the magnetic attractions of vice. Some of his subjects took a more ambitious approach to this problem, however. They did not reform French society, and many of them did not even succeed in reforming themselves. But they took advantage of their positions as members of semi-voluntary communities

---

[152] Cited in Michael Walzer, *The Revolution of the Saints: A Study in the Origins of Radical Politics*, (Cambridge, Mass.: Harvard University Press, 1965), 87.

[153] *Receuil Gén.*, 14:550-3: "Néantmoins comme chacun voit par expérience les jeux des cartes, tarots et dez, au lieu de servir de plaisir et récréation selon l'intention de ceux qui les ont inventez, ne servent à present que de dommage notoire et scandale public, estans jeux de hazard subjets à toute espèce de piperie, fraudes, et déceptions apportans grande despence, querelles, et blasphêmes, meurtres, desbauches, ruynes, et perdition de familles, et de ceux que en font profession ordinaire." "...il est trés difficile, ou plustost impossible, de ce faire."

to seek what they perceived to be a higher standard of personal behavior. Their co-religionists in Scotland, like the royal government of France, were forced to take the more practical path.

CONCLUSION

THE USES OF REFORM

Every parish had a tyrant who made the greatest lord in the district stoop to his authority. The kirk was the place where he kept his court; the pulpit his throne or tribunal from whence he issued out his terrible decrees; and 12 or 14 soure, ignorant enthusiasts, under the title of elders, composed his council.
    - Ewan Cameron of Lochiel (1629-1719), *Memoirs*[1]

Cameron of Lochiel wrote from his experience of Scottish Reformed discipline at the height of its influence. As we have seen, such consistorial tyranny would have been impossible in the sixteenth century. Anticlericalism was one of the driving forces behind the Reformation, and many of the laymen who participated were in no hurry to institute a new kind of clerical domination.

But there were other strains of thought, in addition to anticlericalism, in Reformed ideology. One of the most powerful of these was the idea that society had become too unruly, and that some kind of order had to be restored. To ministers and those laymen who became zealous apostles of reform, order was necessary because God's wrath might lead Him to punish all, the elect as well as the reprobate, with fire, flood, disease, famine or some other angry manifestation of divine power.[2] This idea harmonized with the worldly and pragmatic views of other laymen who held positions of power but whose religiosity was entirely conventional. To them, disorder was more a social problem than an offense to God, although they would have agreed that it was the latter as well. They were concerned about bastardy, poverty, the activities of the poor, and the dangers presented by feuds and quarrels. It was this worldly group, indifferent to theology, which gave the Reformed disciplinary system the support it needed to become a force for change. Without the backing of such authorities the disciplinary apparatus would have been toothless, as it was in northern England, where the Church attempted to enforce discipline through the old system of bishops' courts, and offenders regularly ignored summonses.[3]

---

[1] Cited in G.D. Henderson, *The Scottish Ruling Elder*, (London: James Clarke, 1935), 100.

[2] For a discussion of this "primitive" world-view, see Mary Douglas, *Purity and Danger: An Analysis of the Concepts of Pollution and Taboo*, (London: Routledge and Kegan Paul, 1966), 81.

[3] John Addy, *Sin and Society in the Seventeenth Century*, (London: Routledge, 1989), 10-12.

This helps to explain the Scots' elders apparent obsession with sexuality. When the disciplinary system was first being erected, the ministers of the infant Reformed Kirk knew all too well how dependent they were on the support of local notables. Some of the latter were eager from the start to serve as elders, but others had to be cajoled. They were drawn into the system because with it they could attack what all authorities—Reformed, half-reformed and even tenaciously Catholic—agreed was a leading social problem, even when they could agree on little else. As the population grew, resources shrank, and beggars crowded the roads, even the most traditionalist elders were happy to seize the untraditional reins of church discipline to attack the problem of bastardy, although they had little interest in the rest of the Kirk's program. It was only after kirk sessions had been in place for a generation or more, and the disciplinary system was on firmer footing, that ministers and the more enthusiastic elders had the community support and accompanying self-confidence to take on other issues, such as the Sabbath, vestiges of Catholic piety, or the problem of discord within the community. Even once the disciplinary agenda had moved into these other areas, sexuality was still the bread and butter of Scots discipline, the constant element on the table of misbehavior. It had been the first category of offense taken up in the sixteenth century, and it was the last to go in the eighteenth, when the system withered because the secular authorities on whom it depended withdrew their support.[4] By then, in the lowlands, at least, the discipline of the Kirk was well on its way to being replaced by the disciplines of the military, the school, the state and the capitalistic employer.

In France, the Reformers faced different circumstances. The consistories could rarely count on much "official" support outside of a few firmly protestant towns such as Nîmes, and ministers and elders were aware of the danger that excessive rigor in discipline would drive members of their flocks back into the arms of the Catholics. Sinners in Huguenot communities were only rarely forced to make "reparation publique," while public repentance was a punishment commonly ordered for their Scots counterparts. In place of this reliance on ritual humiliation, the Huguenot ministers and elders chose to scold and reconcile. Their primary concern was to hold the community together while at the same time ensuring that its members would demonstrate godliness in their lifestyles. Discipline became a tool by which a minority population defined itself against a dominant majority.

---

[4] Rosalind Mitchison and Leah Leneman, *Sexuality and Social Control: Scotland 1660-1780*, (Oxford: Basil Blackwell, 1989), 76-8. The Toleration Act of 1712 took away from the Kirk the right to call on sheriffs to imprison excommunicants, although this practice had already fallen into disuse. See *ibid*, 28. See also *ibidem*, "Acquiescence in and Defiance of Church Discipline in Early Modern Scotland," *RSCHS* 25 (1993), 19-37.

This helps to explain the differences in Reformed disciplinary practice between Scotland and France. But despite such differences, the two systems had much in common. Most importantly, in both Reformed Scotland and Huguenot France, as well as in all other areas where some active disciplinary system took root, the lives of average people became subject to a greater degree of official scrutiny than ever before. The process may have been slow, fitful, and in some instances incomplete, but it was the imposition of social discipline which made the Reformation a practical reality, and a force in the lives of the population at large.

The members of that population whose voices we have heard here, as well as some of the elders who sought to change customs and behavior, might have been surprised (had they been alive more than four centuries later) to hear André Biéler claim that the reformers were "entirely driven by the teachings which they had taken from scripture," that the Reformation was, above all, a spiritual movement, and that moral reform was only a byproduct.[5] Could any thinker of the sixteenth—or any other—century have so divorced his or her thinking from the realities of everyday life? To claim that a movement was primarily spiritual, when the majority of the population felt it first in the form of a new authoritarianism, seems myopic, although the process certainly had its spiritual dimensions.

Writing several years after Biéler, Jean Delumeau took another view of the Reformation, both Catholic and protestant. Delumeau suggested that it was only during this period that much of the population of western Europe became truly Christianized. Traditional religious practices and popular beliefs were still loaded with pagan elements, and in the sixteenth and seventeenth centuries Catholic and protestant reformers alike branded many of them as idolatrous or satanic and sought their eradication.[6] Social discipline was only one part of this crusade, but consistorial registers contain many examples of its use to disseminate the new orthodoxies of the later sixteenth century. The thousands of individuals who contributed—through their misbehavior—to this study would undoubtedly be more inclined to agree with Delumeau than Biéler concerning the nature of the Reformation.

But it is not just historians of theology such as Biéler who have misjudged the Reformation by paying too much attention to texts and not enough to contexts. The social historians Emmanuel Le Roy Ladurie and T.C. Smout make the same error when they condemn the Reformed elders

---

[5] André Biéler, *L'Homme et la Femme dans la Morale Calviniste*, (Genève: Labor et Fides, 1963), 7-8: "tout entière conduite par les enseignements qu'ils ont tirés des saintes Ecritures."

[6] Jean Delumeau, *Catholicism Between Luther and Voltaire*, (London: Burns and Oates, 1977), 172, 175-7, 225.

for their tacit toleration of usury, for instance.[7] Certainly, the practice had been classified as sinful for many centuries, was condemned in both the Scots and French Reformed *Disciplines*, and was ostensibly limited by laws on the books in both realms.[8] But some usury was necessary for the purposes of commerce, and there was no real consensus in favor of its elimination. Usury did not lead to disorder; bastardy, popular rituals, feuding and gambling did. Regardless of the higher claims they might make, the Reformed consistories could only work within the confines of what most local powers would endorse or accept.

Heinz Schilling recently suggested that "a sufficient number of case studies from different spheres of European Calvinism...can be used to formulate universal statements concerning the contribution of Calvinist church discipline to the formation of the modern mind."[9] The Calvinist mind of the sixteenth and seventeenth centuries seems far removed from its modern permutations, and the world of the Communion token and the penitent stool distant from that of the driver's license and the state penitentiary. Much of the responsibility once claimed by the Church for the regulation of everyday life is now in the hands of the state. But many modern cultural assumptions may have indeed originated in the new order of social discipline during the Reformation era.[10] Certainly, the interest shown by local and central authorities in the activities of the individual has not waned in the interim.

---

[7] Emmanuel Le Roy Ladurie, *The Peasants of Languedoc*, (Urbana, Ill.: University of Illinois Press, 1974), 171; T.C. Smout, *A History of the Scottish People, 1560-1830*, (Glasgow: William Collins, 1969), 150.

[8] James Cameron, ed., *The First Book of Discipline*, (Edinburgh: St. Andrew Press, 1972), 166-7; James Kirk, ed., *The Second Book of Discipline*, (Edinburgh: St. Andrew Press, 1980), 202; François Méjan, ed., *La Discipline de L'Eglise Réformée de France*, (Paris: S.C.E.L., 1947), 294; *APS*, 3:451, 4:70, 133-4, 228-9; *Recueil Gén*, 11:600, 14:220, 307-10, 319, 428-9, 597, 15:263. It should also be noted that Reformed consistories were no more tolerant of usury than the medieval Catholic Church had been.

[9] Heinz Schilling, *Civic Calvinism in Northwestern Germany and the Netherlands*, (Kirksville, Mo.: Sixteenth Century Publishers, 1991), 40.

[10] For other reflections on this idea, incorporating the pioneering work of Norbert Elias, see Heiko Oberman, "*Europa Afflicta*: The Reformation of the Refugees," *ARG* 83 (1992), 91-111, at 109-10.

BIBLIOGRAPHY

Manuscript Sources:

Archives Départmentales du Tarn, Albi:
  I8 - Délibérations du Consistoire de Labastide-Saint-Amans (St-Amans-Soult), 1587-1604

Bibliothèque de l'Arsenal, Paris:
  6557 - Livre du Consistoire de Clermont, 1603-10
  6559 - Livre du Consistoire de Coutras, 1578-91
  6560 - Livre du Consistoire de Coutras, 1603-21
  6563 - Recueil de l'église réformée de Pont-de-Camarès, 1574-8

National Library of Scotland, Edinburgh:
  Advocates ms 29.2.8 - Balcarres Papers
  Advocates ms 31.1.1 - Extracts from Session Book of Perth

Registrar General's Office, New Register House, Edinburgh:
  OPR 165/3 - Rothiemay Parish Register 1601-49
  OPR 310/1 - Monifieth Parish Register 1562-1620
  OPR 403/1 - Anstruther Wester Parish Register 1577-1601

Scottish Record Office, Register House and West Register House, Edinburgh:
  CH2/1/1 - Aberdeen Presbytery Register 1598-1610
  CH2/121/1 - Edinburgh Presbytery Register 1586-93
  CH2/424/1 - Dalkeith Presbytery Register 1582-1630
  CH2/448/1 - Aberdeen St Nicholas Kirk Session Register 1562-3, 1568, 1573-8
  CH2/448/2 - Aberdeen St Nicholas Kirk Session Register 1602-9
  CH2/450/1 - Edinburgh General Session Register 1574-5, also available in partial transcript: RH2/1/35
  CH2/718/1 - Edinburgh St. Cuthberts Session Register 1586-94
  CH2/722/1-4 - Stirling Presbytery Register 1581-1610 (Microfilm copy of originals stored in Central Regional Archives, Stirling)

St. Andrews University Muniments, St. Andrews:
  B65/8/1 - Court Book of St. Andrews 1588-1592
  CH2/624/1 - Fragments from Minutes of Anstruther Wester Kirk Session 1578, 1587-93, 1598-9
  CH2/624/2 - Anstruther Wester Kirk Session Register 1601-26
  CH2/1056/1 - St. Monance Kirk Session Register 1597-1617
  StAUM ms deposit 23 - St. Andrews Presbytery Register 1586-1605

Finding Aids, Reference Tools:

Donaldson, Gordon and Morpeth, Robert, *A Dictionary of Scottish History*, (Edinburgh: John Donald, 1977)

Grant, Francis J., "Presbyterian Court Records 1560-1935," in *An Introductory Survey of the Sources and Literature of Scots Law*, (Edinburgh: Stair Society, 1936), 154-62

Johnstone, James F.K., *Bibliography of Aberdeen, Banff and Kincardine*, (Aberdeen: Aberdeen University Press, 1914)

Kirk, James, "The Scottish Reformation and Reign of James VI: A Select Critical Bibliography," *Records of the Scottish Church History Society* 23 (1987-89), 113-55

Krakovitch, Odile and Sentilhes, Armelle, *Les Réformes à la fin du XVIe siècle: Relèves de documents dans les fonds d'archives*, (Paris: Société de l'histoire de Protestantisme Français, 1972)

Larner, Christina, et al, *A Sourcebook of Scottish Witchcraft*, (Glasgow: Social Science Research Council, 1977)

Levron, Jacques, "Les Registres Paroissiaux et d'état Civil en France," *Archivum* 9 (1959) 55-100

Mill, Anna, "An Inventory of the Manuscript Records of the Older Royal Burghs of Scotland," *St. Andrews University Publication* 17 (St Andrews: W.C. Henderson, 1923)

Rayner, Patrick, Lenman, Bruce and Parker, Geoffrey, *Handlist of Records for the Study of Crime In Early Modern Scotland (to 1747)*, (London: List and Index Society, 1982)

Simpson, Grant, *Scottish Handwriting: 1150-1650*, (Aberdeen: Aberdeen University Press, 1977)

Stevenson, David and Wendy, *Scottish Texts and Calendars*, (Edinburgh: Scottish History Society, 1987)

Walker, David, *The Oxford Companion to Law*, (Oxford: Oxford University Press, 1980)

Webster, Bruce, *Scotland From the Eleventh Century to 1603*, (London: Sources of History, 1975)

Published Primary Sources:

The Acts of the Parliaments of Scotland, 1124-1707, 12 Vols., (London: HMSO, 1814-75)

Anonymous, *A Compendious Book of Psalms and Spiritual Songs, Commonly Known as The Gude and Godlie Ballates*, (Edinburgh: W. Paterson, 1868), (follows 1578 Edinburgh edition)

——, *A Parte of a Register, Contayninge Sundrie Memorable Matters, Written by Diuers Godly and Learned in Our Time, Which Stande For, and Desire the Reformation of Our Church*, (Middleburg: Publisher Unknown, 1593)

Aymon, Jean, ed., *Tous les Synodes Nationaux des Eglises Reformées de France*, (The Hague: Charles Delo, 1710), 2 Vol.

Bancroft, Richard, *A Sermon Preached at Paules Crosse the 9 of February...1588*, (London: Gregorie Seton, 1588/9)

——, *Daungerous Positions and Proceedings, Published and Practised Within This Iland of Brytaine, Under Pretence of Reformation and for the Presbiteriall Discipline*, (London: John Wolfe, 1593)

——, *Pretended Holy Discipline*, (London: John Wolfe, 1593)

Bannatyne, Richard, *Memorials of Transactions in Scotland, 1569-73*, (R. Pitcairn, ed.) (Edinburgh: Bannatyne Club, 1836)

Baum, G., and Cunitz, E., eds., *Histoire ecclesiastique des églises reformées au royaume de France*, (attributed to Theodore Beza), 3 Vol., (Nieuwkoop: B. de Graaf, 1974)

Bellardi, Werner, ed., "Ein Bedacht Hedios zur Kirchenzucht in Strassburg aus dem Jahre 1547," in de Kroon, Marijn and Krüger, Friedhelm, eds., *Bucer und seine Zeit*, (Wiesbaden: Franz Stainer, 1976), 117-132

Burne, Nicol, *Ane Admonition to the Antichristian Ministers In the Deformit Kirk of Scotland*, (No place of publication given, STC 22031, 1581), reprinted in D.M. Rogers, ed., *English Recusant Literature, 1558-1640* 135 (Menston, Yorkshire: Scolar Press, 1973)

Calderwood, A.B., ed., *The Buik of the Kirk of the Canagait, 1564-1567*, (Edinburgh: Scottish Record Society, 1961)

Calderwood, David, *History of the Kirk of Scotland*, 8 Vol., (Thomas Thomson, ed.) (Edinburgh: Wodrow Society, 1842-49)

Calvin, Jean, *L'Institution de la religion chrétienne*, 4 vol., (Genève: Labor et Fides, 1955-58) (follows 1560 French ed.)

Cameron Annie, ed., *The Warrender Papers*, 2 vol., (Edinburgh: Scottish History Society, 1931-2)

Cameron, James, ed., *The First Book of Discipline*, (Edinburgh: St. Andrew Press, 1972)

The Chronicle of Perth: A Register of Remarkable Occurences From the Year 1210 to 1668, (Edinburgh: Maitland Club, 1831)

Clark, James T., ed., *Genealogical Collections Concerning Families in Scotland*, 2 Vols., (Edinburgh: Scottish History Society, 1900)

Cochrane, Arthur C., ed., *Reformed Confessions of the 16th Century*, (Philadelphia: Westminster Press, 1966)

Commissariat of Edinburgh: Register of Testaments 1514-1600, (Edinburgh: Scottish Record Society, 1897)

Commissariat of Edinburgh: Register of Testaments 1601-1700, (Edinburgh: Scottish Record Society, 1898)

Commissariat of St. Andrews: Register of Testaments 1549-1800, (Edinburgh: Scottish Record Society, 1902)

Cunningham, William, ed., *Sermons of Robert Bruce*, (Edinburgh: Wodrow Society, 1843)

Davidson, John, *D. Bancroft's Rashness in Rayling Against the Church of Scotland*, (Edinburgh: Robert Waldegrave, 1590)

Donaldson, Gordon, ed., "Lord Chancellor Glamis and Theodore Beza," *Miscellany of the Scottish History Society* 8, (Edinburgh: Scottish Historical Society, 1951,) 89-116

——,ed., "A Scottish Liturgy of the Reign of James VI," *Miscellany of the Scottish History Society* 10, (Edinburgh: Scottish Historical Society, 1965), 87-117

"Extracts from the Records of the Burgh of the Canongate near Edinburgh," *Miscellany of the Maitland Club* 2, (Edinburgh: Maitland Club, 1840), 281-359

Extracts from the Records of the Burgh of Edinburgh, 1557-1589, (Edinburgh: Scottish Burgh Records Society, 1875-1882)

Fleming, D.H., ed., *Register of the Ministers, Elders and Deacons of the Christian Congregation of St. Andrews, 1559-1600*, 2 Vol., (Edinburgh: Scottish History Society, 1889-1890)

Fraser, William, *The Stirlings of Keir and Their Family Papers*, (Edinburgh: Privately Printed, 1858)

Gaches, Jacques, *Mémoires sur les Guerres de Religion à Castres et dans le Languedoc, 1555-1610*, (Paris: Pradel, 1879)

Galloway, Bruce, and Levack, Brian, eds., *The Jacobean Union: Six Tracts of 1604*, (Edinburgh: Scottish History Society, 1985)

Henderson, G.D., ed., *The Scots Confession, 1560 and the Negative Confession, 1581*, (Edinburgh: Church of Scotland, 1937)

Isambert, Decrusy et Taillander, eds., *Recueil général des anciennes lois françaises*, 28 Vol., (Paris: Belin-Leprieur, 1824-33)

Kingdon, Robert and Bergier, J.F., eds., *Registres de la Compagnie des Pasteurs de Genève*, (Genève: Libraire Droz, 1964-)

Kingdon, Robert, Reulos, Michel and Mentzer, Raymond, eds., "Disciplines réformées du
    XVIe siècle français: une découverte faite aux Etats-Unis," *Bulletin de la société de
    l'histoire de protestantisme français* 130, (1984), 69-86
Kirk, James, ed., *Stirling Presbytery Records, 1581-1587*, (Edinburgh: Scottish History Soc-
    iety, 1981)
——,ed., *The Second Book of Discipline*, (Edinburgh: St. Andrew Press, 1980)
——,ed., *Visitation of the Diocese of Dunblane and Other Churches, 1586-89*, (Edinburgh:
    Scottish Record Society, 1984)
——,ed., *The Records of the Synod of Lothian and Tweeddale, 1589-96, 1640-49*, (Edinburgh:
    Stair Society, 1977)
Laing, David, ed., *The Works of John Knox* 6 vol., (Edinburgh: J. Thin, 1854-1895)
Lee, John, ed., *Tracts by David Fergusson, Minister of Dunfermline, 1563-1572*, (Edinburgh:
    Bannatyne Club, 1860)
Méjan, François, ed., *La Discipline de l'Eglise Reformée de France*, (includes 1559 Disc-
    ipline), (Paris: Société Commerciale d'Edition et de Librairie, 1947)
Mitchell, Arthur, ed., *Geographical Collections Relating to Scotland Made by Walter MacFar-
    lane*, 3 Vols. (Edinburgh: Scottish History Society, 1906-1908)
Morély, Jean de, *Traicté de la discipline & police chrestienne*, (Lyon: de Tournes, 1562)
    (Reprint Genève: Slatkine, 1968)
Oakley, Ann, ed., *Actes du Consistoire de l'Eglise Française de Threadneedle Street, Londres,
    1571-1577*, (London: Huguenot Society of London, 1969)
Paton, Henry, ed., *Dundonald Parish Records: The Session Book of Dundonald 1602-1731*,
    (Edinburgh: Bute Society, 1936)
Pauck, Wilhelm, ed. and trans., *Melanchthon and Bucer*, (Philadelphia: Westminster Press,
    1969)
Penry, John, *A Briefe Discovery of the Untruthes and Slanders (against the true Governement
    of the Church of Christ) Contained in a Sermon, Preached the 8 of February 1588, by
    D. Bancroft*, (London: n.p., 1589)
Pitcairn, Robert, ed., *Ancient Criminal Trials in Scotland*, 3 Vol., (Edinburgh: William Tait,
    1833)
——, ed., *Autobiography and Diary of Mr. James Melville*, (Edinburgh: Wodrow Society,
    1842)
Quick, John, ed., *Synodicon in Gallia Reformata*, (London: Parkhurst and Robinson, 1692),
    2 Vol.
Register of the Privy Council of Scotland, 1545-1625, 14 Vol., (Edinburgh: Register House,
    1877-98)
Richter, Aemilius Ludwig, ed., *Die evangelischen Kirchenordnungen des sechszehnten Jahr-
    hunderts*, 2 Vol., (Nieuwkoop: De Graaf, 1967)
Robertson, David, ed., *South Leith Records, 1588-1700*, (Edinburgh: Andrew Elliot, 1911)
Row, John, *The Historie of the Kirk of Scotland*, 2 Vol., (Edinburgh: Maitland Club, 1842)
Soman, Alfred, ed., "Le registre consistorial de Coutras, 1582-1584," *Bulletin de la société
    de l'histoire du protestantisme français*, 126 (1980), 193-228
Spottiswoode, John, *History of the Church of Scotland*, 3 Vol., (Edinburgh: Bannatyne Club,
    1847-51)
Stuart, John, ed., *Extracts From the Council Register of the Burgh of Aberdeen, 1398-1625*,
    2 Vol., (Aberdeen: Spalding Club, 1844, 1848)
——, ed., *Selections From the Records of the Kirk Session, Presbytery and Synod of Aberdeen*,
    (Aberdeen: Spalding Club, 1846)
——, ed., "The Chronicle of Aberdeen, MCCCCXCI-MDXCV," *Spalding Club Miscellany*
    2, (Aberdeen: Spalding Club, 1842), 29-70

——, ed., "Summons Against the Magistrates of Aberdeen, 1591," *Spalding Club Miscellany* 3 (Aberdeen: Spalding Club, 1846), 155-71

Sunshine, Glenn, ed., "French Protestantism on the Eve of St. Bartholomew: The Ecclesiastical Discipline of the French Reformed Churches, 1571-72," *French History* 4 (1990), 340-377

Sutcliffe, Matthew, *Ecclesiasticall Discipline*, (London: Bishop and Newberie, 1590)

Thomson, Thomas, ed., *The Booke of the Universal Kirk of Scotland*, 3 Vols, (Edinburgh: Bannatyne and Maitland Clubs, 1839-45)

"Visitation of the Kirk of Holyroodhouse, by the Presbytery of Edinburgh," *Wodrow Society Miscellany* 1, (Edinburgh: Wodrow Society, 1844), 453-67

Warden, Alexander, ed., *Burgh Laws of Dundee*, (London: Longmans Green, 1872)

Watson, Charles, ed., *Roll of Edinburgh Burgesses and Guild Brethren 1406-1700*, (Edinburgh: Scottish Record Society, 1929)

Wendel, François, ed., *De Regno Christi (Martini Buceri Opera Latina*, Vol. XV), (Paris: Presses Universitaires de France, 1955)

Wood, Marguerite, ed., *Book of Records of the Ancient Privileges of the Canongate*, (Edinburgh: Scottish Record Society, 1956)

Secondary Sources:

Abray, Lorna Jane, *The People's Reformation: Magistrates, Clergy and Commons in Strasbourg, 1500-1598*, (Ithaca: Cornell University Press, 1985)

Addy, John, *Sin and Society in the Seventeenth Century*, (London: Routledge, 1989)

Ainslie, James L., *The Doctrines of Ministerial Order in the Reformed Churches of the 16th and 17th Centuries*, (Edinburgh: T&T Clark, 1940)

Anderson, Michael, *Approaches to the History of the Western Family, 1500-1914*, (London: Macmillan, 1980)

Anonymous, *The History of Stirling, From the Earliest Accounts to the Present Time*, (Stirling: M. Randall, 1817)

Babbage, Stuart Barton, *Puritanism and Richard Bancroft*, (London: Church Historical Society, 1962)

Baker, J. Wayne, "Church Discipline or Civil Punishment: On the Origins of the Reformed Schism, 1528-1531," *Andrews University Seminary Studies* 23 (1985), 3-18

Balfour, Sir James, ed., *The Scots Peerage*, 9 Vols., (Edinburgh: David Douglas, 1904-14)

Bardgett, Frank, *Scotland Reformed: The Reformation in Angus and the Mearns*, (Edinburgh: John Donald, 1989)

——, "The Monifieth Kirk Register," *Records of the Scottish Church History Society* 23 (1987-89), 175-195

——, "John Erskine of Dun: A Theological Reassessment," *Scottish Journal of Theology* 43, (1990), 59-85

Benedict, Philip, *Rouen During the Wars of Religion*, (Cambridge: Cambridge University Press, 1981)

——, *The Huguenot Population of France, 1600-1685: The Demographic Fate and Customs of a Religious Minority*, (Philadelphia: Transactions of the American Philosophical Society, 1991)

Bertheau, Solange, "Le Consistoire dans les eglises reformées du Moyen Poitou au 16e siècle," *Bulletin de la société de l'histoire du protestantisme français* 116 (1970), 332-359, 513-549

Biéler, André, *L'homme et la femme dans la morale calviniste*, (Genève: Labor et Fides, 1963)

Bingham, Caroline, *James I of England*, (London: Weidenfield and Nicolson, 1981)

Black, William G., and Christie, James R., *The Parochial Ecclesiastical Law of Scotland*, (Edinburgh: William Hodge, 1928)

Bossy, John, *Christianity in the West, 1400-1700*, (Oxford: Oxford University Press, 1985)

Bouwsma, William, *John Calvin: A Sixteenth-Century Portrait*, (Oxford: Oxford University Press, 1988)

——, "The Quest for the Historical Calvin," *Archiv für Reformationsgeschichte* 77 (1986), 47-57

Brackenridge, R.D., "The Development of Sabbatarianism in Scotland, 1560-1650," *Journal of Presbyterian History* 42 (1964), 149-65

Brigden, Susan, *London and the Reformation*, (Oxford: Oxford University Press, 1989)

Brown, Keith M., *Bloodfeud in Scotland 1573-1625: Violence, Justice and Politics in an Early Modern Society*, (Edinburgh: John Donald, 1986)

——, "In Search of the Godly Magistrate in Reformation Scotland," *Journal of Ecclesiastical History* 40 (1989), 553-81

Burke, Peter, *Popular Culture In Early Modern Europe*, (London: Maurice Temple Smith, 1978)

Burnett, Amy Nelson, "Church Discipline and Moral Reformation in the Thought of Martin Bucer," *Sixteenth Century Journal* 22 (1991), 439-456

Calvet, Jean, *Histoire de la ville de St-Amans*, (Castres: Lucien Granier, 1887)

Cameron, James K., "Scottish Calvinism and the Principle of Intolerance," in Gerrish, B.A. and Benedetto, Robert, eds., *Reformatio Perennis: Essays on Calvin and the Reformation In Honor of Ford Lewis Battles*, (Pittsburgh: Pickwick Press, 1981) 113-128

——, "The Office of Superintendent in the First Book of Discipline," in Bernard Vogler, ed., *L'institution et les pouvoirs dans les églises de l'antiquité à nos jours* (*Miscellanea Historiae Ecclesiasticae* 8), (Bruxelles: Nauwelaerts, 1987), 239-250

Clark, Ivo MacNaughton, *A History of Church Discipline in Scotland*, (Aberdeen: Lindsay, 1929)

Collinson, Patrick, *The Elizabethan Puritan Movement*, (Berkeley: University of California Press, 1967)

——, *The Religion of Protestants*, (Oxford: Oxford University Press, 1982)

Courvoisier, Jacques, *La notion d'église chez Bucer dans son développement historique*, (Paris: Félix Alcan, 1933)

Cowan, Ian, *The Scottish Reformation*, (New York: St. Martin's Press, 1982)

——, *Regional Aspects of the Scottish Reformation*, (London: The Historical Association, 1978)

——, "Church and Society in Post-Reformation Scotland," *Records of the Scottish Church History Society* 17 (1971), 185-201

Cullen, L.M., Smout, T.C., and Gibson, A., "Wages and Comparative Development in Ireland and Scotland, 1565-1780," in Rosalind Mitchison and Peter Roebuck, eds., *Economy and Society in Scotland and Ireland, 1500-1939*, (Edinburgh: John Donald, 1988), 105-116

Dainville, Oudot de, "Le consistoire de Ganges à la fin du XVIe siècle," *Revue d'histoire de l'église de France* 18 (1932), 464-485

Davis, Natalie Z., *Society and Culture In Early Modern France*, (Stanford: Stanford University Press, 1975)

——, *The Return of Martin Guerre*, (Cambridge, Mass.: Harvard University Press, 1983)

Dawson, Jane E.A., "'The Face of Ane Perfyt Reformed Kyrk': St. Andrews and the Early Scottish Reformation," in James Kirk, ed., *Humanism and Reform: The Church in Europe, England and Scotland, 1400-1643*, (Oxford: Blackwell, 1991), 413-436

Delumeau, Jean, *Catholicism Between Luther and Voltaire*, (London: Burns and Oates, 1977)

Di Folco, John, "Discipline and Welfare in the Mid-Seventeenth Century Scots Parish," *Records of the Scottish Church History Society* 19 (1977), 169-183

Donaldson, Gordon, *The Scottish Reformation*, (Cambridge: Cambridge University Press, 1960)

——, "The Church Courts," in *An Introduction to Scottish Legal History*, (Edinburgh: Stair Society, 1958), 363-373

——, *Scotland: James V-James VII*, (Edinburgh: Mercat Press, 1987) (first published 1965)

——, *All the Queen's Men: Power and Politics in Mary Stewart's Scotland*, (London: Batsford, 1983)

——, *Scottish Church History*, (Edinburgh: Scottish Academic Press, 1985)

Douglas, Mary, *Purity and Danger: An Analysis of the Concepts of Pollution and Taboo*, (London: Routledge and Kegan Paul, 1966)

Dunlop, A. Ian, "The Polity of the Scottish Church, 1600-1637," *Records of the Scottish Church History Society* 12 (1958), 161-84

Durkan, John, "The French Connection in the Sixteenth and Early Seventeenth Centuries," in T.C. Smout, ed., *Scotland and Europe, 1200-1850*, (Edinburgh: John Donald, 1986)

Fleming, David Hay, *St Andrews Cathedral Museum*, (Edinburgh: Oliver and Boyd, 1931)

Flinn, Michael, ed., *Scottish Population History From the 17th Century to the 1930s*, (Cambridge: Cambridge University Press, 1977)

Foster, Walter Roland, *The Church Before the Covenants: The Church of Scotland 1596-1638*, (Edinburgh: Scottish Academic Press, 1975)

Friedeburg, Robert v., "Sozialdisciplinierung in England? Soziale Beziehungen auf dem Lande zwischen Reformation und 'Great Rebellion', 1550-1642," *Zeitschrift für Historiche Forschung* 17, (1990), 385-418

——, "Reformation of Manners and the Social Composition of Offenders in an East Anglian Cloth Village: Earls Colne, Essex, 1531-1642, *Journal of British Studies* 29 (1990), 347-85

Garrisson, Janine, *Les protestants au XVIe siècle*, (Paris: Fayard, 1988)

Garrisson-Estèbe, Janine, *Les protestants du Midi, 1559-1598*, (Toulouse: Privat, 1980)

Gatrell, V.A.C., Lenman, Bruce and Parker, Geoffrey, eds., *Crime and the Law: The Social History of Crime in Western Europe Since 1500*, (London: Europa, 1980)

Gervaise, Andrew, and Gammack, James, *Memorials of Angus and the Mearns*, 2 Vol., (Edinburgh: David Douglas, 1885)

Gillespie, James, *Dundonald: A Contribution to Parochial History*, 2 Vol., (Glasgow: John Wylie, 1939)

Gillis, John, *For Better, For Worse: British Marriages, 1600 to the Present*, (Oxford: Oxford University Press, 1985)

Graham, Michael, "The Civil Sword and the Scottish Kirk in the Late Sixteenth Century, " in W. Fred Graham, ed., *Later Calvinism: International Perspectives*, (Kirksville, Mo.: Sixteenth Century Publishers, 1994), 237-48

——, "Equality Before the Kirk? Church Discipline and the Elite in Reformation-era Scotland," *Archiv für Reformationsgeschichte* 84 (1993), 289-310

Greengrass, Mark, *The French Reformation*, (Oxford: Basil Blackwell, 1987)

Guggenheim, Ann, "The Calvinist Notables of Nîmes During the Era of the Religious Wars," *Sixteenth Century Journal* 3 (1972), 80-96

Haigh, Christopher, *Reformation and Resistance in Tudor Lancashire*, (Cambridge: Cambridge University Press, 1975)

Haws, Charles, *Scottish Parish Clergy at the Reformation 1540-1574*, (Edinburgh: Scottish Record Society, 1972)

——, "The Diocese of Aberdeen and the Reformation," *Innes Review* 22 (1971), 72-84

——, "The Diocese of St. Andrews at the Reformation," *Records of the Scottish Church History Society* 18 (1974), 115-132

Hazlett, W. Ian P., "The Scots Confession of 1560: Context, Complexion and Critique," *Archiv für Reformationsgeschichte* 78 (1987), 287-320
Hein, Kenneth, *Eucharist and Excommunication: A Study in Early Christian Doctrine and Discipline*, (Bern: Herbert Lang, 1973)
Heller, Henry, *Iron and Blood: Civil Wars in Sixteenth-Century France*, (Montreal: McGill-Queen's University Press, 1991)
Henderson, G.D., *The Scottish Ruling Elder*, (London: James Clarke, 1935)
Hewitt, George R., *Scotland Under Morton: 1572-80*, (Edinburgh: John Donald, 1982)
Höpfl, Harro, *The Christian Polity of John Calvin*, (Cambridge: Cambridge University Press, 1982)
Houlbrooke, Ralph, *Church Courts and the People During the English Reformation 1520-1570*, (Oxford: Oxford University Press, 1979)
Hsia, R. Po-chia, *Social Discipline in the Reformation: Central Europe 1550-1750*, (London: Routledge, 1989)
Ingram, Martin, *Church Courts, Sex and Marriage In England, 1570-1640*, (Cambridge: Cambridge University Press, 1987)
——, "Religion, Communities and Moral Discipline in Late Sixteenth- and Early Seventeenth-Century England: Case Studies," in Kaspar von Greyerz, ed., *Religion and Society in Early Modern Europe, 1500-1800*, (London: German Historical Institute, 1984), 177-93
Karlson, Carol, *The Devil in the Shape of a Woman: Witchcraft in Colonial New England*, (New York: Norton, 1987)
Keith, Alexander, *A Thousand Years of Aberdeen*, (Aberdeen: Aberdeen University Press, 1972)
Kingdon, Robert, "The Control of Morals In Calvin's Geneva," Lawrence Buck and Jonathan Zophy, eds., *The Social History of the Reformation*, (Columbus, Ohio: Ohio State University Press, 1972) 3-16
——, *Geneva and the Coming of the Wars of Religion in France, 1555-1563*, (Genève: Droz, 1956)
——, *Geneva and the French Protestant Movement, 1564-1572*, (Madison, Wisc.: University of Wisconsin Press, 1967)
——, "The Control of Morals by the Earliest Calvinists," in Peter de Klerk, ed., *Renaissance, Reformation, Resurgence*, (Grand Rapids: Calvin Theological Seminary, 1976) 95-106
——, "Calvin and the Family: The Work of the Consistory in Geneva," *Pacific Theological Review* 17 (1984), 5-18
Kirk, James, *Patterns of Reform: Continuity and Change in the Reformation Kirk*, (Edinburgh: T&T Clark, 1989)
——, "The Polities of the Best Reformed Kirks: Scottish Achievements and English Aspirations In Church Government After the Reformation," *Scottish Historical Review* 59 (1980), 22-53
——, "The 'Privy Kirks' and Their Antecedents: The Hidden Face of Scottish Protestantism," W.J. Shiels and Diana Wood, eds., *Voluntary Religion*, (Oxford: Basil Blackwell, 1986), 155-170
——, "The Influence of Calvinism on the Scottish Reformation," *Records of the Scottish Church History Society* 18 (1972-4) 157-179
——, "L'apparition d'une ecclésiologie réformée. Le cas de l'Ecosse, " in Bernard Vogler, ed., *L'institution et les pouvoirs dans les Eglises de l'antiquité à nos jours*, (Bruxelles: Nauwelaerts, 1987), 251-8
Knox, R. Buick, "A Scottish Chapter in the History of Toleration," *Scottish Journal of Theology* 41 (1988), 49-74
Labrousse, Elisabeth, "France 1598-1685," in Menna Prestwich, ed., *International Calvinism, 1541-1715*, (Oxford: Clarendon Press, 1985), 285-314

Ladurie, Emmanuel Le Roy, *The Peasants of Languedoc*, (Urbana: University of Illinois Press, 1974)

Larner, Christina, *Enemies of God: The Witch-hunt in Scotland*, (London: Chatto and Windus, 1981)

Leneman, Leah, "'Prophaning' the Lord's Day: Sabbath Breach in Early Modern Scotland," *History* 74 (1989), 217-231

Lenman, Bruce, "The Limits of Godly Discipline in the Early Modern Period with Particular Reference to England and Scotland," in Kaspar von Greyerz, ed., *Religion and Society in Early Modern Europe, 1500-1800*, (London: German Historical Institute, 1984), 124-45

Lenman, Bruce and Parker, Geoffrey, "Crime in Early Modern Scotland: A Preliminary Report on Sources and Problems," (End of Grant Report, Social Science Research Council, London, 1977)

Levack, Brian P., *The Witch-hunt in Early Modern Europe*, (London: Longman, 1987)

Lewis, Gillian, "Calvinism In Geneva in the Time of Calvin and Beza, 1541-1608," in Prestwich, ed., *International Calvinism*, 39-70

Lienhard, Marc, "L'église aux mains de l'état? Magistrat et église évangélique à Strasbourg de la Réforme à la guerre de trente ans," *Bulletin de la société de l'histoire de protestantisme français* 130 (1984), 295-318

Lyall, Francis, *Of Presbyters and Kings: Church and State in the Law of Scotland*, (Aberdeen: Aberdeen University Press, 1980)

Lynch, Michael, *Edinburgh and the Reformation*, (Edinburgh: John Donald, 1981)

——, "Calvinism in Scotland, 1559-1638," from Prestwich, ed., *International Calvinism*, 225-255

——, "From Privy Kirk to Burgh Church: An Alternative View of the Process of Protestantisation," in Norman Macdougall, ed., *Church, Politics and Society: Scotland 1408-1929*, (Edinburgh: John Donald, 1983), 85-96

——, ed., *The Early Modern Town in Scotland*, (London: Croom Helm, 1987)

Lythe, S.G.E., *The Economy of Scotland In Its European Setting, 1550-1625*, (Edinburgh: Oliver and Boyd, 1960)

Makey, Walter, *The Church of the Covenant 1637-1651: Revolution and Social Change in Scotland*, (Edinburgh: John Donald, 1979)

Malcolm, J., *The Parish of Monifieth in Ancient and Modern Times*, (Edinburgh: William Green, 1910)

Marshall, Gordon, *Presbyteries and Profits: Calvinism and the Development of Capitalism in Scotland, 1560-1707*, (Oxford: Clarendon Press, 1980)

Martin, François, "Ganges, action de son consistoire et vie de son église aux 16e et 17e siècle," *Revue de théologie et d'action evangéliques* 2 (1942), 17-40, 130-159

McKay, Denis, "Parish Life in Scotland, 1500-1560," from David McRoberts, ed., *Essays on the Scottish Reformation 1513-1625*, (Glasgow: J.S. Burns, 1962), 85-115

McKie, Elsie Anne, *Elders and the Plural Ministry: The Role of Exegetical History in Illuminating John Calvin's Theology*, (Genève: Librarie Droz, 1988)

McLennan, Bruce, "The Reformation in the Burgh of Aberdeen," *Northern Scotland* 2 (1974-7), 119-44

McMahon, George I.R., "The Scottish Courts of High Commission, 1610-38," *Records of the Scottish Church History Society* 15 (1965), 193-209

McNeill, John T., *The History and Character of Calvinism*, (New York: Oxford University Press, 1954)

McNeill, Peter and Nicholson, Ranald, eds., *An Historical Atlas of Scotland c.400-c.1600*, (Edinburgh: Conference of Scottish Medievalists, 1975)

McRie, Thomas, *Life of Andrew Melville*, (McRie's Works, Volume 2), (Edinburgh: William Blackwood, 1856)

Mentzer, Raymond, ed., *Sin and the Calvinists: Morals Control and the Consistory in the Reformed Tradition*, (Kirksville, Mo.: Sixteenth Century Publishers, 1994)

——, "Disciplina nervus ecclesiae: The Calvinist Reform of Morals at Nîmes," *Sixteenth Century Journal* 18 (1987), 89-115

——, "Le consistoire et la pacification du monde rural," *Bulletin de la société de l'histoire de protestantisme français* 135, (1989), 373-390

——, "Ecclesiastical Discipline and Communal Reorganization Among the Protestants of Southern France," *European History Quarterly* 21 (1991), 163-83

Midelfort, H.C.E., *Witch Hunting in Southwestern Germany, 1562-1684*, (Stanford: Stanford University Press, 1972)

Mitchison, Rosalind and Leneman, Leah, *Sexuality and Social Control: Scotland, 1660-1780*, (Oxford: Basil Blackwell, 1989)

——, "Acquiescence in and Defiance of Church Discipline in Early-Modern Scotland," *Records of the Scottish Church History Society* 25 (1993), 19-39

Mitchison, Rosalind, "The Historical Use of Kirk Session Registers," *Scottish Local History* 12 (May 1987), 4-6

Monter, E. William, *Calvin's Geneva*, (New York: John Wiley, 1967)

——, "The Consistory of Geneva, 1559-1569," *Bibliothèque d'Humanisme et Renaissance* 38, (1976), 467-484

Mours, Samuel, *Le Protestantisme en France au XVIe siècle*, (Paris: Librairie Protestante, 1959)

Mullan, David George, *Episcopacy in Scotland: The History of an Idea, 1560-1638*, (Edinburgh: John Donald, 1986)

Münch, Paul, *Zucht und Ordnung*, (Stuttgart: Klett-Cotta, 1978)

Nimmo, William, *The History of Stirlingshire*, 2 Vol., (London: Hamilton, Adams & Co., 1880)

Oberman, Heiko, "*Europa Afflicta*: The Reformation of the Refugees," *Archiv für Reformationsgeschichte* 83 (1992), 91-111

Oestreich, Gerhard, *Neostoicism and the Early Modern State*, (Cambridge: Cambridge University Press, 1982)

Ozment, Steven, *The Reformation In the Cities: The Appeal of Protestantism to Sixteenth-Century Germany and Switzerland*, (New Haven: Yale University Press, 1975)

——, *The Age of Reform: 1250-1550*, (New Haven, Yale University Press, 1980)

——, *When Fathers Ruled: Family Life in Reformation Europe*, (Cambridge, Mass.: Harvard University Press, 1983)

Parker, Geoffrey, "The 'Kirk By Law Established' and the Origins of the 'Taming of Scotland': St. Andrews 1559-1600," from Leah Leneman, ed., *Perspectives in Scottish Social History: Essays In Honour of Rosalind Mitchison*, (Aberdeen: Aberdeen University Press, 1988), 1-32

——, "Success and Failure During the First Century of the Reformation," *Past and Present* 136 (1992), 43-82

Paterson, James, *A History of the County of Ayr With a Genealogical Account of the Families of Ayrshire*, 2 Vols., (Ayr: John Dick, 1847-52)

Peronnet, Michel, ed., *Les églises et leurs institutions au XVIᵉᵐᵉ siècle: Actes du Vᵉᵐᵉ colloque du Centre d'Histoire de la Réforme et du Protestantisme*, (Montpellier: Université Paul Valery, 1978)

Prestwich, Menna, "Calvinism In France, 1555-1629," in Prestwich, ed., *International Calvinism*, 71-108

Rankin, W.E.K., *The Parish Church of the Holy Trinity, St Andrews*, (Edinburgh: Oliver and Boyd, 1955)

Roper, Lyndal, *The Holy Household: Women and Morals in Reformation Augsburg*, (Oxford: Oxford University Press, 1989)

Reid, W. Stanford, "French Influence on the First Scots Confession and Book of Discipline," *Westminister Theological Journal* 35 (1972), 1-14

——, "The Coming of the Reformation to Edinburgh," *Church History* 42 (1973), 27-44

Reulos, Michel, "L'histoire de la discipline des églises réformées françaises, élément de l'histoire du droit ecclésiastique réformé," in Leo Olschki, ed., *La Storia del diritto nel quadro delle scienze storiche. Atti del Primo Congresso internazionale della Societa Italiana di Storia del Diritto*, (Firenze: Olschki, 1966), 533-44

Ross, Anthony, "Reformation and Repression," in McRoberts, ed., *Essays on the Scottish Reformation*, 371-414

Sabean, David, *Power in the Blood: Popular Culture and Village Discourse in Early Modern Germany*, (Cambridge: Cambridge University Press, 1984)

Salmon, J.H.M., *Society in Crisis: France in the Sixteenth Century*, (London: Benn, 1975)

Sanderson, Margaret H.B., *Scottish Rural Society in the Sixteenth Century*, (Edinburgh: John Donald, 1982)

——, *Mary Stewart's People: Life in Mary Stewart's Scotland*, (Edinburgh: Mercat Press, 1987)

——, "Some Aspects of the Church in Scottish Society in the Era of the Reformation Illustrated From the Sheriffdom of Ayr," *Records of the Scottish Church History Society* 17 (1970), 81-97

——, "Catholic Recusancy in Scotland in the Sixteenth Century," *Innes Review* 21 (1970), 87-107

Schilling, Heinz, "History of Crime or History of Sin? Some Reflections on the Social History of Early Modern Church Discipline" in E.I. Kouri and Tom Scott, eds., *Politics and Society in Reformation Europe: Essays for Sir Geoffrey Elton on His Sixty-Fifth Birthday*, (London: Macmillan, 1987), 289-310

——, "Reformierte Kirchenzucht als Sozialdisziplinierung? Die Tätigkeit des Emder Presbyteriums in den Jahren 1557-1562," in Heinz Schilling and Wilfred Ehbrecht, eds., *Niederlande und Nordwestdeutschland: Studien zur Regional- und Staatgeschichte Nordwestkontinentaleuropas im Mittelalter und in der Neuzeit*, (Köln: Bohlau, 1983) 261-327

——, *Civic Calvinism in Northwestern Germany and the Netherlands*, (Kirksville, Mo.: Sixteenth Century Publishers, 1991)

Schmidt, Heinrich Richard, "Die Christianisierung des Sozialverhaltens als permanente Reformation. Aus der Praxis reformierter Sittengerichte in der Schweiz wahrend der frühen Neuzeit," in Peter Blickle and Johannes Kunisch, eds., *Kommunalisierung und Christianisierung: Voraussetzungen und Folgen der Reformation 1400-1600*, (Berlin: Dunker und Humblot, 1989), 113-163

Schnucker, Robert, ed., *Calviniana*, (Kirksville, Mo.: Sixteenth Century Journal, 1988)

Scott, Hew, *et al*, eds., *Fasti Ecclesiae Scoticanae*, 9 Vol., (Edinburgh: Oliver and Boyd, 1915-51)

Seaver, Paul, *Wallington's World: A Puritan Artisan in Seventeenth-Century London*, (Stanford: Stanford University Press, 1985)

Shaw, Duncan, *The General Assemblies of the Church of Scotland 1560-1600*, (Edinburgh: St. Andrew Press, 1964)

——, ed., *Reformation and Revolution: Essays Presented to Hugh Watt*, (Edinburgh: Saint Andrew Press, 1967)

Sinclair, John, ed., *The Statistical Account of Scotland, 1791-1799*, 20 Vols., (Wakefield: E.P. Publishing, 1978-83)

Smith, David B., "The Spiritual Jurisdiction, 1560-64," *Records of the Scottish Church History Society* 25 (1993), 1-18

Smout, T.C., *A History of the Scottish People, 1560-1830*, (Glasgow: William Collins, 1969)

Solt, Leo F., *Church and State in Early Modern England, 1509-1640*, (Oxford: Oxford University Press, 1990)

Stevenson, David, *The Origins of Freemasonry: Scotland's Century, 1590-1710*, (Cambridge: Cambridge University Press, 1988)

Stevenson, Stephanie, *Anstruther: A History*, (Edinburgh: John Donald, 1989)

Strohl, H., "La théorie et la pratique des quatre ministères à Strasbourg avant l'arrivée de Calvin," *Bulletin de la société de l'histoire de protestantisme français* 84, (1935), 123-144

Thomas, Keith, *Religion and the Decline of Magic*, (New York: Scribner's, 1971)

Torrance, T.F., "The Eldership in the Reformed Church," *Scottish Journal of Theology* 37 (1984), 503-518

Tyacke, Nicholas, *Anti-Calvinists: The Rise of English Arminianism, c. 1590-1640*, (Oxford: Clarendon Press, 1987)

Vodola, Elisabeth, *Excommunication in the Middle Ages*, (Berkeley: University of California Press, 1986)

Vogler, Bernard and Estèbe, Janine, "La genèse d'une société protestante: Etude comparée de quelques registres consistoriaux languedociens et palatins vers 1600," *Annales economies, sociétés, civilisations*, 1976, 362-387

Vogler, Bernard, "Europe as Seen Through the Correspondence of Theodore Beza," in Kouri and Scott, eds., *Politics and Society in Reformation Europe*, 252-65

Walton, Robert, *Zwingli's Theocracy*, (Toronto: University of Toronto Press, 1967)

Walzer, Michael, *The Revolution of the Saints: A Study in the Origins of Radical Politics*, (Cambridge, Mass.: Harvard University Press, 1965)

Warden, Alexander, *Angus or Forfarshire: The Land and People*, 5 Vols., (Dundee: Charles Alexander, 1880-5)

Watson, Harry D., *Kilrenny and Cellardyke: 800 Years of History*, (Edinburgh: John Donald, 1986)

Watt, Jeffrey R., "Marriage Contract Disputes in Early Modern Neuchâtel, 1547-1806," *Journal of Social History* 22, (1988-89), 129-147

——, "Women and the Consistory in Calvin's Geneva," *Sixteenth Century Journal* 24 (1993), 429-39

White, Allan, "Queen Mary's Northern Province," in Michael Lynch, ed., *Mary Stewart: Queen in Three Kingdoms*, (Oxford: Basil Blackwell, 1988), 53-70

Williamson, Arthur H., *Scottish National Consciousness in the Age of James VI*, (Edinburgh: John Donald, 1979)

——, "Scotland, Antichrist and the Invention of Great Britain," from John Dwyer, Roger A. Mason and Alexander Murdoch, eds., *New Perspectives on the Politics and Culture of Early Modern Scotland*, (Edinburgh: John Donald, 1986), 34-58

Wilkie, James, *The History of Fife From the Earliest Times to the Nineteenth Century*, (Edinburgh: William Blackwood, 1924)

Wood, Walter, *The East Neuk of Fife: Its History and Antiquities*, (Edinburgh: David Douglas, 1887)

Wormald, Jenny, *Court, Kirk and Community: Scotland 1470-1625*, (Toronto: University of Toronto Press, 1981)

Wright, Ronald Selby, *The Kirk in the Canongate: A Short History From 1128 to the Present Day*, (Edinburgh: Oliver and Boyd, 1956)

Unpublished Theses and Dissertations:

Demura, Akira, *Church Discipline According to Johannes Oecolampadius in the Setting of His Life and Thought*, (Th.D. Thesis, Princeton Theological Seminary, 1964)

Flett, Iain E.F., *The Conflict of the Reformation and Democracy in the Geneva of Scotland, 1443-1610: An Introduction to Edited Texts of Documents Relating to the Burgh of Dundee*, (St. Andrews University M.Phil. Thesis, 1981)

Kirk, James, *The Development of the Melvillian Movement in Late Sixteenth Century Scotland*, (Edinburgh University Ph.D. Thesis, 1972)

Smith, Mark C., *The Presbytery of St. Andrews, 1586-1605: A Study and Annotated Edition of the Register of the Minutes of the Presbytery of St. Andrews*, (St. Andrews University Ph.D. Thesis, 1986)

White, Allan, *Religion, Politics and Society in Aberdeen: 1543-1593*, (Edinburgh University Ph.D. Thesis, 1985)

INDEX

Abercorn, earl of, 273

Abercrombie, 221, 223

Aberdeen, 29, 32, 49, 63-66, 73, 92-3, 97, 109, 114-26, 128-9, 133, 136, 159, 170, 213, 247, 281-2, 288-9; disciplinary ordinances in, 61-3; early reformation in, 57-60; presbytery of, 159

Aberdeenshire, 263

Aberfoyle, near Stirling, 164

Abernethy family, 246-9, 272

Abernethy, James, bailie in Rothiemay, 246

Abernethy, Jean, in Rothiemay, 246

Abernethy, Isobel, in Rothiemay, 247

Abortion, 45, 239

Acheson, Molly, midwife in the Canongate, 285

Adam, John, in Kippen, 171

Adamson, Patrick, archbishop of St. Andrews, 69, 116, 150-3, 186, 189-91, 196, 207, 222, 296

Adie, Beatrix, in Pittenweem, 307

Adie, Marion, in St. Andrews, 217

Adie, Walter, in St. Andrews, 91

Adultery, 19, 24, 27, 42, 46-7, 81-2, 84, 95, 111, 121, 127, 129, 145, 169, 173-4, 175-6, 179, 213, 217, 242, 261, 271, 276, 281, 284, 286, 289, 332, 334, 342

Aird, William, minister in Edinburgh, 184

Aleander, papal nuncio, 11

Alexander family, 222

Alexander, John, merchant and elder in Anstruther Easter, 224

Alexander, Margaret, in Logie, 180

Allane, Jonet, near Stirling, 171

Alms, 112-3, 127, 146, 233-4, 238, 244

Alric, Jehan, in Pont-de-Camarès, 327

Alva, near Stirling, 173, 182-3

Amalrique, Anne, servant in Labastide-St-Amans, 334

Ambrose, bishop of Milan, 19

Anabaptists, 23

Anderson, James, minister in Stirling, 169, 177, 282

Andrew, John, in Dundonald, 303

Angus, Archibald Douglas, 8th earl of, 140, 189

Anstruther family, 221-2, 224

Anstruther, John, reader in Kilrenny, 222

Anstruther Easter, 221-4, 297

Anstruther Wester, 126, 220-40, 245, 248-9, 257, 272, 285, 289, 292-3, 304-5

Arbuthnet, Alexander, principal of King's College, Aberdeen, 206

Arnauld, Catherine, in Coutras, 330

Arnauld, Perrine, in Coutras, 331

Arran, James Hamilton, 3rd earl of, 56, 138, 310

Arran, James Stewart, 4th earl of, 138-40, 152

Arthur/Smith feud, 217, 296-8

Arthur, Henry, in St. Andrews, 297-8

Arthur, James, in St. Andrews, 296

Arthur, Patrick, in St. Andrews, 297-8

Arthur, Patrick, minister in Monimail, 194-5

Arthur, William, in St. Andrews, 296-8

Atholl, John Stewart, earl of, 69, 262-3

Augsburg Confession, 14

Auchinleck, Andrew, minister in Barry, 241

Augustine of Hippo, St., 10

Averons, Pierre, in Labastide-St-Amans, 336

Baird, James, in Muckhart, 171

Balcanquhal, Walter, minister in Edinburgh, 109, 151, 184

Balfour, David, laird near Logie, 179

Balfour, Thomas, elder in St. Andrews, 80, 93-4

Balfour, William, in Leith, 56

Bancroft, Richard, 153-5, 159

Barclay family, 222-3

Bardgett, Frank, 239-40

Baron, James, merchant in Edinburgh, 37

Basel, 10-13, 26

Beaton family, 31, 221-2

Beaton, David, cardinal and archbishop of St. Andrews, 33-4, 222

Beaton, John, laird of Balfour, 143, 224

Lovell, James, reader in Monifieth, 241
Lovell, William, laird of Ballumbie, 127
Low, William, shipmaster and elder in
  Anstruther Easter, 224
Lowrie, Pat, in Dundonald, 304
Luther, Martin, 11, 13, 40
Lyall, Katie, in Monifieth, 285
Lyell, Margaret, in St. Andrews, 217
Lynch, Michael, 51-2, 64

MacCalzean, Thomas, laird of Cliftonhall,
  108, 269-71
McCrechane, Ninian, cook in Edinburgh,
  56
McGeachen, John, in Dundonald, 256
McGill, James, clerk of register, 109
MacGregor family, 33
MacKerrill, James, in Dundonald, 293
MacKerrill, William, laird of Hillhouse and
  elder in Dundonald, 251
McNab, Marion, near Stirling, 304-5
MacTeir, Katherine, in Dundonald, 301-4
Makey, Walter, 133, 260-1
Mar, David, elder in Aberdeen, 59, 61,
  117
Mar, John Erskine, earl of, regent (d.
  1572), 68, 166
Mar, John Erskine, earl of (d. 1634), 140,
  181
Marausse, B., in Pont-de-Camarès, 327
Mardi Gras, 316, 330
Marjoriebanks, James, in Edinburgh, 113
Markets, on Sabbath, 47, 157, 177-8, 187,
  286
Marprelate Tracts, 153
Martial, Pierre, in Ganges, 341
Martin, captain in Labastide-St-Amans, 335
Martin family, 79
Martin, John, bailie and elder in St. An-
  drews, 81
Martin, Steven, 81
Mary I, Queen of England, 28, 38
Mary, Queen of Scots, 33-5, 63, 98, 106,
  114, 251, 268, 311
Mary of Guise, 33-5
Mas, Antoine, elder in Labastide-St-Am-
  ans, 335
Maxwell, John, 8th lord, 186, 188-9
Mazars family, 325
Mazars, Guilliame, in Pont-de-Camarès,
  325

Mazars, Simon, elder in Pont-de-Camarès,
  326
Melville, Andrew, elder in Anstruther
  Wester, 232-3, 238
Melville, Andrew, principal at St. An-
  drews, 80, 94, 131-2, 139, 141, 150-2,
  156, 190-2, 196-7, 201, 205-6, 209-10,
  264, 270, 310-11
Melville, James, minister in Kilrenny, 94,
  97, 110, 141, 156, 161, 190, 196, 206,
  220, 222-6, 228, 234, 239, 259, 264,
  279, 281, 296-7
Melville, John, minister in Crail, 82
Melville, Nannis, in Anstruther Wester,
  235-9, 305, 307
Melville, Patrick, wright in Anstruther
  Wester, 292
Melville, Robert, laird of Murdocairny,
  293
Menteith, Helen, in Dollar, 294
Menteith, Madie, in Clackmannan, 183
Mentzer, Raymond, 5-6, 337, 339-40
Menzies family, 58-9, 115-6, 123, 125
Menzies, Gilbert, bailie and elder in Aber-
  deen, 118
Menzies, Gilbert, son of provost Thomas,
  59, 118
Menzies, Thomas, laird of Pitfodels and
  provost of Aberdeen, 58-9, 61, 63, 114-
  5
Menzies, Thomas, son of provost Thomas,
  117
Methven, Paul, minister in Dundee and
  Jedburgh, 49-50
Mill, Jonet, in Anstruther Wester, 235-7
Milne, David, minister in Dundonald, 252
Mitchell, Jonet, near Stirling, 305
Mithau, Jean, in Pont-de-Camarès, 327
Moncrieff, Andrew, minister in Crail, 193
Monifieth, 97, 126-9, 239-45, 248-9, 257,
  271-2, 285, 295, 306
Mont, Jonat, in St. Andrews, 284
Montauban, 260, 338
Monter, E. William, 5
Montgomery, Robert, minister in Stirling
  and archbishop of Glasgow, 138, 164,
  173, 186, 262-3
Montrose, 64, 264
Montrose, John Graham, earl of, 277
Montpellier, 317
Moody, Mirrabel, in St. Andrews, 217

STUDIES IN MEDIEVAL AND REFORMATION THOUGHT

EDITED BY HEIKO A. OBERMAN

Recent volumes in this series:

Prospectus available on request

E.J. BRILL — P.O.B. 9000 — 2300 PA LEIDEN — THE NETHERLANDS